Something to Do with Power

The John Hope Franklin Series in African American History and Culture

Waldo E. Martin Jr. and Patricia Sullivan, *editors*

The best scholarship in African American history and culture compels us to expand our sense of who we are as a nation and forces us to engage seriously the experiences of all Americans who have shaped the development of this country. By publishing pathbreaking books informed by several disciplines, the John Hope Franklin Series in African American History and Culture seeks to illuminate America's multicultural past and the ways in which it has informed the nation's democratic experiment.

A complete list of books published in the John Hope Franklin Series in African American History and Culture is available at https://uncpress.org/series/john-hope-franklin-series-african-american-history-culture.

Something to Do with Power
Julian Mayfield's Journey toward
a Black Radical Thought, 1948–1984

....

DAVID TYROLER ROMINE

The University of North Carolina Press   Chapel Hill

*This book was published with the assistance of the Authors Fund of
The University of North Carolina Press.*

© 2025 David Tyroler Romine
All rights reserved

Set in Charis by Westchester Publishing Services
Manufactured in the United States of America

Library of Congress Cataloging-in-Publication Data
Names: Romine, David, (David Tyroler) author
Title: Something to do with power : Julian Mayfield's journey toward a Black
   radical thought, 1948–1984 / David Tyroler Romine.
Other titles: John Hope Franklin series in African American history and culture
Description: Chapel Hill : The University of North Carolina Press, [2025] |
   Series: John Hope Franklin series in African American history and culture |
   Includes bibliographical references and index.
Identifiers: LCCN 2025001941 | ISBN 9781469685120 cloth alk. paper |
   ISBN 9781469685137 pbk alk. paper | ISBN 9781469685144 ebook |
   ISBN 9781469687476 pdf
Subjects: LCSH: Mayfield, Julian, 1928–1984 | African American civil rights
   workers—United States—Biography | African American political activists—
   Biography | BISAC: BIOGRAPHY & AUTOBIOGRAPHY / Cultural,
   Ethnic & Regional / African American & Black | SOCIAL SCIENCE /
   Activism & Social Justice | LCGFT: Biographies
Classification: LCC E185.97.M394 R66 | DDC 323.092 $a B—dc23/eng/20250305
LC record available at https://lccn.loc.gov/2025001941

Cover art: *[Portrait of Julian Mayfield]*, by Carl Van Vechten, 1959. Library of
Congress, Prints & Photographs Division, Carl Van Vechten Collection,
LC-USZ62-114419 (b&w film copy neg).

For product safety concerns under the European Union's General Product
Safety Regulation (EU GPSR), please contact gpsr@mare-nostrum.co.uk or
write to The University of North Carolina Press and Mare Nostrum Group
B.V., Mauritskade 21D, 1091 GC Amsterdam, The Netherlands.

Contents

Introduction, 1
Which Way Does the Blood River Run?

1 The Making of a Radical, 1928–1954, 10

2 Invisible Island, 1954–1959, 31

3 The End of Summer, 51
Literature and Activism, 1959–1960

4 An Unbelievable Kind of Revolution, 70
Cuba and the Black Liberation Movement in the United States, 1960–1961

5 In Every Sense a Stranger, 91
Community and African Unity in Accra, 1961–1967

6 The Black Militant in Theory and in Practice, 1967–1968, 112

7 *Uptight* in Cleveland, 130
The Black Militant Goes to Hollywood, 1968–1971

8 The Nation and the Pan-African Ideal, 152
Nationalism, Sovereignty, and Identity in Guyana, 1971–1973

9 The Black King Must Be Black, 176
Hollywood and the Haitian Revolution, 1973–1976

Epilogue, 193
I Am Not Resigned, 1976–1984

Acknowledgments, 199

Notes, 203

Bibliography, 263

Index, 277

Something to Do with Power

Introduction
Which Way Does the Blood River Run?

Our pens and our typewriters are our guns, and all our words must be bullets aimed to draw blood, not from our people but our enemies.
—Julian Mayfield, 1968

"From the beginning," cultural critic Hollie I. West wrote in 1975, "Julian Mayfield, the writer, and Julian Mayfield, the political activist, have been one."[1] In this profile, published in the *Washington Post*, West went on to emphasize how writing was a political act for his subject and confirmed this thesis by describing Mayfield's recent role of propagandist and journalist for the Ministry of Information and Culture in Guyana. Among the duties Mayfield assumed in Georgetown was to convince young Guyanese people to stay in their home country and build the "cooperative republic" that Prime Minister Forbes Burnham had proclaimed in 1970, but West also described how Mayfield had been working on a biography of Burnham as well as a draft of a script for a proposed film on the Haitian Revolution.

With his characteristic economy of words, West then captured the vicissitudes of Mayfield's career from his time as a Broadway actor and rank-and-file member of the Communist Party of the United States of America (CPUSA) in his twenties, an advocate of Fidel Castro and Kwame Nkrumah in his thirties, and a radical nationalist who sought to unify the competing strains of Black Power politics in his forties. The profile captured a life of artistic struggle, revealing it to be one that defiantly reflected the spirit of the times in spite of attendant personal and professional consequences in doing so. The quotations that West offers in this profile reveal a man whose life does not neatly map onto any established category of American artist. There were, of course, Black artists who chose to leave the United States behind, but those who did rarely worked for foreign governments and advocated for nation-building projects. The postwar struggle for liberation saw numerous Black American activists take up the causes of postcolonial nations—from Tanzania to Algeria—but few among them were novelists or actors. For Black artists in the midcentury United States, producing art that reflected their lived experiences remained a revolutionary act, and none captured the difficulty of inhabiting this position more than Julian Hudson Mayfield.

Nearly two decades prior, the then thirty-year-old Mayfield had first identified this precise contradiction as a pressing issue facing a generation of Black writers. During a conference he helped organize in New York, Mayfield joined the likes of Saunders Redding, Samuel W. Allen, John H. Clarke, Arna Bontemps, Lorraine Hansberry, and Sarah E. Wright in considering the relationship between African American writing and the American dream. In a panel organized by Mayfield titled "Social Responsibility and Social Protest," he went further than most in questioning the utility of the American dream as either a cultural aspiration or an intangible political goal. At a moment when the potential for full citizenship for African Americans seemed more viable than it had since the early 1870s, Mayfield's panel presentation was indicative of a radical, youthful faction of Black men and women who were increasingly disenchanted with the stated political objectives of their older colleagues. The alienation that young writers expressed was the fear that the primary objective of mainstream civil rights organizations—equal rights under the law—would not improve the material conditions and cultural status of Black people in the United States.[2]

At the same moment when the House Un-American Activities Committee and its Senate counterpart were persecuting suspected communists and their sympathizers, Mayfield loudly and boldly challenged widespread assumptions about the United States of America, its racial order, and its economic foundations. Speaking for the other young writers on the panel, Mayfield identified how the contemporary conditions of the Cold War and domestic American politics did provide a narrow opening for moral and legal challenges to segregation and Jim Crow.[3] Nevertheless, he questioned whether a widespread embrace of the American mainstream by African Americans was the best means to achieve the political and economic benefits of full citizenship or even if that citizenship had any real value.

Optimistically, Mayfield stated, the best possible outcome for Black Americans was "submersion in what is euphemistically called the American melting pot."[4] In order to maintain their sense of independent self and cultural and social mores, he argued, "the Negro writer may conclude that his best salvation lies in escaping the narrow national orbit—artistic, cultural and political—and soaring into a space of more universal experience."[5] Mayfield had only recently returned from four years of living in rural Puerto Rico, and his searing critique of the dominant modes of US racial politics positioned him as an early and fierce advocate for the kind of transnational, radical Black politics that would come to dominate discussions of liberation efforts in the decade to come. Reflecting on Mayfield's life spent seeking escape beyond the "narrow national orbit" of American racial capitalism, Jim Crow, and the vast geographic reach of white supremacy reveals much about the intellectual and political spaces that he inhabited. His career of peripatetic literary radicalism illuminates the contours of Black radicalism that was shaped by the constraints and conditions of the global political, economic, cultural, and social conflict that would define his life: the Cold War.

Cedric J. Robinson's notion of the "Black radical tradition," first articulated in his 1983 book *Black Marxism*, presented these ideas as the antithesis of the racial capitalism embodied in slavery, sharecropping, and Jim Crow. Building off W. E. B. Du Bois's concept that the role that Black men and women played in asserting their humanity was part of the broader trajectory of American history, Robinson's tradition was not a static notion of resistance but rather a dynamic process that reflected dominant political and cultural precepts. Although Mayfield's own political art and activism was focused on alternatives to integration politics, forging solidarity among men and women of the Global South and nation building in the so-called Third World, the Cold War shaped the discursive and political horizons of these movements, and a close reading of Mayfield's work revealed a dynamic and deeply historical process. He embraced communism as a young actor in New York and forged a career as a novelist, a political journalist, a social critic, an intellectual, and a government functionary, which emphasizes not only how artists cannot avoid being a product of their times but also Mayfield's own significance as a radical thinker and architect of Black liberation as an ideology.

Spanning five decades and four continents, Mayfield's output also closely tracks multiple interwoven trajectories of Black intellectual history. With writing that was representative of Black communism, Black nationalism, Black internationalism, Pan-Africanism, decolonization, and Third World solidarity efforts (to name a few), Julian Mayfield's emphasis on marshaling art and politics to excavate usable pasts and articulate potential futures for Black peoples throughout the African diaspora underscores his importance as an intellectual and a thinker in the post–World War II era. This approach also highlights the salience of biography as a methodology in understanding the linkages between the Cold War and concomitant Black freedom struggles during the latter half of the twentieth century. This can be seen in a 2005 interview in which professor of Africana studies Gerí

Augusto cautioned the interviewer's attempt to direct links between transnational movements and individual politics "because these things are not straight lines and arrows." Speaking about the 1972 African Liberation Day march in Washington, DC, Augusto concluded that despite ideological and political differences, "we [activists] came together where there was mutual interest."[6] In identifying the dynamics of political and ideological movements, Augusto's emphasis on discrete shared goals among activists who might differ broadly on ideology, approach, or tactics offers a method of reading and writing about these intellectuals and activists that is honest and open about their position.

Julian Mayfield's embrace of the communist Left, of Black internationalism, of Pan-Africanism, and of Black nationalism demonstrates this need to consider lives beyond straight lines and arrows and illustrates the ideological and personal role of "mutual interest" in shaping literary and political activism. Mayfield's own life maps a circuitous, intersecting path through the social movements, personalities, and politics that demonstrate the incomplete nature of histories of the Black Left on American culture as well as the efforts to navigate the often contentious relationships between intellectual traditions. What drove Mayfield was both personal and professional, ideological and strategic, and was coupled with an abiding interest in the manifestations of power. He was fascinated by charismatic Black radicals who were seeking power, providing insight into the conditions for his career on three continents that existed almost entirely within the context of Cold War anticommunism and the twentieth-century Black freedom struggle. Beyond power, however, what also drove him was a search for belonging, a unity that had the power to defy the "virus of white supremacy" and the space and means to perfect his art. Although not as explicit in his writings as was power, this desire to connect with his heritage and a like-minded community was a central pillar of the struggle and helped define his movements—intellectual, geographical, and otherwise—throughout the four decades of his adult life.[7]

Mayfield was an artist and an intellectual who lacked both academic credentials and elite status, and thus his marginality within Cold War historical narratives is contrasted by the importance of his archive in constructing those histories. Despite having a sizable portion of his personal papers seized and presumably destroyed in Ghana following the 1966 coup, the Schomburg Center for Research in Black Life currently houses nearly forty linear feet of Mayfield's papers, a gift of his widow, Joan Cambridge, upon his death. This archive, one of the most oft-consulted collections at the Schomburg, is cited frequently in histories of the Black Left, the influence of the Cuban Revolution in the United States, the Black Power movement, and studies of modern African American literature and film. Taken together, Mayfield emerges as a key primary source for modern American history where Black radical activism and Black American interest in the Third World are concerned.[8]

However, Mayfield is only nominally present in many of those works, moving silently through these narratives as a source, not an actor. At the same time, his career was defined by his own interest in the crises that he saw developing in the United States and abroad. His work focused exclusively on Black peoples and the impact of broader political trends on their lives, mentalities, and lived experiences. And yet, his writing is often judged as being devoid of context, meaning, or historical background. The quotes from "Into the Mainstream and Oblivion" reveal why it remains one of Mayfield's most-cited works, yet the intellectual history of the ideas expressed within have received little engagement outside of a small subset of historians. Although his early experiences in the CPUSA influenced his rejection of mainstream Black liberal politics, his experiences living in Puerto Rico with his wife, an ardent Puerto Rican nationalist during the height of antinationalist repression in the mid-1950s, remain obscured or ignored.

Furthermore, Mayfield's position as a Black leftist and a "card-carrying" member of the CPUSA from 1948 to 1956 also highlights how intellectual history has tended to foreground elite intellectuals—W. E. B. Du Bois, Carter G. Woodson, and Booker T. Washington, among others—and exclude radical, feminist, and queer thinkers such as Pauli Murray, Hubert Harrison, Claudia Jones, Gloria Joseph, and Alphaeus Hunton. Professor of Africana studies Michael Hanchard noted this trend in a 2006 analysis of Black political thought, emphasizing that "it is not just the dominant ideals and political practices, but the marginal, the implausible, and the unpopular ideas that also define an age."[9] Mayfield's ideas, as expressed through both his art and his political writing, were not just radical critiques of an irredeemably racist society but were also often disputed, unpopular, or ignored during his lifetime. Put simply, Julian Mayfield did not always fit neatly into the communities he joined.

Mayfield was a bookish young man growing up in a working-class home in Washington, DC, and his early experiences with segregation and white racism, combined with the colorism and classism he observed in school, fostered a perspective on political economy that was inseparable from race. As the son of a chauffeur for the State Department and a domestic worker,

Mayfield's life was a product of migration and striving, the hopes of his parents for him and his sister, Dorothy, to achieve more than they had. He was drawn to writing as a vocation from an early age, and his path is also reminiscent of that of other autodidact, working-class intellectual peers such as Harold W. Cruse and John H. Clarke. A working-class upbringing and the lack of a college degree immediately placed Mayfield outside of many of the established, elite-driven networks that existed at the time for Black artists and intellectuals. His working-class sensibility, coupled with his early training as a journalist, nevertheless provided him with a unique eye for the motivations and concerns of others. This work was also shaped by the class and color distinctions he recognized within the African American community writ large as well as the intelligentsia who claimed to speak for them.

This biographical approach also demands a reconsideration of the intellectual history that Mayfield's published works offer, making an examination of the personal experiences, travel, and interactions with others during its production not only relevant but also necessary. In addition to Mayfield's papers at the Schomburg, the archive holds the papers of many of his peers and friends, including the aforementioned John Henrik Clarke as well as Maya Angelou, John O. Killens, and Tom Feelings. Their correspondence offers a window into the trajectory of Mayfield's artistic and political pronouncements. Perhaps the most significant collection besides those at the Schomburg is the Federal Bureau of Investigation's (FBI) two-hundred-page file on Mayfield, which offers further context and information about his movements, associations, and roles in various groups.

Uncritical consideration of either of these two archives—one a deliberate product of a life of a man and the other constructed by opponents bent on his marginalization and neutralization—further complicates the task of retracing the circuitous routes of Mayfield's unsettled radicalism. If the goal is to understand the intellectual histories of Black intellectuals that came to the fore in the context of the Cold War, then neither archive can be taken at face value. The papers sometimes offer clearer insights into others than they do into Mayfield. He was a keen observer of human interaction with a focus on the quotidian—and frequently prurient—aspects of the human experience, and his archive is replete with accounts of the politics, actions, histories, and stories of others. In addition, as many accounts are products of sporadic attempts at autobiography and memoir writing, the stories emerge through the hazy lens of memory and are refracted through the constant remaking of self that characterized a long and varied career as an artist and a public figure.

The FBI, which conducted surveillance on Mayfield and his family intermittently from 1955 until 1977, produced several hundred pages of material that documents a life lived knowingly under the watchful gaze of agents of the state. A product of FBI director J. Edgar Hoover's obsession with African American activists of all political persuasions, the surveillance campaign against Black critics of segregation, institutionalized racism, and anti-Black racism began at the moment of the FBI's founding. This decades-long project involved the surveillance, intimidation, and persecution of African American activists who dared to publicly challenge the nation's racial and social status quo. Writers were of particular interest to Hoover; files on Frank London Brown, Gwendolyn Brooks, Harold W. Cruse, Langston Hughes, Lorraine Hansberry, Claude McKay, Alice Childress, and John A. Williams demonstrate an unyielding preoccupation with the influence and import of Black writers as agents of social and political change in the United States.[10] While this particular archive centers Mayfield as a subject, what it reveals is often inaccurate and produced within a historical moment in which anticommunism became inescapably intertwined with anti-Black racism.

Furthermore, for Black intellectual history scholarship, the significance of the Cold War also illustrates how the globe-spanning conflict offered opportunities for activists pursuing civil rights even as it curtailed the freedom to travel, work, and live for others who pursued activism beyond the narrow lines delineated by anticommunist ideologies. Viewing this era through the lens of a single person, activists' work and their intellectual commitments illustrate the political, cultural, and social dynamics that allowed a lifetime of radical struggle to persist in spite of the ruptures of anticommunist repression. In light of the biographical approach that I have opted to take, this book unfolds in a largely chronological fashion. Chapter 1 examines Mayfield's roots, the origins of his vocational goals of artistry in the service of radical politics, and how early travels cemented his own idiosyncratic antiracism and understanding of himself as a radical. Chapter 2 considers Mayfield's decision to break with the CPUSA and his relocation to Puerto Rico upon meeting and marrying his first wife, Dr. Ana Livia Cordero. It was the influence of Dr. Cordero and the experience of life in Puerto Rico that shaped Mayfield's incipient anticolonialism and a concomitant interest in transnational forms of activism in service of Afro-diasporic modernity, a fact that previous historians have neglected somewhat.

Beginning after Mayfield's return to the US mainland in 1959, chapter 3 delves into the real-life political struggles that inspired his third novel, *The Grand Parade*. While Mayfield's previous fiction writing was influenced by current events, *The Grand Parade* offered an early critique of racial integration as a strategy for African American political activism. Chapter 4 traces his developing interest in revolution, following him to Havana during the second year of the new Cuban government under Fidel Castro as solidifying Mayfield's support for the North Carolina–born radical advocate of armed self-defense Robert F. Williams. Mayfield's advocacy on behalf of Williams eventually led to a hurried flight to Canada and later to Ghana, where Mayfield joined his wife, Dr. Cordero, in offering his skills as a writer and a journalist to the government of Kwame Nkrumah. Chapter 5 considers the nearly five years Mayfield spent as a guest of the Nkrumah government and Mayfield's idiosyncratic approach to African unity. In particular, as an agent and advocate of the Ghanaian government, Mayfield deployed his pragmatic realism when it came to the difficulties of forging political alliances across the diaspora.

Chapter 6 picks up after the coup in Ghana and focuses on Mayfield's return to and reintegration into the United States. The chapter considers his intellectual response to the militant mood of Black Power, which had surged to the foreground of popular discourse in the United States in his absence, and Mayfield's efforts to mediate the intellectual conflicts of that movement. Chapter 7 explores his most prominent acting role: the lead in Jules Dassin's explosive portrait on the Black Power movement in the United States, *Uptight*. Mayfield's return to the expatriate life, this time in Guyana, is the subject of chapter 8. In Guyana, Mayfield once again engaged in a nation-building project for a Black leader while continuing to pursue the kind of political art that defined his career. Chapter 9 is focused on Mayfield's attempt to marshal the history of the Haitian Revolution to serve as a lesson to postcolonial governments in the African diaspora and to make a Hollywood film on the subject. Joined by veteran actor and friend William Marshall, Mayfield challenged Hollywood's inherent white supremacy once again with his script for *King Christophe*. In the aftermath of Mayfield's abrupt return from Guyana in 1975, his professional career sputtered, and the epilogue considers the last nine years of his life in light of his early death at the age of fifty-six.

Taken together as a whole, Julian Mayfield's life of radical self-fashioning and artistic reinvention offers a novel perspective on both US politics and the Black Atlantic even as it challenges many of the conventions that define this concept. As for Mayfield, he considered himself a pragmatist whose interest in theory was as an instrument of social change. A writer and a propagandist, Mayfield saw himself as an active participant in the Black freedom struggles he celebrated and advocated for in his writing. As Walter Rideout noted in 1969, "the black writer by the conditions of his existence has been made intensely aware of a white 'civilization,' which, whatever its virtues, nevertheless does impose its domination on the black body and mind."[11] Resisting, undermining, and toppling that domination by art, literature, and journalism is perhaps Julian Mayfield's most significant and lasting contribution to American and Afro-diasporic history.

1   The Making of a Radical, 1928–1954

Because, Mr. Norton, if you don't know *where* you are,
you probably don't know *who* you are.
—Ralph Ellison

During the summer of 1950, the interracial cast of the Broadway musical *Lost in the Stars* made numerous stops as they toured the United States, capitalizing on the popularity of their musical adaptation of *Cry the Beloved Country*. Playing the character of Absalom, a young Julian Mayfield wrote of his surprise in encountering the familiar contours of anti-Black racism beyond the borders of the Deep South. Born in South Carolina, Mayfield believed himself knowledgeable about how white people might diminish or threaten his community, but the expansive, differentiated geography of Jim Crow caught him off guard. Upon arrival in Omaha, which he disparaged as the "ugliest nastiest city we played during the tour," the interracial group of actors and crew were refused service at a hotel they had booked.[1] Mayfield and costar William Greaves set out to look for another hotel and, finding none, decided to make some phone calls. They ducked into a nearby restaurant to make change when the cashier, infuriated at the Black men's violation of unspoken racial codes, refused to serve them. The men asked for change for a ten-dollar bill, and the cashier responded by slamming the change on the counter in lieu of an answer.[2]

Recounting the incident in his autobiography, Mayfield admitted that while the cashier's response surprised him, it was he who had the last laugh. In her rage, the cashier left his original ten-dollar bill on the counter, effectively doubling the men's money for the night. Describing this encounter two decades later, Mayfield found humor in the incident but recounted it to demonstrate how the rules of race operated in familiar ways beyond the familiar spaces of his youth.[3] Omaha was not southern, but its white population remained committed to enforcing the color line. The stop in Nebraska was not the only incident on that tour that confirmed this assessment, as stops in Cincinnati, Louisville, St. Louis, and Chicago demonstrated the geographic breadth and creativity of white supremacy in the United States. No stop, however, demonstrated this as clearly as Los Angeles.

In September toward the end of the tour, the cast was leaving a restaurant in the City of Angels when they were stopped and searched by a group of police officers including a Mexican American lieutenant.[4] Despite the presence of well-known white actor Neville Brand, the men and women of the cast were held for over two hours on the side of the road as police searched their vehicle and their persons for narcotics. Eventually, officers gave up and released the cast members without charge.[5] When Mayfield expressed his surprise at the lieutenant's ancestry, the locals explained that he was a "special case" and that the Los Angeles Police Department (LAPD) relished its ability to stop and harass well-known actors and interracial groups.[6] Travel, though not a central thematic element of Julian Mayfield's writing, shaped his observations about race, solidarity, ideology, and political economy. The mobility Mayfield possessed was a significant component of his developing political awareness, his understanding of his place as a Black man in the United States, and aided his conception of himself as a writer, activist, and critic.

The *Lost in the Stars* tour, which covered the fall and winter of 1950 and the first few months of 1951, preceded a turn to radical politics for Mayfield. Beyond illustrating that the United States beyond the South was also avowedly racist, the variety of people and situations that the young actor encountered spurred the development of his nascent anticapitalist and antiracist ideas. Mayfield was a shrewd observer of human behavior with an abiding interest in the "seedier side" of life, and his autobiographical manuscript was full of anecdotes—humorous and ribald—that illustrated how race, gender, and political economy shaped human relationships and state policy. These experiences would become the foundation of subsequent arguments on the interrelated dynamics of race and class in the mainland United States and elsewhere in the African diaspora. In the manuscript, which was written in two stages between the periods 1969–70 and 1979–81, Mayfield described his dawning awareness of the extant racial hierarchies even in spaces without a legally defined color line, such as during his time as a soldier in Hawaii (1946–47). His decision to join the Communist Party of the United States of America (CPUSA) in late 1950 or early 1951 was informed by these experiences that rooted his developing radicalism in the fertile soil of early travels. His subsequent rejection of the postwar liberal order rested upon those same stanchions, buttressed by frustration and disgust with the status quo. These earliest journeys sketch an initial intellectual history of postwar Black radical thought while contextualizing Mayfield's shifting political commitments and the expansion of his concept of self as a part of something greater.

Among twentieth-century Black writers, travel played a significant role in narratives of awakening and self-fashioning. Autobiographical accounts are replete with examples of how space and location challenged preconceptions and shaped political views.[7] Some of the more well known of these accounts include those of Chester Himes, Josephine Baker, Richard Wright, and James Baldwin, all of whom sought refuge from American racism in France with varying degrees of success. Langston Hughes's early experiences in Haiti and Cuba revealed to him the broader currents of Black artistic and social thought that pervaded the African diaspora, while Pauli Murray's and Maya Angelou's experiences in West and North Africa helped remake their sense of what constituted justice and community. Although often perilous for African Americans, travel offered some solace from the frustrations and difficulties of everyday life in the United States.

Often overlooked in favor of international encounters, regional variations within the United States offered domestic Black travelers analogous experiences, as Mayfield's tour with *Lost in the Stars* shows. In 1944, W. E. B. Du Bois recalled in haunting turns of phrase his journey into West Tennessee during his time at Fisk University in the 1890s. "I traveled not only in space but in time," Du Bois wrote, noting that "I touched the very shadow of slavery" during his encounters with illiterate sharecroppers.[8] No amount of reading, historian David Levering Lewis writes in his account of Du Bois's experience, could have prepared the young sociologist and teacher for the dehumanization of "a zone where time had stopped the day after the day of jubilee."[9] Mayfield, in experiencing anti-Black racism in Omaha where he had not expected it to exist, inverts Du Bois's observations in rural West Tennessee. In both cases, a well-read young Black man was confronted with the complexity, variety, and geography of race in the United States beyond what he expected. For Du Bois as it did for Mayfield, race in the United States remained as intimately tied to geography as it did to political economy.

In spite of observations such as these, scholarship of the past twenty years has minimized the relationship between racial oppression and geography, as scholars have tended to flatten regional differences in favor of grand, inclusive narratives. Scholarship on the long civil rights movement is emblematic of this trend. Work produced under this broad category has charted a trajectory of interconnected activism from the Red Summer of 1919 to the militant movements of the 1970s to illustrate how the continuities of radical ideas, liberatory movements, and individual relationships survived the anticommunist and anti-Black efforts of governments and private citizens in the United States. This in turn amplified the dissolution of periodization and geographic specificity.[10] Historiographically speaking, this has been a generative process, highlighting the intergenerational transmission of ideas and the dogged determination of Black people to realize their own liberation, but it has not been without its critics. Historians Sundiata Cha-Jua and Clarence Lang are among the most prominent to take issue with this thesis for its failure to consider "the role of space and political economy in shaping specific, historically bound modes of social interaction."[11] Julian Mayfield's autobiographical account of his early travels and his subsequent exploration of communist spaces in New York illustrates how place contributed to both Mayfield's politics and his personal relationships. By contextualizing the role of location in his critiques of political economy, race, and activism, this chapter argues that geography shaped Black radical intellectual and political discourse during the late 1940s and early 1950s.

It goes without saying that anti-Black racism permeated the United States during the twentieth century, but the shifts in emphasis, social mores, and expectations over space revealed for Mayfield the absurdity and variation of racial rule-making. Experiencing these differences, as Mayfield did on his tour with *Lost in the Stars*, provided him with a perspective on how necessary it was to carefully consider the differences when making claims or passing judgment. These skills would later be put to the test in his travels in the Caribbean and West Africa as he struggled to make sense of the difficulties of constructing racial solidarity among differing social, cultural, economic, and linguistic groups. Black liberation for Mayfield was not a destination but rather a process that was produced historically and cannot be disentangled from the spaces, ideas, and people in which it developed.

A Radical in the Making

Julian Hudson Mayfield was born on June 6, 1928, in Greer, South Carolina. He had few kind words for his hometown, sardonically asserting that "there is no doubt that I am the most important person ever born in Greer, South Carolina, but there is no record of that fact [there]."[12] Although Mayfield would only spend a brief period residing in the Deep South, he returned sporadically throughout his life to visit his extended family. Despite his cosmopolitan pretensions, he nurtured a deep connection to his Black southern roots. Lamenting the fact that he had no Nat Turners or

Harriet Tubmans in his past, he acknowledged that he was the product of "generations of people who mostly struggled and got by."[13] This explicit awareness of working-class origins informed his subject matter and his approach to storytelling. The young Mayfield's voracious appetite for reading material and his systematic approach to his own education were foundational to his later political writing and intellectual debate as well as his own aesthetic sensibilities.

According to papers provided by Mayfield's son, Rafael Hudson Mayfield, the Mayfield family was deeply rooted in South Carolina. In a newsletter from a 1983 family reunion, the unnamed writer joked that "there's a common saying that the Mayfields owned half of Greer," but research into land records suggests that this was something of an exaggeration.[14] Nevertheless, census records reliably date the family's presence to early nineteenth-century South Carolina, where Joseph Mayfield, Julian's great-grandfather, appears as a laborer in the 1870 census.[15] Joseph's grandson, Julian Mayfield's father Hudson Mayfield, was born in 1905. Hudson met and married Annie Mae Prince in 1926. She was a domestic worker at the time but had done a variety of jobs including picking cotton. Hudson briefly attended Allen University in the state capital of Columbia but had dropped out by the time Julian was born in 1928.[16] Solidly working class, the Mayfields made do in Greer until the Great Depression set in. Early in 1930 the family left the South Carolina town, settling in Asheville, North Carolina, where Hudson took a job as a hospital orderly.[17] A daughter was born in February but died seven months later.[18] When the Mayfields relocated to Washington, DC, in 1933, Hudson found work as a taxi driver and had steady employment by the time their third child, Dorothy, was born. The family changed apartments frequently during the 1930s, staying mostly within northeastern Washington, but in 1942 they were able to purchase a home on Fourth Street in southwest near the Navy Yard. Hudson and Annie Mae would go on to reside at that address for more than forty years in a house that also gave Julian a measure of consistency during his teenage years.[19]

From the age of five until the age of eighteen, Julian Mayfield made his home in the nation's capital, living under its recently imposed regime of Jim Crow. "I have never known why black people always breathe a sigh of relief when they finally reach Washington, D.C.," Mayfield reflected later in life, as police there were "as trigger-happy, bloodthirsty and vicious as they are anywhere else in the United States." Washingtonians knew that their city was southern in culture if not in geography.[20] They also knew that it had not always been so. In the aftermath of the American Civil War, the capital's federal patronage system thrived under the nearly unbroken line of Republican administrations from President Ulysses S. Grant to President Willian Howard Taft. The party of Abraham Lincoln rewarded African American political loyalty with relatively fair civil service exams, allowing many to rise to positions of prominence within the federal bureaucracy. With secure well-paying jobs at the US Post Office, the Treasury Department, and the Government Printing Office, this small group of men nurtured an African American community in the nation's capital that was among the nation's wealthiest and socially intricate at a time when Harlem was still a Jewish and Italian enclave.

Historian Eric S. Yellin, who has documented the history of Washington's Black community, places the beginning of its decline at the inauguration of Woodrow Wilson in 1913.[21] Born in Virginia and raised in eastern Georgia, the former president of Princeton University arrived in Washington determined to whiten the federal service and the district itself. Wilson undid the work of previous administrations, ending patronage systems for African Americans and enacting Jim Crow laws that segregated the city's transportation system, theaters, hotels, restaurants, and other public accommodations. Wilson also segregated the federal bureaucracy and law enforcement. By the time the Mayfield family arrived in 1933 Jim Crow was well established, but older residents of the nation's capital would remember that things had not always been thus. Once the home of middle-class Black postal inspectors and high-ranking Black treasury officials, Depression-era Washington differed from Greer and Asheville only in its sprawling urban environment and cosmopolitan population. The color line was enforced with the same alacrity and naked violence that it was in South Carolina.

Despite this fact, Mayfield recalled fondly his parents' attempts to shelter him and his sister from the difficult racial reality of the United States. "We children never thought of ourselves as actually living in a 'ghetto,'" he wrote in his autobiography and recalled that he only became familiar with the concept of the "ghetto" from reading about the wartime plight of Jews in Europe. The world of his youth was a world of Black faces, and he characterized his childhood in Washington as a "fairly tranquil business." He praised his parents for their work ethic and their educational aspirations for him and his sister.[22] Despite living a short distance from a municipal garbage dump, his hardworking parents ensured that he lived a life of stability and free from hunger, but the family nevertheless "always knew which way the wind was blowing."[23]

In southwest DC the Mayfields found a community of fellow Black southerners who "went to church services, weddings, funerals, and gave picnics where the dominant food was always pigs feet, chitterlings, ham and potato salad." Washington's southernness was not only a product of its white supremacist regime but was a reflection of family histories of its large African American minority. Unlike the rural township of Greer, the concentration of Black communities meant that "we were black, and the people who ran everything were white." That, Mayfield reflected, "was a fact of life, like the wind and the sun, not a main preoccupation."[24] Although he decided to be a writer from an early age, Mayfield was no star pupil. In recounting his early education, he credited a young teacher, Mr. Jenkins, with encouraging him to write and giving him the confidence to believe that such a career was possible. In contrast, Washington's white population never let Mayfield forget who he was.

In 1942 at the age of fourteen, Mayfield applied for a position as a copy boy at the *Washington Post*. Standing before the white receptionist, he received an obdurate reminder of the space he was allowed to occupy under Jim Crow when the receptionist responded brusquely to his inquiry: "We don't hire colored boys here." The following year Mayfield found a job at the Library of Congress, where he did menial work pasting labels onto books and reshelving volumes. Ironically, it was this job, and not his schooling, where he was first exposed to modern African American literature. Working in the stacks one afternoon, a young Mayfield discovered Richard Wright's searing autobiography, *Black Boy*. According to Mayfield, he surreptitiously slipped the volume into his bag, reading the book in a single night before ensuring that it was back on the shelf the following day.[25]

After Wright, Mayfield read his way through the wealth of Black literature produced by the Harlem Renaissance. Cullen, Locke, Hughes, Hurston, and others inspired Mayfield and even provided him with his earliest education about the relationship between class and race and how these distinctions shaped relationships within the African American community. This understanding, accompanied by Mr. Jenkins's faith in his writing, encouraged Mayfield to pursue educational opportunities beyond the vocational track of his peers. Enrolling in Paul Laurence Dunbar High School in 1942, Mayfield found himself in an environment quite unlike that of his neighborhood or his previous schooling. Modeled after private college preparatory schools of the era, the publicly funded Dunbar's high academic standards exempted its graduates from taking college entrance exams, a factor that contributed to its appeal for middle-class African American students with aspirations of attending college.[26]

Dunbar's reputation attracted the children of Washington's Black middle class and those of ambitious working-class families, but by the time Julian Mayfield arrived, its standards, like its student population, were firmly in decline. The imposition of Jim Crow undercut the federal support for the publicly funded school, and the remaining community struggled to make up the shortfall. Harlem's concomitant rise also meant that ambitious young men and women began to leave Washington for New York upon graduation. For Dunbar's students, often the best and the brightest of their communities, segregated streetcars still made their long commutes fraught with violence and daily indignities. Racial barriers in theaters, amusement parks, restaurants, and concert halls diminished their ability to make full use of the cosmopolitan city in which they lived. Finally, a series of funding crises took their toll on the school's ability to hire well-qualified teachers. Nevertheless, it was Dunbar that put Mayfield on his path to becoming a writer and an actor.

Mayfield wrote extensively about Dunbar in his autobiography, but only some of those pages have survived. In other sources, he recalled that the memories of greatness still haunted its decaying halls and that at its core it was "a school for the elite."[27] Reflecting the values of the previous century, the students studied Greek and Latin, read poetry, took diction classes, learned musical instruments, and practiced debate. Despite graduating with a middling record at Dunbar—he finished with a C+ in 1946—Mayfield excelled in oratory and dramatics.[28] He was the winner of the American Legion National Americanism Committee's award during his senior year, which provided him with a small windfall and the confidence to pursue a career in the theater.[29]

Julian Mayfield's parents' commitment to a college education for him and his sister signaled a middle-class sensibility, but their inability to provide financially left him with few options. He was aware that a college degree would not allow him to bypass the constraints of Jim Crow, but his ambition to write reflected his belief that this profession would allow him freedom of expression to make up for his lack of social liberty. Aware that his parents could not afford college, he nevertheless "confidently expected lightning to strike somewhere in the next three years."[30] Military service in the peacetime US Army and, more importantly, passage of the Servicemen's Readjustment Act of 1944, commonly known as the G.I. Bill, proved to be his bolt from the blue.

Unlike that of many of his contemporaries, Mayfield's brief military career occurred during the interlude between World War II and the Korean War, and he saw no combat.[31] His service record was limited to secretarial work, performing in a military band, and, as he recalled in his autobiographical writing, illegal games of chance. He did his basic training at Fort McClellan in Anniston, Alabama, and spent his leave before deployment studying dice-throwing and becoming "a third-class pad roller." Gambling allowed him to avoid difficult and demeaning labor and provided him with welcome distractions from the tedium of service.[32] As a private first class in the 926th Engineering Aviation Group, Mayfield departed Alabama for leave in Washington before reporting for duty in San Francisco in early 1946. The army then shipped him to Hawaii, where he was appalled by the conditions that native Hawaiian communities experienced. Drawn to the residential streets of Honolulu, far from the haunts of Waikiki favored by GIs, he had his first experience with the reality of American empire. On Oahu, he recognized the similarities of the experiences of African Americans and Hawaiians in the poor-quality housing, substandard education, and malnutrition. After a brief illness, he was sent back to the mainland for medical leave and was honorably discharged in November 1947.[33]

Despite the short duration of his military service, the peacetime army gave Julian Mayfield the opportunity to attend college, although he found that the experience was not to his liking. In 1947 he enrolled in Lincoln University near Oxford, Pennsylvania, and attended the school for a single semester. Lincoln had been founded in 1854 as the first US degree-granting historically Black university.[34] After nearly a century of white leadership at Lincoln, Horace Mann Bond was appointed as the institution's first Black president in 1945, and he set about challenging both the university's hidebound traditions and the racial composition of its faculty and staff. Bond was popular among students, but his efforts were less appreciated by the tenured white faculty. The new president also faced difficulty in attracting Black faculty replacements. Lincoln's facilities were small, and segregation in nearby townships limited housing options for potential Black faculty, making Bond's pitches to potential employees difficult.

The stifling formal atmosphere of the all-male college did not mesh with Mayfield's gregarious, outgoing personality and interest in romantic relationships with women. Lincoln's distance from Washington and New York City made for long travel times on segregated buses, and the impoverished Mayfield was effectively trapped at Lincoln for the duration of the semester. Deciding to drop out sometime in the fall of 1947, Mayfield relocated to Manhattan, where he stated his interest to study radio broadcasting at New York University. However, upon arriving in Harlem he found himself drawn to the bustling postwar theater scene, and he began taking acting classes and won several small parts at the Blackfriars Theatre.[35] He never reenrolled or completed his bachelor's degree. Bound by institutionalized racism and second-class citizenship, he chafed against the constraints imposed on him due to the color of his skin but also assigned to him by his working-class roots. Although Mayfield did not embrace radical politics or associations at Lincoln, the staid curriculum and atmosphere of conformity spurred his search beyond the boundaries of Black middle-class society for solutions to the persistent racial problems he bore witness to each day.

Harlem, in contrast, was an exciting, invigorating place that shined with promise and potential. Taking acting classes with Frank Silvera, Mayfield befriended other young African American men and women with designs on the theater and careers in the arts. The lifelong friendships he forged with men such as William Marshall, William Branch, Sidney Poitier, William Greaves, Brock Peters, and Robert Slater had an enormous impact on the direction and scale of his career aspirations. It was also Mayfield's involvement in the Black theatrical community in Harlem that brought him into contact with the Black leftist circles that coalesced in the neighborhood's postwar cultural ferment. He made himself a member of the group of young men who orbited the legendary singer, actor, and activist Paul Robeson, and early theatrical success also afforded him the ability to tour the country.[36] This mobility, combined with a budding association with the CPUSA, aided the development of his criticism of capitalism and its relationship to racial oppression in the years that followed.

Lost in the Stars

Julian Mayfield's first major acting role ironically proved more significant for his understanding of American racism than it did for his acting career. In the summer of 1949, Mayfield was cast as the understudy for Sidney Poitier in the Kurt Weill musical *Lost in the Stars*. Adapted from Alan Paton's 1948 novel *Cry, the Beloved Country*, the production featured lyrics by Maxwell Anderson and direction by Rouben Mamoulian. *Lost in the Stars* also had the distinction of having one of the largest Black casts in Broadway history at that time. This meant that Mayfield had faced stiff competition for the part of Absalom Kumalo and was overjoyed to be Poitier's understudy. Unbeknownst to Mayfield, Poitier had secretly auditioned for the role of Dr. Luther Brooks in Joseph L. Mankiewicz's *No Way Out*. When Poitier received that part, Mayfield was promoted to the lead, marking his first time performing on Broadway.[37]

Opening in October 1949, the show quickly earned critical and popular acclaim. The producers, sensing a hit, made the unprecedented move to take the show on the road in the middle of its planned Broadway run, plotting a course through the American Midwest and Plains to the West Coast. The production's clarion calls for racial reconciliation in early twentieth-century South Africa resonated with the interracial politics of the American Left in the late 1940s. With South Africa's apartheid standing in for American Jim Crow, the play directly addressed the ways that racial inequality and segregation bred poverty, crime, and disregard for human life without directly criticizing the white supremacy that dominated the United States.

Weill's adaptation of Paton's novel follows the Anglican reverend Stephen Kumalo's journey from his small town to Johannesburg where he hoped to keep his son, Absalom, from losing his moral compass in the hostile gold mines where he toiled for a meager wage. Rev. Kumalo, much to his chagrin, arrives too late. Absalom, about to be a father, has already joined a gang and, while leading a robbery, shoots and kills a white man. Caught and imprisoned for his crime, Absalom faces the death penalty. Confronted with the prospect of losing his son, Rev. Kumalo undergoes a crisis of faith and receives spiritual guidance, appealing to the judge on his son's behalf. Intent on setting an example, however, the judge finds the young man guilty of murder and sentences him to death. At the end of the play, with his son facing the hangman's noose, Rev. Kumalo is visited by the father of the murder victim, and the two men make peace with each other. Despite Absalom's execution, the reconciliation between the two men—one as the father of a criminal and one as the father of a victim—presents the possibility that forgiveness and reconciliation could be the first steps to mending a social fabric rent by racism and segregation.[38]

As an ambitious young man suddenly thrust into Broadway fame, Julian Mayfield recalled with pride that his role in *Lost in the Stars* provided his first regular paycheck since arriving in New York. Payment aside, the show's national tour significantly broadened his intellectual and cultural horizons. Although Mayfield's anecdotes from this tour placed a heavy emphasis on prurient encounters and ribald humor, his account also highlighted how geography and economic conditions shaped race relations in unique and identifiable ways in different parts of the country. Among the cities the show toured were St. Louis, Chicago, San Francisco, Omaha, Louisville, Cincinnati, Columbus, Omaha, and Kansas City. Mayfield's recollections offer insight into his developing understanding of race, sexuality, gender, and criminality. Despite the effort that he made to portray his younger self as cosmopolitan and self-aware, he would later confess that the young man in his stories still had a great deal to learn.

With an interracial cast, *Lost in the Stars* was unable to play shows anywhere in the Deep South, but as the encounters in the introduction show, this fact did not limit confrontations with racial segregation. The job also whetted Mayfield's interest in leftist ideologies and informed his understanding for the necessity of socially conscious art. Both of these can be seen most clearly in one of the tour's first stops: Chicago. Despite the absence of laws banning African Americans from public accommodations in Chicago, Mayfield did not take long to grasp that the Windy City violently enforced the color line. In his autobiography, he related several encounters in bars and juke joints in which costar Van Prince provoked the ire of dangerous-looking white men by socializing with white women. Concerned with his safety, Mayfield urged Prince to leave the bar after recognizing that being well-dressed Black men in a majority-white bar was not a recipe for finishing out the tour. Even as Mayfield's accounts illustrated the regional variations of Jim Crow, they also showed how locals were resisting those strictures.

After narrowly avoiding violence on his first night in Chicago, Mayfield was leery of the city's nightlife, and on his second night in town he chose to accompany costar William Greaves to a gathering of participants in the local arts scene. There, Mayfield was introduced to Margaret Taylor-Burroughs and her husband Charles Burroughs, forming a friendship that would last for decades.[39] The couple then lived in a converted carriage house behind a "grand mansion" on Michigan Avenue that served as a base for art-related activism on the South Side. It also functioned as an informal boarding house for visiting artists and activists.[40] The couple was already well known in Chicago as advocates for Black art, the curation of Black history, and radical causes at the time, and Margaret later went on to be instrumental in the foundation of the DuSable Museum for African American History in 1961.

Charles, the son of communist activist Williana Burroughs, had been raised in Moscow, and Mayfield recounted with humor how Charles spoke English with a pronounced Russian accent. This accent, Mayfield recalled, grew thicker and more incomprehensible with every shot of vodka Charles consumed.[41] The Louisiana-born Margaret saw her art as a means to improve racial pride and racial solidarity; she used her associations with community leaders, white and Black, to call attention to injustice and force the city to act on issues in education. In addition to her artistic work, she was a public school teacher, and Mayfield wrote with admiration that she was "a thorn in the side of any elected official, including the governor."[42]

This encounter with Margaret and Charles Burroughs would later pave the way for Mayfield's subsequent entrance into the CPUSA, but at the time he derived more enjoyment from the free-flowing liquor and the attractive young women who came and went in the house. He lauded the slight, soft-spoken Margaret Burroughs for her activism and the passionate way in which she spoke about art and art education. He also recalled with glee that she "had a knack for making everybody who came to the apartment work . . . and you soon found yourself ironing or washing dishes and not minding as long as Margaret was there rapping in her flat Midwestern tones."[43] It was also in this former carriage house on Michigan Avenue that Mayfield first met Gwendolyn Brooks and Langston Hughes, who were but a few of the Black intellectuals and artistic luminaries who made it a point to stop by the Burroughs home when in town.

Whatever hope Mayfield had of avoiding a potentially violent conflict by visiting the Burroughs home, however, quickly evaporated on that first night. Shortly after his arrival, the phone rang, and Mayfield and five other young men were drafted to attend to some "trouble" in Trumbull Park. Mayfield's recollections are vague here, but the implication in the text is that Burroughs herself instructed Mayfield to accompany these men to the neighborhood that, unbeknownst to Mayfield, was at the front lines of a white terror campaign directed at nearby Black residents. Ignorant of Chicago's ongoing battle over desegregation, Mayfield agreed and was already in the car when he was given a short primer on the state of race relations in Chicago—information that prompted him to regret his decision.[44] Trumbull Park was a vast residential complex that had been constructed in 1938. It consisted of 55 buildings and 434 apartments and, despite its location in South Deering on the far South Side of Chicago, had an unofficial racial covenant. The Chicago Housing Authority only rented to white families, and attempts to desegregate the complex prompted increasingly violent attacks from white residents.[45] Mayfield described Trumbull Park as a "symbol in the struggle for civil rights," since the complex had been built with public funds, and happily reported in his autobiography that the "trouble" had mostly subsided when he and his new comrades arrived at the site. The rock and bottle throwing had stopped, and the two groups of men—one white and one Black—instead hurled insults at one another from parked cars across a wide boulevard. For him, the desultory attempts at desegregation by the Chicago Housing Authority symbolized the hollow promise of integration as a political solution to American racial conflicts.[46]

Mayfield's experiences in downtown Chicago with Van Prince and the episode in Trumbull Park painted a vivid portrait of the reality and the limits of the North's racism. After a brief run in Chicago, *Lost in the Stars* headed west.[47] St. Louis and Kansas City were consistent with Mayfield's experiences in Washington and Chicago, and Omaha did not even have a cohesive segregated neighborhood, leaving the nonwhite actors and crew entirely bereft of accommodation. After being rejected from several hotels and treated poorly by local whites, the actors were finally welcomed by the local Black community, who were generous enough to put the cast up in their own homes. When the cast reached San Francisco, Mayfield breathed a sigh of relief. After playing thirty shows, the show closed to rave reviews in Los Angeles in September 1950.

Back in New York, Mayfield unsuccessfully auditioned for several roles, but after a series of rejections, he concluded that *Lost in the Stars* had been an aberration.[48] Broadway producers continued to develop productions that lacked roles for Black actors, but the parts that were written were usually nonspeaking roles or humiliating caricatures. Realizing that he might not be able to continue in his newly chosen profession but wanting to remain in the theater, Mayfield set out to become a writer. He described his newfound enthusiasm for the profession as a product of the "relative independence" of writers. Also, writers "could turn out their great works at home, [and] hate their enemies without apology."[49] At this time, his given address was on West 99th Street on Manhattan's Upper West Side, and his interest in writing and his experience in the theater, along with his proximity to Harlem, steered him in the direction of the Harlem Writers Guild, a small group that formed in Harlem only the year before.[50]

John Henrik Clarke once wrote that the Harlem Writers Guild "was born out of the radicalism that followed the Second World War" as men and women sensed the shifting mood of African Americans in the nation.[51] Today, the guild's roster reads as a who's who of Black playwrights and authors of the mid-twentieth century, but in 1950 it was one of several similar groups based in upper Manhattan.[52] Organized by John O. Killens, Rosa Guy, John H. Clarke, Willard Moore, and Walter Christmas, the Harlem Writers Guild served as midwife to the work of dozens of Black literary figures, including Alice Childress, Lorraine Hansberry, Ossie Davis, and

Audre Lorde. The guild fostered the creative energies of generations of Black writers and artists who recognized that if they wanted their voices heard, working together was the only way to rise above the din of a Broadway that prioritized white stories and white actors.

The writers, directors, and actors who participated in guild activities not only helped organize space for the discussion and production of cultural work but also aided in the basic material needs of writers living in what was perhaps the most expensive neighborhood in one of the costliest cities in the United States. Providing Mayfield with a circle of talented collaborators and spaces in which to work on his art, the Harlem Writers Guild also connected him to the leftist circles that existed uptown. Shortly after joining the guild, Mayfield found himself sitting on the Committee for the Negro in the Arts and contributing to *Freedom*, the leftist magazine founded by Paul Robeson. At some point between 1950 and 1951, Mayfield became a formal, card-carrying member of the CPUSA and added his budding radical political voice to the vibrant cultural scene in New York.

The Black Cultural Left

Freedom, Julian Mayfield would write in 1969, was a magazine dedicated to the "furious exchange of ideas" between men and women who were "deeply and angrily and sometimes violently concerned about the issues of the day and the world."[53] Edited by Louis E. Burnham, the magazine ran for a tumultuous five years amid an increasingly hostile climate of anticommunism, blacklisting, and loyalty oaths. Such a space of political and ideological ferment proved intoxicating to the young Mayfield, spurring the development of political and artistic ideas that he would later use to attack the injustices and inequality to which he had been awakened on his tour with *Lost in the Stars*. *Freedom*, however, offered little in the way of remuneration.

The struggling publication—its founder, writers, editors, and readership hounded by the House Un-American Activities Committee and privately funded anticommunist publications such as *Red Channels*—could barely afford to publish its issues, much less pay its staff. As a result, Mayfield worked a variety of jobs, saving his evenings for writing, but any hopes he had of making it big as a writer were dashed by the hard truths of surviving in New York. "Except for a brief stint as a Post Office employee and as a taxi-driver," Mayfield recalled with a touch of bitterness, "I could not remember earning a week's salary."[54] Money, "the bane, the curse, the plague of most writers," was inevitably in short supply.[55]

In spite of these financial tribulations, the early 1950s were productive for the young writer, and he made full use of the spaces and connections that the Communist Party offered its members in the early 1950s. Along with the urban institutions of the Harlem-based Black Left, which included the offices that housed *Freedom*, the Committee for the Negro in the Arts, and the Harlem Writers Guild, Mayfield attended classes at the Jefferson School of Social Sciences in Chelsea, spent summers at the Communist Party–run Camp Unity in upstate New York, and collaborated with fellow guild members in small productions for the American Negro Theater and other neighborhood arts groups. There were also his political party duties, "the furious activity as a rank-and-file member of the Communist Party," which included committee meetings and, as the chairman of a committee on unemployment under the umbrella of the Committee for the Negro in the Arts, research about the employment prospects of his fellow Harlem residents.[56]

In *Black Art and Activism in Postwar New York*, her prosographic portrait of these Black men and women living in Harlem, Rebeccah E. Welch named the loose coalition of playwrights, authors, directors, actors, and novelists the "Black cultural Left" and historicized their origins in "urban institutions and movements that explicitly advanced the role of culture in political struggle."[57] The urban nature of this movement was a product of the demographic changes wrought by the Great Migration, which increased New York City's Black population by a factor of ten between 1910 and 1950.[58] The lack of affordable housing, a product of segregation and restrictive covenants, combined with the rapidly increasing population, led to prohibitively high rent prices and poor living conditions as homes were subdivided into rooms that seldom included even basic amenities. The Black cultural Left's artists and writers not only addressed these conditions in artistic appeals to Harlem residents but lived them as well. As an intellectual vanguard, the Black cultural Left emphasized how race and political economy were related by portraying the contradictions and hypocrisy of the American racial reality. Julian Mayfield's experiences as writer and actor reflected these challenges.

In one of his earliest published pieces, Mayfield pointedly attacked the disingenuous media coverage of the Korean War. "The official concern for the welfare of the civilian population, far less the enemy militia," he wrote to the editor of the *Washington Post* in February 1952, "has not been one of the features of the Korean adventure."[59] Disputing the US State Department narrative that war was being conducted to protect Korean citizens, Mayfield called attention to how public media portrayals of the war were silent about the massive air bombardment campaign in underway

Korea, which indiscriminately killed civilians and soldiers alike. Having offered little in the way of criticism of US foreign policy prior to his involvement with the Communist Party, Mayfield developed a critique of postwar militarism that offers insight into how time spent in the newsroom-like atmosphere of the *Freedom* offices shaped his growing awareness of world events. *Freedom* was Mayfield's apprenticeship. It allowed him to hone his writing talents even as it fostered a space for his political education. Perhaps more important than the anecdotes and stories contained in his autobiographical manuscript, however, were the relationships Mayfield forged during this time.

The tribulations of fellow Black radical writers and artists that Mayfield befriended in Harlem not only make up the bulk of the recollections in his autobiographical manuscript, but these writers and artists also influenced many of his life choices between 1950 and 1954. Those men and women whom Mayfield knew during this era include John H. Clarke, William Branch, Loften Mitchell, Walter Christmas, and John O. Killens.[60] According to Mayfield's recollections, it was Childress who had the greatest impact on his radical education. Born in Charleston, South Carolina, in 1916 and "the only African-American woman to have written, produced, and published plays for four decades," Childress was also deeply enmeshed in the world of the Black cultural Left in the 1940s and 1950s and helped introduce to her peers the struggling young actor with dreams of writing.[61]

In addition to directing Mayfield in several plays, the most notable of which was Ossie Davis's *Candy Store*, Childress encouraged him put his own ideas down on paper.[62] Between 1951 and 1952, performances of *Candy Store* were staged for the benefit of the United Electrical Workers Union and to raise money for the Civil Rights Congress. Mayfield acted in the play for no money, relying on other jobs to make ends meet.[63] According to literary historian Kathleen McDonald, Childress also taught dramatic workshops at the American Negro Theater and led creative forums on Black art and culture at the Jefferson School of Social Science in Chelsea. Evidence suggests that it was Childress who invited Mayfield to the Communist Party's flagship educational project, located on Sixth Avenue and 19th Street, to further his radical education.

The "Jeff School," as it was known, was named after Thomas Jefferson and was the direct successor to the CPUSA's earlier adult education effort, the New York Workers School. The Jeff School offered low-cost or free classes for adults in an environment that was avowedly Marxian. The school opened in 1944 and was funded by the CPUSA as part of an effort to expand teaching Marxist thought to the working class. Like the Abraham Lincoln School in Chicago (founded by lawyer and activist William L. Patterson), the Samuel Adams School in Boston, and the Tom Paine School in Philadelphia, the Jeff School's mission was to "educate and inform the whole mass of the people, [as] they are the only sure reliance for the preservation of our liberty."[64]

Operating openly, the school was a bugbear of New York anticommunists and almost immediately came under surveillance by the Federal Bureau of Investigation (FBI). In a breathless article published in the 1949 *Saturday Evening Post*, white reporter Craig Thompson described the school as an open conspiracy. "Everyone speaks and acts on the assumption that everyone else is already a Communist or about to become one," Thompson wrote, and, most frustrating for him, "people who, elsewhere, will go to jail rather than admit to being party members here openly proclaim it."[65] Mayfield would spend two years taking night classes at the Jeff School, but like Dunbar, the Jeff School's fortunes were already on the decline when he began. At its peak in 1948, the school ushered more than five thousand students— mostly longshoreman and trade unionists—through its programs, but as the McCarthy era progressed, state and federal pressures mounted. A burdensome court case sapped its meager monetary reserves, while leadership changes within associated unions and bad press convinced many workers to avoid the school entirely. The Jeff School closed to little fanfare in 1956.[66]

Another key space of furious intellectual debate and ideological ferment was Camp Unity, a "worker's summer camp" near the New York–Connecticut border. Located approximately twenty miles east of Poughkeepsie, Camp Unity was an ideal retreat from the fetid conditions of New York City in the late summer, and Mayfield spent the warmer months of 1951 and 1952 there writing and acting. An advertisement placed in *The Crisis* of July 1941 encouraged readers to "deal yourself a health glow with a stiff set of tennis on a well-kept, fast court or a brisk swim in the clear, cool waters of Lake Ellis." The ad declared "every weekend a no-trump weekend" and proclaimed rates of $22 per week and $3.75 per day with "efficient chambermaid services."[67]

Camp Unity was part of an archipelago of resorts funded by the Communist Party and labor unions designed as an affordable retreat for working-class peoples from the tightly packed working-class neighborhoods of New York, Philadelphia, Boston, and Baltimore.[68] These resorts were integrated, a rarity for vacation resorts of any kind in the continental United States, reflecting the CPUSA's official policy on interracial organizing. Camp Unity attracted many of its attendees by offering musicians, actors, and directors free room and board in exchange for their work. As a result, many performers often came to the camps to get away, allowing Camp Unity to claim that it "featured the best jazz music within a hundred miles."[69] That fully integrated camp was a welcome respite for leftist and working-class African Americans, but some accounts indicate that relations within the camp did not lack friction.[70]

Camp Unity's encouragement of interracial leisure in the post–World War II United States appealed to not only working-class Black people and Black leftists but other marginalized groups as well. One of the most infamous of these guests was noted Harlem gangster Ellsworth "Bumpy" Johnson, known as the "Harlem Godfather" due to the control he exerted over the numbers racket, the drug trade, and prostitution rings above 110th Street. Mayfield claimed that Johnson regularly vacationed at the camp in the 1940s.[71] Whereas Italian, Jewish, and other white gangsters vacationed in Palm Springs and Miami, Johnson drove up to Camp Unity every summer and rented a cabin by himself because he felt safe "among a bunch of radical nuts."[72] Although one could rent private homes in Florida or travel to Cuba and Puerto Rico, Mayfield reported that Johnson preferred Camp Unity, as it did not require a long trip through the segregated South or a segregated plane ride.[73]

Mayfield, ever the optimist, wrote that he attempted to recruit the aging gangster to the Marxist cause, but the older man rebuffed him; Johnson explained that he opposed the Communist Party because he believed that leftists "didn't understand power, that power belonged to the person who had the guns."[74] In an unsubstantiated claim, Mayfield stated that Johnson had been the one driving the car that carried Paul Robeson to and from his second concert at Peekskill, which had resulted in a violent response by local whites and increased Mayfield's estimation of the man.[75] Johnson told Mayfield that "he had no patience with a non-violent philosophy and that he was damned if he was going to see one of his heroes killed because he was surrounded by a bunch of non-violent quacks."[76] Johnson's easygoing nature and status as the Harlem Godfather left a deep impression on the young Mayfield, and he would subsequently make the numbers racket, a key income stream for Johnson, a major plot point in both of his first two novels.

The ambivalence Mayfield expressed in his autobiography about Camp Unity reflected the complexity of his experience, but criticism of his first forays into writing by white leftists planted the seeds of his eventual rejection of interracial social movements. "The staff was integrated," Mayfield recalled fondly. "We even had a couple of Orientals among the waitresses, and an honest-to-god Eskimo waitress who took in good humor all the dumb questions she was asked."[77] This focus on interracial harmony, however, frustrated Mayfield, as it re-created many of the racial hierarchies at work outside of the ideological homogeneity of the camp. In a confrontation with a woman following the first production of his one-act play, 417, Mayfield articulated his unspoken frustration for the first time.

The woman, whom he called Edith, complimented his play, but she confessed that she was uncomfortable with the fact that "there were no white people in that play, no white people at all." Momentarily flummoxed, Mayfield recalled feeling embarrassed at the oversight. Camp Unity was one of the few truly interracial resorts in the country, and "the theme of all the [party] faithful was black and white racial unity." The issue seemed to upset Mayfield as much as it had Edith, and in spite of himself, he apologized for not including a single white character. As the conversation progressed, however, it dawned on Mayfield that the Harlem in which 417 was set had few white people, and those present were the business owners, landlords, and police officers. Mayfield also recognized that no one would have batted an eye if the company had produced a play about a white family living in the United States that included no Black characters. "Whites and Blacks don't really have much to do with each other in this county," Mayfield wrote, and in spite of working together, using the same transportation and market facilities, whites and Blacks, "hardly know each other."

Edith's comment, reconsidered nearly twenty years later, got at the heart of this fact. The artifice of including white characters in Black stories, when "their literature usually ignores Blacks [. . .] as human beings," became transparent to Mayfield. "If our writing is too much preoccupied with [whites]," he commented in his unpublished autobiography, "it is because their power too often impinges on our lives culminating in dramatic confrontations."[78] Mayfield's frustration and resentment with Communist Party dictates on Black art developed into a full-throated critique of American literature over the course of the 1950s and informed much of his thinking about political art and race and his publications for the remainder of his life.

In an article written about fellow Harlem Writers Guild member and friend Lorraine Hansberry in a 1979 issue of *Freedomways*, Mayfield recalled that "she only became a playwright because she was so disappointed, and often angered, by other plays written about Afro-Americans."[79] Mayfield's drive to produce art for the Black working class reflected these same frustrations; his first two novels—*The Hit* and *The Long Night*—had only incidental white characters who served as antagonists and embodiments of repression. In a 1974 letter to Mark Crawford, Mayfield recalled his frustration with working within "multi-racial organizations." Describing how he been active in such organizations since 1947, he asserted that his rejection of such groups had become "a matter of principle." Although multiracial organizations might have a balanced membership of white and Black Americans, Mayfield recognized that "the whites would usually end up boss man, because they supply the money."[80]

In these spaces provided by the Communist Party—the Jefferson School, Camp Unity, and *Freedom*—Julian Mayfield developed his own radical project, fusing art with politics to encourage solidarity across socioeconomic and racial divisions—without strict adherence to orthodox dogma. Like many of his contemporaries in the Black cultural Left, he challenged American anti-Black racism through art, although much of that paralleled the Communist Party line. A relatively minor figure among African American communists, Mayfield recalled that he had little fear of being blacklisted or having to take a loyalty oath. "None of this black listing involved me personally," he confessed, "for blacks never worked very much anyways, and I had no reputation worthy of mention."[81] Self-deprecation aside, Mayfield's choices would soon place him squarely in the crosshairs of the FBI. In 1954, the FBI initiated surveillance on Mayfield, his friends, and his family. Fearing further collaboration between African American radicals and communist groups in Puerto Rico, FBI agents watched closely and investigated Mayfield as he began a new chapter of his life.

2 Invisible Island, 1954–1959

Es Borinquen la hija, la hija del mar y el sol, del mar y el sol
—Puerto Rican National Anthem "La Borinqueña," 1903

Groups like Negroes in the U.S . . . occupy what is really a colonial status and make the kernel and substance of the problem of minorities.
—W. E. B. Du Bois, 1945

Julian Mayfield's radicalism may have been born in New York City, but it was in Puerto Rico that it came of age. Yet this time period is largely absent from Mayfield's own reminiscences and the scholarly work that mentions him. When he returned to New York in early 1959, the thirty-one-year-old writer had already published two novels and was invited by conference organizer John O. Killens to chair a panel at the upcoming conference "Social Responsibility and Social Protest" hosted by the American Society of African Culture. This provided Mayfield with a venue in which he could express his anxiety and frustration with the integrationist project, especially as it pertained to the ongoing struggle against colonialism. Accompanying him on that panel were fellow writers Lorraine Hansberry, Sarah E. Wright, and James Baldwin.[1] Mayfield's contribution, "Into the Mainstream and Oblivion," later published in the American Society of African Culture volume *The Negro Writer and His Roots*, analyzed the issues facing African American writers in the midst of five years of civil rights struggles and spoke directly to those who were disenchanted with the limited objectives presented by the movement's leadership.

"Into the Mainstream and Oblivion" began with an anecdote of a conversation between an African student and his African American friends. When the African asked his American compatriots what would they do "in the unlikely event that the United States becomes involved in a colonial war in Africa," their answer was clear.[2] Laughing, they proclaimed, "Man, we will shoot you down like dogs!" What troubled Mayfield about this exchange was the apparent enthusiasm of young African American men to go to war to protect European colonial power in Africa. This fact presented him with "a most perplexing dilemma," as it was evident to him that the modern African American "does not know who he is or where his loyalties belong." Explicitly positioning Black Americans as another colonized people, Mayfield expressed frustration that the awareness of this reality was lost on many of the young people he knew. If nothing was done to convince African Americans that their natural allies in the struggle for liberation were in the colonized nations of Africa and Latin America, he argued, such struggles would wither and die on the vine.

It was not the first time Julian Mayfield had spoken out on international matters. In 1951, he penned a scathing editorial published in the *Washington Post* in which he condemned the United Nations' invasion of Korea and characterized the "police action" as a novel form of US imperialism. In this piece, his argument echoed those made by A. Phillip Randolph a decade prior when the labor leader had decried US involvement in World War II. Black soldiers, Mayfield wrote, were still fighting for the "freedom" of a nation while suffering the indignity of segregation and second-class citizenship at home. Eight year later, essays such as "Into the Mainstream and Oblivion" reframed these arguments to decry the false hope that many Black writers found in becoming part of the American mainstream. African Americans in search of freedom should hesitate and consider, Mayfield argued, whether first-class citizenship would ever end the dominance of white society and Black alienation. Instead, he concluded that what integration would produce was not freedom but rather "submersion in what is euphemistically called the American melting pot." Even as he stopped short of calling African Americans a colonized people, he exhorted African Americans to look beyond the borders of their nation for models and allies, noting that white Americans had consistently demonstrated that integration was acceptable only on their terms. Only solidarity with the colonized peoples of Earth, Mayfield argued, had the potential for meaningful change and true liberation. This change in tone marked a profound shift in his writing and activism and also illuminates how Puerto Rico influenced radical trends among African Americans and others opposed to American empire.

This chapter focuses on the political transformation during the five years that Julian Mayfield spent in Puerto Rico, where he married, became a father, and wrote his first two novels. Contemporary biographical sketches and subsequent historical monographs typically portray these ideas as having emerged fully formed in 1959. If any attribution was offered, such as by the Federal Bureau of Investigation's (FBI) surveillance reports on Mayfield, it centered his radical politics in the Communist Party and his close working relationship with the Black cultural Left in New York. However, this pivot to what John H. Clarke would call the "new Afro-American nationalism" went hand in hand with Mayfield's growing interest in the struggles in the Third World, the disenchantment with both US capitalism and Soviet communism, and the search for alternatives to cooperation with white supremacy. The ideas Mayfield expressed in the late 1950s may appear at first glance to be built on his work with *Freedom* magazine and his time at the Jefferson School but should be read as his own encounter with the colonial experiences of Puerto Ricans in the rural village of Naranjito.

Uncovering the Puerto Rican roots of Mayfield's radical embrace of Third World liberation movements, this chapter also centers the relationship between Mayfield and his first wife, Dr. Ana Livia Cordero, as an integral component of his radical political transformation. A lifelong nationalist and an advocate for Puerto Rico's poorest and darkest residents, Cordero nurtured Mayfield's nascent internationalism, a fact largely ignored by historians and even Mayfield himself. This has been due in no small part to the paucity of sources, as Dr. Cordero's archive was only retrieved by Dr. Sandy Placído in 2014 and processed by archivists at Harvard University's Schlesinger Library the following year. But this absence also highlights another important aspect of Mayfield's radicalization in Puerto Rico, that of Puerto Rico and its status as a colonized space in US political and economic history.

This phenomenon is not new and has in fact been named. Boricuan scholars Frances Negrón-Muntaner and Ramón Grosfoguel coined the phrase "Puerto Rican invisibility" in 1997 to describe the "general unawareness concerning American colonial history" in mainland popular culture, politics, and academia.[3] Even Mayfield was not aware of Puerto Rico prior to his marriage and would confess that he knew virtually nothing about the island before meeting Dr. Cordero. This invisibility can be seen most clearly in historians' ignorance of the nationalist struggle for the independence of the island that raged through much of the post–World War II years and the failure to include those struggles in historical analyses of the postwar era. When the history of Puerto Rico's nationalist movement after 1947 is considered, this invisibility takes on political meaning.

Beginning in 1950, a series of armed uprisings rocked the island; nationalist party members and other independence-oriented groups staged violent attacks with the hopes of forcing the US-backed government of Luis Muñoz Marín to demand independence. These were not incidental efforts, nor were they confined to Puerto Rico. On November 1, 1950, two nationalists attempted to assassinate President Harry Truman in

Washington. Subsequently, on March 1, 1954, four nationalists drew weapons on the Ladies Balcony of the House of Representatives and sent a hail of bullets into the chamber while it was in session, wounding five congressmen. These violent attacks are rarely discussed, and even today many citizens of the US mainland are unaware that Puerto Ricans are US citizens, lack congressional representation, and cannot vote in national elections unless they reside on the mainland, to say nothing of how US capital has effectively exploited the island for more than a century. Mayfield's own journey from ignorance to awareness, documented in autobiographical fragments and letters, served as the raw material that he would later shape into a critical analysis of the politics of armed self-defense in service of Black liberation in the United States and, later, in the West African nation of Ghana.

Leaving New York in 1954 as a rank-and-file communist, Mayfield returned to the United States in 1959 as an internationalist-minded radical committed to the liberation of all the world's colonized peoples. He recognized that an overt focus on the domestic and the local was inadequate; instead, "the Negro writer may conclude that his best salvation lies in escaping the narrow national orbit—artistic, cultural and political—and soaring into a space of more universal experience."[4] Without considering the impact of Puerto Rico and the nationalist inclinations of Dr. Cordero, Mayfield's subsequent embrace of an Afro-diasporic writing lacks historical context and appears sui generis. Considering these changes in light of the role of Puerto Rico clarifies the interrelated interests of African Americans and Puerto Ricans at the height of the Second Red Scare.

Love and Marriage

Dr. Cordero's role in Julian Mayfield's archive is limited to a few recollections and documents related to the couple's acrimonious divorce in the early 1970s. Her own papers and her own intellectual and political development reveal her influence on his intellectual and political growth, especially during the first decade of their marriage. Their relationship also offers a glimpse into the broader relationship between African American and Puerto Rican radical movements of the 1950s, which shared not only physical space in New York but also ideological and economic concerns based on racial strictures and white perceptions that they were not fully American. For Mayfield, this meant his recognition of the similarities between colonization in the Caribbean and the Jim Crow South.

In Puerto Rico, Mayfield witnessed an island that did not enforce a color line in public accommodations and yet remained sharply divided by race. The influence of Cordero's nationalism also contributed to Mayfield's ultimate rejection of the Communist Party in 1956 or 1957. Through his experiences in Puerto Rico, Mayfield recognized the utility of nationalist organizations for the purpose of overthrowing the ruling class, challenging Communist Party orthodoxy. Furthermore, Dr. Cordero's indefatigable commitment to her own island's liberation and her concern with its poorest and neediest inhabitants provided Mayfield with arguments and themes that would appear regularly in his writing over the coming decade. Love and marriage thus shaped the contours of his radical anticolonialism during the 1950s and contributed to his public statements, published works, and the activism that would catalyze his self-imposed exile in West Africa in the 1960s.

Mayfield met Cordero by happenstance at a friend's party on Central Park West sometime in late 1953. Dr. Ana Livia Cordero was, he recalled, "an attractive, brilliant young woman who usually finished first at school," and Mayfield was smitten. He later wrote that he told a friend after their first meeting that he would marry her. Cordero, born in 1931, attended the University of Puerto Rico at Río Piedras and then Columbia University Medical School, graduating with honors from both. Mayfield explained with pride that she had refused to attend her graduation from Columbia because former President Dwight Eisenhower, then serving as the university's president, gave the commencement speech. Cordero, he explained, "did not want to accept a diploma from a person for whom she had little respect."[5]

In the midst of a divorce to her first husband when she first met Mayfield, Cordero welcomed his advances.[6] Their courtship was brief and intense. Her work at Sydenham Hospital meant that "she was usually on the run, eating faster than anyone I ever knew."[7] Fortunately, Mayfield kept writers' hours and was available to spend time with her late at night or early in the morning, and he recalled fondly their conversations at barbecue joints along 125th Street. "Whenever we had a chance," Mayfield recalled, "we talked and talked and talked, which would have been all night if it had stopped there."[8] Once her divorce was finalized, sometime in early 1954, Cordero and Mayfield decided to make a life together and began planning their wedding. This announcement was not welcomed by their friends and family. Cordero's parents expressed misgivings about having a struggling writer as a son-in-law. Their engagement also became a source of contention among their comrades in the Communist Party. When they announced their plans to move to Puerto Rico, Mayfield's friends voiced their displeasure. Several of them told him that they "felt [he] was copping out of the class struggle" because the couple had decided to relocate so Cordero could finish her medical training.[9]

Despite her age (she was only twenty-two when she met Mayfield), Cordero had been involved in the island's nationalist politics for many years before moving to New York. This political sensibility was her birthright. Cordero's father, Rafael I. T. Cordero, trained as an economist and was appointed comptroller by President Franklin Roosevelt in the early 1940s. During World War II when a series of student uprisings rocked the Río Piedras campus at the University of Puerto Rico, Don Rafael publicly supported the students. He did so without fear of dismissal, because the US federal appointment prevented the island's governor from removing him from his position.[10] Despite their progressive politics, Don Rafael and his wife, Doña Vivi, were uneasy with their daughter's new fiancé. They couched their concern over the nuptials in economic terms. "Although writing was respected," Mayfield said of his Puerto Rican in-laws, "it was considered more a hobby than a profession."[11] With her parents worried that he could not support her and with his friends worried that he was leaving the struggle, the couple's decision to forge ahead was proof of their mutual affection.[12] After leaving New York in March, they settled in the outskirts of San Juan and were married there on November 6, 1954.[13]

Mayfield had few prospects when the couple arrived in Puerto Rico, and it was Cordero's network of friends who were able to help him find work. In his first job, Mayfield traveled the island conducting surveys on radio audiences for a marketing firm. "In this way I saw most of the towns on the island," Mayfield recalled. There, he also "encountered poverty on a level I had never imagined while I lived in the United States."[14] Familiar with working-class privation in Washington and having seen the conditions facing native Hawaiians on Oahu, Mayfield painted a vivid portrait of the plight of Puerto Ricans. Even on Oahu "there had been no place like El Fanquito," he wrote of San Juan's notorious slum, where "people lived in huts on stilts above greenish, brackish swamp and mud." In settlements outside of the central highland city of Caguas, he saw "pretty little black and brown-eyed kids romp[ing] in the ankle-deep open drainage which ran past their front doors after a heavy rainfall."[15]

The recognition that it was Puerto Rico's poorest and blackest residents who lived in these conditions marked a shift in Mayfield's politics. It also had profound repercussions on his personal and professional life. He became adamant that despite US claims to the contrary, Puerto Rico was recognizable as a colonial possession. Lacking sovereignty, Puerto Ricans were beholden to a legislature and an executive that received virtually no input from the people it governed. That it was dark-skinned people who occupied the lowest rungs of the socioeconomic ladder was further proof of the intransigent and transnational nature of white supremacy. In contrast to many of the positive articles in African American newspapers, most of which were the result of short visits, Mayfield noted that these conditions existed in spite of the lack of a defined color line or a system such as Jim Crow.

In linking color with socioeconomic status on an island that prided itself on not having a legal color line, Mayfield challenged contemporary accounts of how the island lacked the racial bias of the US mainland and slowly began to understand the tense political situation he now lived within.[16] As a Black man raised in the United States, Mayfield was familiar with poverty and coded racial rules, but he was unprepared for the violent suppression of the island's struggle for self-governance and sovereignty. His relationship with Cordero not only helped him gain employment but also offered him a close-up view of the nationalist struggle that proved formative to his nascent politics of liberation.

The evening after their arrival in mid-March 1954, Mayfield and Cordero dined at the home of César Iglesias and his wife Jane. The couple were old friends of Dr. Cordero from her time at university.[17] Two days later, Mayfield and Cordero received news that their hostess was among the people arrested in a series of police raids. Jane Iglesias was charged with sedition and taken to La Princessa, the infamous and violent prison, but her husband César and three of his associates—Juan Santos Rivera, Juan Saez Corales, and Pablo Garcia Rodriguez Cordero—escaped the police and remained on the run for several weeks before eventually turning themselves in at newspaper offices.[18] "If you are a political prisoner it is safer that way," Mayfield noted wryly as he recounted this incident. Turning yourself in at a newspaper office was a common practice among nationalists because "the reporters can attest to the state of your health before the cops go to work on your head."[19] Although Mayfield considered himself educated and worldly, he acknowledged that prior to meeting his Puerto Rican wife, he was entirely ignorant of the conditions and politics of the island. He did not involve himself directly in the Puerto Rican nationalist movement, but his close proximity gave him insight into how the United States imposed its politics and culture on the small island, a sentiment that was reflected in his subsequent articulation of a new Black radicalism.

At the time, Mayfield opted to simply keep his head down and work on his novels. This was in part a financial decision. The newlyweds were poor, making due with shipping crates for furniture and a single chair until Mayfield was able to secure full-time employment as a journalist. In the meantime, they relocated to a postwar housing project called Puerto Nuevo that had recently been built outside the small town of Naranjito. Located in a hilly region some fifty kilometers south of San Juan, the development comprised "acres and acres of little concrete houses with three small bedrooms [whose] uniformity was relieved by the individual tastes of the owners."[20] Despite their relative privation, Mayfield's infrequent recollections of the time indicate that the couple was happy and very much in love. Dr. Cordero worked in a nearby hospital, and Mayfield began adapting his play *417*, communicating frequently with colleagues such as John Henrik Clarke in New York.

Despite the early association with nationalists such as Jane and César Iglesias, Mayfield avoided close contact with Puerto Rican nationalists other than his wife. As a journalist he nevertheless found himself reporting on their activities and recognized the similarities and differences between the Puerto Rican nationalist struggle and the African American freedom struggle on the mainland. Critical of the latter, especially of the Southern Christian Leadership Convention's (SCLC) strategic use of nonviolence and the politics of respectability, he was primarily focused on the violence that the repression that nationalist violence generated in his new home. Puerto Rico provided a stepping stone to his embrace of the new Afro-American nationalism in the late 1950s as well as his critique of integration politics, as he believed that he had seen the results of integration firsthand on the island. The influence of the postwar Puerto Rican nationalist movement on the African American freedom struggle remains poorly understood, but Mayfield's experiences offer a means to better understand the connections between the two movements.

La Revolución Nacionalista Puertorriqueño

What is perhaps most surprising about the nationalist uprisings that challenged US authority in Puerto Rico during the 1950s was not the vigor with which the authorities attempted to suppress the movement but rather how that struggle for self-determination remains absent from popular recollections of the era. Between 1950 and 1960, dozens of attacks by nationalist insurgents were launched on military bases, police stations, and other symbols of colonial domination. There were several assassinations attempts of prominent elected officials in Washington, DC, and as a result, hundreds of Puerto Ricans were killed and thousands were jailed in an effort to suppress this relatively popular grassroots movement. The first democratically elected governor of Puerto Rico, Luis Muñoz Marín, worked closely with US law enforcement agencies, especially the FBI, to detect and suppress the networks of nationalists responsible for these uprisings. However, the complete absence of discussion of the nationalist tradition in Puerto Rico, especially in the wake of the ongoing debt crisis and the two devastating hurricanes of 2017 and 2018, is indicative of how Puerto Rico's invisibility remains one of the most significant barriers to change.

Rooted in nineteenth-century criollo demands for autonomy from the Spanish Empire, the nationalist movement that arose after World War II differed markedly from its earlier incarnations. This was due in part to the differences between the two empires. In contrast to the Spanish Empire's limited involvement in the backwater island territory, the United States arrived in Puerto Rico in 1898 with intentions to "modernize" the nation. Like Spain, the United States not only limited Puerto Rico's ability to trade with other nations but also opened the nation up to American industries that eyed the abundant cheap labor and the minimal government oversight the island offered. Although limited land reform measures were undertaken in the wake of World War II, the postwar era unleashed massive socioeconomic changes on the island, prompting nearly one-third of the population to relocate to the United States in order to survive. The nationalist uprising that Mayfield witnessed in the mid-1950s was the product of two interrelated factors: the "rising wind" of anticolonialism that followed World War II and the release of Puerto Rican nationalist Pedro Albizu Campos from prison in 1947. As historian Brenda Gayle Plummer notes, colonized peoples took advantage of the propaganda deployed by the allied nations during the war, attempting to hold the imperial powers to their claims that they were fighting a "war for democracy." In Puerto Rico, this wind fanned the spark provided by the return of Campos to national politics until it was a raging wildfire.

Born in 1891, Campos was raised in Ponce, a city on the island's southern coast. He studied chemical engineering at the University of Vermont and later transferred to Harvard University in 1913. Following the outbreak of World War I, Campos volunteered to serve in the US infantry and was assigned to the all-Black 357th Infantry Regiment. After surviving the anti-Black racism in the army, he returned to the island in 1919 and joined nationalists in organizing against US hegemony. By the 1930s, he had become known for his embrace of violent spectacle to agitate for national sovereignty. Following the Río Pedras Massacre of 1935, in which four nationalist party members were gunned down by police at a rally on the campus of the University of Puerto Rico, Campos embraced a punitive response toward state violence. In a 1936 speech, he declared that "the present imperialist policies which want to dissolve nationalism through terror and assassination is a provocation and an act of imperialist foolishness aimed at satisfying a handful of North American corporations."[21]

Later that year, Campos was arrested and convicted of conspiracy to overthrow the US government. He was sentenced to ten years in prison. Despite being held at the Atlanta Federal Penitentiary during the Ponce Massacre of March 21, 1937, Campos publicly pledged to kill a continental American citizen in retribution for every nationalist killed.[22] His sentence was later increased to twenty-five years for sedition after statements such as these were smuggled out of prison and printed in pamphlets that were distributed on the island. Despite these additions to his sentence, he was quietly released from prison in 1947 and deported to Puerto Rico. Now fifty-six years old, Campos was the elder statesman of the nationalist movement, but neither age nor his decade-long prison sentence had dulled his revolutionary fervor. He resumed his position as the president of the Partido Nacionalista de Puerto Rico (Puerto Rican Nationalist Party) and immediately began organizing a new campaign to force the United States to grant Puerto Rico unconditional independence. In the fall of 1950, the nationalist movement launched simultaneous attacks on military bases and police stations spread throughout the country. Although those insurrections were quickly and brutally suppressed, nationalists on the island were invigorated.

The relative obscurity of the violence of the postwar nationalist movement—in particular of the two violent incidents in the mainland United States related to it—emphasizes the accuracy of Negrón-Muntaner and Grosfoguel's nomenclature. The idea of Puerto Rican invisibility not only offers a useful shorthand to communicate the surfeit of discussions on matters related to the island's quest for national sovereignty but also offers a stark contradiction between the popular perception of the island's conditions in the 1950s and the US government's role in stifling nationalist aspirations. The two incidents in Washington, DC, mentioned in the introduction are integral to understanding the repression that Mayfield and Cordero witnessed on the island in the mid-1950s. The first occurred on November 1, 1950, after two nationalists, Oscar Collazo and Griselio Torresola, attempted to assassinate President Truman as he napped in Blair House, just down the street from the White House.

Truman was unaware of the attack, but one of the attackers and a police officer were killed in what has become known as "the biggest gunfight in Secret Service history" despite lasting less than a minute.[23] The incident drew Truman's attention to the island but did not substantively alter economic and social policy. It took another incident to push the US government to intervene. On March 1, 1954, four Puerto Rican nationalists smuggled semiautomatic pistols into the US Capitol and fired on the House of Representatives while it was in session.[24] No one was killed, but five representatives were wounded in the attack. The police crackdown that Mayfield and Cordero witnessed upon their arrival in Puerto Rico was an immediate response to these incidents. The nationalist movement could no longer be ignored, and the FBI joined forces with local law enforcement to initiate a campaign of surveillance, imprisonment, and torture to stop the nationalist attacks.

In addition to the crackdown on nationalists, Puerto Rico was also in the midst of a rapid economic and social transformation. The sugar industry, the largest employer and owner of the majority of the land on the island, had become the focus of reformist policies initiated by the island's governors beginning in the 1930s. Governors Theodore Roosevelt Jr., Blanton Winship, and Rexford Tugwell "enacted policies to stifle the growth of large canefarms" in hopes of improving access to land for local farmers. These changes signaled the slow decline of the sugar industry, and beginning in the late 1930s, the productivity of the industry began to decline until by the 1940s it had effectively collapsed.[25] The demise of the sugar industry further increased out-migration, as sugar production had required a great deal of agricultural labor, but its decline also led to the government of Governor Marín encouraging US manufacturing firms to relocate to Puerto Rico to take advantage of its youthful population, low wages, and lack of trade unions.

In addition to the difficult economic and labor situation on the island, Governor Marín inherited deeply unpopular social laws that criminalized nationalist speech and activity. In 1948 the previous governor, Jesús T. Piñero, implemented a law that criminalized nationalist advocacy, activism, and discourse. The Ley de la Mordaza, also known as the "Gag Law" and the "Little Smith Act," made it illegal to advocate the overthrow of the government and was crafted to eliminate the leaders of the nationalist and independence movements and intimate their followers. Furthermore, the law made it illegal to display or even own the Puerto Rican flag, speak out or write on the subject of independence, meet with anyone or organize an assembly in favor of Puerto Rican independence, and even sing a patriotic song. Explicitly modeled after the Smith Act (1940), the Gag Law infuriated nationalists and further spurred the rebirth of the nationalist movement. Marín's response to protests and sporadic violence, as Mayfield concluded, was simply "to lock everybody up, communists, nationalists, socialists alike, anybody who didn't like the government."[26] Not only did this anger citizens, it also placed these groups—which often violently disagreed with each other—on the same side of a nationalist struggle.

Mayfield, acutely aware of how the Smith Act had been used to attack communists and leftists in the United States, recognized the familiar contours of the law that had resulted in the blacklisting and imprisonment of many of his American colleagues. In the autobiographical fragment "La Boriqueña," Mayfield noted that the law was crafted because of the nationalists' objections to the presence of manufactured goods and cultural imports from the mainland. American television shows, films, dress, and pop culture were cited as examples of "Yankee Imperialism" that undermined local culture, causing young people, in Mayfield's words, to "emulate the youth of the colonial power."[27] This cultural hegemony was exacerbated by the influx of industry owned by mainland Americans, which sought to transform the agrarian rural economy into a modern industrial one. However, those economic imperatives also pushed the core of the nationalist movement beyond the shores of the island.

In a case of historical irony, the massive out-migration of Puerto Ricans that paralleled the slow collapse of the sugar industry shored up the foundations of what was a sputtering nationalist movement. Those who fled were able to pursue nationalist activism with less fear of direct police repression. Public displays of Puerto Rican nationalism, such as flags and meetings of the nationalist party, were not banned in the diasporic communities of Chicago and New York. Neither were associations and social clubs, which allowed men and women to organize their communities in the burgeoning diaspora. Wages on the mainland were also higher than those on the island and worker protections were better enforced. Puerto Ricans in the diaspora also developed a stronger sense of their own national identity in light of their minority status in the United States. Restrictive laws and an inequitable relationship with the federal government in Washington prevented Puerto Ricans from not only developing their own industries but also even acknowledging their own culture, something diasporic communities did not have to deal with.

Although limited in scope, Mayfield's observations about the island recognized how colonial subjugation combined with racial and economic repression to shape the high rates of poverty and economic dislocation on the island. These disparities also catalyzed a nationalist movement that Mayfield compared favorably to the political activism he had been a part of in New York. "The difference (in those days) between US radicals and those in the Caribbean and Latin America," Mayfield wrote with an eye toward his own experiences, "was that nearly everyone in the latter group had been in prison several times and took it as a matter of course." Unlike communists and other radicals in the United States "most Latin American revolutionaries do not expect their relatives and comrades to knock themselves out raising bail to get them out of prison."[28] Contrasting the peaceful attempts at revolutionary in the United States with the militant liberation in the empire's periphery, these observations informed Mayfield's criticism of contemporaneous social movements and guided his developing embrace of militancy and armed self-defense as an effective strategy.

Despite his fiery rhetoric, Mayfield appears to have been inactive in politics during his time in Puerto Rico and with good reason. In 1956, Dr. Cordero became pregnant with the couple's first child. Later that same year Mayfield was hired by William J. Dorvillier, a veteran newspaper editor who had run the *Puerto Rican World Journal* from 1940 to 1945. When Dorvillier restarted the publication in 1956, he hired Mayfield as the paper's theater critic. Although it was the only English-language newspaper on the island, the *Puerto Rican World Journal* sold poorly, and its revival lasted only three years. Dorvillier personally favored the nationalist cause, and his paper was circumspect about its support for the nationalist party platform. As a result, Mayfield's columns—a total of seven published between 1956 and 1957—were bereft of political opinions or observations and provided only lighthearted reviews of theatrical productions touring the island.

Later that same year Mayfield was hired at the English-language radio station WHOA, which broadcast news and discussion programs. His reporting on current events attracted the attention of the FBI, but no transcripts or recordings of those broadcasts survive, and I can only speculate as to their content. Mayfield credited this fast-paced environment with the development of his journalism skills and his ability to write on a deadline. The birth of the couple's son, Rafael, in April 1957 did not appear to affect Mayfield's writing schedule, and over the subsequent eighteen months he submitted the finished manuscripts for his first two novels to Vanguard Press. Publication of those two novels, *The Hit* and *The Long Night*, garnered Mayfield significant publicity, and as Dr. Cordero's residency came to an end, he convinced her to return to the heart of the American literary scene in New York.

Despite the development of his career as a journalist and a fiction writer, interviews with and publications about Mayfield ignored the fact that he was in Puerto Rico for most of this time. This invisibility stands in contrast to the island's central role in the FBI's version of Mayfield's activities. Biographical accounts of him published alongside reviews of his novels rarely mentioned the fact that he was living on the island, but the FBI saw his quick relocation as a sign of deepening political commitment. The following section considers the visibility of Mayfield's time in Puerto Rico to the federal government's anticommunism apparatus. The FBI's early files on the writer-activist were intensely concerned with the potential of his associations with Puerto Rican nationalists, *independentistas,* and the Puerto Rican Communist Party. Ironically, the FBI's chronicle of Mayfield's time on the island is more comprehensive than his own reminiscences.

FBI Blues

Julian Mayfield came under surveillance by the FBI due to his political and artistic activities in New York, but it was in Puerto Rico that the FBI made its earliest observations and reports of his politics and his activism and speculated on the threat his words could pose. This surveillance was part of the Bureau's broader effort to monitor and negate the impact of Black cultural and political work, a project that began under the direction of John Edgar Hoover in 1919 when the agency was still known as the Bureau of Investigation.[29] As head of the General Intelligence Division, also known as the Radical Division, Hoover used his resources to monitor Black radicals like Marcus Garvey and Cyril Briggs. After being appointed acting director of the Bureau of Investigation in 1924, Hoover devoted substantial resources to surveilling, monitoring, and interfering with the activities of perceived Black radicals. The Counter Intelligence Program (COINTELPRO), which ran from 1956 through 1971, is perhaps the best known of these efforts, though numerous other smaller programs existed and continue to exist.[30] In an ironic turn of events, the concerted effort to observe, influence, and disrupt the production of African American literature also shaped its construction, especially between the 1950s and the 1970s, as Black writers became aware of the surveillance that was used to discredit them and wrote about their experiences. The FBI's surveillance also shaped a culture of mistrust and paranoia, as many writers and activists discovered that they were being informed upon by their friends and families. The surveillance had salutatory effects on Afro-diasporic solidarity, influencing the development of national and global Black consciousness as African American writers, aware of the surveillance, began to resent and write about the presence of FBI informants and surveillance tactics.[31] Read alongside Mayfield's account of his story, the history of the FBI's surveillance on Black writers and How it influenced their artistic production highlights a relevant aspect of Afro-diasporic intellectual and political projects originating in the United States: How attempts to forestall revolutionary literature helped shape it.

The FBI's files on Mayfield were typical in that they reveal that the bureau was particularly concerned with how radical African Americans were physically moving through the diaspora in search of solidarity. The agents reporting back to the Washington, DC, office focused on their collaborations with other African-descended peoples, although they did not recognize the meetings between anticolonial and anti-imperialist activists as racial solidarity but instead viewed it as ideological consanguinity. These connections, agents worried, would undermine US State Department efforts to discourage various nationalist and independence movements from seeking aid and close relationships with the Soviet Union; such diasporic connections also affected domestic activists' perspectives on civil rights struggles. By keeping abreast of African American literature, Director Hoover and his subordinates believed that they could get a head start on blunting the influence of these literary works before they were published.

Like FBI files on contemporary writers, including James Baldwin, Alice Childress, Chester Himes, John O. Killens, Maya Angelou, Harold W. Cruse, and Frank London Brown, memos and reports contained in Julian Mayfield's FBI dossier reflected common and typical tactics employed by the bureau. Mayfield was dubbed a "Security Matter-C" ("Communist") when the FBI became aware of his residing in Puerto Rico; the FBI was keen to discover his links to nationalists because it considered him a potential threat. The first memo in his FBI file, dated August 16, 1954, reports on his background, his family, his time in the military, and his stint at Lincoln. An initial investigation revealed no evidence of early radicalism, although it accurately concluded that Mayfield had embraced "the communist line" in New York. These early reports in the file lacked significant analysis; they primarily offered background information and were presumably provided to field agents to prepare them for surveillance. This is contrasted with subsequent reports of Mayfield's activities in Cuba and Ghana in the 1960s, in which the FBI considered his writing as part of a broader effort to encourage support for Fidel Castro's revolution and Kwame Nkrumah's African socialism.

Instead, these early reports offered information about Mayfield's biography, material circumstances, and political activities until that point. The reports included short descriptions of his work on the Committee for the Negro in the Arts and *Freedom* and the appearance of his name in the *Daily Worker* for advocating for "various left wing causes."[32] The Washington, DC, field office also conducted background checks on Mayfield's father and mother, included Mayfield's medical records, and even reported an arrest at the age of eleven.[33] The agents writing the report made note of Mayfield's marital status—single—and current address on West 99th Street, New York, without realizing that he had already left for Puerto Rico. A follow-up report, filed by agents in the San Juan field office in June 1955, notified the FBI of Mayfield's whereabouts and marriage to Cordero but completely ignored her activism and her nationalist ties, rendering her invisible on her own island.[34] The San Juan field office subsequently conducted interviews with his neighbors and initiated surveillance of Mayfield and Dr. Cordero's home in Naranjito while keeping close tabs on the people with whom Mayfield associated in Puerto Rico.

Writing by Black authors was a priority for Director Hoover's agents, and Mayfield's work was the primary subject of interest for the San Juan field office agents who surveilled him. Information gathered by an unknown informant, designated T2 in the files, nevertheless offered little in the way of actionable intelligence. "The subject stayed in his house most of the time and appeared to occupy much of his time by typing," one of the early reports stated.[35] The informant designated T2 "did not know what material the subject was typing" but recommended that agents discover a way to find out. In July, an agent informed the Washington office that he had made some recordings of Mayfield on the radio in New York, during which Mayfield was "making a joke" of the American way of life, and provided the recordings to the FBI.[36] Agents then reported that Mayfield was employed as a radio announcer for WHOA and was writing for "a Puerto Rican newspaper," but the file did not identify which one.

This absence of revolutionary content did not deter the FBI, and its agents soon shifted to Mayfield's association with the local Communist Party and the potential for radical cross-pollination. Subsequent reports described Mayfield as unemployed and linked him to the Nationalist Party after agents discovered his attendance at the dinner party mentioned earlier in this chapter.[37] Mayfield's files received wider distribution in 1956 when a meeting with an acquaintance from New York named Esther Rand briefly connected him to a Soviet spy ring.[38] Rand, a Communist Party member and the founder of the East Side Tenants Association in New York, met with Mayfield while visiting Puerto Rico regarding a play she was attempting to produce. Nothing came of their meeting, and the lead provided little in the way of useful information but did not stop the FBI from pursuing this line of inquiry. This information gathering was not without its consequences. Subsequent reports indicated that the agents conducting interviews were drawing unwanted attention to themselves. Because of the questioning of neighbors, acquaintances, and previous superiors, the report hinted that Mayfield and his family had become aware that he was the subject of scrutiny and urged agents to be more discreet in their inquiries.

Per FBI policy, agents did not approach Mayfield directly, but one memo, absent from the file provided by the FBI, appears to have requested permission to do so. A strongly worded rejection, addressed to the special agent in charge in August 1957, denied the request of that agent to interview Mayfield based on the agents' apparent incompetence in gathering material on him. "Authority to interview the subject is denied," the memo stated. "You do not know the subject's employment for the past three years, nor the subject's marital status." This rebuke, apparently from somewhere higher in the FBI's ranks, was coupled with instructions. "Make an effort to develop new sources who would be in a position to furnish information to you concerning his activities." Once this additional investigation was complete, the memo concluded, "you may wish to request again authority for an interview."[39] But no further request to interview Mayfield was found in the files, and memos decreased in frequency as 1958 approached. Having found little in the way of evidence of revolutionary activity or communist association, the FBI gradually decreased its surveillance of Mayfield until 1960.

This reduction in surveillance was closely connected to the publication of Mayfield's first novel in 1957 suggesting that the lack of "subversive" content in the novel rendered it ineffectual in the eyes of the FBI's leadership. *The Hit* received favorable reviews from critics, including Langston Hughes, and the piece's lack of communist themes and revolutionary discourse apparently mollified the FBI.[40] In contrast to the decreasing interest of the FBI, the literary community eagerly embraced the debut novel. In the *New York Herald Tribune*, Hughes himself called *The Hit* "a powerful little novel . . . of unusual interest." Literary critics also praised the novel's prose and its insight into the informal gambling pervasive in Harlem. Narrating a momentous day in the lives of the Cooley family in Harlem, the novel opens with the family patriarch winning the local illegal lottery, known as the numbers racket or "the numbers." The remainder of the novel examines how that "hit" affected his psyche, his familial relationships, and his sense of self. The numbers game was a significant component of life in Harlem and one that fascinated Mayfield; it was also one of the primary businesses of Bumpy Johnson, generating thousands of dollars a week in profits, allowing the Harlem Godfather to bribe police officers and politicians to ignore it and his other illegal activities.

The Hit's protagonist, Hubert Cooley, is a melancholy man who plays the numbers daily, daydreaming about winning the titular hit that will make him rich enough to leave his wife and run off with a woman from his church.[41] In "simple straightforward prose," Hughes wrote, the novel's characterization of winning at the numbers is an allusion to African Americans' interminable wait to access the "American Dream."[42] Like that dream, when Hubert's number does hit, the result is disappointment. Learning of the win, Hubert proclaims his love for a woman who is not his wife, throwing the Cooley family into turmoil. Despite her rejection, Hubert makes plans for his newfound wealth and finalizes his decision to leave his family. His son, who is dealing with his own strained relationship, discovers that the numbers banker who sold him the ticket has learned of Hubert's win and has packed up and left town, meaning his father will never see that money. In spite of this reality, the novel closes on Hubert waiting on his stoop, bags packed, refusing to reconcile with his wife and with no sign of the winnings that he so desperately needs to begin his life anew.[43] Although Mayfield wrote both *The Hit* and *The Long Night* in Puerto Rico, they are more reflective of Mayfield's time in Harlem and make only passing mention of Caribbean themes.[44]

Despite the absence of explicitly revolutionary discourse in these novels, the positions that Mayfield articulated upon his return to New York in essays such as "Into the Mainstream and Oblivion" illustrate the influence of his Puerto Rican sojourn obliquely. This is evidence of the influence that his brush with the anticolonial, nationalist politics on the island had on his subsequent political activism. During the four years he spent in the Caribbean, Mayfield began to regard the struggles for independence in Puerto Rico as elements of larger projects that linked the Caribbean to Africa and to the United States, a position that echoed the arguments that Cordero had articulated since they met. The solution to these interconnected problems, joined by race and organized by economic power, was for Mayfield the acquisition of political power. This was evidenced in the similarities between the nationalist struggles in the United States and in Puerto Rico during the 1950s and 1960s, a subject that the FBI recognized as well.[45]

The Song of Freedom Must Prevail

Following Mayfield's relocation to New York in early 1959, his prose took on a newfound urgency. In challenging not only the status quo of white supremacy but also the civil rights movement's focus on integration, his writing predicted the subsequent turn toward a diasporic frame in matters of liberation and freedom that was to emerge from the movement in the mid-1960s. His time in Puerto Rico corresponded with the slow ascendance of civil rights as the dominant form of African American politics in the United States, but Mayfield recognized that organizations such as the National Association for the Advancement of Colored People (NAACP) and SCLC were focused more on the symbolic value of integrating public accommodations and did not adequately address the critical and related issues of economics, social class, and culture. At best, he argued, these trappings would yield only token changes. At worst, they would leave behind those African Americans who lacked the financial resources to leave segregated neighborhoods and substandard schools and abandon African American authors to the predations and racism of white publishers. It was this last issue that Mayfield, as a writer, objected to most strenuously. "Into the Mainstream and Oblivion" identified the problem, noting how the limited acceptance of African Americans into white spaces would lead to cultural marginalization and "submersion" into the American melting pot.[46]

To avoid the slow destruction of African American culture and self, Mayfield began work on a piece that would address what he had labeled as an "insoluble dilemma," a shot across the bow in the form of narrative fiction that would explore the impact of integration strategies in striking detail.[47] The novel was centered on how the top-down approach of the NAACP and the SCLC would play out in a fictional town; Mayfield used the story to emphasize the inability of school integration to challenge the social and historical forces that kept African Americans politically marginalized, mired in poverty, and vulnerable to white violent reprisals. The novel that resulted from this project, *The Grand Parade*, was published in January 1961. It challenged the solutions to racial oppression and economic inequality offered by liberals, white and Black alike. At the same time, the novel demonstrated that Mayfield's internationalist consciousness, shaped by his time in Puerto Rico, was now joined to a new Black nationalist consciousness in which the struggle of African Americans was likened to those in Algeria, Ghana, Puerto Rico, Guinea, and South Africa.

English professor James Emmanuel, writing in 1968, argued that "Into the Mainstream and Oblivion" prefigured "a decade of insistence by American black men that the varied preciousness of their group identity be publicly recognized and turned into [a] racial project."[48] Yet Emanuel's short introduction to Mayfield's piece, which appears in the anthology *Dark Symphony*, omitted Mayfield's past association with the Communist Party and made scant mention of Puerto Rico. These erasures of the spaces and narratives of Mayfield's development as a radical writer consumed with the mission of sharing political art obscured an accurate accounting of his radical perspective. Between 1959 and 1961, Mayfield would deepen his association with political activism that eschewed the interracial cooperation of the civil rights movement and argued publicly against nonviolence as a tactic. Informed by his experiences in the Communist Party and his close proximity to anticolonial uprisings in Puerto Rico, Mayfield would emerge as one of the young radical writers who insisted that integration was not a liberatory force but instead was a political project whose benefits were limited by design.

3 The End of Summer

Literature and Activism, 1959–1960

Nothing succeeds like power—the ability to control
votes, money, and jobs—and nothing fails like the
man, group, or party that controls nothing.
—Julian Mayfield, ca. 1960

Julian Mayfield's third novel, with a plot that hinged on a school integration crisis in a fictional American city, laid bare the political machinations that lurked beneath racial integration projects in the post-*Brown* era. Begun shortly after his return from Puerto Rico, the book examined the civil rights advances made in his absence and found them lacking. At over 440 pages, the story captured Mayfield's disaffection with strategic nonviolence as a political tactic while also exploring how the destruction of the organized Left weakened the ability of Black working-class communities to defend themselves. Even as the primary narrative focused on the fictional town's liberal mayor, who initiates the integration project, secondary narratives examined how different racial and class factions variously support or decry the coming changes to the city's racial order. Coupled with the nonfiction pieces and activism that accompanied his fictional output for the era, Mayfield's work offers a trenchant critique of traditional leadership in the African American community, as it situated him as a young radical writer desperately in search of an alternative to mainstream political options.

This can be seen clearly in an article for *Commentary* magazine that ran shortly after *The Grand Parade*'s publication. Warning that the "traditional" middle-class "Negro leadership" was "in danger of losing its claim to speak for the masses of Negroes," Mayfield was quick to draw distinctions between the goals of various groups with the broader Black freedom struggle.[1] A challenge to the National Association for the Advancement of Colored People (NAACP) and the Southern Christian Leadership Conference, the piece confronted the class divisions obscured by the civil rights protests of the era. Despite *The Grand Parade*'s sharing of the dispiriting portrait of integration and Black political marginalization laid out in the *Commentary* piece, the novel was hailed by some critics as "an objective view of the racial crisis."[2] For other critics, however, the novel's literary flaws and seemingly unwieldly, disjointed plotlines diminished its artistic impact. And yet read today, Mayfield's critical portrait of the asymmetrical nature of alliances between ambitious white liberals and Black elites offers a critical perspective on the limits of grassroots organizing and up-from-below movements that emerged in the early 1960s even as it emphasized the central role that traditional political structures played.[3] In other words, as a political critique, *The Grand Parade* offers insight into civil rights efforts beyond well-known mainstream movements.

Analyzing *The Grand Parade* alongside Mayfield's embrace of armed self-defense in North Carolina, his support for Castro and the Cuban Revolution, and his subsequent flight from the United States helps fill gaps in his intellectual and political biography while documenting his transformation into a transdiasporic activist. Critical of the civil rights struggle's leaders and their failure to consider the plight of Black workers, Mayfield would soon emerge as a leading figure in a budding Black radical movement, one that embraced nationalism and Pan-Africanism and saw explicit parallels between movements for independence in southern and western Africa with battles for citizenship in the United States. Above all, this transformation further deepened the relationship between Mayfield's art and his politics. Explicitly abandoning "protest fiction" and many of the tenets of the socialist realism, *The Grand Parade* emphasized how political and social conditions constrained by liberalism weakened grassroots local movements even as they remained imperative to meaningful social change.

While the novel elaborates an intellectual and activist project, it also emphasizes the intersection of the personal and the political. Mary Washington, among the few scholars to discuss *The Grand Parade* in any depth, noted how Mayfield's semiautobiographical character Alonzo "Lonnie" Banks makes the novel one of a handful of works from midcentury Black writers that examine "the personal testimonies of black Leftists who were there." This kind of eye-witness testimony, Washington adds, was placed within art and literature so that activist writers could "protect themselves from further intimidation and reprisals."[4] Despite Mayfield's well-earned reputation as a fearless teller of embarrassing or unobserved truths, he also placed many private thoughts in his fiction, revealing them only in unpublished autobiographical work. *The Grand Parade*, then, serves as a key analytic frame of the early growth of Black Power even as it offers a narrative account of the dynamics of nationalism, integration, and Black radical thought and discourse in the mid-twentieth century.

An Objective Look at the Racial Integration Crisis

When he returned to New York in early 1959, Julian Mayfield was well aware of liberal efforts to integrate public facilities, but he did not immediately set out to write the novel that critiqued and skewered that project. Buoyed by the positive critical reaction to *The Hit* and *The Long Night*, Mayfield immersed himself in New York's literary scene and sought to adapt both novels into films with the help of his friend, Sidney Poitier.[5] Through his connection with the Bahamian-born actor, Mayfield had dipped his toes into Hollywood the previous year. Cast as the vivacious band leader Pat Jackson in the John Cassavetes film *Virgin Island*, Mayfield had less than two minutes of screen time in comparison to Poitier's significant supporting role, but the impact was apparent on Mayfield's subsequent work.[6] A one-off role for Mayfield, the part led to a brief association with Cassavetes, which included a stint writing for the actor's noir television drama *Johnny Staccato* in 1959.[7] Filmmaking dovetailed with Mayfield's authorial ambitions, and between 1959 and 1960 he was involved in negotiations to write film adaptations of both *The Hit* and *The Long Night* even as he screen-tested for the part of Jim in the MGM production of *Huckleberry Finn*.[8] When the film projects based on his novels failed to materialize and he lost the *Huckleberry Finn* part to Archie Moore, Mayfield began work on the project that would become *The Grand Parade*.

Having followed events in the United States closely as a journalist and a radio announcer in Puerto Rico, Mayfield expressed exasperation and frustration at the rhetorical response to urgent and insistent African American political demands. In his first published pieces following his return to the mainland United States, he indicated strong support for the growing mobilization of African American peoples in boycotts and public protests, but the limited objectives of these movements concerned him. Having experienced the freedom from an overt color line in Puerto Rico, he expressed disdain toward mainstream civil rights advocates and their fight for access to public accommodations. The increased visibility of Black writers in New York reinvigorated Mayfield's concerns over their methods of protest and the impact of their social commentary. In writing a novel that would ostensibly be marketed to all Americans, Black and white, Mayfield sought a route out of the "insoluble dilemma" he had identified at the Henry Hudson

Hotel in February 1959. How, he wondered, could he criticize liberal political objectives and still appeal to the largely white and liberal audience who had the means to purchase his book?

As Mayfield wrestled with this conundrum, the novel that he submitted to the press paradoxically fulfilled editors' demands to broaden his appeal beyond "Negro themes," even as it was critical of the movement that demanded integration of public accommodations, housing, and schools. Mayfield had set to work challenging the emergent post-*Brown* liberal consensus on race through art, and the resulting book did just that. As a challenge to the status quo, Mayfield regarded integration as a cynical collision of social, political, and cultural factions vying for power with little concern for African American communities' material needs. The resulting behind-the-scenes portrait adapted real-life examples of integration—with key details changed to suit his narrative—to support his thesis that integration would not fundamentally alter the socioeconomic conditions of the majority of African Americans. Examples, such as the integration of Clinton High School in Tennessee, not only lent veracity to his narrative but also provided him with characterizations and situations that allowed him to level criticism at all of the participants involved. Delving into the nitty gritty of racial integration politics, *The Grand Parade* emphasized the moral and social bankruptcy at its heart even as it demonstrated the fundamental inadequacy of desegregation of public accommodations to fundamentally alter the lives of African Americans.

In his frustration with the white literary establishment, Mayfield recognized that despite James Baldwin's eulogy for the "protest novel," a piece of narrative fiction that limited its focus to "Negro-ness" would be unable to escape that designation.[9] He therefore spent time writing a novel that was primarily populated with white characters while marketing himself "as an American, as opposed to a Negro writer." In an interview with *New York Courier* literary critic Evelyn Cunningham shortly after the book's publication, Mayfield noted how his experience growing up behind the veil legitimized the perspectives he advanced in his writing. "I have been exposed to two different worlds within the same society," he explained to Cunningham, and argued that "talent permitting, I can reveal a certain truth about both."[10] The "certain truth" that unfolded in *The Grand Parade*'s convoluted narrative was that the process of racial integration was less about improving the conditions of African Americans and more about the ambitions of liberal politicians and social elites whose concern was white liberal voters.

Although the NAACP's national president, Roy Wilkins, also criticized the "token integration . . . [of] . . . four, or 12 or 20 Negro students" into white schools, his whiggish perspective that the presence of Black students could "only be regarded as a beginning of school desegregation" infuriated Mayfield so much that he took pains to address it directly in *The Grand Parade*.[11] The novel flipped Wilkins's argument on its head by exposing the machinations behind the battles over racial integration. Mayfield repeatedly portrayed integration of white spaces as failing to alter the material and social conditions of the African American community in meaningful or measurable ways. Being allowed entry to schools, theaters, restaurants, and other public accommodations would not, Mayfield's novel showed, challenge white dominance in social, economic, and political life in the United States. Rather, *The Grand Parade*'s contention was that these legal challenges to segregation would allow some African Americans access to white institutions and accommodations while leaving the majority behind.

In *The Grand Parade*, a sprawling work, the primary plot was interwoven with a disorienting number of subplots illustrating a cross section of structural shifts in the postwar American economy, political realignment within the Black and white working classes, the abandonment of the Democratic Party by wealthy whites, and the beginnings of white flight to suburbs. The manuscript also reflected Mayfield's arguments that these issues were simultaneously regionally specific and national in scope, challenging popular perceptions that struggles over racial integration and "the Negro question" were limited to the Deep South. The fact that Mayfield deployed this critique at the very moment the mainstream civil rights movement was seizing the moral high ground in national politics provided a direct challenge to the movement's leadership and its tentative white allies, which were focused on the South and not on their own northern and midwestern neighborhoods. However, movement leaders and their white liberal allies proved to be difficult targets, as evidenced by the confused critical response. Nonetheless, in probing these ideas in depth through a piece of narrative fiction, Mayfield delved into the social and cultural impact of the structural changes, evincing a deep frustration with the options currently available, although he did not offer potential solutions.

The Grand Parade opens with a short vignette that vividly portrayed the changes wrought by the postwar economic boom. After extolling the wealth of postwar America, the third-person omniscient narration described two unnamed men settling a traffic dispute by repeatedly smashing their automobiles into one another. Their gladiatorial contest leaves their cars destroyed, but the men are uninjured. Exhausted and exhilarated, the men emerge from their battered vehicles to embrace before a cheering crowd. In this age of abundance that followed World War II, Mayfield's introduction emphasized how a celebration of national prosperity narrowed the definition of social advancement to a naked consumerism, masking the unevenness of its distribution. Implicit within the novel and in this section in particular was a challenge to this national narrative of progress. African Americans, the novel demonstrates, had seen little improvement in their economic status, whereas white Americans were in the midst of an age of abundance.

Although leaders in Washington, DC, had begun to take notice of African American demands for full citizenship since the 1930s, rhetoric did not easily give way to policy. Five years after Harry Truman's President's Commission on Civil Rights had issued its scathing report, "To Secure These Rights," Republican presidential candidate Dwight D. Eisenhower had pledged "to build a sure foundation for sound prosperity for all here at home" in his acceptance speech at the Republican National Convention. Yet following his inauguration, his administration's recalcitrance and uneven attention to civil rights made it clear to African Americans that they could expect little in the way of meaningful policy changes from the first Republican president elected since Herbert Hoover.[12] Many in the Black elite, however, remained committed to the idea that liberal political power on the local level could be marshaled to make incremental changes in employment, education, and public accommodations, changes that would eventually result in new opportunities for advancement. Mayfield's fundamental disagreement with this position was explicitly informed by his experiences in Puerto Rico and the Northeast, where he had experienced how informal color lines were enforced—not by law but instead by custom—in ways that negatively affected African-descended peoples. These ideas informed prose that lay bare the machinations of power in which the Black elite played a subordinate role even as they demanded that all African Americans place their hope within the confines of liberalism.

For this third novel, Julian Mayfield opted for a setting that was far different and far more expansive than the Harlem of his first two novels. *The Grand Parade* is set in an unnamed border state in the fictional medium-sized town of Gainesboro.[13] Its story opens with the city's ambitious, liberal mayor, Douglas Taylor, who decides to initiate a platform of reform and integration that, he hopes, will give him a chance at a Senate run. Across town, Taylor's African American counterpart, City Councilman Randolph

Banks, publicly praises Taylor's plan and throws his political weight behind the young mayor. Cynically, Banks recognizes that by delivering Black votes to Taylor, he too could rise in city politics and perhaps even become mayor. Initially, this reform program is met with little in the way of opposition. News of the plan to integrate the city's schools, however, soon attracts activists from elsewhere who bring their own objectives to the city.[14]

In the weeks after Mayor Taylor announces his integration plan, two traveling segregationists arrive in Gainesboro to organize resistance in the form of the White Protection Council, deliberately modeled after the real-life White Citizens Councils that emerged in the wake of the *Brown* decision.[15] The men, Clarke Bryant and his young associate Hank Dean, appeal to the city's wealthy elite while stoking fears of unfettered Black male sexuality among the city's white working class. Bryant and Dean are successful in their efforts, and the seeds of resistance to Taylor's plan grow quickly in the fertile soil of racism and bigotry. Incidents of racial violence are met with swift retribution, escalating the conflict from street harassment to public beatings and eventually murder. Reticence from Black parents to subject their children to the process of integration reflects fears of jeers, taunts, and assault, mirroring the experience of many of the children who integrated schools in Arkansas and Tennessee during the previous decade. Working methodically, Mayor Taylor eventually wins over a handful of Black parents who agree to integrate the school, only to discover large crowds of white and Black protesters blocking their way into the building. The final pages contrast the school's successful integration with the assassination of the mayor at the hands of Bryant's young acolyte, ending on the perspective of a young Black girl inside the school struggling to fit into the mostly white class. Integration, Mayfield implicitly warns in *The Grand Parade*, could be successfully implemented, and the costs would be great, but the benefits for the African American community would remain minimal.

Despite the decidedly cynical pictures that Mayfield painted of liberal politicians, Black community leaders, and the political machinations that resulted in integration, a number of critics missed the book's critical perspective entirely. Steven Preston of Worchester, Massachusetts, celebrated the heroism and sacrifice of Mayor Taylor: "The reader ends the book with the feeling that the battle will be won in time because some white people care enough, even giving their lives, for a fair deal for the coloured race."[16] A more negative review in the *New York Times* took Mayfield to task for the novel's poor organization but nonetheless praised his detailed presentation of the social forces of "racism and bossism, of ambition and corruption."

The problem, the *Times*'s critic Joseph Blotner noted, was how Mayfield's portrayal "produce[d] a dulling effect that ultimately defeats the purpose they are meant to achieve."[17] Blotner's comment suggested that the real heroes of the book were the leaders able to bring about integration as a meaningful compromise between segregationists and radicals bent on upending the social order. By minimizing the heroics of these brave liberal politicians, Blotner implied, Mayfield's novel did the integration movement a disservice. Reviews such as these reinforced the perception that the novel was a straightforward account of an integration struggle with a sympathetic portrait of the white liberals who sought to improve the lot of African Americans and were challenged by white segregationists and Black radicals alike.

Reading the novel in the twenty-first century, however, reveals a distinct lack of sympathy or regard for the white social workers, ambitious liberal politicians, and white community leaders. Portraying the white characters who are in favor of integration as conniving, racist, and guided by fear and guilt rather than belief in the humanity of their Black neighbors, Mayfield's writing links their calls for change to personal ambition rather than moral suasion. White support for racial integration, Mayfield concludes, stems from naked self-interest, political gamesmanship, and paternalism rather than genuine concern for the conditions endured by Black people. Black leaders are not spared from critique in Mayfield's novel. Virtually all named characters are portrayed as ineffectual, morally bankrupt, or unwilling to break free from the white institutions and organizations that had economic and political power over them. While not explicitly nationalist or separatist in orientation, *The Grand Parade*'s narrative dismissed the possibility of the existing Black elite acting as leaders in any meaningful struggle, a view Mayfield would make explicit in pieces published during the same time frame in venues such as *Commentary* and *Dissent*. Hopelessly tainted by their association with white power structures and institutions, these Black characters offer evidence of the growing influence of nationalism on Mayfield's radical leftist critique of class relations.

Although *The Grand Parade* fell short of publishers' sales projections and expectations, as one of a handful of books to express these sentiments in narrative fiction, it remains an important early articulation of an emergent resentment and frustration with liberalism that would culminate in the coming decade. The novel prefigured a growing chorus of critiques of liberalism's inadequacy in addressing the economic and class components of oppression, ideas that would gain broad acceptance in the mid-1960s with both Martin Luther King Jr.'s Poor People's Campaign and Stokely Carmichael's call to Black Power. *The Grand Parade* is also significant in that only one other Black writer, Frank London Brown, examined civil rights struggles beyond the Deep South during the early years of the civil rights movement.[18] Unlike Brown's nuanced and poignant narrative of struggles over integration in Chicago's Trumbull Park neighborhood, *The Grand Parade* cast a broad net, an effort to attract a wider readership while resisting the label of "protest novel" even as its prose challenged the liberal sentiments of its white readers.

As his comments to Cunningham and Wolfe demonstrated, Mayfield presented the story of Gainesboro from multiple angles, examining the reasons behind actions by politicians, community leaders, and grassroots activists through detailed character portraits. However, instead of a single, polemical narrative arguing that integration was liberal grandstanding or simply inadequate to combat the history of institutional racism in the United States, what emerged was a complex, interlocking character study of a medium-sized American city. There was a downside to this intricate structure. Compelling backstories for minor characters and a plot that threatened to capsize under its own weight unmoored the book from its central arguments, diffusing its message. Literary shortcomings aside, the novel showed that the tragedy of integration was its potential to succeed. To get at the implications of that argument, however, it is necessary to historicize the novel's construction.

Writing *The Grand Parade*

Unlike much of Mayfield's published works, the genesis and the construction of *The Grand Parade* can only be inferred from the final published product.[19] No early drafts or correspondence relating to its origin are known to exist. In the absence of such material, the context of Mayfield's life, writings, and travels during this time must stand in to explicate his motivation and goals. *The Grand Parade* drew heavily from real-life examples of integration, a fact that facilitates the task of deciphering Mayfield's creative process and intentions and offers insight into the novel as a portrait of Black intellectual politics and activism surrounding racial integration at a key moment in the civil rights movement. The reforms of the fictional character Mayor Taylor were clearly based on examples of desegregation efforts in Louisiana, Arkansas, and Tennessee, where the *Brown* decision prompted local activists and school boards to initiate changes through legal channels. Mayfield did not simply copy these real-life examples; he crafted Gainesboro's fictional desegregation fight to enhance narrative coherence and highlight specific objections that he had to mainstream civil rights activism in 1960. The most obvious of Mayfield's influences was the climactic confrontation at the heart of the novel, based on the integration of Clinton High School in East Tennessee.

Located in Anderson County near Knoxville, Clinton was only a short distance from the federal nuclear research facility at Oak Ridge, where that town's one high school was desegregated in 1955.[20] In 1956, Federal Judge Robert Taylor, responding to a group of African American claimants, noted Anderson County's failure to comply with the *Brown* decision and ordered the high school to desegregate with "all deliberate speed."[21] White leaders called on the population to resist the measure, and subsequent protests by white parents' groups heightened tensions in the area. The announced plan for desegregation also drew itinerant white supremacist John Kasper to the town in late August, accompanied by his young associate Asa Carter, and the two men took the lead in organizing a White Citizens Council. Kasper, a protégé and close friend of poet Ezra Pound, encouraged local whites who objected to school integration with the tacit approval of city authorities.[22] Kasper held public rallies and lobbied local politicians, encouraging people to take increasingly violent measures to maintain the status quo. As a result of these efforts, several Black students were assaulted on a street near the high school in June 1956. Police arrested Kasper but did not file charges; he was soon released. Local whites threatened other African American students who declared their intention to attend Clinton High School, but authorities continued their inaction.

Over the remainder of the summer of 1956, Kasper and Carter continued organizing local whites in preparation for the beginning of the school year. On September 1, Kasper and Carter held a rally at the Anderson County Courthouse, days before the school year was to start. Their group was met on the courthouse lawn by counterprotesters, both Black and white, and the two factions escalated their rhetoric into a violent melee, resulting in numerous injuries but no deaths. Kasper was jailed again and released on bail, and he left town soon afterward but not without a contempt charge. Kasper subsequently traveled to Washington, DC, and then Florida where he joined forces with and drew the ire of fellow segregationists.[23] Despite Kasper's departure, his influence remained after he was no longer present. Although violence against Black students dissipated, on October 5, 1958, an unknown person or persons set off a bomb in Clinton High School, destroying the building. Ironically, during the two years it took to rebuild, students in Clinton were bused to Oak Ridge's already-desegregated high school.[24]

The Grand Parade's traveling segregationist, Clarke Bryant, differed significantly from his real-life inspiration. The changes highlighted Mayfield's interest in how struggles for racial justice beyond the Deep South were affected by internal forces and shaped by external actors.[25] Unlike Kasper, the fictional Bryant hailed from Mississippi but had been active in organizing White Citizen's Councils in nearby Washington, DC, prior to his arrival in Gainesboro. In place of Asa Carter, Mayfield created troubled acolyte Hank Dean, who was driven by his abusive father to prove his masculinity through racial violence.[26] The distinctions between the real-life figures and their fictional counterparts were many, but a comparison between the novel and Kasper's own language in Clinton and elsewhere indicates that Mayfield drew the fictional Bryant's voice directly from Kasper's own.

For example, the fictional Bryant articulated common refrains from ardent segregationists in the Deep South who celebrated Jim Crow as a gift that the South had bestowed upon a nation troubled by the threat of racial integration. Bryant's words also served as the vehicle by which Mayfield was able to insert some African American criticisms of northern segregation. Furthermore, Bryant's character illustrates how the inaction of the state in addressing segregationist organizing allowed violence against Black citizens to continue unabated. Mayfield also used this character to point to the similarities between liberal integrationists and segregationists. Although the former may have officially opposed Jim Crow, both were driven by the same underlying anti-Black racist beliefs: African Americans constituted an unruly, undisciplined, and violent minority whose unfettered freedom threatened all whites.

To bolster this point, Mayfield offered an exchange between Bryant and Gainesboro's leading white philanthropist, Rosalia Stanley, that illustrated how a commitment to philanthropy and anti-Black racism are not mutually exclusive. Although Stanley identified as a liberal and claimed that "everything Bryant said was repulsive to [her]," the meeting between the two was genial. Advocating for an intensification of segregation in Gainesboro and the imposition of formal Jim Crow–style laws, Bryant cautioned Stanley that there would be dire consequences if his demands went unheeded. "Integration in the schools will lead to interbreeding, which you know will only weaken the white race," he explained, parroting race science pamphlets and widespread southern beliefs. Although Stanley expressed concern about the deplorable conditions of Gainesboro's Black ward, Greenpoint, her exchange with Bryant revealed those concerns to be paternalistic in nature. Despite the privations of the neighborhood's residents, Stanley believed that they were ultimately responsible for their poverty and poor living conditions.[27]

Stanley also pointed out that the North had successfully integrated, but Bryant ironically responded with a refrain common among Mayfield's radical contemporaries: "Only the facade of racial integration existed in the North," he asserted in the text. That region's misguided upending of the racial and social order, Bryant explained, had resulted not in harmony but instead in white flight, soaring crime rates, juvenile delinquency, illegitimate births, and moral degeneracy. "Integration does not work in the North," Bryant concluded, with the implication being that it would not work in Gainesboro.[28] And while Stanley professed her "love" for the "benighted Negroes of Greenpoint," she was swayed by her discussion with Bryant, revealing the paternalistic and racist assumptions that Mayfield believed lay beneath the philanthropy and charity that white liberals championed.[29] Although Bryant was unable to convince Stanley to publicly support his program, she took a principled stand of neutrality on the matter, lending legitimacy to Bryant's organization at a critical moment in the plot. Perhaps the most significant aspect of this exchange was in the subtly of Stanley's shift: their meeting prompted her to curtail her support for the mayor's integration plan, signaling the city's white liberal elite's tacit approval of the growing backlash against integration.

In making Clarke Bryant a product of the Deep South who headed north to stop a school integration, Mayfield sought to both create a more convincing foil for Mayor Taylor and Councilman Banks. Bryant also intended to substantiate how the battle over integration was becoming a struggle of national significance. Early cases, such as those in New Orleans and Little Rock, revealed how the Deep South was a crucial battleground, but Mayfield's goal was to predict how the border states would soon face similar conflicts. Mayfield's words in the Clarke-Stanley dialogue also echoed C. Vann Woodward's analysis that the battle over integration was also an interregional battle.[30] Bryant envisioned a clear and present danger to racial segregation in the Deep South if the de facto expressions of Jim Crow were to crumble in border states. Presenting segregation and social harmony as mutually constitutive, Bryant's arguments convinced many of Gainesboro's businessmen and politicians that the divisions formed by Mayor Taylor's integration announcement were not a recipe for future stability.[31]

Bryant's arrival in Gainesboro also symbolized a broader trend of men like him who spurred the development of mass opposition to integration and how they were able to operate without government interference. Notably, no organized mass movement appeared to oppose Bryant and Dean's efforts. In the fictional town of Gainesboro, like in small towns throughout the South, Black political and religious leaders made speeches and objected to the formation of the White Protection Council, but they lacked a mass movement to address the segregationists directly. Although such movements had been successful in Montgomery and would become a key factor in the civil rights movement's strategies in Mississippi, Georgia, and Alabama with the Freedom Riders and later the Student Nonviolent Coordinating Committee (SNCC), *The Grand Parade* emphasized how the racial justice struggles of the late 1950s lacked broad-based support from groups that had the most experience organizing across class and racial lines: those on the Left. This argument was also the most overlooked aspect of the book. In *The Grand Parade*, Mayfield pointedly examined the marginalization of the American Left through the character of Alonzo "Lonnie" Banks, and Banks can be seen as a precursor to the political arguments he would subsequently make about the decline of the Left and the implications of anticommunism within mainstream Black freedom struggles.

The New Politics of the Old Left

In 1970, Julian Mayfield expressed ambivalence about his decision to join the Communist Party of the United States of America (CPUSA) as a young actor in New York. Having grown up immersed in the writing of Langston Hughes and Richard Wright, Mayfield explained to interviewer Malaika Lumumba that he had been drawn to the CPUSA because he felt that it "offered the best advantage, the sharpest weapon by which to attack society."[32] Experiences in New York in the early 1950s soured him on the revolutionary nature of the organization, and during his time in Puerto Rico, he quietly retreated from active participation.[33] From his vantage point, the CPUSA's actions during the late 1940s and early 1950s stood in stark contrast to its radical rhetoric, and he came to believe that the party was more committed to reform than revolution.[34]

Implicit in Mayfield's recollections of his time in the CPUSA at the height of the Second Red Scare was a deep longing for the halcyon days of the 1930s and the Popular Front.[35] Although Mayfield had been a child during the

Great Depression, his introduction to the party had come at the hands of men and women who had directly experienced the vibrant, popular, organized, and militant interwar Left. Paul Robeson, one of Mayfield's personal heroes, had been among those Black radicals who had successfully mobilized men and women to directly confront mistreatment of workers, violence toward African Americans, and American imperialism.[36] In his reflections, Mayfield contrasted these forms of direct action to the anemic "passive resistance" of the civil rights movement, which he saw as lacking the necessary critiques of both class and political economy. Acknowledging the central importance that economic justice had in the movement, he nevertheless disagreed with the nonviolent tactics embraced by activists such as Bayard Rustin. Marches, boycotts, and legal challenges were inadequate solutions for the development of the Black political power that Mayfield sought for his community. He was vocal with these sentiments, loudly proclaiming them in his nonfiction work, but it is in his third novel that the reasoning behind these proclamations emerges with the most clarity. In *The Grand Parade*, the narrative arc of secondary protagonist Lonnie Banks, the younger brother of city councilman Randolph Banks, offers a fictionalized account of the marginalization of leftists, especially Black leftists, in the United States during the early years of the Cold War. This narrative reveals Mayfield's arguments about why the destruction of the organized Left was the immediate precursor to the rise of nonviolent civil rights activism.

This can be seen as soon as Bryant and Dean arrived in Gainesboro. There was no existing organized group to challenge their organizational efforts, a consequence of the persecution and blacklisting of the town's leftists and labor organizers. Over the course of the novel, much of the resistance to their white supremacist goals comes from either Black elected officials or white liberals. The lack of organized labor and an organized Black community prevents Black citizens from mounting a successful defense. Even the climactic confrontation at the school is a poorly organized ad hoc effort by a Black community stymied by its lack of a mass organization. This narrative also reflected Mayfield's belief in the inadequacy of Black leaders in politics, the church, and the community, who lacked the organizing skills and connections to the Black working class necessary to lead them. This absence, his narrative illustrates, had important ramifications for the movement as well as its history. The men and women who had marched in the streets and fought for their rights—while resisting reactionary forces—were no longer around, Mayfield would explain in interviews.

This lack of historical knowledge had profound effects on the nature of the movement and how it was perceived by historians. It was, he lamented, "as if the civil rights movement in the South grows out of nowhere, as if—as if nothing had happened before."[37]

Recent scholarship has examined this claim in more depth, especially that of proponents of the "long civil rights movement" thesis. Such scholars, especially Jacquelyn D. Hall, Robin D. G. Kelley, and Glenda Gilmore, have argued that the immediate postwar Black Left formed key linkages between the 1930s and the civil rights movement, bringing with them traditions of organizing and longer historical perspectives on segregation and violence. In positioning both the Popular Front and the civil rights movement as elements of *longue durée* history of a broader Black freedom struggle, "long movement" scholarship has also argued that the role of the Left, particularly the Black Left, has been overlooked and silenced as a consequence of anticommunist sentiment in popular culture and the academy. In presenting Mayfield's own experiences through the character of Lonnie Banks, *The Grand Parade* humanized this argument, portraying Black leftists at the end of the 1950s, a time when most Americans believed the domestic Left to be effectively extinct. More than simply contextualizing their activism as part of a continuous movement or evidence of rupture, the experiences of people such as Mayfield complicated this dichotomy, revealing how the interpersonal relationships were affected by the continuity of activism and disabling ruptures of anticommunist persecution.

In addition to exploring the intersection of personal ambition, paternalism, and cynical disregard for African American peoples, *The Grand Parade* appears intended to serve an educational role. Leaning into his new role as a movement elder, Mayfield argued that it was his job to "constantly remind [the younger generation] of where they came from and how they got to be what they are now."[38] Writing at the beginning of the 1960s, he frequently expressed his desire to educate the younger activists in the movement, yet even then this impulse was tempered by the ever-present threat of persecution and blacklisting. The lack of source material on the writing of *The Grand Parade* does not allow for a definitive answer, but I speculate that Lonnie Banks's story was intended to fulfill the role that he spoke of a decade later. In weaving Banks's story into the rich tapestry of political and social life in Gainesboro, Mayfield appears to be emphasizing what was lost as a result of anticommunism, red-baiting, and the blacklisting of former members of the Popular Front and communists in particular. Even as Mayfield's narrative illuminated a missing component of the Black freedom struggle, the political pressure on publishers and writers appears to have remanded Banks's story to the background. Although Mayfield used many autobiographical details from his own life and the lives of the Black communists he had known to construct the character, Lonnie Banks differed substantially from the young communist who spent time walking Harlem's sidewalks alongside Paul Robeson and reminisced about his clumsy attempts to recruit Bumpy Johnson, the Harlem Godfather, to "the cause."

Mayfield never stated that Lonnie Banks represented his own embrace and rejection of the CPUSA, but the parallels are too numerous to overlook. Like many characters and events in *The Grand Parade*, it is difficult not to see the similarities. For example, when Banks is introduced into the narrative of *The Grand Parade*, he is bereft after having recently been expelled from the Communist Party. Giving voice to the bruised and battered perspective of the Black Left in the post-McCarthy era, Banks's sense of loss contrasts with Mayfield's clean break from the party after his move to Puerto Rico. But both Banks and Mayfield expressed concern following the death of Joseph Stalin and subsequent revelations by Nakita Khrushchev in his "secret speech."[39] Unlike Mayfield, who left the party quietly and voluntarily, the fictionalized Banks is forced to resign after he gives a paper titled "The Americanization of the Communist Party of the USA." In it, Banks emphasizes the need for "ideological and tactical independence from the Soviet Union," a heretical notion anathema to party orthodoxy.[40]

Although Mayfield does not explicitly reference labor leader and activist A. Philip Randolph in his narrative account of Banks's heterodox arguments and subsequent expulsion, the fictional paper described in the novel bears more than a passing resemblance to Randolph's final speech before the National Negro Congress (NNC) in 1939.[41] As head of the Brotherhood of Sleeping Car Porters, Randolph had chosen to resign from the NNC following the Soviet invasion of Poland and the subsequent signing of the Molotov-Ribbentrop Pact. "Negroes," he told fellow members of the NNC, "do not reject the Communist Party because it is revolutionary or radical or because of its alleged extremism. They reject the Communist Party because it is controlled and dominated by a foreign state whose policy may, or may not, be in the interests of the United States or the Negro People." Furthermore, Randolph argued that "American Negroes will not follow any organization which accepts dictation and control from the Communist Party . . . [or] which accepts dictation and control from any white organization."[42] The notion of local control of the CPUSA was also central to Harold Cruse's criticism as laid out in his 1968 book *The Crisis of the*

Negro Intellectual. Like Mayfield, Cruse left the party in the mid-1950s in part due to what he perceived as the overwhelming influence of whites and Jews on doctrine and strategy as well as a lack of consideration for the specific racial and social conditions of African Americans. Unlike Cruse, however, Mayfield remained convinced of the utility of Communist Party tactics and strategies and avoided criticizing the party publicly.

In *The Grand Parade*, the consequences of Banks's expulsion played both an ideological role, as described above, and a practical role in advancing the plot.[43] For one, the expulsion brings the long estrangement of the Banks brothers to an end. The elder Banks sympathizes with his younger brother's predicament and reaches out, although his efforts are thwarted by Lonnie's pride and his status on the local blacklist. A touching tale of an attempt at fraternal reconciliation, Lonnie's story following his expulsion also highlights the "social death" of leftists in post-McCarthy American. Lonnie's past associations have a material effect after his expulsion from the party. He is blacklisted throughout town, and all but the most menial laboring jobs are unavailable to him. Over the course of the novel, his past repeatedly prevents him from securing employment, finding housing, or even having anything approaching a community to fall back on in times of need.

The insular nature of the Communist Party in real life also informed events in Mayfield's plot. In the novel, the party's lack of connection to the broader Black community dovetailed with anticommunist repression to explain the lack of Gainesboro's organized leftist movement. This lack of a mass movement, versed in tactics and strategies to resist interlopers such as Clarke Bryant, left the town's population vulnerable to the violent influence of the White Protection Council. As a result, the integration of Black students into white schools, initiated not by the Black community but instead by white liberals, becomes the only viable option for progress. What Mayfield demonstrated in this novel reflected the sentiments he espoused in his nonfiction writing, namely that the marginalization of an organized antiracist Left limited collective action and kept those actions segregated by race and silent on matters of class difference. The inclusion of a character such as Lonnie Banks in *The Grand Parade* also offers a fictionalized portrait of the Black Left in the aftermath of one of its most significant ruptures. Historically, accounts of African American communists have been shaped by Richard Wright's famous renunciation of the party. Originally published in the *Atlantic Monthly* in August 1944, Wright's polemical essay "I Tried to Be a Communist" repudiates his early association with the party.[44] Other important Black leftists who publicly rejected their past affiliation with the party include Max Yergan and Langston Hughes, but Wright's public attack made him a lightning rod for praise from anticommunist liberals and criticism from former colleagues.[45]

Unsurprisingly, white critics ignored the character of Lonnie Banks in their reviews, but Mayfield's friend Shirley Graham Du Bois recognized the importance of the character and highlighted him in her discussion of the book in *Freedomways*. In the summer 1961 issue, Graham praised the novel's "symphonic" voice as accurately capturing the "tempo, confusion, speed, noise, violence, bad and good, frustrations, fears, vitality, hopes, dreams, and love—which is our country today."[46] Mayfield's perspective on the complicated politics of integration was refreshing in that it demonstrated how "being a Negro in the United States *is* something distinct and different." More importantly, Graham wrote that unlike Wright, Mayfield "does not write out of despair" but instead writes "with vision," hinting at his positive view of the Left even in its fractured condition post-McCarthy.[47] Graham's comparison of Mayfield to Wright was particularly timely, especially as the Black literary community was still reeling from Wright's sudden death the previous December. In drawing a comparison between Wright and Mayfield, Graham worked toward remedying a reductive view of Black leftists in order to broaden the horizons of readers and critics alike.

In writing the character of Lonnie Banks for *The Grand Parade,* Mayfield challenged readers to understand how the young man remained steadfast in his adherence to and investment in the tactics and strategies deployed by the Communist Party, despite his frustration with its ideological and institutional orthodoxy. Although he was let down by his comrades and his party, Banks is like Mayfield himself in that he does not give up on his commitment to economic and social justice for African Americans in the United States. Banks's character was written neither to garner sympathy for the downfall of the American Left nor to explain to readers the appeal of the party. On the contrary, his story arc emphasizes the ramifications of the Left's marginalization in post-McCarthy America. In widening the frame of available perspectives, Lonnie Banks allowed Julian Mayfield to examine the difficult compromises that ideological radicals faced after a decade of successful anticommunism campaigns. The character also reflected Mayfield's attempts to make sense of his own move away from the party in the mid-1950s even as he advocated for the Cuban rebels hiding in the Sierra Maestras in the latter half of the decade.

Although the subject of the Cuban Revolution does not figure in *The Grand Parade*'s expansive narrative, Mayfield's connection with the revolution and its impact on his thinking influenced the novel's pessimistic conclusion. If integration could not work, what else was there? Examining Mayfield's experiences with Cuba and Fidel Castro's visit to New York in 1960, which occurred in the midst of writing *The Grand Parade*, highlights how Mayfield's rejection of liberalism and the strategic nonviolence of the civil rights movement was intertwined with his embrace of revolutionary nationalism in Cuba and his burgeoning friendship with North Carolina activist Robert F. Williams. Power, however, remained central to Mayfield's intellectual project. Summing up this focus in *The Grand Parade*, Mayfield gave the character of Randolph Banks—the Black city councilman with his eyes on the office of mayor—a singular line that reflected Mayfield's own views on the subject: "Nothing succeeds like power—the ability to control votes, money, and jobs—and nothing fails like the man, group, or party that controls nothing."[48]

4 An Unbelievable Kind of Revolution
Cuba and the Black Liberation Movement in the United States, 1960–1961

· ·

> It is at the heart of national consciousness that international consciousness lives and grows. And this two-fold emerging is ultimately the source of all culture.
>
> —Frantz Fanon, 1961

The impact of Cuba's revolution on the development of African American militancy and nationalist fervor has been a topic of some fascination in the decades since 1959. Historians such as Ruth Reitan, Carlos Moore, and Van Gosse have demonstrated how revolutionary racial discourse and policies were not only intended to redress Cuba's long history of anti-Black racism but were also calculated to resonate with African Americans across the Florida Strait, spurring them to action.[1] Julian Mayfield was an early advocate for the revolution and its goals, and his writing has often figured into the evidence offered in support of these conclusions. Fidel Castro's explicit antiracism and call to action fostered radical political commitments and subsequent activism that challenged the civil rights movement's moderate liberalism.

Literature scholar Cynthia A. Young has drawn from the writings and reflections of Black nationalist intellectuals Harold Cruse and Amiri Baraka, examining how their initial disagreements with one another on the subject of Cuba's revolution gave way to "common intellectual and political ground" over the course of the 1960s.[2] The intellectual transformation of those two men, one a young Beat poet and the other a dour social critic, elaborates how Black radical thought coalesced in parallel with the rising New Left, a consequence of the limitations of liberalism in the United States and the insistent call of Third World nationalism. But Cruse and Baraka were just two among fourteen African American writers and thinkers who visited Havana in the summer of 1960. Expanding the focus of Young's analysis to include the experiences of Mayfield, Robert Williams, and Ana Livia Cordero, this chapter highlights how the terrain of this "common ground" was shaped by a wider variety of experiences and impressions of Cuba's revolutionary fervor.

Mayfield's association with Cuba grew out of the relationships he maintained with fellow Black leftists in New York, especially that of Richard Gibson. In March 1960, Mayfield received a phone call from Gibson inviting him to sign his name to an advertisement that the organization the part-time journalist had founded with fellow CBS newspapermen planned to run in the *New York Times*.[3] Under the aegis of the Fair Play for Cuba Committee (FPCC), the ad, which ran on April 6, accused major US journalists and news outlets of bias in reporting on the subject of Cuba. Joining Mayfield in asking "What is really happening in Cuba?" were other intellectuals, authors, and dissidents, including James Baldwin, John Henrik Clarke, and Robert F. Williams.[4] The ad was also the world's introduction to the FPCC, and the organization declared its members' solidarity with Cuba's revolutionary government and announced their intention to counter bias in media accounts of the revolution's sweeping changes to the island nation.[5]

Not only did the statement's repudiation of US foreign policy signal the beginning of a new leftist movement, but subsequent reports contained in Federal Bureau of Investigation (FBI) files of many of the signatories also illustrated a renewed effort by the federal government to identify and blacklist radicals who publicly criticized US foreign policy. Mayfield's association with the Cuban Revolution helped to refine and refocus his activism, shifting his perspective on the relationship between the United States, African Americans, and the Third World. Despite being in the midst of writing *The Grand Parade*, Mayfield found time to visit Havana with Cordero during the summer of 1960. The experience reoriented Mayfield's thinking toward the changing relationship between the US government and antiracist activism. At the same time, the FBI's renewed interest in Mayfield following the appearance of his name in the FPCC advertisement offers insight into his actions and highlights how the Eisenhower and Kennedy administrations sought to disrupt the relationships being forged between African American radicals and Cuban revolutionaries.

In March 1960, the modest home Mayfield shared with Cordero and their son in Queens received a phone call from an FBI agent posing as a credit inspector. A memo in Mayfield's FBI file documents the call, indicating that it was answered by a Spanish-speaking woman who answered a series of questions related to Mayfield's credit. "Julian Mayfield is always at home," the unnamed agent wrote, basing his statements on conversations with the unnamed woman. "He does not go to work; however, he does his writing at his residence."[6] Echoing earlier reports gathered by the FBI's San Juan office, the memo is significant not for what was discovered but instead for the timing of the call. The date of this report and the phone call that inspired it suggests that even before the FPCC ad ran in the *New York Times* in April, the FBI was aware of the organization's existence and those who were associated with it. Until recently, how the FBI came by this information was a mystery, but a 2018 article in *Newsweek* magazine, outing Gibson as having been on the payroll of the Central Intelligence Agency (CIA), suggests that Gibson himself may have provided information to the FBI.[7]

Renewed surveillance on Mayfield indicated that the domestic response to the formation of the FPCC was sudden and significant. Early in 1960, FBI director J. Edgar Hoover expressed his worries that the FPCC had "the capacity . . . to mobilize its efforts in such a situation so as to arrange demonstrations and influence public opinion."[8] According to historian Athan Theoharris, a few days after the publication of the April advertisement, William K. Harvey, head of the CIA's Cuban Affairs department, assured FBI counterintelligence chief Sam Papich that "this Agency has derogatory information on all individuals listed in the attached advertisement." Harvey's statement bolsters the conclusion that surveillance had begun in advance of the advertisement's publication.[9] In gathering information on suspected "communist subversives," the FBI provided intelligence for the two committees that served as the primary locus of state anticommunist efforts: the Senate Internal Security Subcommittee and the House Un-American Activities Committee.

In July 1959, just seven months after Cuba's revolutionaries had ousted dictator and American ally Fulgencio Batista, Senator James O. Eastland of Mississippi opened up the first public inquiry on communism within the Cuban Revolution. Cuban defectors, such as Major General Pedro L. Díaz Lanz, were called to give testimony about Moscow's influence in the island's new government.[10] African Americans' public declarations of solidarity with the revolution did not go unnoticed, and several African Americans were subpoenaed to appear before the Senate Internal Security Subcommittee and the House Un-American Activities Committee between 1959 and 1962, including Mayfield and Gibson.[11] However, this growing backlash did not deter radicals such as Mayfield, Cordero, and LeRoi Jones. In Cuba, they saw the potential of forging bonds of solidarity with an antiracist and anticolonial government a short flight away from the US mainland.

Among the most influential of these radicals was Robert Franklin Williams of Monroe, North Carolina, a signatory of the April letter. In June 1960,

Williams left for Cuba at the invitation of Gibson. Spending the month of June as a guest of the state, Williams returned to the United States and made a series of public speaking appearances in which he extolled the revolutionary potential of the island, especially as it related to its Afro-Cuban inhabitants. He also expressed his intention to return. When questioned by John H. Clarke, Williams explained that he wanted to return "because [he] wanted to see this social miracle again." The North Carolina–born Williams saw in Cuba something that he characterized as "unbelievable to a Southerner—particularly a Southern Negro," a place where the government was actively antiracist and intent on not only integrating public facilities but remaking those institutions out of whole cloth to undo white supremacy and anti-Black racism once and for all.[12]

On July 4, 1960, an issue of the Cuban literary magazine *Lunes de Revolución* was published that highlighted writings by "Los Negros des USA." With contributions by Julian Mayfield, Langston Hughes, Sarah E. Wright, Maya Angelou, Harold Cruse, James Baldwin, and Richard Gibson, the magazine explored how the experiences of these Black writers challenged the claims of the United States as a "land of the free."[13] Even as the magazine was making waves in the United States, the FPCC was planning another public relations statement to capitalize on the interest generated by Cuba's outreach to African Americans. Two weeks later sixteen African American writers and intellectuals arrived in Havana, where they would be guests of the Cuban state for ten days. In addition to Mayfield and Cordero, these guests included among others John H. Clarke, Sarah E. Wright and her husband Ed Clark, John O. Killens, LeRoi Jone, Robert Williams, and Richard Gibson. Although some twenty-four people had been invited, several, including Alice Childress, Langston Hughes, and James Baldwin, declined the invitation. Their reasons were varied, but concerns about the impact of a resurgent anticommunism figured prominently. Their refusal, however, was not without consequences for broader Afro-diasporic solidarity efforts.[14]

Mayfield observed that what the visitors found was astonishing. "Many of those who refused to go just could not credit the accounts of the revolution we brought back," Mayfield wrote upon his return. "It was an unbelievable kind of revolution and it was happening just ninety miles from the Florida coast."[15] What many had long considered impossible had become, in Cuba at least, a reality. Staying in the chic Hotel Presidente, the visitors mingled freely with the local population, who came and went amid the grand columns in the hotel's enormous art nouveau lobby. Mayfield and Cordero witnessed families in the process of converting the opulent, now-empty homes in Habana Vieja into multifamily dwellings and saw how new laws were putting an end to legal segregation in public accommodations and employment. They saw Black faces in officer's uniforms and in positions of civilian power, giving orders to multiracial groups of Cubans. The trip, which began with cocktail parties and tours touting the accomplishments of the fledgling government in Havana, culminated in a nationwide celebration of the anniversary of the Movimento 26 de Julio in Santiago de Cuba, on the island's far eastern end.[16] For many of the visitors, experiencing Cuba just one year after its successful revolution proved to be a significant moment in their ideological outlook and public politics. LeRoi Jones's account of his visit, "Cuba Libre," declared that "the Cuban trip was a turning point in my life."[17] The Beat poet praised the government's commitment to radically remaking the Cuban nation and wrote of the impact it had on the people he met on the trip. Busy attempting to meet his publisher's deadline for *The Grand Parade*, Mayfield was unable to write about the political and social ramifications of the encounter until the following summer.

Unlike Jones's piece, Mayfield's essay "The Cuban Challenge" focused less on his personal transformation and instead lauded the racial, social, and economic convulsions initiated by the new state. The essay focused on the Cuban government's antiracist policy developments, which challenged common anti-Black practices in hiring, education, and public accommodations. Far from merely attempting to erase the color line, an approach Mayfield had seen in Puerto Rico, Cuba's new government was radically and systematically remaking the social order by placing Afro-Cubans in positions of power. In Cuba, liberal calls for fairness and "color-blindness" were summarily ignored. Mayfield scoffed at claims that the practices were violating the rights of white Cubans, insisting that "the only right [the government] violate[s] is the right to be a bigot."[18]

Even as Mayfield celebrated Cuban antiracism publicly, his private musings reflected concerns with Fidel Castro's grasp on the politics of race in the United States. In his published works, Mayfield defended Castro and celebrated his outreach efforts toward African Americans. Privately, though, Mayfield questioned the depth of Castro's understanding of racial conditions in the American southland. Mayfield called Castro's faith in the revolutionary potential of African Americans "naive and unrealistic" and portended a clear and present danger to the struggle in the United States. In one instance, Mayfield recalled a speech in which Castro proposed a revolutionary uprising of African Americans in the South. Given Russian rifles, Castro argued, an armed uprising of Black southerners could solve the "Negro problem" in the United States once and for all. The idea that such an insurrection could possibly succeed was met with derision by Mayfield, who was shocked when he saw other visiting African Americans nodding along with Castro. When Mayfield expressed skepticism at such a plan, he noted that he was called cynical for stating that "if the rifles passed into [African Americans'] hands on Monday, the United States government would be that much richer on Tuesday."[19] In spite of the history of racist institutions and violence, the majority of Black Americans, Mayfield believed, retained a deep attachment to the American nation-state and feared jeopardizing their second-class status.

The dominance of nonviolent civil rights efforts in the United States was evidence enough for Mayfield that African Americans were not yet ready to take up arms against their government. "Blacks had fought like tigers for the US government in every one of her wars," he mused in his autobiography, "but they always laid down their arms when they came home."[20] Mayfield had also made the betrayal of African American patriots a theme in *The Grand Parade*, where he pointed to how Black citizens of the fictional city of Gainesboro did not see violence action as necessary or even possible in terms of changing their political and economic status. If Cuba represented a model to be emulated, those who touted its potential would have to consider the specificities of the African American experience beyond the small group of radicals in attendance. It was thus somewhat unsurprising for Mayfield to watch as Cuba's new government attempted to radically remake its society and continued to run up against familiar limitations of white supremacy and institutional inertia.[21]

By mid-1961, Mayfield reluctantly concluded that revolutionary Cuba, despite its impact on the burgeoning global Afro-diasporic solidarity movement and its domestic antiracist policies, had not yet undone the centuries of racist and imperialist policies that kept Afro-Cubans at the bottom of the nation's racial hierarchy. Recognition of Cuba's historical anti-Black racism had shifted the conversation in Cuban public life, sometimes with strange results, but racism remained deeply entrenched in the island's social, economic, and culture life.[22] Ultimately, Mayfield came to agree with LeRoi Jones's assessment of the revolution as transformative but focused on how it was remaking Afro-diasporic solidarity rather than his personal sentiments. The broader importance that Mayfield placed on developing this transnational cooperation prompted him to publicly minimize Castro's flaws, especially during the Cuban leader's infamous visit to Harlem.

An Oasis in the Desert

Seldom has the visit of a world leader to the United States made such an impression as when Fidel Castro visited New York City during the last week of September 1960. His first tour of the eastern United States in April 1959 was, by comparison, a positively lighthearted affair. In 1959, the Cuban leader was famously photographed visiting the Bronx Zoo, eating ice cream with American children, paying his respects at the grave of George Washington, and laying a wreath at the Lincoln Memorial. Castro asserted his anticommunist credentials to an overflow audience at Harvard's Dillon Field House after accepting the invitation of Harvard president McGeorge Bundy. "We are against all kinds of dictators," Castro explained to the assembled crowd just four months after the revolution had deposed Batista, "[and] that is why we are against communism."[23]

Castro's second visit proved far more controversial. Due to speak at the United Nations (UN) on September 27, Castro arrived on Sunday, September 18, to wildly enthusiastic crowds at LaGuardia Airport. However, the Cuban delegation's feelings of welcome quickly soured after settling in at their hotel. Less than a day after arriving at the midtown Hotel Shelbourne, Castro's delegation became embroiled in a conflict with the management and relocated uptown to Harlem's Hotel Theresa.[24] Castro's decision to relocate to Harlem, diplomatic historian Brenda Gayle Plummer has argued, "constituted a watershed" in US–Cuban relations, "not only because it coincided with a critical juncture in the history of US race relations, but also because it marked a departure in conventional ways of perceiving, and prosecuting, the Cold War."[25] In making Harlem his base of operations for the UN speech, Castro inverted the city's usual racial hierarchy by inviting world leaders to travel uptown. He also made it clear that he and his delegation were not constrained by traditional notions of diplomatic etiquette.

In contrast to the staid confines of the UN headquarters in tranquil Turtle Bay, Castro's move uptown meant that Cold War diplomacy played out along bustling Lenox Avenue as Indian prime minister Jawal Nehru, Guinean president Sekou Touré, Egyptian president Gamal Abdul Nasser, and Soviet premier Nikita Khrushchev made pilgrimages to meet with Cuba's fatigue-clad, cigar-chomping leader. This spectacular reversal of normal relations of diplomatic relations embarrassed the US State Department even as it drew attention to the second-class citizenship of African Americans in New York City. Mayfield wryly noted that Hotel Theresa was hardly luxurious, calling it "as dingy a place as you can find" in his autobiographical account of the event. Instead, he argued that Castro's stay at the Harlem institution was less about the accommodations and more about making a statement about US race relations, something that few world leaders except Khrushchev had dared to do.

The move also legitimized Castro's rhetoric about solidarity across the African diaspora for many Harlem residents. In a nation that assumed foreign leaders would avoid inflaming already delicate race relations, Castro's dramatic move, according to contemporary journalists, was "a direct slap in the face of US racial practices." Calling Harlem "an oasis in the desert," Castro made the most of the controversy, entertaining Third World leaders and local Black radical activists and perhaps most famously meeting with the Nation of Islam's fiery leader, Malcolm X. The fact that African Americans remained an oppressed minority in the United States had been a public relations problem for the State Department for nearly two decades at this point, but Castro's visit to Harlem elevated those issues to front and center for the whole world to see. Castro himself was well aware of what his visit had accomplished and noted that his visit was "a big lesson to people who practice discrimination."[26]

Perhaps most shocking, especially for white Americans, were the cheering crowds that greeted Cuba's delegation upon their arrival at Hotel Theresa. Black newspapers were quick to reassure readers that the throngs of cheering bystanders were merely curious, while Mayfield pointed out that even those who had no love for Castro were sympathetic to his move uptown. Mayfield acknowledged that while many were ignorant about Cuban politics, Castro was appealing because African Americans "know a little something about being mistreated in hotels and having their rights restricted."[27] Mayfield himself was in a position to document the visit firsthand and was at home in Queens when he received from Richard Gibson the news of Castro's move. Mayfield jumped into his car and set out for Harlem, and although he arrived at the hotel before the Cuban delegation did, a crowd had already gathered outside and was waiting when Castro emerged from a rented limousine.

Local residents were not the only ones curious about the Cuban leader setting up shop in Harlem. Influential African Americans came to either pay their respects or protest Castro's presence in their neighborhood. Ambassador Ralph Bunche and baseball trailblazer Jackie Robinson both spoke to the crowds outside of Hotel Theresa, criticizing Castro's use of Harlem for his own "grandstanding." While acknowledging that many residents were suspicious of Castro's motives and critical of his politics, Bunche pointed out that few could disagree with how Castro's visit shined a spotlight on Harlem at a key moment in African American political history. The presence of a world leader at Hotel Theresa also affected daily life on Seventh Avenue in novel ways, drawing further crowds who were there to watch. Cordons of police protected the hotel throughout the visit, the sidewalks were shut down, and many businesses nearby were forced to close due to security concerns and foot traffic. One exception was the nearby Chock Full O'Nuts franchise that, Mayfield joked dryly, must have done record business that week.[28]

Castro's UN speech, the reason for his visit, appears almost as an afterthought in Mayfield's account. Mayfield was not alone. Much of the discussion of Castro's presence in New York focuses on his meetings with Malcolm X, Nehru, and other world leaders, but the speech itself should not be ignored. The Cuban leader used his platform to decry US interference in the affairs of a sovereign nation, and he spoke at length about the conditions facing Caribbean states in the shadow of El Grande Norte. Although well received by other Third World leaders such as Nehru, Touré, and Nkrumah, the speech did little to alter US foreign policy toward the small island nation. Media accounts indicated that despite the circus-like atmosphere outside Hotel Theresa, Harlem residents and African Americans throughout the nation were paying very close attention to the visit. This was revealed most clearly in the aftermath of Castro's departure. That week, the *Chicago Defender* published a lengthy article on the impact of the Cuban delegation's stay.

This article and several others like it appeared to have been written to explain the appeal of the Cuban leader while reassuring readers that the crowds who haunted the sidewalks outside Hotel Theresa did so out of novel interest rather than a prelude to revolution. "Harlem Labels Castro's Visit as Propaganda" reported the statements of working-class men and women who expressed curiosity and mistrust at the Cuban leader's presence. Herman Griffin, a laborer, revealed an ambivalent patriotism when he told the *Chicago Defender* that he resented Castro's presence: "He did it for a publicity effect on Negroes. I don't like the way he has attacked this country." Despite recognizing the performative nature of the visit, Griffin nevertheless agreed with some of Castro's criticisms about the United States: "I think that Castro is right . . . about some of our government's policies towards Latin America's countries in the past and I can't denounce Castro for taking a stand on that."[29] In light of the virulent anticommunism seen in the United States during the previous decade, many Harlem residents quoted in the article took pains to delicately parse the reasons that crowds of African Americans from all over the city had made the sidewalks around Hotel Theresa impassable. An unnamed assistant supermarket manager insisted that the presence of the crowds was not necessarily indicative of support. Many were motivated by curiosity, "the same as anybody would have.... It doesn't mean anybody agrees with him," the anonymous man reassured readers.

What might have been lost on non-Harlem residents was the significance of that corner of Lenox Avenue and 125th Street. Long a site of radical street speeches and lively debates between Black nationalists, Garveyites, leftists, and communists, the corner also hosted the African Memorial Bookstore, founded by Lewis H. Michaux in 1932.[30] In addition to the corner's history as a gathering place for public political discourse, people came, as Herman Griffin asserted, because the Cuban government had initiated a propaganda campaign aimed at African Americans shortly after the revolution. In January 1959, Castro told hundreds of reporters that "as revolutionaries and idealists, we are against discrimination in any form." He pledged that the new Cuban government would "work to eliminate every kind of discrimination in Cuba."[31] Castro's claims about the changes in his government drew praise and scrutiny in African American newspapers, especially when he admitted to audiences that "we do have a problem [in Cuba], but not anything like that in the South in the United States."[32]

Although Castro's statements were calculated to appeal to Black Americans, as articles in the *Chicago Defender* and *Baltimore Afro-American* revealed, many among his intended audience remained suspicious. Their statements revealed an openness to the possibility of radical social change in Cuba but skepticism at Castro's methods and rhetoric. Harlem residents interviewed by the *Chicago Defender* reflected this internal conflict. "If there is no discrimination against the Negro there now," Arnold Earle tentatively concluded, "there must have been a major change in Cuba—there was discrimination there before Castro took over." Another man, responding to claims by the Castro regime to have eliminated racism, demanded proof: "He'll have to show it to me.... I don't believe it."[33]

As if anticipating the ambivalence from Harlem residents, Julian Mayfield was ready with his own defense of Castro and Cuba's antiracist revolution. Mayfield's article in the *Baltimore Afro-American*, published the same day as the *Defender* piece, announced boldly that "Cuba Has Solution to Race Problem." Countering the concerns of those Harlemites interviewed by the *Defender*, Mayfield recounted his own experience in Cuba with

Dr. Cordero three months prior. Mayfield stated that he had seen "proof that it doesn't take decades of gentle persuasion to deal a death blow to white supremacy." Cuba's racial hierarchy had been thrown down in a matter of months, and while racist sentiments had not been eradicated, the government's extensive efforts to counteract centuries of institutionalized racism in hiring, firing, economics, and culture had seen them muted. In direct contrast to the US government, which publicly expressed a desire for social change but rarely acted, the new Cuban regime had taken decisive action to "[snatch] away [white Cubans'] power to deny a man a job, a house to live in, or a chance to realize his best potential because of his color." Harlem residents, Mayfield believed, should recognize that "the important lesson in the Cuban experience is that great social change need not wait on the patient education of white supremacists."[34]

In contrast to the tepid response that African Americans had toward the Democratic and Republican candidates in the upcoming election in November 1960, Mayfield argued that Afro-Cubans stood decisively for the revolution "and [were] willing to die to keep it."[35] Their fervent support derived from Castro's commitment to a meaningful antiracism and the revolutionary state's willingness to fundamentally remake Cuban society to benefit the impoverished masses. Cuba's new leadership proposed showing to working-class African Americans that the US government was neither as committed to nor as supportive of racial progress as boosters led them to believe. The apparent success of Cuba's revolutionary governance and the frustration it caused to the US government contributed to Mayfield's sense that harnessing or gaining state power would have to be a key element of antiracist activism. This fascination with the state as a means for liberation dovetailed with Mayfield's growing obsession with the power and influence of Black male leaders on the future of the movement for Black liberation.

As a light-skinned Cuban, Castro did not fit the profile of the kind of strong, revolutionary Black man that Mayfield championed. And although Castro's seizure of power and his proclamations inspired Mayfield's public rhetorical support, neither he nor Cordero considered making plans to relocate to Havana despite concerns raised by the FBI in its surveillance reports. Instead, Mayfield found inspiration much closer to home. In the months after his return to the United States, he had closely followed the career of North Carolina–born radical Robert F. Williams. Having had the opportunity to sip rum with Williams in Havana, Mayfield found a man whose interests, concerns, and objectives were closely aligned with his own. Frequent reports of violent confrontations between Williams and local white terrorists in Monroe, North Carolina, prompted Mayfield to see for himself what was going on and offer support—both rhetorical and material—to Williams.

Challenge to the Negro Leadership

Mayfield's first public show of support came in April 1961, when he published an article in *Commentary* decrying the National Association for the Advancement of Colored People's (NAACP) recent expulsion of Williams. "Challenge to the Negro Leadership" recounted the reasons for Williams's expulsion, namely his refusal to walk back comments about "meeting violence with violence" and "stopping lynching with lynching."[36] Mayfield cautioned that the NAACP's political dominance in the civil rights struggle was waning and that Robert F. Williams was a more legitimate voice, one in line with the sentiments of the working-class Black majority.[37] The failure of mainstream actions and movements to "produce more substantial and immediate results in the field of civil rights," Mayfield continued, undermined the organization's legitimacy. An overly legalistic and highly symbolic approach did not endear the NAACP to many African Americans, and the "rapid growth of the militant, white-hating Muslim movement among working-class Negroes" was, to Mayfield, evidence that the NAACP's claim to speak for all African Americans should no longer be taken at face value. Instead, Mayfield urged readers to listen to Robert F. Williams as a representative of working-class African Americans whose frustrations and resentment were even then boiling over into direct action against Jim Crow.

Echoing his portrayals of ineffectual and out-of-touch Black leaders in *The Grand Parade*, Mayfield pointed out how grassroots sit-ins and direct action in service of voting rights in the Deep South by youth organizations such as the Student Nonviolent Coordinating Committee were gradually supplanting the NAACP's methodology of legal challenges to segregation. In contrast to the slow, gradual process of lawsuits, injunctions, and minor victories, these grassroots movements presented "a united front to their common enemy, the system of white supremacy."[38] Mayfield saw the "negro leadership" of the NAACP undermining that united front by insisting on staying the course with regard to legal challenges and attempting to utilize the federal government to offer national solutions to local and regional problems. Nowhere, he wrote, was the undermining of local struggles more blatant than in the NAACP's treatment of Robert F. Williams.

Born in the town of Monroe, North Carolina, in 1925, Robert Franklin Williams was a veteran of both the US Army and the US Marine Corps with a wife and two sons. Monroe, the seat of Union County, was located along the Seaboard Air Line Railroad, making it an attractive town for manufacturing. The railroad had also given the town's African American population a handful of decent jobs, allowing some, such as Williams's father, to purchase property. Located some thirty miles southeast of Charlotte, the town had a slim white majority by the early twentieth century but few opportunities for young Black men. After a stint in the army and searching for work in Michigan and upstate New York, Williams joined the Marine Corps in 1954 with the hopes of getting ahead in journalism or radio. However, once he arrived in California for training, he was furious to learn that the Marine Corps excluded Black marines from information services.[39] Extricating himself from the Marines Corps after only sixteen months, Williams made his way back to Monroe feeling dejected but hopeful about the previous year's *Brown* decision. In Monroe, however, he found an emboldened Ku Klux Klan chapter terrorizing the Black community. Williams joined the local NAACP chapter determined to do something.

After being elected president of the NAACP chapter when no one else wanted the job, the rest of the organization abandoned Williams. This left him, in the words of his biographer Tim Tyson, "virtually a one-man NAACP chapter."[40] Williams responded by recruiting local World War II veterans, such as Woodrow Wilson, B. J. Winfield, John W. McDow, and Dr. Albert E. Perry, to join him in resisting white violence and terror. After a series of confrontations over local segregated public accommodations, Williams's frustration with local white supremacists boiled over, and he decided to act. Following the resolution of a court case in which a mentally challenged African American man had been sent to prison for two years for "attempted rape" the same month that two white men had been released after assaulting Black women, Williams took to the steps of the Union County Courthouse and declared, "We cannot take these people who do us injustice to the court and it becomes necessary to punish them ourselves. In the future we are going to have to try and convict them on the spot. We cannot rely on the law. We can get no justice under the present system. If we feel that injustice is done, we must right then and there, on the spot, be prepared to inflict punishment on the people."[41]

The widely publicized statement resulted in a quick response from NAACP national president Roy Wilkins, who suspended Williams from the organization.[42] Despite attempts to silence him, Williams raised questions that resonated with many African Americans, especially in northern cities. If state and local governments would not adhere to the rule of law and the federal government would not intervene, what were local movements to do in the face of violent attacks by white residents? If the system was unjust, what could law-abiding people hope to accomplish through legal, peaceful means? Men such as Williams, Mayfield argued in *Commentary*, were going to "play an increasingly vocal role in the social maelstrom that is the American Southland." In contrast, leaders such as Wilkins had proven themselves inadequate to the task of leadership by ignoring the sentiments Williams embodied and expressed. As such, Mayfield suggested that "a closer look at [Williams], his views, and the environment that produced him, may be revealing," and he proceeded to do just that.

To get this closer look, Mayfield began raising money for Williams in New York. Along with John H. Clarke and Hudson Mayfield, Julian Mayfield made his first trip in April on behalf of the newly formed Monroe Defense Committee, transporting food, blankets, and other supplies in his car.[43] In July of that year, Mayfield was able to secure press credentials from the *Cleveland Call & Post*, although he had never published a story there. Since the publication of Mayfield's *Commentary* article, there had been a virtual media blackout of Monroe, and Mayfield argued that his reporting could put Williams back in the public spotlight and bring more attention to his strategy of armed self-defense.

In the months preceding Mayfield's arrival, the situation in Monroe developed into a simmering cauldron of tension. After decades of segregation, an invigorated local NAACP led by Williams had begun a multipronged assault on the edifice of Jim Crow. The group successfully integrated the Union County Library in 1957 and then set its sights on the city's swimming pool, built with federal resources under the Works Progress Administration.[44] There they hit a snag. The Monroe government refused to offer a solution to the unsafe swimming conditions for African American children, two of whom had drowned the previous year after swimming in local quarries and ponds. Additionally, this refusal was accompanied by renewed white violence in the form of night riders and terror attacks on Black residents in Monroe. The so-called kissing case of 1958 further inflamed tensions, as two Black boys were threatened with imprisonment and lynching for engaging in a kissing game with two white girls. In the summer of 1960, Williams wrote directly to President Dwight Eisenhower, but the president's response was less than encouraging.

"As much as the president deplores an instance of this nature and is constantly striving toward the time-honored principles of American equality," Eisenhower wrote to Williams in an article later published in the *Baltimore Afro-American*, "it is not within the purview of his office to act officially upon such cases."[45] The failure of the federal government to act, coupled with the regular and persistent threats by white terrorists, night riders, and Klansmen, prompted Williams to adopt a new strategy. He rejected the strategic nonviolence utilized by the Southern Christian Leadership Conference and Dr. Martin Luther King Jr. and instead expressed his goal to "[meet] violence with violence" and "[stop] lynching with lynching."[46] Writing to the National Rifle Association, Williams received a charter to found his own chapter and began arming the men and women of the local NAACP chapter with M-1 carbines and .38-caliber police special revolvers. A veteran himself, Williams drilled the men of Monroe in military tactics and organized them into platoons to form a "black militia."[47] Effective resistance, he believed, required organization, patience, and—most importantly—good marksmanship.

When Julian Mayfield met Williams in Havana in July 1960, he only knew the square-jawed southerner from the newspapers. "I expected to meet some sort of wild man," Mayfield recalled, noting that "for in every Southern town there has always been at least one black man who let it be known that he was willing to die if he could take a few white men with him."[48] Those men, Mayfield wrote, were "rarely political" in the formal sense. Instead, they "kept to the shadows," leaving the main thoroughfares for whites. Williams, in contrast, "belonged to a new breed of Southerner who wanted not only peace in the shadows . . . but demanded complete access to the main street also because his taxes helped maintain it." In Williams, Mayfield discovered a steely resolve that was neither affect nor exaggeration.

Confronting Williams about the arsenal of guns he allegedly maintained as the men shared Cuban rum on a balcony overlooking Havana's famous Malecón, Mayfield recalled that Williams responded with a soft chuckle. "Man, everybody knows that. The Crackers know it. The cops know it, and Roy Wilkins knows it. The next time you're in the states, come on down and see for yourself."[49] Mayfield was taken by Williams's cool demeanor, and Mayfield's public advocacy increased Williams's name recognition and contributed to his rising influence on Black radicalism.[50] Even as Martin Luther King Jr. dominated print and visual media with peaceful marches in Alabama and Georgia, Williams's quiet fury and military-style organization served as a welcome example for many southern African Americans who did not relish accepting the indignity and violence of local whites to prove a moral point.

Mayfield's account of his time in Monroe has served as one of the most essential primary source documents of the events that would transpire in August 1961, and his version of events is corroborated by other historical accounts. Yet his own role in the events has often fallen by the wayside in favor of a (well-deserved) focus on Williams's leadership and tactics. "There are some of us who might participate in struggle, but almost never lead," Mayfield wrote in reference to Williams, and the thirty-three-year-old journalist was an eager participant.[51] Lumping himself in with other authors, journalists, organizers, and propagandists, Mayfield considered that his own novels and newspaper articles may challenge segregation discursively but not directly. This contrasted with what Mayfield saw in Williams: a charismatic, practical man who had resolved that he would no longer be a second-class citizen and would do so with a rifle in his hand. Implicit in Mayfield's recollections was a sense of dissatisfaction with his own rhetorical challenges to white supremacy. His decision to join Williams and engage in armed self-defense alongside members of a community reflected a newfound sense of purpose and a desire to not only "see for himself" but also do something tangible.

For Mayfield, Williams's cold, calm anger whenever he heard of a new injustice marked him as a man who was not to be trifled with. During the Havana trip, Mayfield was with Williams when Robert Taber and Richard Gibson received news that they had lost their jobs due to their support of Castro, and Williams's fury took Mayfield by surprise. It was not loud or boisterous anger but instead was cold, calculated, and patient. Mayfield's recollections make multiple mentions of Williams's mastery of his effulgent rage. Here was someone, Mayfield believed, who knew the injustices of the past as well as anyone else and had experienced many of them directly but felt "just as outraged at the last injustice or atrocity as [he was] at the first."[52] This anger did not debilitate or confuse; it demonstrated a resolve forged in cold steel. More than that, Mayfield reflected, "it was Rob Williams's plain speech and undoubted sincerity and commitment which took me to Monroe." Monroe also represented the kind of movement that Julian Mayfield had wanted to be a part of since he joined the Communist Party of the United States of America in the late 1940s, and he confessed wryly that "there might have been a little romantic appeal" in joining an armed revolutionary fighting for a community of Black people.[53]

Although Mayfield would speak highly of the town of Monroe, it was not the aesthetics that drew his praise. He confessed that he "fell in love with Monroe," but that "wasn't easy because Monroe was one of the most unaesthetic-looking towns in the South."[54] It was instead "a love affair with the town's black population," who, by the time Mayfield arrived, were organized and united in defense of their community. In Monroe "a man who did not carry a pistol or a rifle was considered foolish," and Mayfield took to carrying a pistol for the first but not the last time in his life.[55] On his second day in town, he attended the funeral of a young Black man who had been killed when his car had been run off the road into a ravine. "It was tit for tat," Mayfield noted, as "young Black men regularly engaged in the same practice" when they caught a white man alone on a dark country road. The difference, however, "was [that the Black community] didn't have the police force of Chief Mauney . . . on their side."[56]

Sporadic skirmishes, occurring throughout 1961, maintained an uneasy stalemate until August. That month, a group of Freedom Riders, which included members of the Congress of Racial Equality, arrived in Monroe hoping to defuse the tensions and integrate the town through nonviolent tactics. Veterans of police and civilian violence in Anniston and Birmingham, the Freedom Riders ignored Williams's advice and set up the Monroe Nonviolent Action Committee. Lead by James Forman, they began implementing their own ideas for how to help the citizens of Monroe, with little input from those citizens. Ironically, the Freedom Riders' presence upset the precarious balance of power and stoked the flames of violence. Demographically speaking, most of the Freedom Riders were white, and many had recently been released from prison for testing *Boynton v. Virginia* by integrating interstate transport. Their presence increasingly angered local whites and confused local Blacks, a fact that did not escape Williams or Mayfield.[57]

Despite Williams's urging that the Freedom Riders avoid public protests, the group organized a picket line on August 20, 1961, resulting in a week of arrests and police violence. The following weekend, Monroe's white citizens initiated a riot that occurred with tacit support from the local police after the Freedom Riders organized a picket of the Union County Courthouse. On Sunday, August 27, the Freedom Riders arrived at the courthouse, where they were met by the sheriff, his deputies, and a large group of white civilians.[58] When the local police realized that the protesters were unarmed, Mayfield recalled that "the white boys of Monroe had a field day."[59] Williams had refused to take part in the picket after he was told that he was not permitted to bring weapons, but when calls started coming in begging for help and describing the bloody assaults of protesters by white police officers and citizens, he quickly sent out a caravan of cars to rescue them.

Having arrived with Mae Mallory from New York the previous night, Mayfield was one of those who drove out to rescue the Freedom Riders as they were being brutally beaten by police and local white residents. Accompanied by John Lowery, a young white man from the Bronx, the two men joined a caravan of eight cars headed to the center of Monroe. On the way there, a carload of local whites pulled up beside them. Mayfield recalled that "[they] shrilly invite[d] us to go back to New York or Moscow where we came from," but "they [did] not attack for they recognize[d] that these are the crazy niggers who carry and use guns" and drove off without incident.[60]

Managing to pick up several bruised and battered protesters from the site of the melee, Mayfield drove without incident until the car was sideswiped by another car "filled with white boys," who pushed his car into the railing of a bridge. Terrified of the one-hundred-foot drop, Mayfield kept his hands on the wheel until his car was rammed again. The men, seeing Mayfield's New York license plate, asked him, "What are you doin' down here?"[61] According to Mayfield's account, he reached for his revolver but was stopped by Lowery, who implored him to lower the weapon. Mayfield wrestled his arm away from Lowery, slapped the man, and pointed his pistol at the car beside him and answered their question: "I came to see your mother, motherfucker!" Before Mayfield could get off a shot, however, a local man traveling in a car behind him fired his pistol into the air. The car full of white men, now realizing that they were not attacking nonviolent Freedom Riders, disengaged and sped away.[62]

In the aftermath of the violent confrontation as several Freedom Riders (including James Forman) lay bleeding in the Monroe County jail, the remaining nonviolent protesters regrouped at Williams's residence in the Black neighborhood of Newtown. At the same time, Mr. and Mrs. Bruce Stegall, a white couple from nearby Shelby, North Carolina, were on their way to Monroe. The Stegalls later told reporters that they wanted to see for themselves what was happening in Monroe and that they cruised slowly down the town's streets.[63] As they drove down Boyte Street, where the Williams house was located, their car was stopped by a crowd of Newtown residents who forced the couple out of the car and onto the street. Some began hurling epithets at them, while others called for their murder. Fearing for the couple's safety, Mallory approached the crowd and demanded that they let the couple go, while Williams let them inside his home, a decision that would have serious and unexpected consequences. At Mrs. Stegall's request, Williams telephoned the Union County sheriff to explain the situation. The sheriff in turn informed him that a warrant had already been issued for his arrest on the charge of kidnapping despite the fact that the Stegalls left his house and made their way home without incident. A short while later, a neighbor came over and reported that the lieutenant governor had just been on television declaring that he had ordered the National Guard to arrest Williams for "insurrection." Williams immediately began making plans to flee Monroe.[64]

Escape to Africa

As darkness fell on the warm August night, Julian Mayfield waited nervously in his car by the entrance to Newtown. A few hours before, Williams had sent him to the home of a supporter and asked the two men to hide two submachine guns that had recently been smuggled down.[65] While the man dug a hole for the weapons in his backyard, Mayfield telephoned his pregnant wife to tell her what was going on in Monroe. He remembered that the call was made "rather dramatically, to say goodbye, just in case, because there was the sound of gunfire." At six o'clock Williams telephoned Mayfield again, telling him that "if [they] didn't leave Monroe there would be a bloodbath." Under the cover of darkness, Williams, his family, and fellow militant Mae Mallory crept down the road, where Mayfield was waiting with his Nash Rambler. As Mayfield's battered car left Union County, it passed trucks full of "armed white men putting on their uniforms, pointing toward Monroe."[66] A few days later after dropping Mallory with friends in New York City, the group crossed over into Canada and to safety.

Exile was not what Julian Mayfield had intended when he joined Robert Williams in Monroe. In Puerto Rico, Mayfield had sought to build a new life with his wife far from the blacklisting of McCarthyism and the stultifying effects of American racism. Instead, he discovered the pervasiveness of white supremacy and the oppressive reality of colonialism. Returning to New York, Mayfield put his talents as a writer to work in order to warn African American communities outside the South about limitations of liberal integrationism, but his message largely fell on deaf ears. Despite some reservations about Cuba's young revolution, he reveled in the freedoms that the antiracist revolution offered him, in particular the freedom from FBI surveillance. He saw the calls of solidarity and revolution's challenges to

American foreign policy as an effective means to criticize liberals, both Black and white, and he became an active and vocal supporter. Monroe too served to demonstrate the flawed logic of nonviolence as a tactic and encourage his embrace of armed self-defense as a way to protect and preserve Black communities. Robert F. Williams offered compelling reasons to confront white supremacy on its own terms and to reject Black elites who were unwilling to address the economic and social issues affecting Black masses.

In his account of his flight from Monroe to Toronto, Mayfield noted with frustration that little of the support he and the Williamses received en route to exile came from African Americans. Much to his chagrin, it was white leftists who shielded Mayfield and the Williams family during their flight to Canada, a fact that further darkened his view of the potential for revolutionary solidarity in the United States. From Toronto, the Williams family chose to depart for Havana, where they would spend the next seven years as Williams encouraged African Americans with his radio program, *Radio Free Dixie*, and Mabel taught English while raising their two sons. Like the Williams family, Mayfield was reticent to return to the United States and with good reason. Between September and November 1961, FBI files indicate the bureau not only utilized "technical or microphone surveillance" to watch the home that Mayfield shared with Dr. Cordero in East Elmhurst, Queens, but also paid informants to question her on his whereabouts.[67]

In spite of these efforts, Dr. Cordero skillfully eluded the FBI and protected her husband. According to the FBI's unnamed informant, Cordero lied about Mayfield's whereabouts, stating in September that he was "back down South" and claiming that the family had "postponed [the] trip [to Ghana] until December and that they have decided to wait until the baby is born."[68] Cordero also suggested that she might "pack up and go to Venezuela with her parents," deflecting the informant and the FBI's attention. Remarkably, she was even able to retrieve the family's Nash Rambler. FBI agent C. H. Stanley reported that "she stated that the car was returned to her by a friend whom she declined to identify."[69] Dr. Cordero's deception provided Mayfield with time to cross back over the border and acquire a passport in New York on September 11, 1961, but he had nowhere else to go.[70] He could not safely return to the United States without facing federal charges, but he remained separated from his family. He had nothing to do but wait.

Having already been offered a job at the Ministry of Health in the West African nation of Ghana, Dr. Cordero contacted the ministry and requested that she be able to begin her position at an earlier date. Cordero put the family's affairs in order and flew to London with the couple's four-year-old son, Rafael. Once Mayfield received the news, he flew from Toronto to Newfoundland and then to the Prestiwick airport in Scotland and from there made his way to London, where the family was reunited after being apart for nearly six months. Despite the fact that she was nearly thirty-eight weeks pregnant when they arrived—long past the point where airlines allowed pregnant women to fly—Cordero was somehow able to convince airline staff that she was earlier along than she appeared to be. From London, the family flew to Accra, where they began their new life. Mayfield, Cordero, and their children would spend nearly five years in Ghana. During this self-imposed exile, Mayfield would become an even more vociferous critic of US foreign and domestic policy. He worked to raise the profile of African American freedom struggles at home and abroad while functioning as an informal leader of an African American expatriate community in Accra. Finding employment in Flagstaff House, the Ghanaian president's residence, as a political journalist, Mayfield wrote extensively for the government of Ghana in both official and unofficial capacities.

In retrospect, Mayfield's harsh critique of integration policies proved distressingly accurate. In the decades that followed, previously all-white schools accepted Black students but maintained white administrators and faculty. Formerly all-Black schools closed down, fracturing communities as students attended multiple far-flung schools while also hollowing out the ranks of Black educators and administrators. Black students, now minorities in white spaces, faced new challenges. Having concluded that the integration of African Americans into white spaces would be an ineffective means of challenging the economic dislocation and violence endured by Black peoples and their communities, *The Grand Parade* made it clear that "the goal of integration was based on an incorrect assessment of reality."[71] But by the time this became obvious to others in the United States, Julian Mayfield had already moved on to addressing larger issues, particularly the expansion of his geographic focus. Having begun looking beyond the borders of the United States with Cuba, Mayfield found in Ghana a space to develop arguments for the instrumentalization of state power as a tool for revolutionary social and economic change. A Black nation with a Black president who spoke of the importance of solidarity and welcomed dissenting African American voices to join in their revolution proved to be a powerful influence on Mayfield's intellectual projects and his personal life.

5 In Every Sense a Stranger

Community and African Unity in Accra, 1961–1967

> To me the independence of Ghana will be meaningless unless it is linked up with the liberation of Africa.
> —Kwame Nkrumah, 1956

> Black Americans need to understand their relationship to Africa, but they need . . . to understand the forces which stand between them and the dignity only a free, strong Africa can assure them.
> —Hoyt W. Fuller

After nearly two months in Canada, Julian Mayfield was impatient to reconnect with his wife and son. In early November, he flew from Toronto to Halifax, Nova Scotia, and from there to Prestwick Airport in Scotland, where he planned to rendezvous with Ana Livia and Rafael.[1] On the last leg of his flight, Mayfield found himself seated next to a man who spoke with a thick Scottish brogue. Despite having immigrated to Canada over half a century before, the man declared that he was returning "home" to Scotland and poured some of his Canadian whiskey into his seatmate's cup as they made small talk. Upon discovering that it was Mayfield's first trip to Africa, the man suddenly became accusatory and exclaimed: "You told me you were *from* Africa!" When Mayfield tried to explain, the man continued: "Well, if you're not from Africa where are you from? And what the hell are you anyway?" Mayfield's answer that he was "an American Negro, or an African-American, or an Afro-American, or—if you prefer—I am an American of African descent" only confused the man further. "Lad," the man chuckled, "I don't give a damn what you are. I just wish *you* would make up your mind and let me know."[2]

This anecdote, from an essay titled "Ghanaian Sketches," was chosen by Mayfield to highlight the discomfort that many white Americans and Europeans had with ongoing shifts in African American identity.[3] In his 1944 book *An American Dilemma*, Swedish sociologist Gunnar Myrdal had argued that the solution to de jure racism in the United States was a shift to a deracialized American identity shorn of racial and ethnic difference.[4] A decade later as many African American elites and white liberals pivoted toward a national narrative of colorblindness, the drive toward independent statehood in colonial Africa, Asia, and the Caribbean increased identification and participation of African Americans in liberation struggles. These contradictory impulses drove a wedge between groups even as they opened up new horizons of possibility for African Americans seeking freedom beyond the boundaries of the nation-state. The confusion that Mayfield relayed was emblematic of a broader discomfort about the relationship between Africanness, Blackness, and Americanness that would play out in the United States, Africa, and the diaspora over the coming years as liberation struggles and civil rights efforts shaped social movements and generated opposition throughout the Atlantic world and beyond.

In considering the years Mayfield spent in Ghana, this chapter historicizes how the ideological parameters and day-to-day reality of diasporic community were reshaped by these prolonged encounters between Afro-diasporic peoples and Africans. This embrace of African unity at the height of the Cold War also reveals how this process is rooted in the diasporic experience and shaped by African Americans and Afro-Caribbeans working on behalf of an African government. Ghana also sharpened Mayfield's focus on the subject that he had begun wrestling with in New York: power. In talking about the Ghanaian nation-state, Mayfield argued that "we are talking now about power[,] . . . a singular key for understanding the relations that exist between men and nations and societies." He concluded somberly that when talking about power, "we are, unavoidably, also talking about race."[5] That relationship, between power and race, came to consume his activities in Ghana from his arrival in September 1961 to his departure in January 1966.

Mayfield recognized that within that nexus of race and power, the existence of a Pan-African nation-state could fundamentally challenge the global Cold War order by providing an alternative to white supremacy originating in either the Soviet Union or the United States.[6] Synthesizing distinct strands of Pan-African writings with the individual experiences of Africans, Europeans, and Afro-diasporic men and women, Mayfield's intellectual project, often laden with symbolism, resisted abstraction and ideological orthodoxy. Instead, he focused on the practical task of forging African unity on an interpersonal level among peoples divided by language, culture, class, and ideology. Of singular importance to Mayfield's effort was how the nation-state afforded radicals like him the space in which to realize the forms of sovereignty that they hoped to enact, even as it often constrained their expressions of cooperation.

In Every Sense a Stranger

Julian Mayfield and Ana Livia Cordero, along with their son Rafael, were relieved when they finally landed in Accra after the long flight from London, but they had arrived at a singularly chaotic moment. Queen Elizabeth II and Prince Phillip had arrived in the country two days earlier for their first state visit to the new nation of Ghana.[7] As Mayfield and Cordero made their way from the airport to the home that the Department of Health had arranged for them at Achimota College, they had to contend with streets crowded with well-wishers hoping to catch a glimpse of the British monarch.[8] After getting Rafael to bed, Julian and Ana Livia were enjoying the cool night air on their veranda when a Russian-made limousine pulled up to their bungalow. The window rolled down, and they were greeted by none other than Shirley Graham and W. E. B. Du Bois, there to welcome them to Ghana. This greeting by the Du Boises, who had arrived in October, was Julian and Ana Liva's introduction to the unique network of people who would become their new community.

Fifteen days later on November 26, Ana Livia gave birth to a healthy baby boy, whom the couple named Emiliano. Mayfield recounted how later that month, a group of the family's neighbors celebrated the baby's arrival with an "outdooring ceremony." This celebration was a Ewe rite that Mayfield compared to a Catholic christening except that it began in the dark, cool hours before dawn and involved the consumption of a great deal of alcohol. Because baby Emiliano arrived "kicking and screaming on a Sunday," the neighbors bestowed upon him the African name "Kwasi" and welcomed the child and the family with open arms.[9] The spontaneous celebrations surrounding Emiliano's birth had a profound impact on Julian and Ana Livia and their sense of belonging in Ghana. This heartfelt welcome by the community, Mayfield explained, belied claims about the insurmountable differences—cultural, national, and ideological—between Africans and African Americans.

Such accounts of relationships between Africans and African Americans had been an established genre of nonfiction writing for decades prior to the publication of "Ghanaian Sketches," but a book by one of Mayfield's major literary influences loomed large in his imagination as he wrote this essay. *Black Power*, Richard Wright's account of his 1953 tour of the Gold Coast colony provided an opposing viewpoint to argue against. Published in 1954, *Black Power* contrasted Wright's strident anticolonialism with his tepid enthusiasm for African independence and cultural practices. At the time, Black critics of the book seized on Wright's dismissive tone toward West Africans and his focus on their impoverished material conditions and superstitions and the vast cultural gulf that separated him from his hosts.[10] White critics were equally dismissive but with important distinctions. Michael Clarke's biting review in the *New York Times* criticized Wright's "caricature of British colonialism . . . drawn . . . from the dreary old arsenal of Marxist slogans" while the political scientist David E. Apter wrote that Wright "demonstrates little understanding of the difficulties of social transformation" in the criticisms Wright offered of the "backwardness" of Gold Coast residents.[11] Wright's travel narrative struck nerves on both sides of the color line precisely because the author rejected the Cold War liberalism of the United States and the Pan-African socialism of Ghana.

Although he did not mention Wright by name, Mayfield in several of his early essays challenged the conclusions that Wright expressed in *Black Power*, which bore the dismissive subtitle "A Record of Reactions in a Land of Pathos." In contrast to Wright's statement that "I'm of African descent and I'm in the midst of Africans, yet I cannot tell what they are thinking and feeling," Mayfield emphasized that there was no special preexisting relationship between peoples of African descent. Instead, any collaboration or communication depended on the individual's acceptance of difference and empathic understanding of others in the diaspora.[12] He rejected Wright's argument that the diaspora was a barrier to a global emancipatory Black consciousness and instead characterized it as a bridge that could be constructed by mutual respect despite cultural and social difference.

"Ghanaian Sketches" also challenged Wright's critical treatment of Pan-African politics, economic disparities, culture, and superstition in the Gold Coast. *Black Power*, critics contended, not only reinforced Western tropes about the continent but also positioned Western modernity and capitalism as the ultimate savior of Africa from both Soviet intervention and Africans themselves.[13] Debating whether capitalism or communism was better suited for the continent, Wright dismissed the "African socialism" promoted by Kwame Nkrumah as Soviet communism wearing blackface. Adding insult to injury, Wright reduced African demands for independence to "assuag[ing] [African] feelings of shame and betrayal" that were a result of the humiliation brought about by colonization.[14] Recalling Dominique-Octave Mannoni's thesis on the crippling psychological effects of colonization, *Black*

Power offered an unflattering perspective on the inferiority of African civilization even as Wright insisted that "none but Africans can perform [liberation] for Africa."[15]

In the decade following the publication of *Black Power*, several white academics and journalists wrote pieces that intentionally (or unintentionally) reinforced Wright's thesis. "Ghanaian Sketches" both identified this genre, which Mayfield saw as part of a broader "campaign to dampen . . . identification among Africans and African Americans," and challenged its basic underpinnings.[16] One significant piece engaged by Mayfield ran in the *New Yorker* in May 1961. Its author, Harold Isaacs, asserted that fundamental national, cultural, and social differences existed between people of the diaspora and people of Africa. In a poignant anecdote, Isaacs related an encounter with an unnamed African American man who lamented, "I came to Africa feeling like a brother, but there I was, I was not a brother. I was not Senegalese or Nigerian or Ghanaian, I was American [and] . . . I would always be an outsider coming in. It's the way anybody looks at a stranger."[17] While he critiqued Wright implicitly, Mayfield challenged Isaacs by name. Mayfield contrasted Isaacs's portrayal of African American discomfort in African society with his own arrival in Ghana.

Instead of apathy or hostility, he cited the celebration of the birth of Emiliano as evidence of how he and Dr. Cordero were welcomed in the burgeoning community of Africans and Afro-diasporic emigres.[18] Among those who extended their hands in fellowship were fellow Afro expatriates, including political activists, intellectuals, doctors, dentists, architects, and artists from throughout the African diaspora who had heeded Ghanaian president Nkrumah's impassioned call "to help us build our country."[19] Like Isaacs, Mayfield recognized the significant cultural and social stumbling blocks to realizing Nkrumah's notion of African unity across the diaspora. Forging relationships based on common goals demanded the right actions, careful discussion, and a willingness to listen. Despite a profound strangeness, it was this dialectic of "attitude and behavior" that served as the foundation of African unity.[20] Those who rejected this Hegelian, idealistic unity, Mayfield argued, would soon find themselves rejected by the African communities they encountered.

Mayfield gave examples of the forms of attitude and behavior that led to rejection. In this essay, he identified one of two groups that failed to connect with their African hosts. Members of this group, upon which he bestowed the unflattering moniker "The Bitchers," exhibited the national chauvinism that Isaacs's article had attributed to African Americans.

Mayfield argued that these travelers to West Africa reaped the consequences of their assumptions and beliefs: these men and women were unable to "adjust to a society where things do not work with the same snap and efficiency as they are expected to in a highly industrialized nation."[21] Mayfield believed that anger at poor sanitation, insensitivity to local cultural norms, annoyance at intermittent electricity and water, and frustration with bureaucratic inefficiency lay at the root of the diasporic conflict that Isaacs claimed to have witnessed. The nationalistic chauvinism of "The Bitchers," Mayfield wrote, meant that their failure to find common cause with West Africans was their own responsibility.

In a subsequent piece titled "Uncle Tom Abroad" and published in *Negro Digest*, Mayfield identified the second group: African American expatriates who arrived "on the payroll of the US government or a private firm."[22] He compared their stated support for African nationalism or socialism with their timid domestic politics. "Back home you could probably not get [their] signature for a petition defending the right of women to have babies," he wrote.[23] The political commitments of these men and women, whom Mayfield gave the mock-Latin name "Uncle Tomus Americanus," were ambiguous and calculated.[24] Despite claims that they were working in the interest of their African hosts, Mayfield noted that they never did "anything that might annoy the local US Embassy" and adhered to a strict philosophy summed up as "Don't Rock The Boat."[25] At best, Mayfield believed, their presence leant legitimacy to the attitudes and policies of cold warriors who dominated US foreign policy. At worst, they subverted the goals of Pan-Africanist politics, aiding neocolonialism and global white supremacy.

Above all, recalling the later-in-life arguments of W. E. B. Du Bois, Mayfield asserted that African Americans who valued their passports and international travel over working toward improving the conditions of their African hosts were helping the United States more than they were addressing African political and economic needs.[26] At a moment when young people in the United States were waking up to realize that "the only way to make progress in a situation of oppression is to rock the boat, and to rock it with such violence that either it sinks or it becomes a decent place in which to live," Mayfield found African Americans' failures abroad dispiriting.[27] It was this disharmony of theory and practice, or in Mayfield's formulation attitude and behavior, that he believed was the source of the disconnection experienced by African Americans in Africa.

The cultural distance between members of the African diaspora was not intrinsic, Mayfield argued, but instead was a product of colonialism and white supremacy on both sides of the Atlantic. Of growing up in Washington, he recalled that "every imaginable pressure had been brought to bear upon me as a child to make me ashamed of any connection I had with Africa." Similarly, Ghanaians who had not been educated in England or America "simply [did] not know what racial discrimination [was]." This had real effects on people's perceptions of racism, as the man or woman "who has lived in such white settler areas as Kenya, the Rhodesias, and South Africa, the West African has never experienced day-to-day naked white oppression."[28] In spite of these epistemological differences, Mayfield's writing in Ghana highlighted the contribution that African Americans made in linking Black radical traditions in the United States with the ideals that Kwame Nkrumah and George Padmore had set forth in their articulations of Pan-Africanism.[29] Confessing that he had arrived in Ghana "in every sense a stranger," Mayfield disputed Isaacs's basic premise by highlighting his own personal experience. "A person's strangeness or his nationality may be an initial barrier to intimacy," Mayfield explained, "but in the end his attitude and behavior will determine whether he makes friends or enemies."[30]

As Shirley Graham Du Bois opined in the pages of *Freedomways*, "building a nation is more than construction in stone and steel. . . . The eyes of the people must be opened, their past given meaning and their future given hope."[31] Throwing himself fully into life in Accra, Julian Mayfield explored the history of West Africa while pursuing a future that would serve African communities throughout the continent in their construction as new modern nations.[32] A great deal of scholarship has been devoted to the meaning, ideology, and long-term effects of Ghanaian sovereignty and the role of Kwame Nkrumah in that process.[33] However, what remains absent from this work is the attempts to overcome the mutual strangeness that Mayfield and his fellow Afros sought. Although central to the work of the Afro expatriates, they remained marginal to scholarship until the early 2000s. However, the experience of Afro expatriates pointedly revealed the hypocrisy of an American state that promoted democracy abroad while stymieing the efforts of domestic Black activists.

Writing for African audiences about the struggles of African Americans and writing for African Americans about the experience of working toward African sovereignty, Mayfield bridged the conceptual chasms that divided the diaspora from Africa. His writing also encouraged the mutual understanding that he struggled with on a daily basis. In published and unpublished works, Mayfield's archive provides numerous insights into the varying components of his process of constructing relationships in the diaspora. His use of African American discourses and embrace of African political ideologies serves to highlight how he navigated multiple discursive and cultural registers. In this challenge to ideas that would divide the diaspora to Africa, Mayfield's sense of purpose shines brightest.

During the first decade of Ghanaian independence, articles that emphasized differences between Africans and African Americans followed one after another. Isaacs's piece in May was followed quickly by a similarly themed piece in May. "Strangers in Africa," by journalist Russell Howe, presented visiting African Americans as being out of touch with African culture and society. Africans, Howe wrote, saw African-descended peoples as "stranger[s] from a different tribe whose ancestry . . . must have been slave."[34] Howe attributed these differences to essentialized notions of identity, such as nationality and American racialism. No matter what beliefs in unity were present, Isaacs and Howe reinforced Wright's and Myrdal's perspective that national identity remained the most salient factor in race relations in the post–World War II era. As Isaacs concluded, "whether [the American Negro] likes it or not, he is American and in Africa he becomes an American-in-exile."[35] In other words, there was no assimilation possible for African Americans in Africa; they would remain outsiders no matter what they tried.

Grounding his analysis of Afro-diasporic relationships in a dialectical understanding of both people and political economy, Mayfield demonstrated in "Ghanaian Sketches" that ideological and political commitments shaped social relationships in Africa as much as racial, cultural, and material conditions. While American racial ideology did not necessarily translate to a nation where the daily dehumanizing violence of white supremacy was unfamiliar to most of the population, the shared experience of second-class citizenship in the land of their birth could, Mayfield argued, effectively unite people divided by geography and history. This perspective reflected Kwame Nkrumah's own unifying framework for Ghana, what he dubbed the "African Personality." Mayfield in his writing clarified that his was not an African perspective but instead was an "Afro-American" one. Still, it was clear that Nkrumah's framework influenced Mayfield's considerations and bookended his framing of African unity in his writing and provided him with a scaffolding upon which to construct his own notion of what constituted solidarity amid the struggle over liberation in West Africa.

The Practical Language of Diaspora

Julian Mayfield's Ghanaian writing served the broader goal of uniting Africa under one government, but a historical exploration of that work also demonstrates the role Mayfield played in the process of constructing Nkrumah's rhetorical framework for African unity, the "African Personality," in the early 1960s. Nkrumah had resurrected the phrase in the 1950s, borrowing it from the nineteenth-century Pan-Africanist and educator Edward Blyden.[36] Expanding Blyden's definition, Nkrumah envisioned the "African Personality" as encompassing cultural and political sovereignty to promote the ideas at a moment in history when both seemed possible. "In asserting our African Personality," Nkrumah told an African American audience in 1958, "we shall be free to act in our individual and collective interests at any particular time . . . to exert our influence on the side of peace and uphold the rights of all peoples to decide for themselves their own forms of government."[37] Rather than be constrained by race, Nkrumah's continental "African Personality" was calculated to be broad enough to encompass the Arab/Berber North and whites exiled from South Africa and Rhodesia.

"For too long in our history," Nkrumah told Harlem crowds in 1958, "Africa has spoken in the voices of others. Now what I have called the African Personality in international affairs . . . will let the world know it through the voices of Africa's own sons."[38] Rather than disqualify him from speaking for the new Ghanaian state, Mayfield's embrace of Pan-African nationalism and Nkrumah's expanded definition of the concept meant that the African American writer was well suited for the task.[39] This commitment to African liberation and Ghanaian Pan-Africanism allowed Mayfield to play a key role in the process of Ghanaian nation building. As a writer for government-published newspapers and speeches for Nkrumah, Mayfield presented his own experiences for African and diasporic consumption, linking struggles in the United States, Africa, and the Caribbean together for African audiences far afield from Accra.

Most of Ghana's bureaucrats, professors, and other professionals had been trained in British and American schools; because of this, Nkrumah rejected them as having been tainted by colonialist thinking.[40] They, in turn, rejected his government for ostensibly discarding the existing colonial relationship. This political disagreement over the future of Ghana turned the campus of the University of Ghana at Legon and various government ministries into hotbeds of opposition to Ghanaian nation building. To counter their influence and power, Nkrumah bypassed them by creating "secretariats" that would answer directly to him. In those secretariats, he placed men and women he deemed sufficiently committed to the cause of Ghanaian economic, political, and cultural sovereignty. As Julian Mayfield's and author and cultural diplomat Maya Angelou's roles in these secretariats demonstrated, this often meant looking to diasporic expatriates for allies.

The Publicity Secretariat, located in the presidential residence at Flagstaff House, housed Mayfield's office from 1962 until his departure in early February 1966. There he wrote newspaper articles, opinion pieces, radio scripts, press releases, and speeches before founding the short-lived journal the *African Review*.[41] This secretariat served as the main propaganda organ of the Nkrumah government, producing and disseminating support for the state through a variety of channels, including newspapers, radio programs, and pamphlets. The Publicity Secretariat's staff reported directly to Nkrumah. In contrast to the Ministry of Information, the Publicity Secretariat had few career bureaucrats and instead was made up of Convention People's Party loyalists and expatriates such as Mayfield. Still, even though Ghanaians and Afro expatriates spoke the same language, they did not always understand one another.

Since English was spoken by most Ghanaians, both the US State Department and many of the Afro expatriates reasoned that "language [gave] Americans a decided advantage over the Russians."[42] G. Mennen "Soapy" Williams, assistant secretary of state for African affairs, saw Ghana as a linchpin of US foreign policy on the continent and was determined to use this lingua franca to his political advantage. Using his department's resources to influence Ghanaian public opinion and national policy through public diplomacy, Secretary Williams nevertheless found himself scrambling to keep up with negative reports in the foreign press about racial turmoil in the United States.

US Foreign Service officers were instructed to emphasize a narrative of progress in US race relations to combat the reports of violence. In a memo dated June 13, 1963, Foreign Service officer A. Morales-Carrion argued that "it is urgent that the US Government make 'sweet uses of adversity' and turn the country's present racial dilemma from a serious liability into a positive asset in foreign relations." Morales-Carrion suggested inviting the Organization of African States Human Rights Commission to the United States to examine the situation there with regard to African American freedom struggles in Alabama and Georgia. Although these visits would reveal the shortcomings of the United States, Morales-Carrion believed that they would also "be an exercise in placing facts in perspective, perhaps even showing the world that the United States has few peers as a guarantor of civil rights."[43]

Morales-Carrion's plan was rejected, but it illuminated how the assistant secretary's office was keen to draw attention away from the Soviet Union's daily fusillade of accounts of white violence against African Americans. In the wake of the violent attacks on Black protesters in Birmingham, Alabama, the Soviet Union had devoted upward of "twenty-three percent of its daily broadcasting to attacks on the American system," and Morales-Carrion's plan formed an aspect of a broader effort to blunt the impact of Soviet criticism.[44] Formal reports contained within Secretary Williams's classified personal papers reveal an organization concerned with the impact that radical voices such as those of Mayfield, Shirley Graham, and other African Americans could have on West Africans and US foreign policy in the region.

In response, the State Department coordinated broadcasts of Voice of America radio and engaged African American musicians, including Louis Armstrong, Dizzy Gillespie, and Duke Ellington, in "jazz diplomacy" to promote African American culture as American culture. The responses to Afro expatriate critiques, however, were more direct. Addressing the articles written by Mayfield indirectly, the State Department wrote press releases and produced propaganda of its own describing the complexities of the American system of state and federal power as a hurdle that could be overcome, leading to the gradual improvement of race relations.[45] This counterpropaganda reveals that since Ghana was an Anglophone country, the authors of these memos saw no need to consider how their language was perceived by African audiences.

In contrast, Mayfield recognized that such assumptions about language obscured important epistemological differences. "The Russian[s] [are] used to dealing with the terms 'colonialism' and 'imperialism' as realities," he wrote, and "[these] are all words that convey certain definite images to people in West Africa."[46] In contrast, Americans understood these words as abstract and theoretical concepts. Public diplomacy efforts by the State Department and its subsidiary organization, the United States Information Service, he believed, failed to consider the tangible experiences with colonialism that West Africans and southern Africans implicitly understood. They did not, in Mayfield's estimation, believe them to be organizing principles of political activism, nor did they see them as anything other than hollow, nationalist rhetoric. The distance between these ideological interpretations indicated that Julian Mayfield's work in the Publicity Secretariat recognized nuanced differences between peoples as he sought to make ideas mutually intelligible across divides of the African diaspora, a form of translation. By offering historical context and accounts of anti-Black racism, white violence, and government inaction, Mayfield's writing emphasized important subjective differences between audiences in Africa and the United States.

Mayfield's earliest writing in the Ghanaian newspaper *Evening News* demonstrates how his superiors in the Publicity Secretariat believed that his personal experiences with racism in the United States could be made relevant to West Africans. In his first series of articles, published between March 29 and April 6, 1962, Mayfield revisited the events that led to his flight from the United States "in an attempt to arouse African support for the defendants in Monroe, N.C."[47] Four articles published over the course of eight days recounted his experiences in Monroe in detail, offering his first public statements of the events of August 1961.[48] Introduced by the editor as "a famous United States author," Mayfield was described as providing "an appeal which should bolster up tremendously Mr. Kennedy's progressive moves for integration." Despite Mayfield's advocacy for revolution and his embrace of liberation, either he or his editors clearly considered that his experiences would be better served as a means of indirectly influencing President John F. Kennedy's domestic racial politics as well as his foreign policy toward West Africa. Not only did this show the international reach of African media in the early 1960s, but it also highlighted a newfound responsiveness of the US foreign policy establishment and its sensitivity to African affairs.

President Kennedy, as historian James Meriwether has demonstrated, shrewdly observed that favorable African policies offered a means to influence African Americans without upsetting Southern Democrats who held sway in the House and the Senate.[49] The articles Mayfield wrote and that his superiors in the Publicity Secretariat published suggest that they recognized this fact as well. Beginning with "Save Mae Mallory! Frame-up in Monroe," Mayfield's first *Evening News* article, the four articles explained the circumstances, historical context, and meaning of the charges arrayed against Mallory in ways calculated to shock and sway Ghanaian popular opinion. "Save Mae Mallory" was followed by "Why They Want to Kill Mae Mallory," "Monroe, No Man's Land," and "Monroe, USA: The Powderkeg Explodes." Describing daily injustices and unpunished and frequent white violence and providing vivid descriptions, such as how Klansmen "would force a black woman to disrobe and dance for them on the sidewalk as they fired bullets near her feet," the articles were well received.[50]

Three subsequent articles followed, each featuring photographs of Mallory, Williams, and Mayfield as the latter detailed the events of the "Monroe Frame-up." By historicizing and contextualizing their role in the violence directed against Monroe's Black population, the visiting Freedom Riders, and the false charges of kidnapping, Mayfield's critique emphasized the futility and waning influence of nonviolent, passive resistance. "What kind of town is Monroe, and why has it been the centre of the bitterest racial tug of war in the United States for the past five years?," Mayfield rhetorically asked before explaining that the city's economic and social segregation made it emblematic of thousands of small towns in the US South where white majority could terrorize an African American community with impunity. Emphasizing the complete lack of control that African Americans in Monroe had over their political and social lives, Mayfield compared their predicament with the African experience under colonialism. The terror of white violence in Monroe that Mayfield presented to Ghanaian readers was designed to shock, echoing the continental experience with European colonial violence. The implication of such comparisons was clear. Colonialism and Jim Crow were products of the ideology that Black peoples around the world faced: white supremacy.

"I began these articles with the intention of telling my readers about Mae Mallory," Mayfield wrote in the fourth and final article in the series. "Yet," he confessed, "I have hardly mentioned her because she played so little part in the events I have described."[51] Although manifestly untrue, Mayfield made this claim with the intention of highlighting the punitive nature of the prosecution's case. He understood that the Black defendants, which also included Monroe residents Richard Crowder and Harold Reape, would face a different justice system than white defendant John Lowery, a Freedom Rider from New York.[52] In emphasizing that point to African readers, Mayfield lamented that "[Mallory] cannot hope to have a fair trial." But the fairness of the legal proceedings was not his only worry. Extrajudicial violence was still a clear and present danger such that Mayfield urged his readers that Mallory must be freed because "no militant black woman can survive a lengthy sentence in a North Carolina prison."[53]

In light of these circumstances, Mayfield wrote that "if [readers] believe that this worthy woman should not be condemned to certain death in the American southland, I urge them to address their pleas to the one man who now holds her life in his hands." The article's final paragraph featured the mailing address of the White House and implored readers to contact President Kennedy directly. Appealing to the president of the United States seemingly clashed with the radical framing of the Monroe armed self-defense movement that, on the surface, suggests an editorial lapse. However, this practical step also points to the fungibility of Mayfield's ideological framework. As in many of his arguments, Mayfield's writing conveyed a cynical realism that recognized that an individual Ghanaian living in Kumasi or Sekondi could do very little to influence domestic policies in the United States aside from making their opinions known. Regardless, President Kennedy did not intervene in the Mallory case. Although Mallory was extradited to North Carolina, convicted, and sentenced to sixteen to twenty years she was eventually released in January 1965 after the North Carolina Supreme Court threw out her conviction.[54]

No evidence of audience reaction exists, but Mayfield's ardent defense of Mallory apparently drew enough of a positive response that the *Evening News* soon announced that Mayfield would be contributing "exclusive" articles three times a week.[55] The column "Plain Speaking" reflected both the paper's colloquial tone and Mayfield's own direct, confrontational style. With a novel in progress, two small children at home, and a wife working long hours as a doctor in the Ministry of Health and as the personal physician to W. E. B. Du Bois and with Mayfield supplementing the family's income by writing articles for US-based publications such as *The Liberator* and *Muhammad Speaks*, what is perhaps most surprising is that the series ran for as long as it did.[56]

Julian Mayfield's journalism in Ghana sheds light on how the aforementioned intralanguage translation worked, making concepts with distinct meanings intelligible to all. Despite the fact that many Ghanaians spoke English, differences in meaning cropped up frequently and were apparent to expatriates and their hosts alike. Concepts such as racism, imperialism, capitalism, and socialism meant different things to different audiences, and so Mayfield, in his writing, sought to recognize and smooth over these distinctions. Perhaps most important, the fact that Mayfield went from guest journalist to regular columnist to chief editor of a government-funded journal in such a short time demonstrates that he not only enjoyed the support of the Publicity Secretariat but also the confidence of President Nkrumah. As Mayfield undertook the intimidating task of starting a journal from scratch, he still managed to find time to write for other audiences, African Americans in particular. Although he believed in the importance and utility of nonfiction writing, he found that fiction allowed him to better connect with his readers and to share the ideas that drove his own activism. In this writing, Mayfield brought these discussions down to the level of individual relationships and how culture, race, and political economy were intimately intertwined.

One short story, "Black on Black," was emblematic of Mayfield's writing. Its focus on a love story between a free-spirited Black American singer and a sober, driven African official examines the tensions that arose between diasporic and African cultures in Nkrumah-era Accra. Unfolding largely through dialogue, an African chieftain of the fictional nation of Songhay, Nana Kwamina Matusi IV, and a "female Belafonte from New York" named Bessie Bates, try and fail to make their relationship work. Throughout, Mayfield's first-person narrator offers context on the history of their relationship through his own knowledge of their lives, focusing on these fictional lovers navigating the hidden shoals of racial and cultural expectations in a romantic relationship. The story presents a unique portrait of the quotidian experience of diaspora for African American audiences even as it demonstrates that factors beyond cultural difference accounted for the ultimate implosion of their love affair.

This short story's unflinching look at the dissolution of a relationship presented an evenhanded, in-depth perspective on the difficulties of traversing the diaspora. The story also offered an early analysis of how these relationships formed at intersections of race, class, and gender and often within conflicting perceptions of Blackness. In acknowledging these deep differences separating people who shared a history, Mayfield implicitly echoed statements that he had made in "Ghanaian Sketches," namely that it was imperative that it was up to individuals to connect across gulfs that the diaspora had created among African peoples and also that there would be conflicts and that they would not always be resolved in a satisfactory way. Based on the real-life relationship between Nana Nketsia IV and Maya Angelou, the fictional relationship in "Black on Black" stood in for many of the marriages and relationships that characterized the experiences of Africans and African Americans in Accra.[57] Although the earliest drafts were written around 1964, "Black on Black" was not published until 1971 at a moment that coincided with the rise of cultural nationalism as a political and artistic statement among Black radicals.[58] It is rooted, however, in the experiences African Americans had in West Africa. The messy personal politics of these relationships not only highlighted the impact of the personal in the politics of diaspora but also pointed to the inadequacies of the subsequent debates between those who espoused Black control and ownership of art and culture and those who emphasized armed revolution as the key to political power.[59]

Within the context of the intellectual history of Black expatriate literature, what was most significant about "Black on Black" was how political economy was interwoven into gender, class, and cultural divisions in the portrait of the focal relationship. Bessie seeks money and stability, while Nana is focused on creating an independent, modern, and decolonial nation. Bessie explodes over being hidden in the kitchen from a white woman, a moment that rubs salt in the wounds of a childhood spent under the specter of Jim Crow. Nana's inability to commit publicly reveals how culture circumscribed his political power. These objectives aligned with Mayfield's arguments that the underlying problems of African unity could not be reduced to the cultural or the social but instead intersected with the economic and political position of modern African nation-states and shifting gender politics on both sides of the Atlantic.

While Mayfield centered political economy as a significant force in these relationships, "Black on Black" was evidence not of its centrality or overriding importance but rather its relationship to culture and gender. In his nonfiction writing about Nkrumah, Mayfield emphasized political economy as a primary reason for African disunity, noting how "the unity which Africans have failed to achieve is more than countered by international financial combines which have managed to bury their differences"; he recognized the bind that African leaders faced.[60] He also centered these ideas in his fiction, especially "Black on Black" and the play *Fount of the Nation*. Political figures such as Nana, Mayfield argued in "Black on Black," knew very well "how little room they have to maneuver in the intricate economic web that has been spun over them by the spiders of international monopoly capitalism whose legs stretch from Washington and New York, to London, Paris, Brussels and Bonn."[61]

"Black on Black" is significant in that it offered a critique of political economy disguised as an examination of cultural and social difference, weaving together these ideas in a piece of popular fiction. Uniting Mayfield's artistic sensibilities with his politics, "Black on Black" illustrated one element of the framework Mayfield had developed to promote an African unity that was based on an intersectional notion of race and class, although his gender politics remained firmly patriarchal in orientation.[62] Cultural differences, linguistic barriers, national sentiments, and political economy played significant and intertwining roles in shaping divisions between Africans and those in the diaspora; none could be discounted. Any solution to those divisions would have to take all these factors into account. However, as "Black on Black" emphasized, relationships and belonging, culture and social relations, and national and transnational identifications could not be disassociated from the material realities facing a postcolonial economy. In foregrounding the political and economic concerns that shaped nation-specific articulations of Black internationalism, Mayfield once again reflected earlier arguments by W. E. B. Du Bois and Kwame Nkrumah.[63]

Mayfield revised "Black on Black" several times during his last two years in Ghana, and its final ending illustrates how the intertwined conflicts had by then become insurmountable. Mayfield's belief that Africans themselves were unable to fully embrace the radical reconfiguration of their society necessary to realizing their stated goals is borne out in the ending of the story as Nana allows Bessie to depart Songhay. Similarly, African Americans were unwilling to sublimate their own desires for a usable past and self-discovery to put themselves fully in the service of their African hosts. The failure of the fictional Nana recalled that of Nkrumah, whose asceticism contrasted with his fiery public persona.[64] Bessie's failure, which was not derived from Maya Angelou's actual reasons for leaving Africa, suggested the lack of commitment and dedication among Afro expatriates that Mayfield witnessed.[65]

Each character rejects the other—and with good reason—but the consequences of their rejection are broader in scope than either care to recognize. A year later, Mayfield's unpublished biographical portrait of Nkrumah, "The Lonely Warrior," concluded that Nkrumah's most significant failing as a leader was not his radicalism or his lack of political will but rather his insulating himself from the complaints and voices raised by the inhabitants of the nation he governed, both native-born and expatriate. In failing to navigate the continuous contradictions that the dialectic of African unity created, Mayfield's fictionalized lovers illustrate the importance of personal relationships to the shaping of diasporic politics.

"Black on Black" also closely examined how Africans and Afro expatriates heard each other's words without listening to their content. Solidarity, Mayfield's story suggested, was more than simply ideological; it also required personal understanding and the development of a meaningful sense of belonging. In writing designed to offer African Americans in the United States a complex, nuanced portrait of diasporic relationships, Mayfield sought to dispel both overly wishful thinking and abject pessimism about the potential for African unity. Viewing culture, gender, and race as refracted through the lens of political economy in "Black on Black" demonstrates that fitting transdiasporic relationships into familiar African or American categories obscured more than it revealed. The forging of diasporic unity, Mayfield's writing suggested, was both more particular and more personal than its critics and its supporters cared to reflect upon.

Fount of a Nation

In his four-act play *Fount of a Nation*, Mayfield revisited the fictional African nation of Songhay in order to consider the impossible position that newly independent African nations found themselves in upon attaining independence. Presenting a thinly veiled version of Kwame Nkrumah as the president of the Republic of Songhay, Mayfield examined his desperate efforts to modernize a country while attempting to sidestep the international pressures of a global Cold War. The character of Robert, the leader's African American adviser, serves as the president's foil. Robert voices the arguments made by Afro expatriates about Ghanaian politics, though fictionalized for the play. In one scene, he expresses his anger after learning that the president has decided to accept American money in order to finance the modern harbor so as to open Songhay to international freight liners. "No matter how much your generation talks about revolution," Robert addresses the president of Songhay accusingly, "it always ends up with you accepting things the way they are. We—my generation—must find another way." To that, the president responds dryly, "When you find it, let me know."[66]

In probing the difficult decisions that African leaders had to make, *Fount of the Nation* also captured the intractable position that Afro expatriates found themselves in during the final years of the Nkrumah government. As many privately decried the cult of personality around Nkrumah, dubbed the Osgayefo (Redeemer), most remained publicly supportive of the government. Even Mayfield refrained from offering any criticism until after the government fell, keeping his increasingly negative opinions to himself between 1964 and 1966. Grounded in his eye for the political roots of everyday life, Julian Mayfield's writing refused to discount or ignore the material realities that framed the contradictions of diaspora, whether they be in the air-conditioned offices of Flagstaff House, the modern lobby of the Ambassador Hotel, or on the crowded dance floor at the Lido nightclub. Similarly, Mayfield rejected calls to foreground class and nationality above race. In telling the story from the inside of the presidential office of Songhay, *Fount of the Nation* once again examined the centrality of personal relationships to the operation of diasporic thought. Collaboration and cooperation in

Songhay and Ghana required careful navigation of difference, and there were limits. But perhaps more importantly, the play demonstrated how Nkrumah's drive toward a simultaneous nationalist and continental notion of sovereignty demonstrated a dramatic, if incomplete, shift in African political history.

That shift was the recognition of the profound need for an organized Africa to resist the neocolonialism of former empires. Writing from Ibiza in the aftermath of the February 1966 coup that toppled Nkrumah's government, Mayfield argued that North Americans and Europeans who celebrated his downfall did so because of his "conscious attempt to transform the entire society into a modern socialist state."[67] Notably, Mayfield did not use the word "nation." He used the term "society," tacitly implying that Nkrumah's goals extended far beyond the tiny West African nation he governed. Mayfield pointed out, though, that the "people of Ghana, especially those in the cities, were quite naturally more concerned with domestic economic stagnation and a dwindling public treasury than they were with their international prestige." The prestige of being a state that stood firm against Soviet, American, and European neocolonialists "means little when there is not enough food for the children, nor enough money in one's pocket to buy that which is available."[68] Overcoming this disconnect between the lofty goals of President Nkrumah and the daily needs of the people of Ghana was the reason for the rhetorical advocacy that Mayfield undertook at Flagstaff House. That the two were never brought into alignment was both the source of Mayfield's frustration and criticism of the government and the foundation for the nationalist rhetoric he would take up in the United States and later in Guyana.

Although Mayfield initially sought to minimize his role in the Nkrumah government, he soon found himself fully "identified not only with Ghana's foreign policy objectives, but also with her domestic affairs."[69] Many of his contemporaries, including Leslie Lacy, David Levering Lewis, Alice Childress, Maya Angelou, Malcolm X, and Preston King, asserted that Mayfield was the de facto leader of the Afro expatriate community, much to his chagrin. In "Tales from the Lido," a series of vignettes written between 1971 and 1983, Mayfield recalls that his work was often interrupted by African Americans who had managed to get themselves in trouble in Ghana. His position also provoked frustration among Ghanaians. Inviting men and women from other nations to Ghana and paying them more than local salaries engendered criticism among many in Ghana, especially in such institutions as the University of Ghana and the military. Similarly, Nkrumah's courting of Kaiser Aluminum and the US State Department in the construction of the Volta River Dam project provoked mixed reactions among Afro expatriates who saw foreign development as compromising nascent African sovereignty, a position that Nkrumah himself would adopt only late in his administration. "To enter such agreements" with former colonizers, Mayfield wrote ruefully, "is the same as inviting the late train robber Jessie James to count your money."[70]

Mayfield was fortunate that he had chosen to leave Ghana almost a month before the 1966 coup, and correspondence between Mayfield and fellow expatriates indicates that his dedication to his work, international travel, and his long absences from home drove a wedge into his relationship with Ana Livia. In light of these exchanges, his move to Ibiza in February 1966 suggests that this desire to find a quiet place to work and write also functioned as a formal separation from his wife as their marriage deteriorated.[71] Although they would not formally sign divorce papers until 1971, Ana Livia and Julian's relationship never recovered from the tensions that emerged in Ghana. Subsequent correspondence alternately reflects anger, frustration, and sadness at the dissolution of their partnership.

In the aftermath of the coup, Dr. Cordero's work with the Nkrumah government drew the attention of the new military regime. She was arrested in May and held for several months before being released on the condition that she leave the country. She returned to Puerto Rico where she would remain for much of the remainder of her life, dedicated to pursuing her own ideas of Puerto Rican nationalism, Pan-Africanism, and Third World solidarity.[72] Her time in Ghana had increased her commitment to Puerto Rican nationalism, and she later served the Movimento Pro Independencia as its representative in Africa. Following her return to Puerto Rico in 1967 with her children, Cordero founded the Proyecto Piloto Trabajo con el Pueblo (Pilot Project of Work with the People), which aided many of Puerto Rico's poorest citizens. A dedicated transnational activist, Cordero continued her insistence on the presence of Puerto Rican representatives at conferences such as the 1966 Tricontinental Conference in Cuba, which helped weave Puerto Rico into the complex web of anti-imperialist activism that spanned the globe.[73]

Contemplating all that had transpired since he had left the United States, Julian Mayfield reluctantly concluded in early 1967 that the community he had been a part of in Ghana was no more. He weighed his options, noting that in Ibiza he'd had ample time to write and few distractions; he considered staying, but his friends would not hear of it.[74] A letter from Maya

Angelou spurred him to action. In impatient script she implored Mayfield, "Come home!" Her reasons were many, but most importantly, she believed that his presence was needed because the struggle for liberation was not in the Mediterranean; as she put it, "The struggle is *here*."[75] Noting that filmmaker Ivan Dixon had expressed interest in producing a film version of *The Hit* and that Black-oriented productions were becoming a real possibility in Hollywood, Angelou wrote optimistically about Mayfield's artistic prospects. In May 1967 after five and a half years away from the United States, Julian Mayfield relented and booked passage to New York, ready once again to challenge white supremacy in the land of his birth.

6 The Black Militant in Theory and in Practice, 1967–1968

> The Black Revolutionary does not embrace violence as a religion, but only as a tactic, and only when he thinks he can win.
> —Julian Mayfield, 1968

When Julian Mayfield arrived in the United States in late May 1967, his return came at an incongruous moment in American cultural and political history.[1] Even as the instruments of state surveillance and repression were aimed squarely at "black nationalist, hate-type organizations and groupings," popular fascination with Black radicalism made it a valuable commodity to film, television, and book-publishing companies.[2] In addition to the culture industry, protests and direct action by a new generation of Black students aimed at primarily white institutions prompted universities to begrudgingly form the nucleus of Black studies programs, hiring Black professors and lecturers to avoid bad publicity and forestall armed takeovers of campus buildings.[3]

Returning to the United States at a moment when a militant posture in Black radical movements dominated headlines, Mayfield concluded that the revolutionary proclamations of the new generation of young radicals were as hollow as the liberal rhetoric he had critiqued in *The Grand Parade*. Despite his long-standing belief in the necessity of revolution and the search for sovereignty as key components of Black self-determination, he did not shy away from the flaws he identified in the masculinist militancy of Huey P. Newton and Bobby Seale, in particular their lack of pragmatism and attachment to a revolutionary fantasy. In his April 1968 keynote address to the writer's conference at Fisk University, Mayfield argued that a single-minded militancy in groups such as the Black Panthers limited the possibility of meaningful revolution.[4]

"The Black Writer and Revolution" was a wide-ranging speech, but prominent in the piece was an epistemological distinction between the figures of the militant and the revolutionary. The militant, Mayfield explained, is irresponsible, immature, unthinking, and needlessly violent. He "risks his own life, and more often the lives of others, in almost suicidal confrontations with superior power." This new militancy was also a reflection of the fragile state of Black American masculinity: "Because he must always be busy proving he is a man, [the militant] can get a lot of black people killed without achieving real objectives."[5] In contrast, the revolutionary "is first and foremost a thinking person who takes his own manhood or her womanhood for granted." Selflessness was only one element of revolutionary status. Mayfield also made the distinction between ideology and tactics, noting that the revolutionary "does not embrace violence as a religion, but only as a tactic, and only when he thinks he can win."[6] The discrepancy between the practical and ideological embrace of violence as a form of direct action was grounded in Mayfield's experiences with Robert F. Williams and Williams's development of armed self-defense in Monroe, North Carolina; it also reflected the kind of pragmatic politics that came to define Mayfield's perspective as he approached middle age.

Delivered shortly before his fortieth birthday, the Fisk keynote revealed how revolutionary ideology was less important for Mayfield than tactics, organization, and strategic planning in the service of fundamental social and political change. The conference, organized by Mayfield's fellow Harlem Writers Guild alumnus John O. Killens, afforded the thirty-nine-year-old writer the platform to expound upon this heterodox intellectual project, in which he prioritized practical revolutionary tactics and strategy over ideological declarations. Developed during and in response to Mayfield's first year as an instructor at Cornell University, a position that helped spur his return to the States, his critique of Black militancy was further refined during the next four years as he taught a lecture series at New York University and occasional courses at the State University of New York at Cortland (SUNY Cortland). Working in the academy would have the additional benefit of bringing Mayfield closer to a generation of students who had come of age amid the civil rights movement and embraced radical alternatives to the politics of nonviolence and appeals to white liberal morality.

The Fisk conference also afforded Mayfield a chance encounter with former acting teacher Frank Silvera that would alter the course of Mayfield's career and take it in a radical new direction. At Silvera's urging, Mayfield met with filmmaker Jules Dassin with hopes of becoming a writer on his upcoming film project for Paramount. Dassin was so impressed with Mayfield that he not only invited him to contribute as a writer but also offered him the male lead. The film that came about as a result of their meeting, *Uptight,* served as a vehicle for Mayfield's ideas about the contradictions in the movement at the height of the Black Power era. Written in early 1968 and shot in the immediate aftermath of Dr. Martin Luther King Jr.'s assassination in April, *Uptight* elaborated on Mayfield's arguments about the limitations and consequences of masculinist militancy, the changing relationship between protest and politics, and the unsustainability of the Black Power project.

If Mayfield's experience with the Freedom Riders and forces of state repression in Monroe had further diminished his interest in the kind of nonviolent activism embodied by Martin Luther King Jr., then his time in Ghana reinforced his preoccupation with masculine articulations of state power. As Mayfield later told actor and director William Marshall, "Since I first went to Africa I have been fascinated by black men who hold power, what they do to get it and to keep it, their life styles, and why they often lose it."[7] Militant rhetoric and direct action taken by groups such as the Black Panther Party for Self-Defense and the Republic of New Afrika, Mayfield wrote, lacked mass broad support, practical tactics, and—most importantly—the ability to exercise meaningful power. In addition to being premature, Mayfield argued, these organizations would succeed only in bringing about a violent and potentially genocidal response from the white majority. Fears of such a response influenced both his writing and the lectures he gave while teaching in New York. By 1969, Mayfield emerged as one of the loudest voices warning against the discourse of "law and order" perpetuated by the Nixon administration and its potential for large-scale persecution—and genocide—of African Americans.

Prior to his involvement in the film, Mayfield sought work in the academy as a means to remain financially independent and afford him the time to continue his own writing. Despite his best efforts, teaching proved a burdensome task and left him with little time for his creative work. Yet in his syllabi for various classes and in the lectures he gave in New York and Ithaca, Mayfield offered compelling arguments about the perils of militancy without strategy, the dangers of collaboration with President Lyndon Johnson's liberal Great Society, and the broken promises of Black studies programs. "The Black Writer and Revolution" was not only an analysis of the state of Black politics but was also an alarm, warning listeners of the effect that continued "unthinking" militancy would have on the African American population. Mayfield believed that the US government not only had the means to initiate the large-scale detention of African Americans and white allies but also was preparing to do so. Existential survival, then, became a primary concern as reflected in his speeches, writing, and public experiences.

This chapter considers a particular period in Julian Mayfield's longer search for a solution to the persistent contradictions and contentious debates that characterized the Black Power movement. His work resulted in a major piece of cinema that examined all sides of the debate and succeeded in pleasing no one. If, as Peniel Joseph writes, historians are to understand Black Power as the means by which Black peoples "challenged the scope of liberalism, democracy, and the nation-state," then an analysis of major Hollywood studios' decision to give carte blanche to a formerly blacklisted director (Dassin), a "communist subversive" under surveillance by the FBI (Mayfield), and a veteran of the Harlem cultural Left (Ruby Dee) offers a compelling narrative of a paradoxical moment in American history.[8] At a moment when Attorney General Robert Kennedy had signed off on the plan to "expose, disrupt, misdirect, discredit, or otherwise neutralize" Black social movements under the FBI's Counter Intelligence Program (COINTELPRO), American culture industries saw profits to be made in portraying the struggles of Black liberation.[9] Ironically, *Uptight* was among a handful of films that sought realism and rejected caricature in its portrait of Black radicalism even as proponents of Black radicalism were persecuted, marginalized, and murdered by state forces.

As the first major Hollywood motion picture to seriously depict Black militancy in the United States, *Uptight* is also an important primary source for the intellectual history of the era. The film challenged the dichotomous historiographical schema of Black-oriented films in the 1960s and 1970s. Films from this era dealing with race have tended to be situated in the historiography as examples of either liberal integrationism (e.g., *Look Who's Coming to Dinner* and *In the Heat of the Night*) or exploitation (e.g., *Superfly*, *Shaft*, and *Cotton Comes to Harlem*).[10] The latter category, typically referred to as "blaxploitation," came to dominate the industry in the early 1970s, much to the chagrin of many Black writers, religious leaders, and social critics.[11] Depicting the intellectual and political divisions in ways that challenge this schematic view of filmic representations of Black Americans, *Uptight* demands a reassessment of this framework. Additionally, Mayfield's role in the film, overshadowed in the historiography by his earlier work in Ghana, is integral to understanding the dynamics of Black revolutionary rhetoric during a pivotal moment in the history of the Black Power movement. A tepid reception and poor box office receipts limited the film's impact and staying power, but in considering Black Power as something other than the "evil twin" of the civil rights movement, the making of *Uptight* offers a new perspective on lesser-known artistic depictions of these political, economic, and social struggles. These conflicts contributed to the explosive rise and lasting influence of Black Power as a political, cultural, and social movement.

Placing *Uptight* and Mayfield's teaching within this historical context further integrates artistic expressions of Black militancy and the development of Black studies into the broader historiography of the Black Power movement. *Uptight* illustrates what historian Tom Sugrue described as the quest for "a political alternative to the racial liberalism that had prevailed through most of the postwar years."[12] Now an outsider returning from six years in Africa and Europe, Julian Mayfield searched for meaningful political and artistic alternatives to both racial liberalism and the rising Black militancy that audiences demanded confront the deep divisions characterizing the late 1960s. In their critical appraisal of the divisive nature of Black politics in 1968, the film's scriptwriters—Dassin, Mayfield, and Dee—believed that by presenting a realistic portrait of the movement, the film could help lead viewers to an understanding of the limitations of specific ideologies. The resulting portrait—concise, accurate, and honest—would allow for the conditions in which the solidarity necessary for liberation could be constructed.

Back in the War

It was a letter from Cornell University that finally prompted Julian Mayfield to accept that his future lay in the United States. At the urging of former Ghanaian University president Connor Cruise O'Brien, Mayfield applied for and received a teaching fellowship at Cornell University at the newly created Society of the Humanities.[13] The formation of the society in late 1966 marked the beginning of Cornell's attempt to address complaints by Black students about the lack of a Black studies program, the low numbers of Black faculty, and the overwhelmingly Eurocentric curriculum. Hiring a nonacademic published writer such as Mayfield was a stopgap measure to address increasingly vocal student demands, and the subsequent armed seizure of Straight Hall by Black students in April 1969 proved that the measure had not been enough. The takeover, prompted by unmet demands by African American students on campus, resulted in the students holding the building for several days before they peacefully departed.[14] Mayfield was inspired to accept the offer because of the promise of a consistent paycheck and his own idealized notions about teaching at the university level, and he began to make plans to return to the United States.

Despite increasing tensions and an uptick in expulsions of foreigners who had been aligned with Nkrumah, Ana Livia Cordero chose to remain in Ghana with Rafael and Emiliano in the aftermath of the February 24 coup. But her position as a specialist at Ghana's Department of National Institute of Health and Medical Research was not enough to protect her from the new military government's purge of Nkrumah loyalists. According to a news report dated June 6, 1966, Dr. Cordero was arrested and jailed on June 3. She was held incommunicado for several days, prompting concern from her friends and family. Released on the condition that she leave Ghana, she nonetheless protested her imprisonment, stating that her "illegal arrest and immediate expulsion was a direct violation of her civil rights and an interference with academic and scientific freedom."[15] She was subsequently put on a plane and sent back to the United States in early 1967. During this difficult time, the estranged couple exchanged increasingly vituperative letters. Julian expressed frustration with Cordero's decision to return to nationalist organizing work in Puerto Rico, and she indicated her displeasure with his decision to remain in Spain while she and the couple's children struggled in the Caribbean. It would be almost a year before he would see his children again.

Unsurprisingly, Mayfield's decision to reenter the United States after almost six years away prompted a great deal of soul-searching and anxiety. His recollections of the day of his return reflected his discomfort living in a nation controlled by a hostile white government. For all of the inconveniences and difficulties posed by living in Ghana, he recalled fondly that it had at least afforded him the rare privilege of "forget[ting] just what it was like to live in a world so directly controlled by whites." Arriving on a Saturday, Mayfield noted that "no sooner had I stepped off the ship . . . and seen my first American policeman in seven years than it all came back to me. I was back in the war."[16]

Mayfield, choosing to fight that war with words instead of guns, presented to Cornell an outline of an intense study of the intellectual history of Black thought through Black literature. Limiting his focus to the twentieth century, Mayfield proposed exposing students to contemporary Black political, social, and cultural thought through fiction and poetry that spanned the twentieth century. W. E. B. Du Bois, David Walker, Waring Cuney, Harold Cruse, Amiri Baraka, Countee Cullen, Frank London Brown, Lorraine Hansberry, Langston Hughes, and Margaret Walker featured prominently on his syllabus, and the seminars sought answers to the question

"What does the Negro want?" Believing that Black writing reflected a profound cultural and social transformation over the previous three-quarters of a century, Mayfield argued that these books were the key to understanding the contours of Black intellectual history. This "current diversity of themes and attitudes," Mayfield wrote, "reflect[ed] the fragmentation of the Negro leadership groups which used to be monolithic in structure."[17]

This first seminar, which began in September 1967, was titled "Negro Goals as Reflected in Negro Writing" and offered a lesson plan consistent with his objectives as laid out in letters to O'Brien. In Mayfield's first turn at teaching, correspondence with administrators indicates that this new career path induced in him a significant level of anxiety. He had received a special waiver to be hired as faculty at Cornell due to his lack of a PhD, and the fellowship granted him $10,000 for the nine-month assignment. In letters he exchanged with Cornell's program head, Max Black, Mayfield outlined his pedagogical goals. Resistant to the idea that "the students will not only be talked to and at," he insisted that his seminar be organized so that "they will be able to participate fully."[18] Black acquiesced to Mayfield's demands, and the latter was given a significant degree of control over his first teaching experience. Correspondence from the immediate aftermath of his first semester teaching at Cornell indicates that his seminar was a rousing success. Not only was Mayfield impressed with his students' work, but his students also indicated their appreciation of his perspective and historical insights in their letters to him during the holiday break. That winter, he was invited to Fisk University for the third Black Writers' Conference and asked to give the keynote address. The theme of the conference was "The Black Writer's Vision for America," and it was scheduled for April 19, 1968.

Mayfield dramatically revised his address in the aftermath of Martin Luther King Jr.'s assassination in Memphis two weeks prior.[19] Even though Mayfield had long been critical of King's tactics, rejecting how the Southern Christian Leadership Conference leader couched protest in the moral language of Christianity and promoted nonviolent passive resistance to white supremacy, the assassination of King had a profound effect on Mayfield. He lamented the reverend's early death as another casualty in the war against white supremacists and took solace in the ways that men and women throughout the country mourned King's passing. The explosions of public protest and violence that followed King's assassination, Mayfield told the Fisk audience, heralded great changes for the nation. In this revised speech, titled "The Black Writer and Revolution," Mayfield expressed his belief that the question of whether revolution was possible in the United States "was never very far from the minds of any person in this auditorium." King's assassination and the riots that had consumed hundreds of American cities in its aftermath convinced Mayfield that the conference and its attendees must find some way to address "the future of black people in America."[20]

In this address, Julian Mayfield expressed the ideas and objectives that would define his writing, public pronouncements, and activism for the next four years. First and foremost, he centered the importance of Black writers in the post–civil rights era. At a time when peaceful marching and morally righteous protest had given way to an explosion of violence, looting, and arson, Mayfield asserted the collective responsibility of Black writers in shaping the horizons of the Black freedom struggle in an increasing violent and hostile environment. "As writers we have a unique role to play in the struggle for Black liberation," he averred. Perceiving the backlash to the evolution of the Black freedom struggle from "Freedom Now" to "Black Power" as an existential threat, Mayfield declared that Black writers had to dedicate themselves first and foremost to the issue of survival. Finally, he clarified that he brought to the table no truly "new" ideas but "only old ideas that I want to discuss in what I hope is a new way."[21] With these objectives stated, Mayfield proceeded to elaborate his vision for the symbiotic relationship between the Black writer and revolution.

In a characteristically freewheeling tone, Mayfield's broader point was in keeping with addressing the divisive mood that characterized African American responses to King's assassination. "The decisions and the actions we take in this next period," he concluded, "may very well determine the direction of the black liberation struggle for the next generation."[22] Mayfield urged attendees to consider what they had in common over what divided them. The disparate responses to King's murder among Black intellectuals and political leaders, Mayfield warned, threatened to further fracture what was an already broken movement.[23] He was not alone in his reevaluation of the movement in the aftermath of King's assassination; other intellectuals, organizers, and radical Black politicians articulated similar ideas in April 1968. The speech that Stokely Carmichael gave the day after King's assassination influenced Mayfield's revised keynote. On April 5, Carmichael told audiences that the death of King had fundamentally changed American political life. "White America made its biggest mistake when she killed Dr. King last night. When she killed Dr. King last night, she killed all reasonable hope. When she killed Dr. King last night, she killed the one man of our race, in this country, in the older generation who's a militant and a revolutionary, and the masses of black people would still listen to. Even though sometimes he did not agree with them, they would still listen to him."[24]

As a longtime critic of King's tactics, Mayfield interpreted his assassination as further evidence that "no matter how many books you published, no matter what professorial post you may hold[,] . . . no matter how polished your accent, how neat your clothing, how straight your hair, how fair your skin . . . when the stuff hits the air conditioner . . . we all go."[25] Linking the fate of all the men and the women in the room with King's, Mayfield concluded that despite all of King's peaceful proclamations and moral rectitude, his rhetoric did not save him from the violence of white Americans. And as Mayfield pointed out, the Black men, women, and children who took to the streets in cities such as Washington, Kansas, Los Angeles, and Detroit to loot, burn, and rage against the assassination of yet another leader were "hitting back in the only way they knew how, taking back what, in a sense, had been stolen from them."[26]

Smoke from burning buildings still shrouded cities beleaguered by riots when Mayfield stood behind the lectern at Fisk and argued that Black writers had to recognize that they were no different than black political leaders, in that both were "lagging behind our people." The deeper lesson that writers should take from the uprisings that followed King's assassination, Mayfield argued, was that the people who risked their lives to set fires, loot merchandise from stores, and take to the streets did so for *"no articulate political goals."* Those men and women represented "unharnessed power," which was "an indictment not only of the so-called intellectuals, but most of our leadership."[27] This failure of Black leaders and intellectuals to harness this power of the people "in order to achieve positive *political, economic* and *social* objectives" revealed a broader failing among the Black intellectual and political elite. Black writers' being caught unaware by the outburst of grassroots anger and frustration indicated that Black writers had to "catch up to our people" before they could hope to lead them.[28]

This perspective of a revolutionary Black proletariat reflected Mayfield's Marxian roots, but in his inversion of the Leninist formulation of the educated, revolutionary vanguard leading the proletariat to revolution there was a scathing critique of his audience. In effect, the people had left the intellectuals and political leadership—the vanguard—behind. "The black people themselves, the cats on the block, have joined the issue," he warned; "they will never really go back home and wait for writers and scholars and politicians to resolve our intellectual differences." The patience of the people, who had waited through years of debate and very little in the way of change, was exhausted. "We writers," Mayfield told his audience, "are going to have to become revolutionaries whether we completely accept the idea or not, if for no other reason than to keep up with our potential readers."[29] In his drafts for his autobiography, Mayfield wrote of the year 1968 that "the writer must either figuratively [or] literally take up the gun, for what is the good of living and writing when you are not free."[30]

The primary objective of this keynote was to convince the audience of Black writers that they must address the fires of revolutionary consciousness that King's assassination had fueled, an idea in keeping with many of his contemporaries. However, in voicing his concerns about the survival of all African Americans and the threat of genocide, Mayfield broke with many of his peers. "For us to come together and talk about lit-ter-raw-teur in the spring of 1968 would be as absurd and as tragic as a group of Jewish writers gathered in 1937 to talk about the future of symbolism in Jewish poetry," he said before pivoting to an argument that "genocide against our race is a very real possibility, that it is actually contemplated at this very moment."[31]

This threat affected all African Americans, Mayfield argued, no matter their profession, their ideological belief in nonviolence, their religiosity, or their location. He confidently stated that there were "26 detention or concentration camps waiting, unoccupied, ready to receive up to 50,000 black and white militants, and that the President in Washington already has the power . . . to declare a national emergency and detain that many people over night."[32] Rhodes Johnson, writing in the *Nashville Tennessean* two days after the conference, reported that "not everyone in the room applauded Mayfield" for these remarks, "but all paid rapt attention" as he spoke.[33]

The King Alfred Plan

The possibility of an African American genocide remains, even today, a persistent idea on the fringes of political discourse in the United States. Mayfield was not the first to theorize about a genocide aimed specifically at African Americans and other nonwhite Americans, but in promoting the idea in college lectures and his artistic output during the late 1960s and 1970s, he became an early and outspoken proponent. Although he does not cite the source, archival sources indicate that Mayfield began to speak on the subject shortly after he read about the 1967 novel *The Man Who Cried I Am*, but the origins of the idea date back to Mayfield's heyday in the

Communist Party and the passage of the Internal Security Act of 1950, better known as the McCarran Act.[34]

Title II of the McCarran Act provided the attorney general with the power to "apprehend and by order detain persons who there is reasonable ground to believe probably will commit or conspire with others to commit espionage or sabotage."[35] As early as 1951 journalists argued that Title II had the potential to lead to concentration camps and genocide on American soil based not on race, but ideology.[36] P. L. Prattis of the *Pittsburgh Courier* even went so far as to state that "the G-men down in Washington have their eyes on 14,000 persons (as a starter) who'll be seized in the middle of the night (or any other time) if and when the President determines that our argument with Russia and the Communists has become serious enough."[37] It is unclear where Prattis received this information, but he linked the number to testimony given by men and women before the House Un-American Activities Committee between 1949 and the publication of his article.

Sixteen years later as the number of Black radical activists and civil rights leaders murdered, maimed, or imprisoned by agents of the state began to rise, John A. Williams seized on this concept as the central plot device for a novel, later titled *The Man Who Cried I Am*. Framed as an account of the last days of Max Reddick, a protagonist loosely based on Richard Wright, the novel takes readers on a journey through Reddick's attempts to make sense of his life as a Black expatriate journalist and writer approaching the end of his life. During the course of the story Reddick, who is dying of cancer, stumbles onto a plot to conceal an explosive memo known only as the "King Alfred Plan" that is somehow connected with his past among the Black expatriates.[38] After visiting old haunts, past girlfriends, and former comrades, Reddick finally receives a copy of this document and is able to read it for himself. He discovers with horror that his country's government has a meticulously planned genocide in store for him and his people. After reading the memo and sending copies out to other friends, Reddick is murdered by a former friend, now revealed to be working for the Central Intelligence Agency.

Williams's novel presents the memo's plan in detail, explaining how the nation will be divided up into ten geographical regions and which "Minority" (African American) organizations will be targeted and which "Minority" politicians will be removed from office, along with a description of how millions of "Minority" people and white sympathizers would be initially rounded up in the eight hours immediately following the president's declaration of a "state of emergency."[39] Subsequently, the text describes how millions more will be detained and sent to their deaths in the days and weeks after the declaration in a systematic fashion and on an industrial scale. The plot device bears some resemblance to accusations leveled at Title II of the McCarran Act, but the novel's release and propagation during the height of COINTELPRO attributed specific figures and plans, contributing to its apparent veracity.[40]

Julian Mayfield was among the first Black intellectuals to speak publicly about the threat of genocide against African Americans.[41] In December 1968, he appeared on a panel alongside publisher and editor Dan Watts, historian Richard B. Moore, author Claude Barnett, and moderator William Greaves on the latter's television news program, *Black Journal*. In response to a longer discussion about the legacy of Dr. King and his shift to economic justice with the Poor People's Campaign, Mayfield posed a question as he argued that structural transformations and industrial progress meant that African Americans were "more and more an obsolete people . . . [and] they do not need our labor anymore."[42] As Black Americans were "more and more unemployed . . . the basic question is what do you do with the people that you don't need anymore?"[43] The implication was that if African American labor was no longer needed, extermination was a very real possibility. None of the other panelists addressed Mayfield's comments or his question, but it was not the last time he would mention it.

Mayfield inserted similar comments into his screenplay for *Uptight*, explicitly connecting Black militancy to a preexisting plan for racial extermination. During a tense debate between Black militants and peaceful civil rights advocates, the latter decry the former's plans for an armed uprising. Violence by Black militants would "bring the whole military machine down on our heads," the integrationist leader argues. "[They] will be the excuse for fascism in this country, [they] will bring on the camps."[44] As Mayfield himself had in his *Black Journal* appearance, his characters give voice to his fears that increasing automation would result in the obsolescence of Black labor, precipitating a genocidal response from the US government. The spectacle of militant Black radicals wielding guns in Sacramento, Cleveland, and elsewhere, Mayfield argued, was the excuse that white Americans were looking for to begin rounding people up for "disposal." In spite of these fears, Mayfield argued that the Black revolutionary, unlike the militant, was aware of this possibility and preparing for its eventuality. Whereas John A. Williams's public appearances were limited, Julian Mayfield was open and vocal about the idea, and his pronouncements and allusions helped cement the idea in Black radical cultural and political discourse.[45]

An early proponent of this idea, Mayfield soon found himself supported by other militants, white and Black. In March 1969, he joined civil rights lawyer William Kunstler, Student Nonviolent Coordinating Committee (SNCC) chairman H. Rap Brown, and the Students for a Democratic Society's Bernadine Dohm in arguing for a connection between the McCarran Act and a system of unconstitutional, preventative detention. Organizing a press conference at the Diplomat Hotel on New York's West Side, the group publicly charged that the federal government was "moving toward a system of preventative detention designed to intimidate the poor, Negroes and dissidents seeking to change the society."[46] They cited President Richard Nixon's recent comments as evidence of Title II being implemented by Attorney General John Mitchell. In January 1969, Nixon had proposed that "dangerous, hard-core recidivists could be held in pretrial detention when they have been charged with crimes and when their continued pretrial release presents a clear danger to the community."[47] While Black radical activists and their allies were not the only critics of these statements, their message was the most dire.

A negative response to Nixon's declaration emerged from a broad coalition of liberal and radical men and women, but it was the groundswell of popular perception that prompted Black journalists and, later, Black leaders and politicians, to take action. In November 1969, *New Pittsburgh Courier* reporter and columnist Ethel Payne reported that Attorney General John N. Mitchell had invited Coretta Scott King, attorney and SNCC veteran Timothy Jenkins, Representative John Conyers, Ralph David Abernathy, Southern Christian Leadership Conference leader Hosea Williams, and Mayor Richard Hatcher of Gary, Indiana, to a secret meeting in Washington to discuss—among other issues—popular perceptions of Title II.[48] Little was revealed about this meeting, and it was clear from the article that Payne had not been present. Subsequent comments by Hatcher and the National Urban League's Whitney Young indicated their growing concerns that the Nixon administration's racially coded calls for "law and order" and drastic changes in the US criminal code had convinced some civil rights leaders that it was a prelude to some sort of mass internment organized on racial and ideological grounds.[49]

By 1971, this concern had reached a fever pitch. Contemporary media coverage featured statements by self-professed spies who claimed to know details of the King Alfred Plan.[50] That year, another controversy would erupt following the publication of *The Choice* by reporter Samuel Yette. In his introduction, Yette echoed Mayfield's comments from *Black Journal*, asserting that any discussion of African American citizenship "must begin with a single, overpowering socioeconomic condition in the society: black Americans are obsolete people."[51] Yette, the first Black reporter hired by *Newsweek* magazine, worked at the organization's Washington desk. He had reported riots and Black militancy of the early 1970s and the response to citizenship demands of the previous decade. Considering President Johnson's Great Society as a project designed to pacify civil rights protesters, Yette linked rising Black unemployment, white flight, and the first signs of deindustrialization to eventual African American economic obsolescence.

The titular "choice" of the book was to either face what Yette called "modern slavery" of continued socioeconomic and political marginalization or rebel and face internment and ultimately genocide. To buttress his argument, Yette cited statements by public officials and connected the US refusal to ratify the Geneva Convention's genocide clause with plans to exterminate large numbers of African American "obsolete peoples." Yette's refusal to back down from the assertions he made in the book as the controversy made waves in major media outlets resulted in his termination by *Newsweek*. He was also mocked and criticized in the press.[52] In the aftermath of the publication of *The Choice*, however, these ideas were ensconced in American popular consciousness. Journalism and film were not the only spaces in which the ideas appeared; poet and musician Gil Scott-Heron composed a poem and later a song titled "King Alfred Plan" that appeared on the album *Free Will*, released in 1972. In "King Alfred Plan," the radical poet spoke frenetically about what was to come:

> Places are being prepared and readied night and day, night and day
> The white boy's plan is being readied night and day, night and day
> Listen close to what rap say about traps like Allenwood P-A
> Already legal in D.C. to preventatively detain you and me
> How long you think it's going to be before even our dreams ain't free?
>   You think I exaggerate? Check out Allenwood P-A.
> Night and day, night and day, the white boy's scheming night and day
> The Jews and Hitler come to mind. They thought the slavery far behind
> But white paranoia is here to stay. Check it out. Night and day
> What you think about the King Alfred Plan? You ain't heard? Where
>   you been, man?

John A. Williams never claimed that the plan was real, but he publicly affirmed the underlying logics of his fictional creation. In an interview published in *Jet* magazine in October 1971, Williams echoed both Yette and

Mayfield in his rhetorical question, "What would any administration do in a situation when a large segment of the population was discontented and tearing down the neighborhood[,] . . . threatening the order and the established regime?" The answer, for Williams, was mass internment and genocide, as laid out in the final pages of *The Man Who Cried I Am*. While the idea was dismissed among white journalists and ridiculed in the pages of major newspapers such as the *Washington Post* and the *New York Times*, public outcry escalated to a point in 1971 where the Ninety-second Congress reluctantly addressed the issue.

Following passage of the Non-Detention Act in September 1971 by the House of Representatives, President Nixon signed the bill into law on September 25, 1971. The bill repealed Title II, the Emergency Detention Act, and stripped the US attorney general of the power to detain any American and non-American citizens for threats to the national security of the United States.[53] Although not mentioned in Yette's book, Julian Mayfield deserves credit for pushing these ideas into the mainstream and considering the existential plight of Black Americans during the late 1960s and early 1970s that prompted Congress to take action to allay these fears.[54]

A Radical in the Academy

Existential concerns for African American survival were also a theme of the lectures Mayfield gave during his employment at New York University and SUNY Cortland between 1969 and 1971. In a talk titled "By Force and Violence," he noted his frustration with white Americans, as opposed to white English colonialists in Africa. "My English friend," Mayfield wrote, "understands that all his privileges and prerogatives are sustained by an infrastructure of force and violence which to survive must keep down a black revolution in Africa."[55] Honest colonialists, he opined, were not concerned with being liked or loved, only obeyed. Aware of this reality, the unnamed English colonist understood that "when the revolution comes they should either split the scene [get out] or use their guns . . . in their own self interest." In contrast, white liberals in the United States, ensconced in "comfortable suburbia," were simply unable to understand the plight and anger of the Black men and women in the "inner colonies just a few miles away." Liberal America, Mayfield wrote, was becoming "terribly aware of its whiteness, and ponders which way it will point its rifle in the inevitable race war."[56] Unaware of or unwilling to accept the forms of coercion and violence that had previously kept nonwhites repressed, Mayfield concluded that white Americans misunderstood and misrepresented Black radical demands.

Subsequent talks, including "The Quagmire of the Black American Writer" and "Everybody Loves the Africans of Rhodesia," embraced Third World nationalisms that publicly disregarded the ideological tenets and political machinations of "great powers" such as the Soviet Union and the United States. Each revolutionary movement, Mayfield wrote after a lengthy discussion of politics in southern Africa, had to build up a base of knowledge about its own particular political and economic history. Furthermore, he argued that no great power—Russia, China, or the United States, for example—should have "priority over the self-interest of any of those nation states."[57] Echoing his character Lonnie Banks, Mayfield emphasized the necessity of local control over revolutionary movements and not relying on or acceding to demands by foreign powers. He also sought to communicate the lessons about what constituted practical revolutionary action and emphasized the need for sovereignty and self-sufficiency to students and listeners.

In a syllabus for a course titled "Black Techniques of Survival," which Mayfield taught at SUNY Cortland in 1970, he laid out his belief that "survival" demanded that African Americans understand the historical actions of white Americans and the influence of racial capitalism. "White Americans have deliberately and systematically attempted to destroy Black Americans as a group, physically, culturally, socially, economically and psychologically since 1865," the syllabus began. More significant than white American policies toward Black peoples was *"the failure of Blacks to grasp [that] the genocidal character of White racism has retarded if not defeated the struggle for Black freedom."*[58] Presaging many of the arguments that Yette made in *The Choice*, Mayfield pointedly critiqued the options historically available to Black peoples: "permanent slave status" and resistance leading to "probable physical extermination."[59] With this historical interpretation as his basis, Mayfield concluded that "a thorough study of the techniques of survival and the mistakes of the past becomes inevitable."[60] Having introduced the subject, Mayfield proceeded to clarify how African Americans and other Black peoples had understood the American project of racial capitalism and how they had struggled against it.

The class was highly structured and emphasized an openness that did not limit students to those pursuing graduate degrees or those with a background in Black literature. Mayfield encouraged nontraditional students, stating that "a student's attitude toward discipline and often independent study is more important" than the subject the student chose to major in or the extent of the student's education. He argued for an interdisciplinary approach to independent study topics he would assign to students, including "self-help organizations," "populist movements," and "Third World nationalism."[61] Between the Fisk conference in April 1968 and the writing of this syllabus, Julian Mayfield's concern for the survival of Black peoples only intensified. The threat posed by COINTELPRO and the factional violence it inspired between Black liberation organizations made the situation even more dire. Mayfield remained committed to communicating these ideas to as many people as possible by whatever means he had at his disposal, reiterating the arguments he had made at the Fisk writers' conference.

It was Mayfield's growing frustration at the inefficacy of his efforts that attracted him to Dassin's film project, despite his reservations. In the interview with music and arts critic Hollie I. West published in 1975, Mayfield noted that his pursuit of a film career in the late 1960s was an obvious move. "You speak to more people in the film than you can in the novel—unless you're an awfully successful writer," he said. "People don't read as much as they used to. Although there are more literate people around, they just don't [read]."[62] Speaking at Fisk, Mayfield had argued that the role of the Black writer was to "articulate all the hopes and the fears and the rage burning in the hearts of our people." But he soon realized that such articulation was not enough. "I believe," Mayfield told the audience at Fisk, that "our responsibilities go even further than that, for we are, in a meaningful sense, more privileged than the majority of our people, with a greater mobility and a greater access to all of the knowledge of the past."[63]

The Fisk writers' conference provided Mayfield with the opportunity to discuss the potential for revolution with other intellectuals. He offered ideas on how Black writers should respond to the present conflagrations in cities such as Detroit, Newark, and Washington, DC, but the conference was perhaps most important in that it provided him a chance encounter with his old acting teacher, Frank Silvera. Having recently joined Jules Dassin's new project as an actor, Silvera explained to his former student that Dassin was looking for Black writers to contribute to his script. Having recently lost actor James Earl Jones for the lead, the director saw Mayfield's imposing frame and charismatic presence and immediately offered him the role.[64] As Mayfield recounted of their meeting, Silvera "talked me into reading for the role . . . and I talked him into signing me on as a writer."[65] Following his meeting with Dassin in April 1968, Mayfield wrote an apologetic note to Max Black at Cornell expressing his regret that this new opportunity would severely restrict his ability to perform the duties of his academic fellowship. Black, for his part, responded positively. He wrote to Mayfield that he was "thrilled by this wonderful opportunity" and released him from his obligations at Cornell.[66] Shorn of his commitments, Mayfield returned to New York City and threw himself into the task of rewriting Dassin's script with costar Ruby Dee and preparing for his first turn as a main character in a Hollywood film.

7   *Uptight* in Cleveland

The Black Militant Goes to Hollywood, 1968–1971

> It was an uptight time. Being Black in America is an uptight situation.
> —Ruby Dee, ca. 2008

During the appearance that Julian Mayfield made on *Black Journal,* he not only discussed his fears of a potential genocide in the United States but also posed a question about future tactics for equality and justice in the wake of the perceived end of the civil rights movement: "Do you continue to work within the system . . . that . . . has neglected you and oppressed you and repressed you for 300 years? Or do you attempt to change the system? And by change, I mean, eliminate it, overthrow it."[1]

Richard B. Moore, a distinguished historian of the Afro-Caribbean, was the first to respond. Moore expressed his disagreement with the premise of the question and set himself up as an ideal foil for the younger and more radical men on the stage. Chiding Mayfield for looking at oppression from a "Euro-American viewpoint," Moore emphasized that "it isn't a question of what we do with them, it's a question of what we do with ourselves." The problems faced by Black people throughout the hemisphere required them to work, in Moore's words, "within the framework of the system and . . . to work on its complete change, its basic change." A smiling Mayfield cheerfully challenged Moore's prescription, arguing that not only did the Afro-Caribbean scholar contradict himself but that his argument hinged on the assumption of a unity of goals among African-descended peoples. As an example of this lack of consensus, Mayfield motioned to his fellow panelists to "look at the unity that is demonstrated around this table here."[2]

The enormous divisions between different Black polities in the United States, marked by class, ideology, gender, and cultural differences, mirrored divisions within Black diasporic intellectual communities. The panelists were a microcosm of these debates. Mayfield continued his critique by citing the seemingly insurmountable odds of addressing and challenging the myriad forms that white power took in the United States. Beyond the federal government, Mayfield reminded the panel, there were fifty state governments and thousands of city, county, and regional governments that remained politically inaccessible to Black people. Realistically speaking, he concluded, "We don't have enough power to do all of these things at once and . . . it seems to me that there is such a basic contradiction that we ought to address ourselves to it." Although he did not mention the film in his televised appearance, the ideas he discussed intersected neatly with the themes explored in *Uptight*, in particular the basic contradiction lying at the heart of the production. The film's story, which follows the drunken, callow Tank (played by Mayfield) and his betrayal of a former comrade offered Mayfield a means to examine contradictions he had explored in his Fisk keynote, namely the problem posed by the new Black militancy, the impotence of the nonviolent civil rights movement after the passage of the Civil Rights Act of 1964, and the rising backlash.[3]

In the first draft of the script, which Jules Dassin had titled "Betrayal," Mayfield saw an opportunity to illuminate and explore the inner workings and conflicts he had witnessed in his two decades of activism. Armed with firsthand experience in these movements, he explained his perspective to journalist Kay Bourne of the *Bay State Banner* after the film's release. "We wanted to write a picture which showed a section of the black community as it is. . . . We wanted to show militants, not as screaming and shouting, but to present a serious argument for revolution in this country."[4] And although he had been a critic of the nonviolent tactics of the civil rights movement since the 1950s, he took pains to offer a faithful account of those groups as well. His perspective as an insider, he believed, made him an attractive collaborator for Dassin and a risk worth taking by Paramount, but Mayfield was well aware of what he was facing. Working with whites invariably required the Black artist to compromise, Mayfield told the *New York Times* in 1969, "the reality he knows before the play or picture is produced." Not only was this because "the black frame of reference is often so totally different from the white" but also because white studios knew that their audience was largely white and would be uncomfortable with certain topics and themes.[5] Limited by the constraints of the original story, an increasingly nervous studio, efforts to disrupt the production by the Federal Bureau of Investigation (FBI), and racial tensions on location in Cleveland, the film was nevertheless completed, a testament to the dedication of its director and stars.

Uptight was a reimagining of the 1935 John Ford film *The Informer*. That film was based on a 1925 novel by Liam O'Flaherty about the Irish Revolution (1919–23).[6] O'Flaherty's book and subsequent films grapple with the travails of "Gypo" Nolan, a former member of the Irish Republican Army (IRA) who is down on his luck and turns informant. At the beginning of the novel, Nolan has recently been expelled from the IRA for refusing to execute a captured British paramilitary. As a result, he is unable to provide financially for his girlfriend, Katie, and is angry at her choice to prostitute herself, and his life is in disarray until a chance encounter with a former comrade, Frankie. Now a fugitive with a price on his head, Frankie solicits aid from his former comrade, but Nolan turns him in for the reward.

With the money, Nolan plans to purchase a berth on a ship to give Katie a better life in the United States. Once he has received the reward, however, the enormity of his deed dawns on him, and he buys a bottle of whiskey to drown his sorrows. His suspicious actions and newfound wealth attract the attention of his former IRA comrades, who capture him, try him in a court proceeding, and sentence him to death. Escaping captivity following his sentence, Nolan returns to Katie's apartment to apologize before the IRA soldiers find and shoot him. Mortally wounded, Nolan staggers to a nearby church, where Frankie's mother mourns her dead son; he apologizes to the mother and receives absolution before succumbing to his wounds.[7]

The success of Liam O'Flahery's original novel and both film versions of *The Informer* were important selling points to Paramount executives, who agreed to Dassin's pitch with minimal negotiating. To the executives, Dassin's project appeared to be an ideal way to capitalize on the fascination with Black militancy while using a proven plot to minimize risk. Both critics and studio executives had reservations about Dassin, who had not made a film in the United States since his blacklisting seventeen years prior, and questioned whether he could rise to the occasion, but his pitch convinced them.[8] In a surprise move, Paramount gave Dassin complete creative control over the project, and the first script that Dassin wrote reflected his interest in US racial conflicts while taking seriously calls for revolution from militants in the Black freedom struggle. In this initial adaptation, Dassin exchanged Dublin for Harlem, Irish revolutionaries for Black militants, and Black and Tan paramilitaries for white American police officers, but the primary narrative arc of betrayal, regret, and absolution in the context of a revolutionary movement remained intact.

Dassin evinced little anxiety about portraying American society after nearly two decades abroad, but the director of noir crime dramas such as as *Rififi* indicated in interviews that he was wary of his limitations when it came to racial issues. "I don't know how capable I am or indeed any white man is of understanding the black man or putting himself in the black's position," he explained to reporter Scott Vernon during production. "I've tried to poke my nose as close to the windowpane as possible because, after all, I am on the outside looking in—as are so many whites."[9] It was this sense of being "on the outside" that prompted Dassin to reach out to Black writers to improve the realism of the script. Dassin first invited Ossie Davis to join him on the project.[10] Davis, then busy adapting Chester Himes's novel *Cotton Comes to Harlem* for MGM, demurred. Instead, he recommended his wife, Ruby Dee. She agreed and began revising Dassin's initial draft. Although she originally joined the project as a writer, she was later cast as Laurie, the protagonist's girlfriend. Dee's early revisions focused primarily on characterization and rewriting Dassin's dialogue in order to convey "an authentic sound to the language and to the feel of the events" in the picture.[11]

At the forefront of Julian Mayfield's mind when he came to the project was making the kind of film that would speak to the rage and frustration of the working-class Black masses he had referenced in the Fisk speech. If lack of "articulate political goals" among those rioting suggested the need for guidance, Mayfield saw in *Uptight* the opportunity to highlight the weaknesses of the movements available to Black peoples, although his script would ultimately offer no solutions. The audience Mayfield had in mind represented the "unharnessed power" he spoke of in his Fisk keynote.[12] By following the lead of the Black masses protesting in the street over Martin Luther King Jr.'s assassination, he hoped that he could communicate their revolutionary objectives to a broader audience. With this lofty goal in mind, Mayfield set to work to "catch up" to the militant mood sweeping the nation and direct it through a careful analysis of the contradictions facing Black activists, emphasizing their mutual enemy in the white power structure and the flaws in both liberal integrationism and Black militancy alike. He offered suggestions to Dassin that he believed would increase audiences' ability to identify with the characters onscreen, hoping to avoid the kind of prescriptive action that had often made socialist realism fall flat with audiences.

Dee and Mayfield fulfilled Dassin's hope that they would bring a level of verisimilitude to his script, and in response, he seriously considered the changes they suggested for the project. Mayfield's contract was finalized on April 25, and he turned around a rewrite of the script by May 5.[13] Subsequent revised scripts were dated May 13 and May 15, with changes in dialogue and action continuing throughout filming. Mayfield's first impression of the script was that it was "well-conceived," but he expressed concerns about the language that the characters, especially the Black militants, were using. The existing dialogue, he told Dassin, made it difficult to understand the motivations of the characters and, more importantly, "who these people are."[14] Among the changes to the final draft of the script was the insertion of a tense encounter between two Black activist groups: an interracial group modeled after the Student Nonviolent Coordinating Committee (SNCC) and the Congress of Racial Equality and a militant group referred to only as "the Committee" that is an amalgam of contemporary revolutionary groups, such as the Black Panther Party for Self Defense. Another significant change was the film's finale: rather than succumb to the wounds inflicted by his former comrades, the protagonist, now going by the moniker "Tank," chooses to throw himself off the high stairway at the steel plant where he had once worked.[15] The film also revisits one of the themes that Mayfield had examined in *The Grand Parade*, reminding audiences once again of the marginalization of the organized Left in Black political movements.

The changes that Mayfield and Dee made did not radically alter the film's overall plot, but they shifted the focus of the film from a character study of an individual to a character study of a social movement. Tank remained a pitiable man expelled from his revolutionary organization for his lack of moral rectitude. A veteran of trade union conflicts of an earlier era, the burly, hulking Tank is nevertheless ill-equipped for this new kind of ideologically driven activism. Lacking physical, moral, and intellectual discipline, Tank responds to King's assassination by drowning his sorrows in alcohol and reaffirming his faith in nonviolence. In the film's opening scenes, the leader of the revolutionary cell that Tank belongs to, Johnny Wells (Max Julien), finds Tank in this abject state. Disgusted, Johnny refuses to let Tank accompany him on the planned heist. The unnamed group of militants, led by Johnny, plan to steal a shipment of guns from a warehouse to be used in a future uprising. In a tense, silent shot that recalls the climactic heist scene in *Rififi*, the militants appear to have successfully carried out their plan when a guard surprises them and is shot dead by Johnny. Even as Johnny and his team successfully escape with the guns, evidence left behind provides enough information for the police to identify Johnny, and the police initiate a manhunt. After discovering that there is a reward for Johnny's capture, Tank is approached on the street by his former comrade, who has holed up in a vacant burned-out building. Johnny explains to Tank that he plans to leave town but not without visiting his sick mother (played by veteran actress Juanita Moore). Tank implores him not to visit his mother, but when Wells indicates that he will do so, Tank decides to inform the Committee about Johnny's decision.

It is here, in the scene of Tank's act of informing, that the writers of *Uptight* made their most substantive alterations to O'Flaherty's narrative. In *The Informer*, Nolan ponders his decision alone before turning Frankie in for the reward. In *Uptight*, Tank interrupts a confrontation between the interracial civil rights group and the militant Committee so that the latter will intercede with Johnny's rash decision and in hopes that his information will put Tank back in the Committee's good graces. The conversation between Tank, Kyle, and the Committee members was created by Dee and Mayfield out of whole cloth and serves as the most significant representation of Black radical politics to appear in a Hollywood film up to that point. Dassin had been the one to originally create the part of the leader of the nonviolent faction, Kyle (Frank Silvera), but it was Mayfield and Dee who explored the conflicts between him and the militants through incisive dialogue, elevating the film from a study of betrayal into a nuanced exploration of the contours and horizons of political discourse among Black activists at the end of the 1960s.[16]

Rather than present a simplified conflict between a "good" form of activism and a "bad" form, the scene examines how recent historical events were shifting the tenor and tone of Black activism. Set in an unused bowling alley, the scene opens on the Committee, whose members are waiting to meet to discuss potential collaboration with an unnamed nonviolent civil rights group. Kyle, the nonviolent group's leader, arrives at the meeting hoping to broker a deal with two leaders of the committee, B. G. (Raymond St. Jacques) and Corbin (Dick Anthony Williams), for their participation in an upcoming nonviolent march downtown. Even before Kyle arrives, though, his position is weakened by his choice to bring along Teddy (Henry Baseleon), a young white man sporting horn-rimmed glasses and a tweed jacket. The men and women of the Committee immediately reject Teddy's presence, and after he is asked to leave, Teddy indignantly accuses his former comrades in the Committee of abandoning him. The subsequent dialogue reveals the characters' backstory, implying that they had once been nonviolent Freedom Riders but had made the transition to armed revolutionaries. Teddy confronts Corbin, his former comrade, reminding him of the Selma march and going to jail, but Corbin rejects his entreaty, stating only that "the times have changed."[17]

Teddy's character functions here as a composite of white liberal activists, especially those who had left SNCC following the decision to reject interracial organizing. The inclusion of Teddy allowed Mayfield to voice his personal frustration with white liberal activists in the late 1960s, and Teddy emphasized for audiences both the rejection and the sense of entitlement whites were experiencing in the movement in 1968. "I have every right to be here," Teddy declared, but the stone-faced members of the Committee simply ignore his protestations until he chooses to remove himself from the meeting. Offering a historical perspective on the Black freedom struggle, the Committee's leader, B. G., implicitly referenced King's assassination in Teddy's rejection but as a capstone to the nonviolent phase of the movement. "Selma, lunch counters, Birmingham. Yesterday. A phase we went through together," B. G. explains to Kyle, refusing to address Teddy directly. "Now we don't walk together anymore. It's policy now. No whites."

Teddy's rejection by the new Black militancy not only symbolizes the responses that many white activists had to the significant shift toward Black separatism among Black liberation organizations but also illustrates the interpersonal impact that the end of interracial organizing had on the movement. Many white activists in SNCC had been frustrated by the December 1966 vote that declared it an all-Black organization.[18] Despite Teddy's initial appearance as an ostensibly antagonistic character, his actions in his final scene complicate the character in a way that would redeem him to audiences. On his way home from the meeting, a dejected Teddy overhears police officers on their way to apprehend Johnny. Teddy calls the Committee's phone line to attempt to warn them, but the woman who answers berates rather than listens to him hinting that the rejection of whites may not always be in the best interest of militant groups.[19]

The shift toward Black separatism among Black freedom activists echoed SNCC's decision and the subsequent "Black Power" position paper that emphasized that white activists should confine their work to white communities.[20] Corbin's response to Teddy's claim that the Black militants "can't do it alone" seems directly drawn from the "Black Power" position paper. As Corbin explains to Teddy, "[Black activists have] got to do it alone. . . . We got to develop our own or die. . . . Go help the white brother. He's in trouble. Change him. That's your job." Following the decision to remake SNCC as an all-Black organization in early 1967, the organization urged its white former members to organize and work within white communities. This exchange between Teddy and Corbin, then, offers the writers' take on how that shift in SNCC would affect existing movements.

Kyle meekly protests Teddy's expulsion but nonetheless stays to negotiate. Kyle voices his opinion on the futility of violence as a tactic, analyzing the militant strategy and finding it lacking. The lines he speaks echo Mayfield's April keynote at Fisk: "You've got no revolution. A revolution is a plan, not a gun." In response, B. G.'s lines echo Stokely Carmichael, asserting that the nonviolent program "is dead. Killed by white violence April 4th 1968 in Memphis." The only thing the two factions can agree on is to stay out of each other's way. The militants agree to leave the civil rights march alone, and Kyle agrees to protect their identities and refrain from exposing them to the police. In writing this scene, Mayfield, Dassin, and Dee refrain from moralizing this confrontation. Each activist group offers arguments consistent with their real-life inspirations, and their dialogue is grounded in current events and intellectual discourse. It is their inability to agree and cooperate, in spite of their differences, that dooms both groups to irrelevance, repression, and persecution.

Inserting a scene in which an embrace of violence for its own sake and an emphasis on an accompanying masculine revolutionary posturing were a bloody dead end serve as a powerful denunciation of contemporary Black revolutionary politics. Without a commitment to armed self-defense, the nonviolent movement was doomed to ineffectual marches, lobbying, and ultimately an inadequate response to the problems facing Black people. The militants' straightforward embrace of violence and belief in armed rebellion as the only solution to the oppressive white supremacy in the United States presaged violent retribution from the state and possibly from white vigilante groups. Lacking unity and the mass participation in politics that characterized the Old Left, this meeting of the strongest factions of the Black freedom struggle exemplified for Mayfield the basic dilemma he had outlined at Fisk and on *Black Journal*. Working within the existing US political system without power would not adequately address Black people's problems, but seeking its overthrow was suicidal. The refusal of either group to look beyond its own narrow ideological perspective would ultimately, the film concludes, lead to the decline of both groups and the potential for retribution on a genocidal scale, as Kyle attempts to warn B. G. that his undisciplined, disorganized militancy would "bring on the camps."[21]

Mayfield and Dee also highlighted the tense relations between the two groups through Tank's arrival at the scene of the confrontation between Kyle and the Committee. Having encountered Johnny in an abandoned house down the street, Tank bursts into the meeting to share the information he has gathered. After Tank is initially dismissed, Kyle insists that Tank be given a chance to speak. When they find out about Johnny's determination to visit his mother, the Committee cuts the meeting short in order to stop him. Even so, the information Tank has shared is not enough to put him back in the Committee's good graces. Expelled from the meeting, Tank wanders the streets in the rain, nursing his rejection.

Tank's character fits the mold that Mayfield cast with Lonnie Banks in *The Grand Parade*. A former steelworker, Tank is a veteran of labor organizing and is proud of his time as a worker who defied the bosses and helped out his fellow men. He revels in the hard work he has done, despite the toll it has taken on his body. Implied in the script and made clear in Mayfield's discussions is that being a steelworker has left him physically unfit to continue in his previous capacity. These credentials were enough for his comrades among the younger generation of Black militants to initially accept him, but his dependence on alcohol and lack of ideological discipline made him a less than ideal member of the Committee. The film also implies that Tank's history of violence and his association with the Left also renders him unfit for a place in the interracial nonviolent civil rights movement. A former labor organizer would make the nonviolent group vulnerable to charges of red-baiting. Representing hundreds of thousands of working-class men fed up with the system but who do not belong to any organized group, Tank's character allows Mayfield to echo his own earlier condemnations of Black movements that did not recognize the importance of the Black working class.

Caught between nonviolent integrationism and militancy, working-class men such as Tank were unwelcome in either camp. Both groups, civil rights organizations and militants, claimed to be speaking for men such as Tank, but *Uptight* argues that neither group listened to his immediate concerns. Following his expulsion from the meeting, Tank encounters his girlfriend, Laurie, standing in a doorway near other prostitutes. He witnesses her greet a man and then enter a hotel with him; this proves to be a final straw. Stepping off the sidewalk into a gutter strewn with trash and rainwater, Tank meanders aimlessly until he finds himself at the police station, where he betrays Johnny for the reward money.[22] The subsequent scene, perhaps the film's most poignant, illustrates the consequences of the failure to utilize mass-movement tactics. After receiving Tank's information, police arrive at the apartment complex where Johnny is visiting his mother. When the police call for Johnny's surrender, neighbors begin to jeer and taunt the police, pelting them with bottles, cans, and other garbage. The angry crowd scatters when the police fire a shot into the air, yet the scene hints at the fear that police had at that moment. Implicit in this scene is the "unharnessed power" of the people who, with the right direction, could be organized to challenge police violence. Exhausted by daily encounters with state violence, the people of the apartment complex wish to thwart the arrest by the police but lack the organization and resources to do so. Late-arriving members of the Committee attempt to direct the people gathered at the railings as they flee the gunshots, but the confusion does not provide Johnny with enough cover to escape. Shot in the back by a police bullet, Johnny dies on a fire escape while on his way to the roof.

The message of this chaotic moment was in keeping with Mayfield's thoughts on Black militancy: local residents, already distrustful of the white police, were primed for action. All they needed was support and organization from committed revolutionaries. B. G. and the Committee, in contrast, don't seem interested in providing assistance or organizing the "lumpenproletariat," to borrow Huey P. Newton's description of the Black working class. In a similar vein, Kyle's interracial civil rights movement is more focused on public protest and formal electoral politics than to consider addressing those whom Mayfield called "the cats on the block." The depiction of the residents as angry and frustrated but ultimately disorganized and ineffective implies the failure of either group to successfully engage with and back the mass of people who could make meaningful social change a reality. *Uptight* effectively renders that the disagreement over tactics—nonviolent protest on the one hand and violent militancy on the other—moot. In each case, the vanguard has alienated itself from the people for whom it ostensibly fights on behalf of and has chosen to lead without listening.

The remainder of the film chronicles Tank's attempt to deal with his guilt over his betrayal of Johnny and his subsequent death. *Uptight*, as mentioned before, ends in a distinctly different fashion than Ford's 1935 production. After spending the night buying drinks in bars and flaunting his wealth, Tank drunkenly attends Johnny's wake. Like Nolan in *The Informer*, Tank's guilty demeanor arouses the suspicions of the Committee, who confront him. After letting him leave, they follow him to the home of a local police informant, then take him back to the bowling alley to beat a confession out of him. The Committee sentences him to death, and while the Committee members drive him to his execution, Tank escapes. Certain that death awaits him, Tank nevertheless returns to Laurie's apartment, where he confesses his crimes. Laurie does not offer absolution, instead condemning him and tearing at his face with her nails before stating the obvious: he is a dead man. Leaving Laurie, Tank heads to the steel mill to which he has given the best years of his life, pursued by the militants assigned to execute him. Scaling a huge crane-like structure, he waves to the men, inviting them to shoot him. When one hesitates, the other takes the gun from him and fires.

Wounded by gunfire, Tank pulls himself over the edge of the railing and throws himself to his death atop the mountain of iron ore ready to be transformed into steel.

The clarity of Tank's narrative arc—from rejection to despondence, betrayal, guilt, and self-destruction as absolution—stands in marked contrast to the writers' resistance to offering a resolution of the conflicts that they had introduced in the film. Echoing Mayfield's speech at Fisk, *Uptight* emphasized his arguments that the nonviolent movement's effort to work within the white power structure to recognize the citizenship and basic humanity of African Americans would never result in economic or social advancement for the masses of African Americans. Conversely, Mayfield shaped the film's plot to show militant characters whose lack of a meaningful, mass-oriented revolutionary program led only to meaningless violence and death. The film's message was cynical, bordering on hopeless. Although it offered criticism and nuance, it did not demonstrate anything resembling a solution. "Black Power," a bystander tells a reporter in the film as a crowd gathers after the murder of Johnny Wells by police. "That's what it gets you. Dead."[23]

Uptight in Cleveland

Art imitated life in Cleveland during the summer of 1968 as police violence, declining living conditions, and a lack of social services contributed to the formation of new Black militant groups. Even as Mayfield took his critique of militant groups and civil rights organizations public, the film's production illustrated how tensions inherent in the business of making movies, especially between an all-white film industry and a story on Black militancy, contributed to an explosive situation in Cleveland that summer. *Uptight* presented Mayfield with the opportunity to explore militancy and civil rights with the monetary backing of a major Hollywood studio, one that was white-owned, had hired a white director, and offered a white crew. That contradiction was not lost on him, nor was it lost on the people who watched the production unfold on their streets. Dassin had originally planned to shoot the film on location in Harlem, but sometime in early 1968 he settled on Cleveland as an example of a "more typically American" city.[24]

The move served the film's plot and its cinematography, and as Cleveland had been a key destination for southern Blacks migrating north, the race relations in the city mirrored those of the film's script. As in many other northern cities, Cleveland's racial demographics had changed dramatically in the previous two decades as working-class and middle-class whites moved out of downtown neighborhoods and into new developments west of the Cuyahoga River. Even as decreasing tax rolls affected city planning and budgets, the new racial and economic makeup of the city helped usher in the city's first Black mayor, Carl B. Stokes, who claimed a mandate from the city's liberal and Black constituencies. Two months before King's assassination, Stokes announced the "Cleveland Now!" program, an inner-city economic development plan that political scientists have called the "most ambitious program of urban reconstruction in the history of the country."[25]

Not only did Cleveland have a bevy of liberal-minded politicians whom activists such as Bayard Rustin had long called for, but the city was also home to a number of Black nationalist groups. On the campaign trail Stokes had gone out of his way to forge political alliances with these groups, which had sprung up after the devastating Hough Uprising of 1966. Beginning on July 18, 1966, Cleveland saw some of its most impoverished neighborhoods rise up in defiance of police brutality and frustrations over racist treatment by white business owners.[26] By 1968—two years after widespread violence and looting forced Stokes's predecessor, Ralph S. Locher, to call in the National Guard—some of Cleveland's Black residents had formed militant groups with hopes of protecting themselves against the city's brutal all-white police force. The FBI closely watched the development of these organizations, such as the Republic of New Libya, that the FBI considered to have a "great potential for violence."[27] The coalition of liberal interests and Black voters that had elected Stokes saw him as a solution to the strife in the community, but despite his administration's investment in antipoverty programs, the Hough neighborhood remained a seething cauldron of distrust and resentment.

The news that *Uptight* would begin filming on May 27, 1968, was celebrated by Mayor Stokes's administration, but the tensions in Hough had not dissipated in the intervening two years, a fact soon reflected on the set. Residents flocked to the on-location filming as shooting began and were cast as extras. According to Dassin, local poet Norman Jordan organized local Black nationalist groups to aid with crowd control and join in some of the exterior crowd sequences.[28] With seemingly little attention paid to the content of the film, studio policies mandated police officers on set to act as security for insurance purposes. Combined with discriminatory hiring practices in Hollywood, the set was highly segregated and protected by the same police force that had prompted the uprisings two years prior. A white crew guarded by white police officers working on a film with a Black cast, hundreds of local Black extras, and radical themes of Black militancy dashed whatever hopes Dassin had for a smooth shoot.

On June 4, simmering tensions boiled over into violence when a Black police officer attempted to force a young Black man from the set. In response, Hough residents surrounded the officer after he physically removed the young man from the set and demanded an apology. Hearing of the conflict, several nationalist groups massed and began parading down Wade Park Avenue waving banners and protesting the film. To the crew's chagrin, many of the film's extras joined the protest. Although no arrests were made, Dassin met with Stokes the next day in order to calm tensions and resolve the matter.[29] The damage had been done, however, and white crew members and many white police officers refused to continue working on the set, citing security concerns. In response, Black actors denounced the white crew members for "subconsciously trying to sabotage the production" and provoking tensions.[30] Some accounts cynically dismissed the clashes as controversy designed to promote the film, but recent publications have revealed that it was not only the white crew members and Cleveland police officers who were upset by the production's themes. Behind the scenes, the FBI had assigned agents on-site who attempted to disrupt the filming of what the bureau considered a film designed to "incite racial strife."[31]

Confidential FBI memos reveal that the special agent in charge of the Cleveland FBI office had received multiple requests to investigate the film in late May 1968. A memo subsequently reported that an informant had contacted the FBI and reported the film's plot; the special agent in charge stated that "the obvious conclusion one draws from the ending [of the film] . . . is that the racial situation in the United States is unresolvable and will result in continued strife."[32] These FBI memos also suggest that the white participants who quit the production may in fact have been encouraged by the bureau to resign.[33]

Paramount employees who were interviewed by FBI agents cited concerns over Dassin's blacklisting and exile in Europe, Dee's membership in the Communist Party of the United States of America, and Julian Mayfield's association with the Fair Play for Cuba Committee, associations that apparently also factored into crew walkouts. FBI director J. Edgar Hoover also approved a plan to pressure Paramount into halting production by supplying damaging information about Dassin to executives, a policy consistent with Counter Intelligence Program practices at the time.[34] No concrete evidence indicates that either of Cleveland's white-owned newspapers—the *Plains Dealer* and the *Cleveland Press*—cooperated with the FBI, but suspicion was rife among local activists. In response to these perceived threats, Paramount shut down production suddenly in mid-July and relocated to the company's lot in Culver City, California.

For the actors and crew the change of scenery happened at a fortuitous time, but for the residents of Cleveland the summer of 1968 would prove violent. On July 23 shortly after the crew relocated the set to Los Angeles County, a fierce gunfight between Cleveland police officers and members of the Republic of New Libya erupted in nearby Glenville, a few blocks from where filming had taken place in Hough.[35] Four days of rebellion and rioting followed. Fearing a repeat of the Hough Uprisings of 1966, Mayor Stokes took the unprecedented step of pulling all police from the nearly six square miles of the city, turning policing duties over to local groups for three days before relenting, and sending in the National Guard.[36] When the National Guard departed on July 27, three Black citizens and four white police officers had been killed. Despite their earlier attempts to quell the violence while filming in Cleveland, once in Los Angeles, neither Mayfield nor Dassin spoke publicly of the move, although the director alluded to the trouble on set in interviews where he stated that "the pressure was too much up there."[37]

The remainder of the film was shot on the Paramount lot, including the climactic confrontation between Johnny Wells and the Cleveland Police Department. Shooting wrapped on August 8, 1968, although editing would continue through October. While Mayfield made no mention publicly or privately of problems on set during filming, correspondence indicates that he appreciated the move to Los Angeles and expressed fondness for the city and was excited to work in Hollywood. Ultimately, the FBI's efforts to undermine the production of *Uptight* were unsuccessful and the film, despite its notoriety, did not enjoy the reception that Dassin, Dee, and Mayfield had hoped it would.

Bad Press for "A Filmic Revolution"

Premiering on December 18, 1968, *Uptight* divided critics and audiences with its raw portrait of Black working-class militancy, conflicts between Black social movements, and an open-ended reflection on the future of the Black freedom struggle. Despite attracting the attention of the FBI, contributing to Black nationalist activity in Cleveland, and earning praise from both Black Arts Movement pioneer Larry Neal and poet Nikki Giovanni, the film languished at the box office. By June 1969 *Uptight* had all but disappeared from movie theaters. Contemporary newspapers indicate that the film was shown on television sporadically through the 1970s, but it was never rereleased in theaters and was largely forgotten until it was released on DVD and Blu-Ray in 2012.[38]

What accounts for this lapse in historical memory? Why did a controversial movie on a contemporary topic fade so abruptly from popular consciousness? Three interrelated factors contribute to the movie's disappearance: a racially divided critical response, ambivalent audience reactions, and a lack of promotion and support by Paramount. Advance publicity, based on the troubled filming on location in Cleveland and the subsequent move to Los Angeles, reflected national anxieties after a summer of violence and property destruction, and many critics predicted that *Uptight* would bring in large audiences based on this fact alone. Following its release, the critical response was split along racial lines. White reviewers found much to criticize, while Black critics urged audiences to see this "highly relevant film." Lindsay Patterson's ambivalent review was indicative of this trend: the *New York Times* film writer criticized Dassin's choice to remake an existing story instead of "starting from scratch with young black writers or existing black materials." Noting that Americans "like nothing better than to exclude [based] on the false issues of race, creed or religion," Patterson damned the film with faint praise, calling it "a hopeful step toward a broader vision."[39] Clifford Terry dismissed the film out of hand: "The acting . . . [was] as stilted as the script," he wrote, and he limited his praise to Raymond St. Jacques's stoic fury as Committee leader B. G.[40]

The *Wall Street Journal*'s John J. O'Connor offered a response that most accurately reflects the film's contemporary context. *Uptight* was "far, quite far, from being 1968's best movie, but it stands a good chance of being the year's most fascinating phenomenon in American film-making," he wrote shortly after the film's release.[41] Other critics, however, did not give the film even this much consideration. *New York Times* film critic Renata Adler savaged the film, stating that "it is never for one instant moving, never lives up even to its initial documentary footage of the voice and funeral of Martin Luther King." *Uptight*'s story was neither "historically or foreseeably real," she wrote. It was merely filled with "personal dramas unrelated to politics."[42] Adler's review, which infuriated both Mayfield and Dassin, illuminated again the insoluble dilemma facing Black writers and artists who had no choice but to reflect the times in which they lived. Although fascinated by Black militancy, white Americans and especially white critics remained unwilling to listen and revealed themselves unable to understand the deeply personal nature of Black political action.

In contrast, Black critics lauded the focus on Black perspectives and experiences as well as the lack of sensationalism or pandering in the film's delivery. Hazel Garland told *New Pittsburgh Courier* readers that "if you don't see another movie this year, don't miss 'Uptight,' the powerful drama produced by Jules Dassin."[43] Activist and theorist Larry Neal penned a nineteen-page review titled "Why Save America?" in which he decisively declared, "[*Uptight*] will probably thrust itself upon the public sensibility in a manner unprecedented in the history of American film."[44] Poet Nikki Giovanni's review, appropriately titled "And What about Laurie?," called *Uptight* "the strongest possibility of a Black movie I have ever seen."[45] She praised Ruby Dee's arresting performance and cited the unique nature of a character who was neither seductive temptress nor supportive partner. Subsequent reviews in the *Amsterdam News*, the *Call and Post*, and the *Chicago Defender* offered similar praise, with critics noting the nuanced, realistic portrayals of Black militants and the film's ability to capture the political shifts that Black Power politics had affected in Black communities and social movements over the previous two years.

If critical opinions were mixed, early audience reactions were almost entirely negative. At the premier, held at the Greenwich Village Loew's Sheridan Theatre on December 18, the audience of students signaled their disapproval of the film's plot early into the showing. Critic Bernard L. Drew, writing for the *Hartford Times*, was present for this showing and published one of the first reviews. Even as he praised the film as a "fine, intelligent, and exciting film produced with savvy," he could not help but note how a young interracial audience immediately expressed their disapproval.[46] Dassin, Mayfield, and H. Rap Brown experienced this audience response firsthand, as they were to host a panel following the film. Joined by Ossie Davis, standing in for Ruby Dee, and Ruth Jett, a longtime Harlem theater activist, whatever hopes the group had for a convivial discussion fell by the wayside as the audience began to yell and hiss at the screen.[47] According to Drew, the crowd began to boo whenever Tank came onscreen and cheered loudly when he met his ignominious death.

After the film ended, the audience was not shy about confronting the filmmakers and their associates onstage about their feelings toward the film. The panel responded defensively, seeking to redirect the hostile line of questions, but the students were adamant in voicing their negative interpretation of the film. One student, speaking of the scene where Johnny

Wells is gunned down by police, asked Brown if he thought it good for "the black masses to see themselves standing on the balconies of their homes . . . for once having the dignity of protecting their interests while they rain down garbage on the police, but who flee at the first shot?" Brown's response, that he had "seen one shot make 5,000 people flee," buttressed his argument that "this is not a picture for the revolutionaries, but the masses, and this is how they act."[48] Dassin was the target of particularly harsh criticism from the audience—being a white director of film about Black militants—but Julian Mayfield, as the lead actor, caught the brunt of their frustration and dissatisfaction.

As Mayfield attempted to answer an audience member's question about his character, Tank, the student angrily interrupted him with another question: "Is the black man so weak and stupid to do all of the things you acted and wrote him doing?" Mayfield again tried to explain Tank's flaws—his drunkenness, his psychological state, his failure at forging meaningful relationships—but the answer fell flat, and the student dismissed the film as "just another gangster story." Another student inquired why the film only showed Black men killing other Black men as opposed to whites. Still another echoed one of the conclusions from Daniel Moynihan's 1965 report *The Negro Family* as he demanded to know why the filmmakers "still have not shown the black man as a masculine, phallic figure. It's still strong women who motivate and run everything."[49] In response to this critique, the students apparently made their approval known with applause. Heckled and challenged by the audience's confrontational questions, the panelists onstage ended the discussion early and retreated backstage.

While one audience's reaction does not in itself provide conclusive proof of why the film failed to resonate with audiences, the precipitous decline in box office receipts suggests that the New York audience's reaction was not exceptional. In January 1969, Julian Mayfield spoke to a *Detroit News* reporter about the film and recalled his Cornell students' response to the film's finale. Mayfield was shocked that "some of the students thought that after [Larry] shoots [Tank], he should have shot his companion because he had been too weak to carry out his task."[50] Christopher Sieving suggests that the film's failure to resonate with audiences was "related to the fact that its formation failed to comply with the rapidly developing standards of the 'black aesthetic,'" and therefore the film was unable to "meet the [Black] nationalists' standards for essentially black art."[51] Yet one of the architects of the Black Arts Movement, Larry Neal, lauded the film, while

SNCC chairman H. Rap Brown spoke approvingly of its portrait of Black militancy.[52]

The film's primary failure was not a lack of the correct aesthetic but rather its refusal to offer a clear and concise vision of the future of the Black freedom struggle. The film's overarching narrative arc, one of frustration and despair at the failure of groups to unite for the good of the community, was not something audiences, especially young people, particularly wanted to hear. By showing that neither faction was correct in its program, the film's writers implied that the failure of both was predicated on their refusal to unite with one another. Almost a year after Mayfield's declaration that Black writers needed to "catch up" with the masses and keep pace with the "cats on the block," *Uptight*'s inability to resonate with audiences suggests that people wanted a clear-cut narrative, not an extended meditation on the nature of protest and political activism and the necessity of mass movements.

Mayfield returned to teaching following the ending of the film's production, and his subsequent interactions with college students points to another important division among the film's audiences. Viewers, Mayfield argued, were also divided along generational lines. Younger audience members not only saw in Frank Silvera's earnest civil rights leader Kyle a sympathetic view of a "bourgeois" movement but they also found the militants to be unrealistic caricatures. In contrast, older viewers regarded the filmmakers' failure to sufficiently condemn the Black militants as inflammatory, with the implication that it tacitly supported Black rebellions in places such as Detroit, Cleveland, and Newark. In short, the film's portrait of Black militants was not radical enough for young people but was unacceptably militant for their parents' generation.

Perhaps the most important element that contributed to the film's short run at the box office was Paramount's apparent desire "to kick [*Uptight*] under a rug."[53] Compared with other films released in 1968, Paramount did little to promote the film. I speculate that studio executives hoped that the controversy over its production would stand in for radio, television, and print advertising and refrained from spending much money on promotion. The studio did try to show the film in large urban markets, making it the first movie shown at the newly constructed Roxbury Cinema in Boston's Black-majority neighborhood. But when compared with the kind of promotion and distribution received by Paramount's biggest hits of that year—*The Odd Couple, Rosemary's Baby,* and *Romeo and Juliet*—the marketing for *Uptight* was decidedly meager.

Part of the problem was the limited release, which prompted film critic Jesse Walker to question what had happened to it just three months after its release. "As far as I can find out [*Uptight*] isn't playing anywhere," Walker wrote in mid-February. "Was it too uptight?"[54] Notably, when the film did receive wider distribution, Paramount paired it with films such as *Skidoo* (1968) and the equally incongruous *Barbarella* (1968).[55] Whether it was generational politics, FBI interference, or the studio's desire to make a controversial film disappear from view, *Uptight*'s lack of success had an overwhelmingly negative impact on the careers of its writers. At the same time, the lack of success reshaped subsequent Hollywood productions that considered the experience of Black Americans. Paramount's financial loss from *Uptight* stalled existing Black dramatic projects at the studio and throughout Hollywood, exacerbating tensions among up-and-coming Black filmmakers and white studios, and filmmakers increasingly turned more toward prurient content such as Herbert Biberman's *Slaves*, starring Dionne Warwick.[56]

In the same way that many critics foregrounded the film's troubled production in their reviews, *Uptight*'s inclusion in Black film historiography focuses less on its script or narrative and more on its production. The film's poor showing at the box office corresponded with a shift in content among films with majority-Black casts. Those films veered away from serious dramas and instead focused on humor, sexual titillation, and violence shorn of politics except for vulgar antiracism and Black revenge.[57] *Uptight*'s most significant impact was the direction that Hollywood took following its failure. Studios, wary of another expensive flop, moved away from complex character-driven stories and toward the kind of plot-driven caricatures consistent with Cedric Robinson's and other intellectuals' later criticisms of blaxploitation as a genre. While some have characterized the film as a blaxploitation film, *Uptight*'s failure to fit neatly into that category contributed to the widening dichotomy of films with Black stories and Black themes.

Ironically, *Uptight*'s production and reception exacerbated the contradictions facing Black artists that Mayfield had pointed out during the panel discussion that aired on *Black Journal*. And Mayfield himself embodied those contradictions; working within the system (Hollywood) while trying to overthrow it (with *Uptight*), he demonstrated the essence of the conundrum he had posed at Fisk. Revealing in many ways the accuracy of Audre Lorde's reflection that "the master's tools will never dismantle the master's house," Mayfield nonetheless remained steadfast in his positive opinion of his work on *Uptight*, as did many of his contemporaries.[58] In an exchange between Mayfield and Dassin in the summer of 1969, Dassin expressed his belief that the three writers "didn't do the job we should have done." Mayfield, however, resisted the urge to admit defeat, defiantly responding that "if you insist on being depressed about our flick, let's say to hell with it and go on to something else."[59] Dassin would not make another movie in the United States and Mayfield spent the next six years trying but failing to realize a series of film projects.

Despite negative reviews, *Uptight* was a personal success for Mayfield. Earning a salary of approximately US$1,000 a week while shooting in Cleveland and Los Angeles, he personally made an additional $40,000, or approximately $340,000 in 2023 dollars, from the deal he had struck with Dassin. All told, Mayfield earned enough to purchase a piece of land in Spencer, New York, near Ithaca. Dubbing his new rural haven "Chaka Farm," he also founded a production company, Chaka Productions, and began aggressively pursuing other film projects. In 1969, he began work on an untitled Marcus Garvey biopic with William Greaves and purchased the film rights to *Walk Hard, Talk Loud* by Ed Lacy, a novel about an antiracist leftist boxer.[60] Dividing his time between Chaka Farm, Cornell, New York University, and SUNY Cortland, Mayfield also submitted several hundred pages of a proposed autobiography in mid-1969, much of which survives in his archive. This financial windfall, however, did not last. A dispute over money with William Greaves put an end to the Garvey project, and Mayfield was unable to find a producer who would take on *Walk Hard, Talk Loud*. In response to these financial pressures as well as Mayfield's preoccupation with the violent deaths of radical Black activists such as Fred Hampton and the imprisonment of his colleague H. Rap Brown, Mayfield began once again to seek escape from the "narrow national orbit" of the United States.

"The Business of Making Revolution"

From 1967 until his abrupt departure for Guyana in October 1971, Julian Mayfield's writing probed the broader trends reshaping Black writing, revolutionary activism, and art in the wake of Stokely Carmichael's call to Black Power. Eschewing ideological debate for discussions of practical steps that African Americans could take to catalyze revolution in the United States, Mayfield remained convinced of the need for solidarity as he criticized the ideological battles that divided the movement. In *Uptight*, he found the ideal platform to dissect the distinctions he had made to the audience in Nashville and illuminated the contradictions, conflicts, and limitations that were present in post–Civil Rights Act Black liberation movements. In the classroom, he challenged students to understand the historical forces that set the nation on its present path. For Mayfield, teaching was another aspect of his long-standing effort to educate the broader public about the ways that thought and action influenced the articulation of Black radical activism.

In these two contexts—the academy and Hollywood—Mayfield's intellectual projects focused on common themes and dispelled misinformation and rumor. Mayfield was easily the most radical leading Black man to star in a major Hollywood motion picture to that point, and his experience making *Uptight* revealed the difficulties he faced in presenting his vision of authentic Black militancy, with both its appeal and limitations, to the world. Hollywood in 1968 remained a bastion of white supremacy, the success of such films as *Look Who's Coming to Dinner* and *In the Heat of the Night* notwithstanding. That *Uptight* was made at all is remarkable, a reflection of a moment in which at least some Hollywood studios and Black writers shared a belief in the necessity of portraying Black radicalism onscreen, though with obviously different objectives in mind. *Uptight*'s negative reviews and unprofitability tell only part of the story of its construction while hinting at a broader impact.

After the film's long relegation to obscurity, a new generation has rediscovered its gritty portrait of Black militancy, the beginnings of urban decay, and what writer Michael A. Gonzales calls "the 1st Blaxploitation Movie." In 2008, the then eighty-four-year-old Ruby Dee introduced a showing of the film at the Brooklyn Academy of Music's theater. "Paramount did not want to release the film," she told audiences, echoing Dassin's later comments about the studio's attempt to bury the film after its release. But, Dee reported, the director's passionate argument convinced the studio.[61] Critic J. Hoberman, after viewing *Uptight* in 2009, praised the film for its "ferocious performances; a vivid, almost allegorical use of location; and a sense of bottled rage that explodes in the movie's apocalyptic final half-hour. . . . Up Tight [sic] effectively capped [Dassin's] career, recapitulating the themes and style of his strongest Hollywood films with a scarcely modulated brute force."[62]

In early 1971, Mayfield noted in the introduction to *Ten Times Black*, a volume of short stories he edited, that while the conditions had changed, the institutional force of anti-Black racism remained disturbingly intact. "Let us be clear about one thing," he wrote. "[The Black writer] is not excluded today because he is Black, but because now the stuff of his work is Black."[63] Paramount had taken a chance on a radical depiction of Black frustration and militancy, and that chance had not paid off to the studio's satisfaction. Subsequent films, such as *Superfly* (1972) and *Shaft* (1971), did not explore the "full range" of Black experience and failed, in the opinion of many writers in the Black Arts Movement, to embody the Black aesthetic. While the films featured predominantly Black casts and scores that foregrounded "Black" musical styles (such as soul, funk, jazz, and blues), they did not seriously wrestle with the themes that Mayfield, Neal, and Giovanni had discussed in their writing. In fact, with the exception of the controversial film *The Spook Who Sat by the Door*, directed by Ivan Dixon, no other film of that era portrayed the Black liberation movement in any meaningful way.

In a provocatively titled essay for Addison Gayle's edited volume *The Black Aesthetic*, Julian Mayfield offered his own thoughts on the subject. "At the risk of sounding superstitious, I know deep down in my gut what [the Black aesthetic] means," but, he professed, "it is easier to define in the negative. I know quite definitively what the Black Aesthetic is not." After dismissing claims by others and declaring that it is not "a way of talking, a secret language invented by black people to confound the whites," musical ability, and sexual prowess, Mayfield concluded that if the Black aesthetic was anything, "it is our racial memory, and the unshakeable knowledge of who we are, where we have been, and where we are going." The Black aesthetic "for those trying to create it today, is necessarily the business of making revolution, for we have tried everything else."[64]

This essay, "You Touch My Black Aesthetic and I'll Touch Yours," laid bare the frustrations that motivated Julian Mayfield's art in 1970. Despite these difficulties, he remained fully committed to "making revolution." Now undeniably middle-aged, he could no longer rely on the energy of his youth, but neither was he old enough for his words to resonate with the appropriate gravitas. As circumstances would have it, an old friend from Ghana reached out and offered him a new opportunity, and Mayfield, longing for the kind of community and belonging he had last experienced in Ghana, took him up on. Leaving the United States not only offered Mayfield a fresh start but also, as he explained to Maya Angelou, gave him the "satisfaction of not having to put up with the bullshit of White Power 24 [hours] a day."[65]

8 The Nation and the Pan-African Ideal
Nationalism, Sovereignty, and Identity in Guyana, 1971–1973

I am always thinking of Guyana. I have a feeling which has always been with me, that it is going to be the centre of the Black World and it is going to be the most effective link between the Continent of Africa and the BLACK DIASPORA.

—Nana Nketsia IV, ca. 1974

National consciousness, instead of being the all-embracing crystallization of the innermost hopes of the whole people[,] . . . will be in any case only an empty shell, a crude and fragile travesty of what it might have been.

—Frantz Fanon, 1961

The arguments that Julian Mayfield advanced in his writing often reflected the politics of the geographic space he inhabited; his time in the South American nation of Guyana was no exception. Arriving in the tropical nation on the northern coast of South America in late 1971, Mayfield challenged elements of Pan-African theory in an ardent defense of nationalist struggles. In an article published in the *Black Scholar* in 1973, he took issue with internal challenges to the Guyanese nation-building project, bluntly stating that "the Pan-Africanist ideal does not exist anywhere in the world today."[1] This argument, a product of his support for the postcolonial government of Prime Minister Forbes Burnham, appears at first glance to be a repudiation of the public statements and political writing that had emerged from Mayfield's typewriter barely a decade before. But Guyana in 1973 was not Ghana in 1961, and the circumstances of the former demanded ideological and tactical revisions.

Even as his work highlighted the powerful effects of Pan-African thought and solidarity on Black nation-building efforts, Mayfield's abiding prioritization of political power prompted him to foreground the postcolonial nation-state in his calls for Black liberation. Integrating the political and social history of Guyana under Burnham with Mayfield's contributions to the Guyanese Cooperative Republic, this chapter demonstrates how the intersection of these ideas was not only generative to Black intellectual thought and political activism in the 1970s but also reveals some of the reasons for the ideological and political disagreements within the Afro-diasporic community that arose as the 1970s came to a close.

Historian Russell Rickford has argued that a study of Guyana's small African American expatriate community reveals "lesser-known currents of transnationalism [that] illustrate black America's romance with the modern nation-state."[2] Mayfield's writing between 1971 and 1975, which produced a slew of government documents, a biography of Burnham, and commentary on the nature of Pan-African thought, demonstrate how the role of the nation-state slowly shifted to the forefront of discussions of African unity in the 1970s. Mayfield's artistic output also served to repurpose historical and contemporary events to support the modern postcolonial nation-state through art. His output in Guyana reveals a moment in which a tactical retreat from Pan-African ideals was seen as the best means to counter US hegemony. In doing so, Mayfield helped force a confrontation between the needs of the nation-state and the ideals of Pan-Africanism. This confrontation was apparent not only in the pages of journals and newspapers but also on the streets of cities such as Georgetown and Berbice. Mayfield's activism and his writings illustrate the ways that these ideas shaped—and were in turn shaped by—the particular geography, history, and socioeconomic conditions of Afro-diasporic polities in the nation of Guyana at a moment of rupture in the Black Power movement worldwide.

When Mayfield departed for Guyana in November 1971, it was out of frustration and "the general sense of powerlessness" he experienced in the United States.[3] Visiting the nation briefly in September, he found a leader and a government that appeared to offer practical and programmatic solutions to the liberatory contradictions that complicated his efforts in the United States. Guyana also promised to alleviate some of Mayfield's personal economic woes, and unlike his flight to West Africa, he arrived in South America with plans to reside in the country indefinitely. His decision to relocate was solidified by the political rhetoric and policies of Guyana's People's National Congress (PNC) as articulated by Forbes Burnham. Mayfield in particular was moved by the ways the party explicitly addressed three overlapping issues that were prominent within Black nationalist movements in the United States: the land question, the education of Black children, and the inseparable nature of politics and economics in questions of national sovereignty. Indeed, it was American Black nationalists who helped convince Mayfield that Guyana was worth exploring as a potential site of resistance to US hegemony and anti-Black racism.

Toward a Guyanese Pan-Africanism

In an open letter to Julian Mayfield, published in August 1971 in *Black World*, the artist, intellectual, and activist Tom Feelings argued that the future of the Black liberation movement was in Guyana. Feelings implored Mayfield to visit and see for himself a nation with clear goals for the future because of Mayfield's familiarity with the "frustrations" of working for a newly formed nation. Despite the fact that Feelings did not have a formal position with the Guyanese government, he recognized that Mayfield's credentials would be attractive to the state, making Mayfield's transition easier. Feelings was also quick to criticize those who spoke negatively of leaders such as Burnham, declaring their perspectives ignorant due to their lack of firsthand experience. "Our brothers in the universities, of the scholarly left, who expound on the romantic theory of the Third World," Feelings wrote disparagingly, "had best come down here and peep at some of our future world problems[;] . . . the theory might sound nice, but the practical terms are, at the least, *difficult*."[4] Feelings's emphasis on practical knowledge over theory was well in keeping with Mayfield's own preferences. Both men possessed experience in living and working in the midst of a nation-building project directed by a powerful and outspoken Black man, and Feelings believed that Mayfield would feel at home in Georgetown.

An artist by training, Tom Feelings had immigrated to Guyana the previous year with his wife, Muriel, and young son, Zamani.[5] To forgo the material comforts of the First World for a role in building the future of Pan-African Third World unity was a small price to pay, he had reasoned. Feelings's decision to relocate was also prompted by his lack of hope for a meaningful future for him and his family in the United States. "We have seen what America has to offer," he wrote to Mayfield, "and can walk away from it." He urged Mayfield to come, "see for yourself," what was going on in Guyana. The decision by editor in chief Hoyt Fuller to publish Feelings's letter in late 1971 reflected the magazine's transformation from the staid *Negro Digest* to a more internationalist *Black World*.[6] African American interest in spaces where meaningful national sovereignty was not only a product of the rising tide of independent nations in Africa and Latin America but also reflected the increase in state repression against radical movements in both the United States and elsewhere in the Western Hemisphere.

But why Guyana? The tiny South American country, scarcely larger than the state of Kansas, is mostly dense, equatorial jungle. Ninety percent of the population resides on the narrow strip of land along the Caribbean Sea. At the time, the nation lacked overland connections to the neighboring nations of Brazil and Venezuela.[7] The decision of men such as Julian Mayfield, Paul Adams, Herman Ferguson, and Tom Feelings to choose expatriate life in Guyana not only expressed a romanticized view the nation-state held by Black radical movements since the 1850s but also illuminates the instrumentalization of a particular Black nationalist politics in the United States at a moment when nationalist movements faced marginalization and state violence. Guyana was to be a haven from white supremacy and from the hegemonic power of the US government. The example of Guyana in the late 1960s and early 1970s also demonstrates how this particular nationalist discourse was shaped by an internationalist impulse in ways that contradicted the previous decade's Pan-African thought. More significantly, the choice to settle in Guyana, as opposed to Julius Nyrere's Tanzania or Sekou Touré's Guinea, reveals how questions of land, geography, and language were central to African American radicals' internationalist aspirations and reveals the practical steps taken to realize those dreams.

Even today, the idea of a Black nationalism is a contentious topic. Historian Daryl Michael Scott has argued that African American nationalism in the United States had become confused with "ethnoracial solidarities" that developed in the 1920s, making it seemingly unique among nationalist movements worldwide.[8] By conflating solidarity among African Americans with nationalism, Scott wrote, "Black nationalism became decoupled from the core concept of sovereignty or even self-government."[9] In arguing that African American nationalism had become sui generis, however, Scott minimized the international contours of that Black radical tradition and how nationalists sought out sovereignty and self-government beyond the borders of the United States based on kinships—fictive or otherwise—with other Black peoples.[10]

In a private letter to Mayfield dated April 1971, Tom Feelings lamented how Black nationalists in the United States failed to reckon with the central problem facing nationalist projects there: the question of land. "Black people in America," Feelings wrote, "are unsure if the land in America belongs to them, or even if they want to die there burning it down."[11] The question of land, long central to African American aspirations to citizenship in the United States, also guided internationalist considerations in the age of decolonization. Feelings's statement also captured the historic ambivalence toward Black nationalism in the United States even as he highlighted the evolution of nationalist politics among African Americans in the late 1960s and early 1970s. The inability to truly control land in the United States meant that domestic Black nationalist schemes were doomed to failure, a fact that Feelings linked directly to the "confusion" among radical groups in that country. Feelings's embrace of Guyana at a moment of declining fortunes in the United States exemplifies expatriates' interest in the availability of land within a sovereign nation dedicated to Pan-Africanism and autarky, and this interest suggests that it would be a mistake to consider this nationalist impulse as being solely limited to the United States. This conflation of nationalism with racial solidarity left many African Americans frustrated, providing an audience for a discourse that emphasized control over land as being fundamental to having control over culture and politics.

Guyana's appeal was based precisely on its promise of the potential for Black political power beyond the borders of the United States. Feelings, Mayfield, and other Afros in Guyana recognized that the sparsely populated nation had the political and geographical characteristics necessary for a sovereign, nationalist project. Unlike Tanzania and Guinea—two important sites for Black radicals seeking sanctuary in the late 1960s—Guyana's unique ethnoracial makeup, colonial history, and the circumstances of its independence offered Anglophone radicals an appealing "land base" from which they hoped to effect change on national and international scales.[12] The changes that Prime Minister Burnham made to the nation's constitution in 1968 and again in 1971 fascinated many Black nationalists, drawing them to Guyana as the Black Power movement fractured and collapsed in the United States.

The Guyanese Cooperative Republic

Guyana's appeal to Black radicals, nationalists, and dissidents has been attributed to the rhetoric of its firebrand prime minister, Linden Sampson Forbes Burnham, but Burnham's embrace of Third World radicalism and Pan-Africanism obscured how Guyana's geography, history, and linguistic and ethnic heritage shaped the rhetoric and practice of postcolonial sovereignty. Unlike most Caribbean nations, Guyana's African-descended population did not constitute a majority; South Asian–descended peoples made up a plurality of the population. Mayfield recognized the central importance of race in its transition from British sugar colony to "cooperative republic," noting that "the racial factor in Guyana was more basic than any apparent ideological differences."[13] The race factor was at the root of the political conflicts that divided the nation during Burnham's nineteen-year administration and was one of the primary features that attracted Mayfield and other Afro expatriates to the nation.

In comparison to Ghana, where linguistic, ethnic, and class divisions had been the primary challenges facing the nation-building project, Guyana's straightforward racial divisions offered Mayfield and Feelings a familiar terrain. A letter to Mayfield's friend, political scientist Preston King, alluded to these social dynamics, and Mayfield listed racial tensions as one source of unease with his planned move. Alien yet familiar, Guyana shared much with other former sugar colonies in the Caribbean and Africa, but the inclusion of another ethnoracial group in the nation would have unexpected consequences.[14] The roots of Guyana's unique racial makeup were a result of planter anxieties over labor shortages as slavery was abolished in the 1830s. As early as 1838, planters began importing indentured laborers from Calcutta. Between the arrival of the first "Gladstone's Coolies" on May 15, 1838, and 1917, over 239,000 men and women were brought to British Guiana from Bengal. The results of this human trafficking had a profound effect on the demographics of the colony in the twentieth century. The colony's population was approximately 375,700 in 1946, of which 143,000 (38.2%) people were of African origin, while 163,000 (43.5%) were of East Indian origin.[15] Unlike the populations of Jamaica, Barbados, and Hispaniola, British Guiana's African-descended population was a minority by the late nineteenth century.[16] The arrival of indentured Indian workers depressed wages as planters stoked tensions between the two ethnic groups for their own benefit. Rivalries among these communities over access to arable land made organizing resistance to colonial rule difficult for the first generation of independence activists, but in the aftermath of World War II, leaders in the Afro-Guyanese and Indo-Guyanese communities attempted to put aside their differences and collaborated on the shared goal of ending British rule.

Among those who rose to prominence following the war were the Indo-Guyanese dentist Cheddi Jagan (b. 1918) and Afro-Guyanese labor leader Linden Forbes Burnham (b. 1923). After receiving their primary- and secondary-school educations in Guyana, both men traveled abroad for advanced degrees. Upon their return to British Guiana in the late 1940s, they led a political unification of the colony's nonwhite ethnic groups under the mantle of the People's Progressive Party (PPP).[17] The party's platform bridged the divisive racialism fostered by the sugar industry and the colonial government in order to concentrate on winning independence.

The PPP was formally created on January 1, 1950, and its members elected Cheddi Jagan as the party's secretary and Forbes Burnham as party chair. This power-sharing agreement was deliberate; it was designed to ensure that no single ethnic group had full control of the party.[18] For a time, the project worked. By welding together the nation's two largest ethnic groups, which made up over 80 percent of the population, the PPP's rapid growth persuaded a recalcitrant United Kingdom to initiate the process of independence. A national election was organized in 1953 in which the PPP won an initial victory, but celebrations were short-lived. Despite the fact that British Guiana was one of the most isolated and neglected regions of the British Empire, reports of Soviet interest in the region were provided to Prime Minister Harold Macmillan by US intelligence agencies. British troops arrived in the colony in October 1953, and the newly approved constitution was suspended indefinitely.[19]

Another election was proposed for 1957, but ideological disagreements and concerns about foreign influence contributed to a growing rift between Burnham and Jagan. In response to the US-backed coup in Guatemala in June 1954, Jagan and his American-born wife, Janet Rosenberg Jagan, adopted a more strident anticapitalist and anti-imperialist stance. The Jagans also offered rhetorical support for the ongoing insurrection in Cuba against the US-backed government of Fulgencio Batista. Publicly, Burnham offered a more moderate approach, supporting British and US anticommunist efforts in the Caribbean and refraining from overt support for the Cuban revolutionaries. For the US State Department and the British Foreign Ministry, Burnham appeared to embody Prime Minister Winston Churchill's self-satisfied assertion that when it came to British Guiana, the Afro-Guyanese's "anti-Colonialism will be more than balanced out by their anti-Communism."[20]

By August 1957, the PPP had begun its split into Burnhamite and Jagaite factions. The election, which awarded seats in the newly created thirty-five-person parliament, was won by Jagan's faction, who received nine seats. Burnham's faction only won three seats. In the aftermath of this loss to Jagan, Burnham broke fully from the PPP and joined with the United Democratic Party to form the PNC. Because Central Intelligence Agency (CIA) and State Department officials considered Burnham a moderating influence on Jagan, his departure signaled to the Eisenhower administration that the continued dominance of a PPP government in Guiana was a threat to US interests in the Caribbean basin. Following the overthrow of Batista in January 1959 and the election of President John F. Kennedy the following year, the State Department began to circulate evidence that Jagan was working closely with the Soviet Union, and diplomats and US Foreign Service officers expressed anxiety at the possibility of another Caribbean nation forging close ties with Moscow.

A subsequent win for the PPP in 1961 only solidified Jagan's parliamentary control. In response, the CIA and the United Kingdom helped forge an alliance between the conservative National Democratic Party, led by business magnate Peter D'Aguiar, and Burnham's PNC.[21] The strategy worked, and in 1964 the PNC/National Democratic Party coalition beat the PPP, controlling twenty-nine out of fifty-four seats. Jagan, however, refused to resign as prime minister until he was forced out by Governor Richard Luyt, who installed Burnham as prime minister. With Burnham firmly in control, Prime Minister Harold Wilson acquiesced to Guyana's calls for independence and set a date for independence: May 26, 1966.[22] The formal recognition of Forbes Burnham as independent Guyana's prime minister marginalized the already weakened PPP. The US–UK honeymoon with Burnham was short-lived. Within a year of independence, Burnham began to make overtures to the Soviet bloc for aid, and after elections in 1968, his government established formal relations with Cuba and Eastern bloc nations and began publicly articulating a Third Worldist position in international affairs.[23]

Following the contested 1968 electoral victory in which he successfully sidelined both the PPP and D'Aguilar's United Force Party, Burnham crafted a new constitution, implemented in 1970, that declared Guyana a "cooperative republic" with two primary goals: the elimination of the "colonial mentality" and the promotion of "self-help economic development program[s] based on a national system of cooperative ventures."[24] Arguments in favor of Guyanese self-sufficiency, including agricultural and industrial modernization, became a mainstay of party-funded newspapers and pamphlets. Burnham also proclaimed his support for Black Power movements in the United States and elsewhere.

At the same time, the PNC began its suppression of opposition parties, leading to a de facto one-party state, although the PPP did govern in local municipalities, especially those with large Indo-Guyanese majorities.[25] Burnham not only recognized industrial and agricultural development as key facets of his envisioned national self-sufficiency project, but he also saw a need for an ideological framework. Guyanese-born artist Bernadette Persaud recalled that "Burnham had his eye on scholars and intellectuals," intimating that he used relationships with them as a means to legitimize his administration and his nation-building project while marginalizing his political rivals.[26]

Burnham of Guyana

Although Burnham's electoral victory was the result of intervention by the CIA and British intelligence, his proclamation of the Guyanese Cooperative Republic and his embrace of Black Power inspired support from men and women throughout the African diaspora.[27] Mayfield, who confessed that he knew little of the nation prior to his visit in 1971, quickly emerged as one of its most vocal advocates. Uneasy with simmering racial violence and having misgivings about how Burnham would achieve his stated goals, Mayfield would nevertheless throw himself into the tasks assigned to him by the Ministry of Information and Culture, where he would be appointed in December 1971. Mayfield would later note with frustration that "nation-builders cannot manufacture history of the kind that will prepare their people for the disciplined march towards a new society."[28] Yet as Mayfield's work in Guyana demonstrated, he was determined to meet that challenge head-on.

In spite of his decision to work closely as a member of the Ministry of Information and Culture's staff, he remained convinced that "Forbes Burnham has an uphill fight on his hands if he seriously intends to get Guyana moving."[29] Burnham's offer of sanctuary for Black radicals from Africa and the diaspora emerged at the same moment when governments throughout North America and the Caribbean began to disrupt Black Power movements, persecuting and sometimes murdering activists who challenged state power and the electoral dominance of the PNC.[30] In offering these men and women asylum, however, Burnham sowed the seeds of his fall from grace from the revolutionary imaginary of Afro-diasporic radicals. Expatriates with differing ideological and political positions brought their disagreements with them and exacerbated internal tensions within the Afro-Guyanese community.

Although Mayfield believed that Burnham had demonstrated a certain sincerity as a revolutionary Afro-diasporic leader by supporting Cuba's intervention in Angola and providing financial support for revolutionary groups that opposed white-minority governments in South Africa and South Rhodesia, Mayfield's decision to relocate was for reasons equal parts geopolitical and ideological as well as personal. Even reports of the CIA's role in Burnham's accession to prime minister were apparently ignored or dismissed, as Mayfield did not mention them at all in his writings or his correspondence. Based on his recollections, the two most significant factors in his decision to relocate to Guyana in November 1971 were his hopes of reestablishing himself in a state free from the pressures of white supremacy and his budding relationship with a Guyanese woman, Joan Cambridge, whom he had met during his September visit.

In a letter to Cambridge from September shortly after his return to the United States, Mayfield declared, "You are the greatest distraction[.] I think if I hadn't had things to do back here [in the United States], I wouldn't have left Georgetown." Expressing his desire to purchase land in Guyana, he inquired as to the feasibility of this plan and invited Cambridge to write back.[31] Cambridge did not reply to Mayfield until late October, which made him anxious about his plans to relocate. "Your letter saved my life," he wrote to her as he expressed his relief at her response. "I have been very changed since I returned here," he continued, pledging his love to Cambridge and writing of his desire to learn from her about Guyana and to work with her upon his arrival.

Ghana also informed Mayfield's expectations and plans for Guyana, and his correspondence echoed concerns about the dynamics of Afro-diasporic relationships. As he had in "Ghanaian Sketches," Mayfield noted that in Guyana it was not just "the attitude of Great American Chauvinism" that threatened the relationship between the Guyanese citizens and Afro expatriates but also a deep resentment "because [Afros] are seen as a threat[;] . . . unlike the Whites, these Blacks from the industrialized nations have usually come to stay."[32] In spite of his own status as an expatriate worker who planned to settle permanently, he cautioned that "the hiring of expatriates is both delicate and dangerous."[33]

Laudatory of Burnham's domestic political instincts, Mayfield nevertheless expressed reservations about the prime minister's choice of political appointments. Recalling his experience with corrupt ministers in Nkrumah's government, Mayfield concluded that these were the growing pains of newly independent nations. In writings both public and private, he linked the colonial system to the "severe handicap[s]" that newly independent nations faced.[34] Despite these early concerns, Mayfield reinforced the image of Burnham as a dedicated, hardworking leader who was unafraid of "getting his hands dirty," a fact that even inspired Mayfield to consider trying his hand at farming.[35] Although he had doubts about the nation's ability to achieve the goals Burnham had set, Mayfield had little doubt about the prime minister's sincerity. The Burnham government had pledged in 1970 "to feed, clothe and house the nation by 1976," and Mayfield wrote in praise of this effort and the nearly "10,000 new jobs" it would create, especially for infrastructure projects.[36] As he had in Ghana, Mayfield also emerged as a verbal pugilist, challenging the government's most vocal critics—in particular former PNC ally Eusi Kwayana—rebutting arguments publicly and privately.[37]

Kwayana had returned to Guyana from Ghana in the mid-1960s and begun organizing Afro-Guyanese peoples in preparation for independence. He was not a candidate, but he was quick to criticize his political opponents and draw attention to their insufficient commitment to the Pan-African educational and social ideals he espoused. In 1973, he publicly criticized Burnham for taking credit for his ideas, asserting that the idea of the Cooperative Republic was originally an idea that grew out of his own organization, the African Society for Cultural Relations with Independent Africa (ASCRIA). Burnham, Kwayana argued, had "co-opted and sabotaged" his plan without giving him credit. Kwayana also argued that the prime minister's Pan-Africanist language was hollow rhetoric, something Burnham used only to win votes.[38] Despite unyielding criticism from the ASCRIA, Burnham's investment in the ministry's propaganda effort began to bear fruit at least internationally. By 1971, the state was heralded by Caribbean and African radicals as both a haven for Pan-African thought and a nation on the cusp of a radical transformation. Successful at promoting Guyana as a sanctuary for Afro expatriates, Julian Mayfield soon had political and personal trouble with many of the Afro expatriates who arrived. Rhetoric and reality did not always align in Guyana.

Appointed to a position in the Ministry of Information and Culture, Mayfield identified solutions to a multitude of problems that he saw. Impressed by Burnham's commitment to self-reliance and self-sufficiency as well as his explicit concern for the attitudes and perspectives of Guyanese citizens, Mayfield embraced his position as a writer in the Publications Division, and his archive is replete with informed analyses of the state of political, social, and racial discourse within the country. Touting autarky and self-reliance in the "cooperative republic," Burnham demanded sovereignty in political, cultural, and economic affairs, noting that one without the others was insufficient. For his part, Mayfield was hopeful that Guyana would offer both the belonging he sought, the radical socioeconomic changes that Burnham promised, and a space for Afro-diasporic solidarity to grow and flourish.[39]

While Mayfield began his time in the ministry by researching public attitudes and perceptions of Guyana abroad, his archive reveals his belief that only the state apparatus offered a means to effect change on both the national and international levels. Already experienced in rhetorical nation building and the application of print and radio media to influence the public, Mayfield accepted the political limitations that Burnham imposed and argued in favor of the steps the prime minister took to marginalize the opposition that challenged his plans. In particular, Mayfield saw in Burnham's rhetoric and political activities a serious concern for addressing the problems of the postcolonial rule he had witnessed firsthand in West Africa. Burnham's cooperative socialism, Mayfield argued, provided a template for how the nation could become self-sufficient, which in turn would lead to the kind of sovereignty as yet unrealized. Recognizing the contradictions between Burnham's Guyanese nationalism and his own Pan-Africanism, Mayfield reasoned that of the two, the former had more potential for success.

The Nation and the Pan-African Ideal

In the aforementioned article published in the July–August 1973 issue of *Black Scholar*, Julian Mayfield dismissed the "pan-African ideal" as an idea whose time had passed, as hollow and nonexistent as the ideals of integration that had dominated the United States in the 1960s. He identified the so-called Pan-African ideal as a strain of imperialist chauvinism, characterizing its adherents' beliefs thus: "Because I am a black man, the moment I set foot on soil anywhere in the world controlled by black men, I am as free as any citizen to come and go as I want, and to propagate whatever I wish." Mayfield's article, a response to an earlier piece by Eusi Kwayana, considered the inherent limitations faced by political refugees who sought sanctuary within sovereign nations. The article also did double duty as a refutation of Kwayana's accusations about the deportation of two African American radicals in the spring of 1973.

In the piece, Mayfield implored readers to recognize that national sovereignty required careful parsing of local political situations, much as he had urged a previous generation of travelers that Afro-diasporic travel demanded cultural and social sensitivity. Political refugees, he asserted, always had to be careful, and he argued that "aliens in any country in the world live there at the sufferance of whatever government is in power. *In reality, they have no rights*, although governments vary in the degree of privileges they allow aliens."[40] In prioritizing national sovereignty within a nation-state that attracted expatriates specifically because of its embrace of the Pan-African ideal, Julian Mayfield captured one of the most persistent contradictions of Burnham's nation-building project in Guyana, one that would later contribute to his decision to leave in late 1974.

Mayfield's response to Kwayana fit neatly into the ongoing debate over nationalism within the framework of Pan-Africanism. In the wake of proclamations of Black Power in the diaspora, some postcolonial governments in Africa and the Caribbean perceived this transnational liberation movement as a threat to their own sovereignty and capital accumulation schemes. Much as he had seen Ghana's sovereignty as key to a "United States of Africa," Mayfield believed that Guyanese sovereignty and national development superseded the transnational freedom dreams of the Pan-African ideal. By the time of his article in the *Black Scholar*, Mayfield had spent two years in Guyana; his work with the Ministry of Information and Culture informed his conclusions in the piece and defined his objectives in that position as both an employee of the government and an expatriate worker with experience in nation-building projects. First and foremost, he argued, the people of Guyana needed to be united in support of their own national project before Pan-Africanism could be realized in practice. Foregrounding national coherence as a core component of Black liberation, Mayfield rejected both Kwayana's Pan-African aspirations and his criticism of Burnham's government, thus echoing Feelings's dismissal of the armchair critics of the "scholarly left."[41]

Mayfield's emphasis on Guyana's domestic politics, public opinion, and support for the Burnham government was vital to the mission that Burnham had laid out in his 1970 proclamation of the Guyanese Cooperative Republic. That said, a "cooperative republic" was not a new idea. During the negotiations on the formation of a West Indian Federation in 1958, Burnham argued for a similar plan to fellow delegates in nearby Port of Spain, Trinidad. "The largeness, or power or importance of a nation," Burnham told the gathered delegates, including Errol Barrow of Barbados, Michael Manley of Jamaica, and Eric Williams of Trinidad, "is not calculated merely by acreage or square miles. . . . There are the human resources which are so important in reckoning the importance of the nation."[42] Critics of Burnham have argued that this populist rhetoric obscured an overriding desire for political power, but Mayfield and other Afros, such as Feelings, believed in the plans that the prime minister outlined in his public speeches and editorials. The legacy of the Burnham government, especially among former PNC members and adherents, suggests that Mayfield's allegiance and faith in his new leader was misplaced.

In a 1989 essay, PNC member and professor of political science Festus Brotherson Jr. characterized Burnham's policies as a Machiavellian pursuit of legitimacy. "The country's foreign policy was not crafted over the years to serve the objective national interest," Brotherson wrote. "Rather, the overriding objective . . . was to do abroad what it had failed to do at home: i.e., to establish legitimacy."[43] Simply put, Brotherson characterized Guyana's foreign policy under Burnham as "determin[ing] the national interest," as opposed to the national interest guiding foreign policy.[44] Subsequent interpretations of Guyanese political history have not substantively challenged this critique, as scholars have been almost uniformly critical of Burnham's obsession with foreign policy and his undue influence over election outcomes that legitimized his government's continued power. Coupled with Burnham's embrace of electoral violence and election tampering, his reputation remains a thorny subject in the nation despite efforts to rehabilitate and celebrate his accomplishments by some of his political successors.

The substantial resources that Burnham invested in the Ministry of Information and Culture also supports this critique. By the time Mayfield arrived in 1971, the ministry was well funded and well staffed, a reality that was indicative of Burnham's commitment to convincing Guyana's seven hundred thousand citizens that their labor and economic sacrifices were necessary for the development of the nation's cooperative republic. Embracing print and radio as the means to convince the population of its role in Guyana's nation-building project, men and women such as Julian Mayfield and Joan Cambridge came to play significant roles in articulating and propagandizing Burnham's vision for a modern Guyana. Mayfield's archive provides a detailed account of what that vision was. Numerous notes and drafts of speeches with his annotations offer his own take on the prime minister's language and arguments. As a communications specialist and later special adviser to the prime minister in the Ministry of Information and Culture, Mayfield took his job—and his proximity to power—seriously.

Beginning in 1972 with this proposal to reorganize the Ministry of Information and Culture and ending in December 1974 when he returned to the United States, Mayfield devoted his daytime hours in Georgetown to researching, parsing, promoting, and perfecting the messages emanating from the ministry. In the meantime, Mayfield and Cambridge were married in a small ceremony in the summer of 1972.[45] Together, they took the lead in promoting the celebration of African heritage in the Caribbean (CARIFESTA '72); organized a response to the Sixth Pan-African Congress in Dar-es-Salaam in 1974; and promoted Burnham's unique brand of agricultural and industrial autarky in a number of formats.[46] Mayfield remembered all too well how Kwame Nkrumah had been undermined not by an invading force but instead from within his own government and was determined that Burnham's plan for self-sufficiency would not suffer the same fate.

Mayfield's archive indicates that in navigating the politics of race and class in Guyana, the relationship between foreign capital and domestic production, and familiar problems facing a postcolonial nation, he maintained a sincere commitment to both Burnham and the tenets of Burnhamism. This devotion was quickly rewarded and, within a year Mayfield was promoted to senior adviser. From there, he worked closely with Burnham in crafting and editing speeches, public pronouncements of ideology, and press releases. At the same time, Mayfield regularly contributed articles and statements to government-controlled newspapers, celebrating his outsider's perspective and offering his own radical interpretation of world events as well as analyses of the impact of such economic and political issues on Guyana. This work has left a rich archive of material that offers insight into the machinations of the Guyanese government's programs and how Mayfield and Burnham intended its policies to be received by citizens of the nation and of the broader African diaspora.

Dismantling Booker's Guyana

Mayfield recognized how public sentiment and foreign influence worked in opposition to Burnham's objectives for the realization of self-sufficiency of the cooperative republic, and Mayfield's writings leave a detailed account of his attempts to undermine this influence and its effect on the public. Burnham recognized that a country as small as Guyana would inherently be vulnerable to foreign market fluctuations and policies; as a result, he emphasized the connection between foreign policy and domestic conditions, and his policies were shaped by this connection. In the wake of independence, domestic agricultural production languished due to the artificially low cost of imported food, while domestic manufacturing faced similar hurdles. Foreign companies owned much of the most fertile agricultural land, current and potential industrial sites, and means to bring material in and out of the country; this meant that domestic policies could not be disentangled from the whims of foreign firms and governments. As Mayfield wrote in the manuscript "Burnham of Guyana," the fact that there existed a division between "foreign" policy and "domestic" policy, while a handy dichotomy for political scientists' analyses, did not accurately convey the conditions facing Guyana in 1972.

Guyana was a small nation where most arable land until the 1960s had been used exclusively for the production of sugarcane for processing and export, and Mayfield wrote extensively about Burnham's obsession with making the nation agriculturally and industrially self-sufficient.[47] In a 1972 speech about the budget edited by Mayfield, Burnham emphasized how reducing the Guyanese dependence on imported food was a fundamental component of Guyanese sovereignty. "There is no need . . . for us to continue to import peanuts after the 31st of December 1972, nor carrots, nor tin fruits, nor jams or jellies," the prime minister argued before his ministers. In addition to these items, Burnham complained that the nation imported $1.8 million (USD) worth of Irish potatoes and nearly as much in English peas but could, with the proper agricultural investments in drainage and land, produce those items domestically.

The major stumbling block to these plans, however, was that Guyana's arable coastal land was largely divided between the British-owned firms of Booker Sugar Estates Limited, Jessels Holdings, and Tate and Lyle, the first of which was also a majority holder of importing, shipping, and retail concerns.[48] Despite the nationalization of fifteen of the eighteen extant sugar plantations by 1970, foreign firms retained their control over imported foodstuffs, which were cheaper than the production of domestic alternatives.[49] Foreign policy with Britain, Ireland, the United States, and other major exporting nations was thus inseparable from domestic agricultural, industrial, and social policy, a source of frustration for Burnham's government throughout the decade.

In addition to writing speeches and newspaper columns, Mayfield worked closely with Elvin McDavid, the minister of information and culture, in curating Burnham's speeches and discourse into ideological documents that laid out the tenets of Burnhamism. Often echoing Mayfield's previous disagreements with orthodox communists in the United States and West Africa, extracts titled "The Ideology of Our Party" emphasized the ways that the "cooperative socialism" of Guyana was profoundly misunderstood in part because it came from the minds and experiences of African-descended peoples. The authors of these documents argued that Burnham's vision was criticized in Western media because it did not fit the European "compartments," favoring policies that addressed the specific material needs of Guyana.[50]

As Mayfield wrote in his edits for one document, when Europeans and North Americans believe that a given politics is communist, "they put you into the Communist compartment, assuming that you are a number of monkeys and that your greatest ability lies in mimicry and copying[,] . . . [that] you believe in everything that is happening in the Soviet Union."[51] The problem, Mayfield wrote, was that "socialism has got so many meanings" that it did not fit into the classification schemes that social scientists and politicians had constructed. In short, Third World socialisms were profoundly misunderstood by both white Europeans and Americans but also by many of the European-trained bureaucrats and former colonial administrators who were now in positions of power in Guyana.

Curating the ideological tenets of Burnhamism, however, was not what solidified Julian Mayfield's respect for the prime minister. Rather, it was the ways that Burnham eschewed ideological discourse in favor of plain speaking about tactics, strategy, and policy. Mayfield wrote at length about Burnham's dogged campaigning during parliamentary elections and how he would take a retinue of ministers and journalists through dozens of sleepy villages that dotted the coast of Demerara and Berbice, stopping to sip rum and inquire about local issues. Praising Burnham's physical stamina, Mayfield also spoke highly of his personability, as the prime minister would easily recall the names and problems of the people he encountered on this campaign trail, often years after a single meeting. Burnham's ability to "organize the most complex ideas and present them to his constituents in simple terms which are not condescending" was, to Mayfield, the sign of a polished and capable politician.[52] Likening Burnham to both Kwame Nkrumah and Fidel Castro, Mayfield believed that the prime minister's frenetic politicking, carefully worded speeches, and policy proposals demonstrated a genuine concern for the welfare of Guyanese peoples.

In contrast to this sincere concern, Mayfield also noted a disquieting paternalism in the prime minister's interactions with citizens of Guyana. During one campaign trip in January 1973, Mayfield recalled that Burnham and his entourage stopped in an unnamed village on the east coast of Demerara. In a crowded rum shop, Burnham spied a young man attempting to leave without being noticed. "Why the hell aren't you at Kuru Kuru," the prime minister asked the young man, and "What are you doing here in a rumshop at this time of day?" The young man complained that "that fork propuh hard to turn," a complaint about the difficulty of plowing a nearby field where the man was currently employed. Burnham responded with a rude comment and exited the shop.[53]

Mayfield goes on to note that not only did Burnham know the young man, but the government had a file on him, a fact that demonstrated a level of personal involvement and an uncomfortable level of paternalism. The man, referred to as Jack in Mayfield's account, had been a petty criminal whose activities had landed him in a Buxton jail. Seeking his freedom, he wrote numerous letters to the prime minister and, in doing so, "literally wrote his way out of jail" by plagiarizing poetry, verse, and songs in praise of Burnham.[54] Despite the prime minister's ability to "spot a rogue a mile away," Burnham personally intervened in Jack's case, promising to release him if he went into farming. Burnham then secured twenty acres of land, known locally as Kuru Kuru, and sent Jack to farm black-eyed peas and cassava. That Jack was now sitting in a rumshop complaining about the difficulties of tilling the soil angered Burnham. "Jack is like thousands of other young men and women who come out of the public schools yearly," Mayfield wrote in his discussion of this encounter. "They are insulted to be offered anything but clerical work," despite the lack of jobs in that area. "Somebody must produce," Mayfield concluded, "and in agricultural Guyana, this means farming and related industry."[55]

Jack's story highlighted the thematic focus of Julian Mayfield's work for the Ministry of Information and Culture. In identifying the structural issues of postcolonial Guyana—poverty, lack of industry, and unemployment—Mayfield's writings combined a Marxian analysis of the productive labor necessary to improve living conditions and a Gramscian critique of how the predominant cultural forces undermined the nation's modernization process. "Burnham of Guyana" contains several anecdotes such as that concerning Jack in which the prime minister personally intervenes in young people's lives to give them an opportunity, only to be rejected when they refuse to perform the necessary labor to turn that opportunity into a means of sustaining themselves. These repeated examples were represented in Mayfield's writing not as personal failures but rather as evidence of the hegemonic influence of colonialism in which young people simply hoped to step into positions of power left by departing colonial managers and bureaucrats.

In declaring Guyana a cooperative republic in 1970, Burnham prioritized the elimination of the "colonial mentality." For Mayfield, Guyanese youths' rejection of farming and agricultural work in favor of bourgeois pursuits was evidence that the nation had far to go in this project. Citing the prevalence of foreign media as part of the problem, Mayfield went so far as to argue against the introduction of broadcast television to the country due to the negative effects such visual displays of wealth and colonial power would have on the mentalities of the people of Guyana.[56] Despite this concern for the colonial mentality, revolution was not an abstract concept for Mayfield. Instead, it was a series of practical actions undertaken by a population that involved labor, shared sacrifice, and unity of goals. Much as he had argued in Ghana, Mayfield's press releases and newspaper articles emphasized, "You must get involved in the revolution on a practical level."[57] To Mayfield, that meant literally "getting ones' hands dirty" in the fields and performing the backbreaking labor that would generate the capital necessary to fully develop Guyana into a modern state.

Ideologies of Practical Revolution

As he had in Ghana, Mayfield made practical contributions to nation building in Guyana. One of these was his role as an unofficial liaison between foreign Black radicals seeking sanctuary and the government. In January 1972, he wrote a letter to Prime Minister Burnham pleading for a stay on the extradition of Mr. David Hill, who had arrived in Guyana via Trinidad the previous month. According to the letter, Hill had been "a leader in organising an effective boycott against white businesses in the black community" in his hometown of Cleveland, Ohio. Mayfield connected Hill's boycott effort to his own struggle in Monroe, claiming that "I am perfectly acquainted with the Cleveland situation because they grew out of our 1961 struggle in Monroe[;] . . . the political organization of which Mr. Hill is a leader is a result of that struggle." Due to Mayfield's intercession, Hill was allowed to stay in the country and later became a close ally of the PNC.[58]

Following the difficult 1973 parliamentary elections, Mayfield expressed discomfort with the prevailing political climate, especially the growing political divisions among the Afro expatriates. Support for or opposition to Burnham played a significant role in the widening of divisions as Afro expatriates took sides, resulting in the deportations of two African American radicals, Mamadou Lumumba and Shango Umoja, in March 1973.[59] Lumumba and Umoja had both been organizing in the San Francisco Bay area since the early 1960s, when Lumumba helped the quarterly journal *Soulbook* along with Donald Warden, Isaac Moore, Carroll Holmes, and Ernie Allen. It was through Warden that they made their connection with Guyana. Tchaiko Kwayana, Eusi Kwayana's African American wife, had worked with radical activist-intellectual Donald Warden in Oakland as a part of the Afro-American Association in the early 1960s. That organization had since become part of the Pan-African Secretariat, a transnational organization dedicated to the exchange of men and women and ideas throughout the diaspora.[60]

In 1973, the Pan-African Secretariat sent Lumumba and Umoja to Guyana to aid the ASCRIA's local mission and teach at the Golden Grove Government Secondary School in Demerara. Although the men were welcomed by the students and the community in Demerara, their connection with the ASCRIA made them pawns in Eusi Kwayana and Burnham's escalating political rivalry. For reasons that are disputed by those involved, Umoja and Lumumba were deported from Guyana in March 1973, and the subsequent controversy divided the Afro expatriates, highlighting the difficulties of squaring Guyanese nationalism with Pan-Africanism. According to Eusi Kwayana, Lumumba and Umoja's deportation occurred "after they had written in the *Sunday Graphic* a lengthy assault on the USA," and their "public utterances . . . exposed the oppression of the black peoples and the Indians of North America."[61] Kwayana also attributed their deportation to their close association with the ASCRIA, which had published accusations of corruption within the highest ranks of the PNC.

The subsequent issue of *The Black Scholar* contained Julian Mayfield's rebuttal of Kwayana's account and interpretation of the case. According to Mayfield, Umoja and Lumumba were visited by the Guyanese police and asked to register at the local police department as resident aliens. Mayfield wrote that the two men physically resisted the police's routine request, and "from that point on their deportation became as inexorable as Greek tragedy, with no one to mourn for them in this country except the cynical opposition groups." Mayfield noted in this essay that Lumumba and Umoja were not at fault and that "the person most responsible for the deportations was Eusi Kwayana." Kwayana, Mayfield wrote, "encouraged them to proselytize his particular analysis of Guyanese politics vis-a-vis United States imperialism" and could have halted the deportations had he simply picked up the phone and called Burnham." In short, Mayfield did not challenge the substance of the case, only the way that Kwayana had portrayed it in international media.

Citing Guyana's national sovereignty as the central factor in the deportation of Umoja and Lumumba, Mayfield also argued that their story "should have an important lesson for many readers of *The Black Scholar* who are contemplating living abroad." Noncitizens and guests of the government "live there at the sufferance of whatever government is in power." Noting that he too had been approached by the police and asked to accompany them to the local station to be registered as a resident alien,

Mayfield identified the men's attitudes toward Guyanese state authority as a "Great American Chauvinism." Echoing his criticisms of African Americans in Ghana, he lamented how many Black Americans arrived in Guyana and immediately began "telling the 'natives' how the country could be improved." Without any irony, Mayfield advised political refugees to "settle down quietly, go to work and hope the authorities forget that you exist."[62]

In private correspondence following the deportations of Lumumba and Umoja, Mayfield's letters highlighted the increasing paranoia and division among Afro expatriates. Following this incident, he wrote to the prime minister on behalf of himself and another Afro, Paul Adams, requesting permission to carry a concealed weapon. Citing recent murders of Black power activists in California, Mayfield explained that neither he nor Adams "would . . . think it unusual if a tourist dropped into Guyana with instructions to knock one or both of us (or you) off, and catch the first plane out."[63] Mayfield recounted other incidents to friends in letters, in which he intimated that Eusi Kwayana intended to bring Black Power militants such as the ones he had portrayed in *Uptight* to Guyana to aid him in unseating Burnham from power. Max Stanford (later Muhammad Ahmad) was one such militant whom Mayfield and Adams had objected to being allowed into the country. In one letter, Mayfield noted that Stanford was close to Lumumba and Umoja, the two African American activists who had been deported in March 1973 and had threatened violence against Mayfield, Adams, and Feelings following their return to the United States. It was their refusal to intercede on Stanford's behalf, Mayfield believed, that led to deteriorating relations between Kwayana's ASCRIA faction and the Afro expatriates aligned with Burnham's ruling PNC.

By late 1974, Mayfield was frustrated that his political rhetoric did little to ameliorate the ongoing political and racial violence in Guyana. That year, the sociologist Walter Rodney and Eusi Kwayana joined with other opposition groups to form the Working People's Alliance (WPA), which sought to challenge the stalemate between the PPP and the PNC.[64] The formation of the WPA and, in particular, the presence of Rodney further split the Afro expatriate community, as those associated with Rodney and Kwayana became targets for violence and deportation by the PNC. What had begun with enthusiasm and promise ended with fears of violent retribution and permanent divisions among African American radical groups.

In a strange twist of fate, the man whom Mayfield helped settle in Guyana in 1972, David Hill, went on to become a paramilitary who perpetuated violence against anti-PNC activists in the late 1970s and early 1980s. Expanding the "House of Israel" in Guyana and granting himself the title of "Rabbi Washington," Hill was linked to numerous attacks on the WPA. Upon learning of Hill's actions, Mayfield expressed regret for the role he had played in aiding Hill's immigration into Guyana.[65]

Ultimately, Guyana did not become the kind of haven for African American radicals in the same way that Ghana had been in the 1960s. However, this was not for lack of trying. According to historian Russell Rickford, the African Americans who chose to visit and settle in Guyana in the early 1970s were not simply searching for sanctuary from political and economic turmoil in the United States. They were, he argues, "engaged in a search for fulfillment—a quest for immersive blackness, self-government, and true social belonging."[66] Unlike others, Mayfield not only sought these concepts for himself but also sought to aid in the construction of a new nation that would welcome any and all Black people. As his writing demonstrates, however, what many encountered was a nation in the midst of a transformation and assertive of its sovereignty in which shifting battle lines and factional disputes left them confused, frustrated, and at the mercy of an increasingly autocratic state.

Julian Mayfield's longing for belonging and his desire to escape the narrow confines of the United States had led him once again to a space far from the center of US empire where the effects of white supremacy and hegemony were diminished. Belonging was only the first step in the broader project that African American expatriates such as Mayfield and Feelings undertook in Guyana. As he had in Ghana, Mayfield continued to write fiction while working at the Ministry of Information and Culture, and although his output was reduced due to the demands of his position, he nevertheless took the task of improving perceptions of Guyana as the starting point on improving the historical perspective among all African-descended peoples.

"Burnham of Guyana" Revisited

In the final chapter of his unpublished biography of Forbes Burnham, Mayfield considered the problems that the prime minister continued to face in his effort to remake the nation into a self-sufficient, sovereign state. Foremost in Mayfield's mind was the "colonial mentality" that Burnham's 1970 constitution sought to eradicate. "Benevolent and self-seeking British traditions," Mayfield wrote, "have left a heavy cross of attitudes which are bound to retard West Indian progress."[67] Citing George Lamming, Richard Wright, and Amiri Baraka, Mayfield carefully dissected the "colonial mentality" and concluded that meaningful change in Guyana required not sophistication and theoretical innovation but rather submission to a "national discipline" to remake the nation."[68] Like Kwame Nkrumah, Jomo Kenyatta, and Sekou Touré, Forbes Burnham demanded the full dedication of the people of Guyana toward a fundamental change in their nation. Burnham's consolidation of power and the increasing corruption of the ministers and politicians he surrounded himself with undermined his authority and popularity.

Julian Mayfield saw how the Pan-African ideal of racial solidarity lacked the kind of programmatic and practical steps necessary to construct a more just and equitable space. However, in putting his faith and labor at the service of the Black nation-state, he ran up against familiar problems. In a 1975 essay, Guyanese activist-intellectual Walter Rodney rejected the idea that it was possible for Guyana under Burnham to be truly revolutionary and instead criticized it as a neocolonial state.[69] The PNC, he argued, was merely the "consolidation of the petty bourgeoisie as a class around the state."[70] The expropriation of sugar plantations did not end low wages for laborers but instead merely redirected the profits of that labor to those who were close political allies of the PNC. Similarly, Burnham's efforts to create self-sufficiency by blocking imports of foreign-made goods enriched the large landowners who produced the substitutes; coincidentally they were members of the PNC. "Using progressive rhetoric, establishing a single 'peoples' party and affecting state ownership," Rodney argued, the government succeeded in re-creating colonialism with a Black face.[71]

Although electoral violence had been steadily escalating since 1973 and Mayfield was having concerns about the presence of African American expatriates in the nation, his decision to flee Guyana in December 1974 was prompted by a quickly deteriorating relationship with the prime minister. In late November, Mayfield submitted a draft of his manuscript "Burnham of Guyana" to the prime minister for review. Because of his close working relationship with Burnham, a direct phone line had been installed in the home Mayfield shared with Cambridge, and according to her, once Mayfield left the manuscript with Burnham, the phone stopped ringing.[72] After two weeks of silence, Cambridge began to worry that Mayfield had lost favor with Burnham. She discouraged him from inquiring directly to the prime minister and instead hastily organized a trip to the United States under the auspices of needing medical treatment.

As Cambridge explained in an oral history in 2019, "I feared for his life—and mine!" Once they had arrived safely in Washington, she had Mayfield see a doctor who diagnosed him with a "moderately severe case of hypertension" and typed up a letter stating this fact. Cambridge then forwarded the letter to the prime minister's office to explain their absence.[73] Later that month, Mayfield formally requested a medical leave of absence from his position while maintaining an apparently cheerful demeanor in his missives. In one letter, he wrote to Burnham that "Burnham of Guyana" was being considered by two publishers and that Joan Cambridge's first novel, *Clarice Cumberbatch Want to Go Home*, was in the process of being published.[74] While Mayfield had written about how quickly the prime minister's moods could shift, the abruptness of departure suggests Burnham's apparent rejection caught him completely by surprise. There was scant mention of Mayfield's final days of his time in Guyana in either his nonfiction writing or his correspondence at the time. And even though he was no longer employed by the Guyanese government, he maintained close contact with Minister McDavid and others in order to keep abreast of current events in Guyana and offer his assistance from afar. Even Mayfield's formal resignation, sent directly to Burnham in 1975, apologized for his departure and cited ongoing health concerns as the reason he had left. Cambridge would not return to Guyana until 1986, a year after Burnham's death from a heart attack.

During his time in Guyana, Mayfield, though inspired by Pan-African ideals, nevertheless challenged those ideals by embracing Guyana's own Burnhamist nationalism. With a land base in South America, a Black-led government, and a population seemingly determined to throw off the yoke of the colonial mentality, Guyana presented itself to Mayfield as potentially the kind of nation he could reside in for the remainder of his life, and he had been determined to play his part in the construction of that new nation. His initial thrill at being part of the dynamic Black-dominated nation gradually transformed into a growing sense of disillusion, especially with mounting factional disputes and increasing street violence. Losing Burnham's favor was the last straw, and fear of retribution convinced Mayfield and Cambridge to give up on the dream, at least temporarily. Returning to the United States, Mayfield attempted to revive his academic career. The couple settled in Washington, and Mayfield quickly landed a job teaching, first at the University of Maryland and then at Howard University, where he served as the writer-in-residence in the university's English Department. Mayfield was never one to rest on his laurels, and his return to the academy saw the continuation of the intellectual, author, and activist's strident critique of American foreign policy, global capitalism, and the perils of Blackness in a white world.

9 The Black King Must Be Black

Hollywood and the Haitian Revolution, 1973–1976

....

> The only successful revolt in history happened in Haiti. The transformation of slaves . . . into a people able to organize themselves and defeat the most powerful European nations of their day is one of the great epics of revolutionary struggle and achievement.
>
> —C. L. R. James, 1938

When Julian Mayfield left his position in Guyana behind and returned to the United States in the winter of 1974, he remained committed to one project he had begun there: a biopic based on the life of Henri Christophe of Haiti. In early 1973, Mayfield had been hired by his old theater colleague William Marshall to aid in developing a film based on the story of the rise and fall of Christophe. In a draft script for *King Christophe,* written while he worked at the Guyanese Ministry of Information and Culture, Mayfield's characters considered the limited political options available to postcolonial leaders at the beginning of the nineteenth century. In an exchange between Christophe and his confidant, Paulin, the two men considered the challenge of leadership in defiance of colonial empire. "If you force a nation to work it calls you a Dictator or Tyrant," Paulin observed, "[but] if you don't it calls you soft."[1] Written at a moment in which Prime Minister Forbes Burnham was exhorting the Guyanese people to grow their own food and develop their own economy to become independent from European domination, *King Christophe*'s draft script addressed the precarious status of postcolonial governments in the Caribbean even as it sought to portray the historical importance and impact of its titular character.

As the autocratic leader of the State of Haiti for twelve years (1808–20), Henri Christophe undertook massive infrastructure projects and forced the Haitian people to once again labor on the plantations they had burned during their revolution. This was necessary, Christophe argued, so that the nation could produce enough capital to stand firm against the empires of Europe. Christophe was not unique in this. Rather, he followed a well-worn path carved by his predecessors Jean-Jacques Dessalines and Toussaint

L'Ouverture, who both had demanded that the Haitian people continue to produce sugarcane and coffee for export.[2] Haiti's nation-building project was enforced with such brutality that in October 1820 the people rose up en masse to overthrow Christophe, putting an end to the Haitian monarchy forever.[3] Written as a celebration of "one of the world's great revolutionaries" *King Christophe* added new layers to Mayfield's continuing interest in power and his continued ambivalence about autocracy, masculinity, and the applicability of historical examples to the modern era.

In much the same way that *Uptight* had offered a nuanced portrait of the intellectual divisions within the Black liberation movement in the United States, the draft script for *King Christophe* addressed political, cultural, and economic contradictions in contemporary postcolonial nations. Shaped by the close working relationship with the prime minister, the Christophe project reflected how Mayfield's understanding of Haiti's postrevolutionary history influenced his perceptions of Guyana's own nation-building project. In the political, social, and economic pressures Burnham faced from both the United States and the United Kingdom, Mayfield saw echoes of those faced by Henri Christophe.[4]

As a piece of political art, *King Christophe* presented the struggles of independent Haiti in starkly nationalist terms. It was the story of one nation standing against a hostile white world founded on colonialism and the subjugation of Black peoples. This struggle dovetailed with the one Mayfield was then working for in his support for the Guyanese Cooperative Republic, in which the former colony of British Guiana struggled to achieve economic, agricultural, and political sovereignty through autarkic policies. In his script for *King Christophe*, Mayfield emphasized many of the same themes found in his writings for the Guyanese Ministry of Information and Culture, especially the primacy of nationalist struggles over transnational ones at a moment in which hard-won independence was threatened by resurgent imperial ambitions.

Like *The Grand Parade* more than a decade earlier, *King Christophe* provided an artistic vehicle for Mayfield's political objectives. Like the novel and *Uptight*, Mayfield incorporated contemporary themes and conflicts that divided activists and policymakers. In contrast to the contemporary setting of *The Grand Parade* and *Uptight*, the historical setting of *King Christophe* and the importance of the Haitian Revolution in Black history proved to be far more challenging to adapt than he had initially anticipated. As the introductory paragraphs demonstrate, the discomfort evident in Hollywood studios' decision-making about portraying the Haitian

Revolution as the subject of a major motion picture remains evident. The inability of numerous filmmakers to fund a film on the Haitian Revolution, with some caveats, is the organizing theme of this chapter and the explanation as to why Mayfield approached the project with such dogged determination.

The Black King Must Be Black

Julian Mayfield did not originate the idea for *King Christophe*, but his efforts were instrumental in the film's development. Furthermore, his archive provides the only extant evidence of the film's existence.[5] William Marshall had been quietly working on the project since the mid-1960s, but a late-night television appearance by Anthony Quinn forced him to take action. On the evening of May 12, 1972, Quinn appeared on Dick Cavett's eponymous talk show and announced to Cavett and the studio audience that he had begun an adaptation of John W. Vandercook's 1928 novel about the life of Henri Christophe of Haiti, *Black Majesty*.[6] Claiming that that he had secured the permission of the government of President Jean-Claude "Baby Doc" Duvalier to shoot on location in Haiti, Quinn also declared that he would play the lead role of Christophe in blackface.[7] As Quinn explained to Cavett, he chose to cast himself in the lead role of the enslaved man who became a king because Black actors would not or could not tackle that role. Cavett praised Quinn's ambition, and the two men moved on to discuss other topics, but over the coming months a growing chorus of African American actors, writers, and directors spoke negatively about Quinn's decision to play a Haitian revolutionary leader in blackface.[8]

In claiming that African Americans were not up to the task of either writing about, starring in, or directing such a film, Quinn's exchange with Cavett laid bare many of the implicit assumptions that framed Hollywood's casting and hiring decisions. For decades, parts for Black actors had been limited to caricatures or supporting roles, limiting their résumés. Consequently, producers were wary about hiring inexperienced talent and, as Quinn's actions demonstrated, would prefer a white man in makeup to an untested Black actor. The following month, Marshall wrote Quinn a letter. Praising his colleague and calling the project an "artistic triumph," Marshall encouraged Quinn to find a qualified Black actor for the lead role. Quinn's response challenged Marshall's arguments, and over the course of several letters, the moods of both men soured. Marshall in particular grew angry over his colleague's insistence that he and he alone was qualified to play Henri Christophe. In his final letter, Marshall concluded his argument with a simple declaration that stressed the inseparable nature of race, Haiti's revolution, and its portrayal in a visual medium: "The Black King Must Be Black."[9]

Despite its importance to the political and racial conditions of the present, Haiti's successful revolt remains an elusive topic for Hollywood studios, but this is not from lack of trying. Multiple projects on Haiti's revolution were underway at the moment in which Quinn made his announcement and some of the most talented African American actors and filmmakers were involved in trying to realize a major motion picture. Two intertwined and persistent problems lay at the heart of these unsuccessful projects: accurate historical representation of revolutionary Blackness and the anti-Black racism present in the US film industry. Both issues have been central to the failure to make such a film, and as of the publication of this book, no film helmed by a Black director or written by a Black writer on the subject of Haiti has been filmed or released, although a handful of films that touch on the story do exist.[10] Analysis of these projects not only reveals the limits of Hollywood's embrace of Black histories and stories but also illustrates the history of the film industry's investment in and construction of a racial regime that privileged white stories or white interpretations of Black stories, remanding those that did not fit dominant narratives to the margins.

This history also reveals how Hollywood studios' interest in projects waxed and waned with the tides of Black liberation discourse. During periods of great interest in the African diaspora, especially in the 1930s and again in the 1970s, attempts at financing artistic interpretations of Haiti's dramatic expulsion of Europeans were made. Finally, the recent recovery and publication of C. L. R. James's long-lost theatrical dramas based on Haiti—*Toussaint Louverture* in 1936 and *The Black Jacobins* in 1967—illustrates the interest in film as a medium of revolution and the transition from stage to screen among activist intellectuals. Revealing history of these unmade films is part of a larger project of reclaiming Black history by Black artists and historicizing a key moment in the history of resistance to white supremacy in Hollywood through embrace of revolutionary Blackness in the Caribbean. This history is not entirely hidden, as Danny Glover indicated in his lamentations of his own stalled project.

In his 2008 interview Glover spoke of his project, *Toussaint*, as the artistic descendant of unmade projects by previous generations of filmmakers including Sergei Eisenstein, Tony Quinn, and a team effort initiated by Sidney Poitier and Harry Belafonte. In addition to these projects, my research has uncovered three other productions in development in the mid-1970s that Glover chose not to mention. The first was the aforementioned William Marshall and Julian Mayfield project *King Christophe*. The second was a script about Toussaint L'Ouverture by soap opera actress Ellen Holly, and the last was concerned with Christophe's fellow rebel, Haitian general Jean-Jacques Dessalines, and was associated with Yaphet Kotto and Brock Peters. All told, there were five projects at various stages of development in the mid-1970s, four of which were organized by African Americans. Thus, between 1929 and 1997, seven films about the Haitian Revolution have been proposed that got no further than the planning stages. Another motion picture set during the Haitian Revolution, *Lydia Bailey*, was shot and released in 1951 but does not fit the criteria set out by William Marshall, and indeed, an analysis thereof reinforces Glover's arguments.

The American-made *Lydia Bailey* demonstrates how a film about the Haitian Revolution could actually be produced. The movie, which ironically featured William Marshall in his Hollywood debut, uses the political and social ferment of the Haitian Revolution not as the center of the story but instead as a backdrop to a love affair between two white Americans. The absence of that film from other analyses is curious, as the authors ruminating on the absence of films on Haiti frequently reference Quinn's and Glover's projects. Some even cite the Marlon Brando film *Queimada/Burn!* as an extended allusion to Haiti's revolution, despite the fact that Gillo Pontecorvo's story is so abstracted from the historical and social context of events on Saint-Domingue as to be a loose comparison at best. *Lydia Bailey* therefore supports the conclusion that the only way for a US film to be made about Haiti is to create white heroes and construct the narrative around them.

Set in the early 1800s and based on the 1948 book of the same name by New England–based novelist Kenneth Roberts, *Lydia Bailey* begins with Albion Hamilton, a New England lawyer played by Dale Robertson. Working on the estate of a recently deceased business magnate, Hamilton finds himself falling in love with a small painting of the man's daughter. He contrives a plot in which he must gain the young Miss Bailey's signature in order to settle her father's estate and sets sail for Haiti to acquire it. Upon his arrival, the naive Hamilton ignores the advice of his ship's captain and goes ashore to locate Bailey. Wandering through the streets alone on an island poised on the edge of a French invasion, Hamilton is assaulted in an alleyway and is nearly killed before being rescued by the mysterious "King Dick," an English-speaking cosmopolitan Black man played by William Marshall. King Dick aids Hamilton in locating Bailey, but the American man soon finds himself mired in the machinations of various warring factions of Haitian revolutionaries preparing for an invasion of French forces.[11] With the assistance of King Dick, Hamilton succeeds in not only advising the leaders of the revolution, including Toussaint L'Ouverture, but also gaining Bailey's signature and finally her hand in marriage.

While Anne Francis, who played the lead female role, and Robertson were established actors in the early 1950s, *Lydia Bailey* was William Marshall's first film role. The film received positive reviews, and critics were impressed with Marshall and predicted that the tall, baritone-voiced actor would have a long and fruitful career. As King Dick, Marshall not only stole the show but also revived a fascinating character of Atlantic history for a new generation. The inclusion of King Dick as a character was first and foremost a pragmatic move by Roberts. The character's knowledge and diplomacy were necessary for the Hamilton character to fulfill his narrative arc, and screenwriters Philip Dunne and Michael Blankfort expanded the role of King Dick in the movie, giving him over forty minutes of screen time. As Marshall's first film role, *Lydia Baily* catapulted him from obscurity to Hollywood fame.

Unlike the characters of Lydia Bailey and Albion Hamilton, however, King Dick was based on a real person who may have been present in Haiti during the early nineteenth century. Richard "King Dick" or "Big Dick" Crafus first appeared in the historical record during the War of 1812. He was noted for his size and strength, and contemporary sources placed him as a leader among American prisoners of war held in Britain between 1813 and 1815. His origins were mysterious; no documents have been found to establish his origins with any certainty. Recent scholarship has written of Crafus as a palimpsest upon whom scholars and fiction writers alike have placed their images of Blackness and otherness in the Atlantic world, but in Jean Negulesco's 1952 film, he serves as both a critical character and an important vehicle for the plot's forward momentum.[12]

William Marshall's turn as King Dick in 1952 was also a celebrated element of the film's reception. White and Black critics alike praised his performance, but Black critics in particular enjoyed his screen time, noting how his performance challenged southern audiences' racial sensibilities. As Julian Mayfield recounted in his autobiographical manuscript some years later, Marshall's part was celebrated in no small part because "[Marshall] had actually been allowed to bang a white man over the head with a stick." Much to the delight of Mayfield and his contemporaries, the character of King Dick faced no comeuppance after he assaulted the two white men attempting to rob and murder the protagonist in an alleyway, a common result in films that featured Black-on-white violence at that time.[13] Marshall's King Dick also demonstrated savvy, expertise, and worldliness that contrasted with Hamilton's ignorance of the politics on Saint-Domingue and life beyond the confines of New England. While the character enters the picture as an untrustworthy guide, he turns out to be critical to not only Haiti's resistance to the French invasion but also Hamilton's love life.

African American critics were not the only ones to be charmed by the picaresque King Dick; the Haitian political and social elite also embraced him and the film in which he starred. The Haitian government of President Paul Eugène Magloire learned of the film as external shots of Haiti were being completed in late 1951. In preparation for the film's release the following May, Magloire offered to host the world premiere in Haiti's Palais National. Paramount Studios accepted the invitation, and in May 1952 actors William Marshall, Juanita Moore (who played Bailey's maid, Marie), and lead actress Anne Francis joined Negulesco on a chartered flight to the island. Upon arrival, Marshall joined Francis in an open limousine as the party made their way through the streets of Port-au-Prince. He later escorted the young white actress up the red carpet to join some nine hundred members of Haitian society in watching the premiere.

It is unclear if the film's ostensible star, Robertson, had been invited or if he had simply been unable to attend, but in providing an escort to Francis, Marshall did something that would have been impossible in New York or Los Angeles. Critic James L. Hicks joked in the *Cleveland Call and Post* that "Governor Talmadge of Georgia would have torn up his wool hat and red suspenders if he could have seen" the couple embrace and bow following the conclusion of the show.[14] In contrast, when the film premiered in New York in July, Francis was escorted into the theater by Robertson, with Marshall arriving alongside Moore, in line keeping with racial rules against showing even the hint of interracial relationships. Although it was possible to flout US racial norms in the periphery, doing so in the heart of the empire was not something that Marshall was able or perhaps willing to do.

Any racist criticisms of Marshall's role, however, were drowned out by praise for his performance. For the *Los Angeles Sentinel*'s film critic Hazel L. Lamarre, the film was "inspiring because somewhere, somehow the production staff captured the fire and the spirit of the Haitian revolutionists and portrayed it with respect and sincerity."[15] Lamarre was joined by others, including Walter White, head of the National Association for the Advancement of Colored People, who expressed their hope that the film's success would inspire further works that celebrated Black history and portrayed

African-descended peoples with dignitary and respect. Marshall, who had until that time been a stage actor, was immediately signed to a seven-year contract with Paramount and was featured in four midbudget films during the remainder of the decade, including *Demetrius and the Gladiators* and *Something of Value*. However, despite being well received by critics and filmgoers alike, *Lydia Bailey*'s clumsy approach to race, its perpetuation of racist stereotypes about Haiti, and the importance ascribed to the fictional Hamilton's efforts to the revolution itself did not endear the film to future audiences.

Largely forgotten today, the film is a footnote in the career of the book's author, Kenneth Roberts, and its breakout star, William Marshall. And although Marshall did not speak publicly about the film during his attempt to make *King Christophe*, letters to potential investors and friends suggest that his desire to tell the full story of the Haitian Revolution was born during his visit to Port-au-Prince. According to Marshall's correspondence, he began exploring his options for the project as early as 1964, the year he purchased the English rights to Aimé Césaire's *Le Tragedie du Roi du Christophe*. It was not until 1972, however, that Marshall was in a position to realize the project. Flush with financial success following the release of the vampire film *Blacula*, he began devoting more of his time to the then-unnamed project in earnest until Quinn's announcement forced his hand. In going public with his criticism, Marshall found that he was not alone in his opposition, nor was he the only African American who was actively pursuing such a project.

Black History Does Not Need Tony Quinn

Shortly after Quinn's appearance on *The Dick Cavett Show*, the campaign to dissuade Quinn from completing his project began in earnest. In June 1972, Ellen Holly penned an open letter critical of Quinn in the *New York Times* titled "Black History Does Not Need Tony Quinn." A star of the groundbreaking soap opera *One Life to Live*, in which she played a Black woman passing as an Italian American, Holly had been an outspoken critic of Hollywood racism for nearly a decade.[16] Her public chastisement of Quinn mirrored many of the arguments that Marshall had brought to the fore, but Holly's attack, published in the *New York Times*, drew far more attention to the subject. Both Marshall and Holly emphasized the denigrating and dehumanizing effects of blackface, the large number of skilled African American actors who could legitimately play the role, and the affront that Quinn's announcement was to Black audiences worldwide. But Holly also noted three other critiques that Marshall had not included: the power differential at work between a project helmed by Quinn versus one led by an African American woman (or man), the nature of film as a visual medium, and the assumption that Black history needed to be explained by white men.

Holly's confrontational missive began by asserting that African Americans were well aware of the double standards involved in Hollywood's reliance on white actors to play roles representing people of color. Declaring it "distressing" that Quinn would choose to play "one of the most remarkable single figure[s] in all of Black history" in blackface makeup, Holly asserted the importance of racial representation onscreen and the particular impact that visual media had. She argued that the continued existence of such a film would have an overall negative impact on generations of Black children who, in her mind, "would learn of [Christophe] for the first time from a screen image that presents him as a white man in makeup." More than simply a question of representation, it was the permanence of film as a physical medium that frustrated Holly. Finally, she attacked Quinn's assertion that if not for him, this history would remain neglected. Asserting that African Americans had a deep concern for their history, Holly demanded that Quinn show some sensitivity to the "emotional needs" of the Black community and find a Black actor to play the lead. Holly's letter, more so than Marshall's exchange, generated widespread opposition and a flurry of correspondence, almost all of them expressing reservations about the project or outright opposition to Quinn's proposed role.[17]

Quinn's response to Holly was as bitter as it was defensive. He argued that Hollywood's long-standing practice of placing white actors in makeup to play Arab, Mexican, and Sudanese characters gave him the right to wear blackface in order to play Christophe. He cited his own Mexican American heritage and the fact that Marlon Brando had played Mexican revolutionary Emilio Zapata in the 1952 Elia Kazan film *Viva Zapata!* without criticism by Quinn. However, Holly's and Marshall's criticisms of Quinn not only challenged Hollywood's shibboleths about the right of white men in makeup to play such roles but also made claims about the ability of these actors to play such roles with accuracy and realism. As broader arguments about representation, race, and constructing the past became clearer and more explicit, these debates also illustrated the private efforts of actors and writers to address racial inequality within and outside of Hollywood.

In September 1972, journalists Emily F. Gibson of the *Los Angeles Sentinel* and Pamela Haynes of the *New Pittsburgh Courier* answered Quinn's rhetorical question that had ended his response to Ellen Holly. In that piece, published in the *New York Times* in June, Quinn wrote to Holly that "[Christophe] has been a hero of mine long before you ever heard of him. I know his worth. I pray I will be worthy of the task. I am willing to accept the challenge. In short, if not me—who? If not now—when?"[18] Haynes, the author of a weekly column titled "Right On," opined that "when James Earl Jones can play Thomas Jefferson . . . without eyebrows being raised, then Anthony Quinn can play [whomever] the hell he wants to on screen."[19] Furthermore, she asserted that his motivation was primarily financial. "When you look at the booming Black film market, it is no surprise that Anthony Quinn wants to slide in and make his pile along with the rest." Financial motivations aside, Pamela Haynes lamented that it was a dark day if "we need a white man in Black face to teach us about revolution."[20]

Emily Gibson not only critiqued Quinn's project but also, in devoting two of her "Revolutionary Reflections" columns to the subject, investigated many of Quinn's claims. In an article published on September 20, Gibson wrote that the actor was financing a Haitian newspaper, *Haiti Hebdo*, to promote the project in Haiti and encourage support among Haitians.[21] She also interviewed Marshall, who told her that "we must do something so that we control the land we are living and functioning on and the lenses that mirror us in the eyes of the world. If not, we're going to continue to get very inferior interpretations of who we are."[22] Rejecting "inferior interpretations" of African Americans in art, Marshall's interview with Gibson also reflected Black nationalist sentiments with regard to land and control over the mechanisms of production. The controversy and criticism surrounding Quinn's project continued through the next year even as the project quietly disappeared from public view. No newspaper articles mention the project after the summer of 1973, and there was no information in the Hollywood trade press. Quinn's silence on the subject is total, however, as neither his official biography nor his autobiography of that time mentions the project at all. William Marshall's and Ellen Holly's campaign had worked, but in Marshall's case, it was only the beginning of a long and difficult road.

This narrative of the efforts to produce a film in the 1970s on the Haitian Revolution highlights how the influence of cultural nationalism encouraged Black writers and actors to work toward realizing projects focused on important elements of Black history. The debate over the representation of the historical figure of Christophe in Hollywood during that era widened existing fault lines in discussions over identity and representation even as they clarified for many the limits of how Black people were to be represented in film. However, one letter published in the *New York Times* highlights an oversight that few if any of the African American participants considered in their impassioned exchanges.

On July 9, 1972, the *New York Times* devoted its entire opinion page to a single question: "Should Tony Quinn Play a Black Man?" The printed responses from both white and Black Americans were uniformly critical of Quinn. There was also a brief letter from two Haitian men, Alix Mathieu and Pierre-Michel Fontaine. Mathieu and Fontaine expressed their pleasure at learning that Christophe's story was to be brought to the screen; however, they noted an important absence in the projects that had been publicly declared. "We are more than a little intrigued," their letter noted, "by the fact that neither Miss Holly nor Mr. Quinn touched upon one of the most fundamental issues contained in the controversy—the obvious fact that Christophe was a Haitian, that his story took place in Haiti and that, consequently, talented Haitians should have an opportunity to make a contribution to the movie if it is to carry a minimum of realism."[23]

Pointing out that neither Holly nor Quinn had indicated their intention to hire Haitian actors for important roles, Mathieu and Fontaine expressed their concern that this film was all too likely to repeat a common tale from Haitian history: the exploitation of Haitian culture by "enterprising Americans who would make money without any of that wealth benefiting Haitians."[24] In collapsing Black and white American identities into that of an imperial power, colonizer, and exploiter of Caribbean nations, Mathieu and Fontaine voiced a frustration that many in the African diaspora had with African American debates over race and power. In centering critiques of anti-Black racism and historical oppression on the experience of African Americans, many outside North America saw such criticisms as how the Pan-African ideal could be unmade by national and imperial realities. This attitude of American superiority, which Mayfield had himself criticized in editorials written while in Ghana, highlighted the limits of Pan-African thought and announcement of solidarity even as it purported to do otherwise. It is unknown what Marshall planned with regard to the hiring of Haitian actors and crew members, but it is unlikely that he would place his project in the hands of anyone but himself.

Christophe of Haiti

An accomplished stage actor and occasional director, Marshall had little experience writing, and so in mid-1972 he wrote to his old friend Julian

Mayfield and invited him to join Marshall as a writer on the nascent effort. Mayfield and Marshall had been friends since the late 1940s, when the two men had worked together in New York. Unsurprisingly, Mayfield jumped at the opportunity to work in Hollywood and immediately began to read deeply on Haiti's revolution and Henri Christophe. Christophe's rise from enslaved child to revolutionary general to monarch of the Kingdom of Haiti showed the power of revolutionary violence in fundamentally changing society. Mayfield also believed that Christophe's struggles to transform and modernize the Haitian economy were relevant to the contemporaneous efforts among newly independent West Indian and African nations.

Mayfield and Marshall's exchanges over the course of the project reflected the profound sense of potential that both men saw in this story. However, more than simply a historically relevant event, Haiti emerged from these letters as a cypher, a blank slate for Mayfield and Marshall to impose their vision of what a film about a slave revolt shot in the 1970s would mean for African Americans and African-descended peoples worldwide. As the revolution that indelibly altered the course of Caribbean history and set the tone for uprisings throughout the New World for nearly a century, the story of Haiti's revolution against the French Empire had long been a potent symbol of rebellion among Afro-diasporic writers. The revolution had also been a watchword for the dangers of unfettered Black rebellion against whites, a divisive subject in any era. Mayfield and Marshall thus believed that at a moment that had seen the articulation of "Black Power" as a slogan, celebrations of Blackness in film and song, and the rise of independent Black nations of the Caribbean and Africa presented the perfect opportunity—and audience—for this story of successful resistance to racial capitalism.

The significance of Haiti as the subject of Marshall and Mayfield's project and the timing of their attempt were the result of several factors. Marshall's own personal success and Quinn's announcement were two of the most significant, but anger at negative portrayals of African Americans on film had begun to generate interest among wealthy African Americans to fund films that resisted portraying African Americans in exploitative and demeaning ways. Additionally, according to Mayfield, the summer of 1973 was the perfect time for anyone interested in making film to make their play because of the ongoing strike of the Screenwriters Guild of America (SGA).[25] In a letter to Tom Feelings, Mayfield reported that the SGA was on strike in May, which slowed production to a crawl, and argued that "now was the time to prepare for the end of the strike when many projects would get off the ground that hadn't a chance before."[26]

Hoping to take advantage of any opportunities created by the strike, Mayfield and Cambridge made the long flight to Los Angeles from Georgetown to join Marshall and his partner, Sylvia Gussin, in writing the first draft of the script. According to Cambridge, Marshall personally appealed to the SGA to allow Mayfield to work on the Christophe project during the strike.[27] The compromise they reached allowed Mayfield to work on the film as long as he stayed confined to Marshall's home. This arrangement, which suited Mayfield just fine, allowed him to complete a first draft of a script in less than two months while Cambridge was able to enjoy Los Angeles, often accompanying Marshall and Gussin on jaunts around the city.

The resulting draft, tentatively titled "King Christophe," was more than simply a movie to Mayfield; it was a project that went to the very heart of Hollywood's pervasive white supremacy. When Mayfield came on board the project, he offered his thoughts on the difficulties in getting such a movie made that reflected a racial power gap in Hollywood. Racism aside, the failure of Black-themed films to come to fruition was evidence of a lack of will. The reason why Black actors, writers, and filmmakers had not succeeded in gaining power in Hollywood was that "when they sit down to make a movie . . . *they do not really believe they belong at the head of the conference table*," he wrote to Marshall. In contrast, Mayfield told Marshall that an "arrogant nigger (like you) who has the nerve to think he belongs at the head of the conference table . . . is in danger and will be continually thwarted."[28] Despite his awareness of the overwhelming odds against the realization of such a production, Mayfield threw himself fully behind it, finishing the first draft of the screenplay in six weeks.

Following his return to Guyana, Mayfield penned a follow-up missive in which he emphasized the primary objectives of his script, now in the midst of a second draft. The story, he argued, should further humanize Christophe, especially in his troubled relationships with his family, the administrators who carried out his edicts, and his relationship with Haiti's impoverished peasantry. Mayfield also pressed Marshall to allow him to write a treatment that, he argued, would better allow Marshall to sell the project to the investors in the United States.[29] This treatment clearly articulated Mayfield's idea of what the film should look like and what purpose it was to serve. Mayfield declared that "the story of Christophe is also the story of the Haitian Revolution," and the treatment also asserted that Christophe was not simply Black but also that he and his comrades in arms were in fact men and women from Africa.[30] Mayfield believed that a combination of novelty and the relevance of the story would sell this project, and he repeatedly emphasized how the format of film, with its stunning visuals and accompanying musical score, would provide a splendid account of the revolution in visual form. Buoyed by an unshakable sense of purpose, he asserted that the picture "cannot fail because it is entirely new, shattering all precedents and reaching far beyond the horizons of so-called 'Black' motion pictures." Mayfield asked rhetorically, "Why make a movie about Christophe?" His answer was that "it's one hell of a story, and it's never been told before."[31]

In early 1974, Mayfield presented his friend and patron with the second draft of *Christophe*. The revised script remained melodramatic and dialogue-heavy, and like much of Mayfield's fiction, was character-driven. The supporting cast were composites of historical actors, which allowed him to discuss the social, economic, and political themes that drove his character's actions. Rather than explore these themes within the limitations of existing historical figures, such as the well-documented Baron de Vastery, one of Christophe's most important advisers, Mayfield introduced enough fiction into the story to allow him to convey the lessons he had gleaned from his time working for leaders of the postcolonial nations of Ghana and Guyana, which he believed would be instructive and useful for modern-day leaders.

Much to Marshall's frustration, Mayfield's second draft continued to sacrifice facts in service of a good story. The Christophe who emerged from the scripts was a dynamic, violent, and unpredictable ruler whose lofty goals were ultimately laid low by hubris. Yet in the midst of his violence and inhumanity toward the citizens of Haiti, Mayfield's Christophe was simultaneously a visionary leader who looked not five years but instead a century into the future. Haiti, Christophe realized, would remain impoverished unless it participated in the world economy on equitable grounds. Without its own economic power—and its own financial capital—its destiny would remain in the hands of European bankers and European armies. The "symphonic" plot combined this kind of relevant historical knowledge with drama, action, scenes of brutalization, and a special emphasis on epic battle sequences, a combination of factors designed to attract a wide variety of filmgoers. The script examined the motivation for Christophe's appalling acts of barbarism and the reasoning behind the reenslavement of the Haitian people for what amounted to financial gain for the state. Acknowledging Christophe's flaws, Mayfield presented a man driven to liberate his people from white rule by any means necessary even if it meant Haitian leadership enslaving Black citizens.

The script opened and closed on the events of 1820, and flashbacks covered Christophe's arrival in Haiti as a young African torn from his mother's embrace, his early life as a slave, his rise to a respectable position as the head chef of a Cap Haitien hotel, and his decision to join Toussaint L'Ouverture and Jean-Jacques Dessalines in their effort to free Haiti from French rule. The choice of events portrayed, however, revealed that *King Christophe* was no morality play. At its core it was an unflinching portrait of power, Blackness, and masculinity in the age of revolutions. Mayfield was driven to present a nuanced and historically accurate portrait of a deeply flawed Black man facing an impossible situation not of his own making. By offering a violent despot as the product of the brutal history of colonization and enslavement, Mayfield's script could be read as justification of the actions that Christophe took in Haiti but offered context and motivation and a realistic account of the consequences of Christophe's brutality. Rather than a rehabilitation, *King Christophe* was a recognition of the titular character's personal history, his impact on the world, and commentary on the society from which he had emerged.

King Christophe's central problem—and the focus of Mayfield's script—was the king's belief in the importance of creating a new nation on the ruins of the French colony of Saint-Domingue. Christophe's inability to construct new modes of production or to transform the political organization beyond a repudiation of colonial anti-Blackness and a resistance to European-dominated enslavement was the central problem faced by the protagonist. As those who have historicized Christophe have noted, the king not only continued with Toussaint L'Ouverture and Jean-Jacques Dessalines's emphasis on large-scale plantation agriculture, primarily through forced labor, but also took his plans a step further by modeling the new government of the Kingdom of Haiti upon the system of an absolutist European monarchy, in contrast to the rival democratic Republic of Haiti that dominated the southwestern portion of the island.[32]

In contextualizing Henri Christophe for Marshall's movie, Mayfield's written correspondence alluded to his previous support for Kwame Nkrumah and implicitly supported his ongoing work for Forbes Burnham, leaders who both attempted to remake the economic and political basis of their respective nations after achieving independence.[33] In particular, the Christophe of Mayfield's script argues with his advisers that his people need to think like Haitians and not like Europeans. Mayfield's Christophe also reflects on the nature of power and the difficulty of being a Black king in a white world. *King Christophe* was more than an epic historical drama; Mayfield's script sought to explain and contextualize the actions of contemporary authoritarian leaders in Africa and the Caribbean, making sense of their aims and the measures they undertook to preserve their national sovereignty even in the face of transnational ideologies such as Pan-Africanism.

After Mayfield submitted his second draft in the summer of 1975, William Marshall's response confirmed that the two men were no longer aligned in their vision for the film. In August 1975, Marshall wrote to Mayfield with significant criticisms. "Let us not violate historical fact," wrote Marshall, referencing Mayfield's decision to take liberties with Christophe's story in service of a more compelling narrative.[34] Marshall's objections were many, but one of the most significant was that King Christophe's death was no longer by his own hand. In October 1820 as a mob of armed peasants gathered in the shadows of his palace, the real King Christophe committed suicide—in some sources by silver bullet—rather than be killed by his own people.[35] Mayfield's script instead envisioned the aged Christophe, paralyzed by a stroke and wracked with disease, demanding to be dressed in his military uniform and placed on his horse so that he could ride against the mob and die a warrior's death in battle. This was not Mayfield's only deviation from historical fact, but Marshall indicated in this letter that this particular challenge to historicity had gone too far. "We believe," Marshall wrote, speaking for himself and his partner, Sylvia Gussin, "that neither of the first drafts enhances the chances of winning support for the production" and claimed that they had not used either of two completed scripts in their efforts to obtain funding from investors.

Calling Mayfield's thoughtful, if long-winded, discourse on the moral contradiction between the slave economy and revolutionary democratic ideology an "unacceptable evasion" of Christophe's story, Marshall emphasized that "gratuitous fictions are of no use to us." After a brief note about the legalities of ownership and rights, Marshall concluded his letter with a statement that clarified the end of the working relationship. Since Mayfield had been paid according to the terms agreed upon, the scripts and work now belonged to Marshall. Despite parting ways, Marshall ended the letter on a hopeful note, declaring that "a friendship that can take the wear and tear of movie-making is a friendship indeed."[36] Marshall and Mayfield did remain friends through the remainder of Mayfield's life, but they declined to work with one another again. Unable to secure funding from Black community leaders and artists despite personal appeals to Berry Gordy and publisher John H. Johnson, Marshall was eventually forced to drop the project completely. Despite a long career in Hollywood, Marshall never wavered from his commitment to celebrating Black history and Black achievement. In spite of repeated setbacks, he continued to demand dignified, historically relevant roles and, when those did not exist, create them for himself.

The end of the *King Christophe* project was Julian Mayfield's last attempt at making a motion picture. It also coincided with his final return to the United States. As detailed in chapter 8, fears over the poor reception of his biography of Forbes Burnham prompted Mayfield and Cambridge to hurriedly depart Guyana in December 1975. Settling in Takoma Park, Maryland, near Washington, DC, Mayfield once again began pursuing employment that would make use of his writing talents. In 1976, he won a Fulbright Fellowship and spent the 1976–77 school year in West Germany and Turkey with Cambridge. Correspondence indicated that Mayfield found teaching abroad enervating, and he and Cambridge enjoyed the travel opportunities they had while in Central and Southern Europe. Following their return to the United States in 1977, however, opportunities began to dry up, and Mayfield once again found himself seeking creative outlets for his political art.

Epilogue

I Am Not Resigned, 1976–1984

I am not resigned to the shutting away of loving hearts in the hard ground.
So it is, and so it will be, for so it has been, time out of mind:
Into the darkness they go, the wise and the lovely. Crowned
With lilies and with laurel they go; but I am not resigned.

—Edna St. Vincent Millay, 1928

The years between 1977 and 1984 were mostly characterized by economic privation and frustration for Julian Mayfield. Despite his impressive résumé and his wealth of connections, he struggled to find regular work following his return from Guyana. Initially, he turned to journalism and wrote for a series of small newspapers in the Washington, DC, area, including the *Washington North Star* and *Time Capsule*, with intentions to start his own paper. However, Mayfield was unable to make ends meet as a working journalist and reluctantly returned to teaching. He was hired at the University of Maryland, College Park, in 1977 and taught there until 1979. Much like his time at SUNY Courtland and New York University, he focused on African American literature and the impact of Black writers on history. In 1979, he was hired by Howard University and later made writer-in-residence. There he would remain for the last four years of his life.

Despite his frustration with the precarious nature of his employment and the chronic underfunding of Howard's English Department, Mayfield's classes, such as "American Negro Literature" and "Twentieth Century American Literature," were popular among students. His creative writing workshops even more so. One of his former students, the African and African American studies professor Wahneema Lubiano, spoke highly of Mayfield and the courses he taught. She described him as "intellectually and pedagogically generous" and considered his teachings and his support fundamental to her move to Stanford and the completion of her PhD. "Julian," she recalled, "was part of what made me realize that I could be an intellectual and political at the same time, that I did not have to slip off the mantle of one to be the other, and that living a life doing work that was an intertwining of the two was not only possible but beautifully enjoyable."[1] A nontraditional student, Lubiano was already in her twenties when she took classes with Mayfield. In 1981, she was accepted in Stanford's PhD program in African American studies and relocated to California. Despite the distance, the two exchanged regular letters and cards until the end of his life.

It was not just students who valued Mayfield's politics at Howard. During his time as writer-in-residence, he worked closely with Eugenia Collier and aided in the struggle against the administration's destructive budget cuts and low pay for adjunct faculty. In spite of a punishing workload, Mayfield continued to demonstrate his commitment to writing fiction and revisited his memoirs. In 1981, he once again began revising his autobiography. He gave it a new title, "Which Way Does the Blood River Run," and again submitted it to publishers. He also began revising many of the sections on Ghana into "Tales of the Lido," a collection of vignettes from his time in West Africa, that he hoped to market as a first-person travel memoir. That piece went through multiple revisions during this period, although he told friends that he would have to spend time in Ghana in order to finish it. He also wrote several short stories, none of which made it to publication. Numerous rejections, few prospects, and his commitment to writing in spite of his other activities took their toll on his relationships and his health, as friends and relatives repeatedly urged him to eat better and drink less.

In 1982 Mayfield's father, Hudson Mayfield, passed away at the age of seventy-six. Later that same year Julian's paternal uncle, J. C., died in Greer. Together with his sister Dorothy (Dot) and his mother, Mayfield drove down to South Carolina in August to attend the funeral. There, he took the time to reconnect with his southern family and began a brief journal in a composition notebook. Visiting where he had lived as a small child and meeting his now middle-aged cousins made him marvel at the changes Greer had undergone in his absence. With great amusement, he recounted how he and his sister Dot even saw a white man jogging on the streets of Greer, a shocking development at a time when exercise remained a largely urban phenomenon. "Under most conditions we permit whites their peculiarities," he reasoned, noting that white Americans had never lived "under the gun" as their Black neighbors had.[2]

Mayfield was overwhelmed with memories and familiar faces. His recounting of the experience reflected his thoughts on his own mortality as well as his life of activism and travel. "Once upon a time in the 1960s, I set out to discover my roots," he wrote on the first page of the journal and "discovered it could be a dangerous preoccupation."[3] Summing up thirty-five years of activism, journalism, and artistic creation, Mayfield mused on his life, minimizing his accomplishments in favor of what he had not yet done. Unsurprisingly, the trip also prompted him to consider the possibility of retirement. He looked into purchasing land in the Sea Islands or elsewhere in South Carolina's Low Country, with the intention of living out his life among other southern Black people. Marveling at his South Carolina relatives and their apparently uncomplicated lives, Mayfield returned to Washington and teaching with a newfound appreciation for what was possible for him. But despite this apparent peace with his past, his pen remained as sharp as ever when it came to the treatment of Black people, in the Americas and elsewhere.

In April 1984, Mayfield was invited to join an ongoing conversation in the *Washington Post* about the relationship between Blackness and Americanness. The controversy had begun in February when Democratic Party candidate Rev. Jesse Jackson had derisively referred to the American Jewish community as "hymies" and complained to aides about the difficulties of campaigning and fundraising in "hymietown" (New York). A young Black reporter named Milton Coleman, although not the intended audience of those remarks, reported them to his editors, who published them in a larger story about African Americans and Jewish Americans in the 1980s. The resulting article stirred up a hornet's nest of criticism aimed at Jackson, and the self-styled "prophet on a political mission" found himself on the defensive. The remarks also strained tensions among African American and Jewish American constituencies within the Democratic Party still smarting from the explosive 1981 runoff election between Atlanta mayor Andrew Young and Jewish state legislator Sidney Marcus.[4]

Jackson responded by lashing out at reporters and questioned the journalistic ethics of Coleman and the *Washington Post*.[5] During an appearance on *Face the Nation* with reporter Leslie Stahl a week later, Jackson denied that he made the remarks and agreed to a meeting between the candidate and the editors of the *Post*. According to reports, the tense meeting included the revelation that Coleman was the source of the quotations. Eight days later on February 27, Jackson gave a speech at the Temple Adath Yeshurun, where he apologized for the remarks. "In part, I am to blame," Jackson explained to the four hundred worshippers at the Syracuse, New York, synagogue, and "for that, I am deeply distressed."[6] Unfortunately for Jackson, the damage had been done. Despite a strong showing in the primaries, where Jackson received 18.2 percent of the votes, he lost the nomination to Walter Mondale in July, signaling the end of Jackson's first presidential run.[7]

The controversy over Jackson's remarks, however, did not dissipate after his apology. Instead, what had begun as a conversation about the relations between African Americans and American Jews soon morphed into a broader discussion about the responsibilities of Black reporters in reporting on Black political leaders. After the Nation of Islam's Louis Farrakhan came to Jackson's defense and called Coleman a "no-good, filthy traitor," veteran African American reporter Carl T. Rowan took to the editorial page of the *Washington Post* to criticize Farrakhan for his remarks. At issue for Rowan was the journalistic ethics of African American reporters, of which he was one of the most senior. Farrakhan, Rowan wrote, was "trying to hold black journalists to a standard of stupid, self-destructive racism" in his attacks on Coleman.[8] No Black reporter, Rowan continued, "has a special obligation to swallow and forget whatever is said in error by a political candidate who is black."[9] On April 15, civil rights lawyer William M. Kunstler and South African writer Clive Leeman weighed in with support for Jackson, distinguishing between the candidate's offhanded remarks and Farrakhan's violent invective, all the while opposing Rowan's call for journalistic colorblindness.

In April an interviewer asked Mayfield, as a regular contributor to the *Washington Post*'s editorial page, to answer whether Jackson and Coleman should consider themselves "Black First or American First." Mayfield's response, "Sorting Us Out," began in familiar fashion with a personal anecdote. "My first three days in the Army were very integrated," Mayfield recalled, describing his train ride to Alabama from Washington, where he played poker with white and Black recruits on integrated train cars. But upon arrival "a tough-looking little white sergeant hardly looked up from his clipboard as he grumbled, 'All right. White troops over heah. Nigra troops over theah.' Reality had set in again." There was little point, Mayfield argued, in asking Jesse Jackson or any other Black person in politics or journalism whether they were Black or American first, because the white questioners were the ones who "know whether Jackson is the black candidate, or an American candidate that happens to be black." If they were forced to respond to this "dumb question," African Americans may demand to "know if there is a contradiction" between their Blackness and their Americanness. "If the answer is yes, they will, of necessity, have to choose blackness."[10] The "choice" of Blackness was, Mayfield revealed, no choice at all but rather a calculated decision that bore the weight of centuries of racism, oppression, and violence. There was no choice in whether or not a person could be Black; there was only the decision to claim it with pride or attempt to distance oneself from it out of fear.

In a final rejoinder to the debate over Jesse Jackson's Blackness versus his Americanness, Julian Mayfield once again wrote to the *Washington Post*; this time it was in response to a column by journalist Joseph Kraft. In that column, Kraft castigated Jackson, calling him "an affront to the white majority." Rather than continuing to defend Jackson, Mayfield instead turned his attention to Kraft, denouncing the columnist for his attacks on Jackson and for giving readers "a refresher course in the arrogant assumptions of white superiority." For Mayfield, it appeared that Rev. Jesse Jackson had the permission of whites to "raise hell about civil rights at home, but when he is seen talking to presidents, premiers and prime ministers, whites are justified in suspecting that he may be talking about something as important as power."[11] Kraft and other critics of Jackson were seemingly unwilling to acknowledge that what Kraft was talking about was the limits of Black political power. Power, the connective tissue that united the far-flung elements of portions of Mayfield's intellectual, artistic, and activist life, could not ever be discounted wherever race was being discussed.

Colorblindness, Mayfield concluded, remained as improbable a solution to white supremacy in 1984 as it had in 1959. That year he had cautioned Black writers to avoid submerging themselves in the American mainstream and acquiescing to the psychological demands of whiteness. Twenty-five years later, a still frustrated Mayfield refused once again to yield, arguing that his Blackness remained inseparable from his identity—and the identifies of millions of others—as an American. The problem, as he described it, was that white Americans did not regard him as a fellow citizen unless he gave up his claims to that Black identity. It was only when Black men chose to operate within a narrow political schema that did not upset the entrenched white power structure that they could be fully accepted. While the United States may have made strides in diminishing public articulations of racism and while some institutional racism had lessened in the quarter century that elapsed between these two arguments, the political, economic, and cultural realities of American racial identity remained distressingly intact.

In early October 1984, Julian Mayfield was admitted to the Coronary Unit at Washington Adventist Hospital in Takoma Park, Maryland, after suffering a major heart attack. Messages of support poured in from friends and family, but after several weeks in intensive care, he passed away on

October 20, 1984. "The Giant That Many Overlooked" was dead at the age of fifty-six.[12] Three weeks after his death, his widow Joan Cambridge wrote a letter to the *Washington Post* to complain about Ronald Reagan, recently reelected as president. "I will not speak for my husband," the typed letter read, "I only know that Ronald Reagan had best mind how he tramples the rights and lives of the people Julian Mayfield loved and defended for his entire life, or the President will find himself plagued by one hell of a revolt among the ancestral spirits now [that] Mayfield has joined them."[13] Even gone, Mayfield's voice and acerbic critique of white supremacy and its champions lived on in those he loved.

In a 1979 interview conducted by Harriet Jackson Scarupa, Julian Mayfield had reiterated his abiding interest in power to the young journalist. "I have got, I am certain, a certain power fixation. I am fascinated now and have been for many years by Black people who wield power—to any extent." Power, for Mayfield, served as a shorthand for the interconnected nature of politics and art, Blackness and Americanness, and how people identified themselves and contested those identities thrust upon them. Power was the solution to the oppression of African-descended peoples and would, he believed, come only to those who sought it out.

Acknowledgments

One thing that I had not anticipated when writing this book was the difficulties associated with writing a section addressing the generosity of people who have aided me on this long journey. It is no exaggeration when I say that this has been the hardest section thus far to write as I am deeply indebted to many, many people. It is my sincere hope that I am able to thank all of them personally, and if I have overlooked anyone it is out of forgetfulness and not malice.

First and foremost, I am grateful to my dissertation committee. Adriane Lentz-Smith, my chair, was generous with her knowledge, probing questions, incisive analysis, and thoughtful comments as if she had been my adviser since the beginning of my journey toward a PhD. She pushed me to be a better thinker and a more deliberate writer and is perhaps most responsible for the historian I am today. Sally Deutsch served as both a sounding board for ideas and a thoughtful, considerate critic in our conversations as I stumbled my way to completion, her many insights pepper this volume. Ronald Williams, who began as a mentor and has become a dear friend, pushed me to better grapple with the complexities and nuances of writing Black intellectual histories of the recent past while refusing to let me rest on my laurels. Tim Tyson's work was my introduction to Julian Mayfield, and this provision of a model for how biography can best be marshaled in the service of writing better history was both inspirational and practical. The support and assistance of teacher, writer, and researcher Bill Chafe over the years has never wavered. In our many discussions, he has been a sounding board and a valuable resource for writing better history. I am most grateful for my dissertation committee's patience and time in shepherding me through this process.

The Department of History at Duke University was my home for eight years, and I owe so much to everyone whose efforts helped me along the way. Special thanks go to John Martin, Robin Ennis Pridgen, Cynthia Hoglen, Phil Stern, and Jamie Hardy for their administrative and practical support in this graduate program. Pete Sigal, who has been a tireless cheerleader and indefatigable supporter in my journey, is owed a great debt. Through my early courses with Jolie Olcott and John French, I was introduced to the rigorous training of historical research, and with the assistance of Nancy McLean, Bruce Hall, Laurent Dubois, and Malachai Hacohen, I was able to gain practical experience in the subdisciplines of history, which formed the basis of my historical practices and methodologies. Despite my lack of formal study with Jan Ewald, Ray Gavins, and Thavolia Glympth, my work has nevertheless benefited from their probing, thoughtful questions and casual discussions over the years. Thank you all.

When I arrived at Duke, I found myself surrounded by not one but three cohorts of colleagues and friends who shared the difficulties and joys of graduate school with me. My thanks go to Caroline Garriot for her warmth, kindness, and generosity of spirit and to Liz Shesko for the green couch and for all of her moral support. Ashley Elrod's and Ashley Young's presence during our difficult slack-based writing efforts will not be forgotten. I also want to thank Jon Free, Claire Payton, Ryan Poe, Tina Davidson, Valerie Wade, Mandy Cooper, Mandy Hughett, Christy Mobley, Meggan Farish Cashwell, Dan Papsdorf, Stephanie Rytilahti, Yuridia Ramirez, Rachel Bessner, Tina Davidson, Tiffany Holland, Will Goldsmith, and Jes Malitoris for their comments, thoughts, and assistance with both my earliest drafts and the germination of many ideas. Ayanna Legros, Artie Braswell, and Josh Strayhorn provided me with insightful comments and helped generate many changes to the final manuscript, and last but certainly not least, I thank Bryan Pitts and Ahab for always being there when I needed a friend (or two).

In the aftermath of graduate school, I was fortunate enough to move quickly into a postdoctoral position at the Samuel DuBois Cook Center on Social Equity. My thanks go to Sandy Darity for providing me with an intellectual home for four exciting years. Thanks also to Gwen Wright, Joanne O'Neal Gray, Keisha Bentley Edwards, and Aaron Colston for making that postdoc position a generative and exciting place to be. To my many friends in the African American Intellectual History Society—Ashley Farmer, Keisha Blaine, Ibram Kendi, Charisse Burden-Stelly, Charles McKinney, and Sandy Placído—thank you all so much for your openness and your presence. Special thanks to Andrew Rosa for guiding my hand in the Schomburg Center for Research in Black Life Reading Room in the summer of 2015 and making sure I read all of Julian Mayfield's autobiography before I went home that day.

I don't think it is unfair to say that without archivists, historians are merely writers. For that reason, I want to thank the many dedicated archivists and librarians whose assistance and labor is present in this dissertation. At the Schomburg Center for Research in Black Life, Steven Fullwood and a superlative team of archivists have made that library a necessary destination for all modern historians. Thank yous are due to the staff at the Robert W. Woodruff Library at Atlanta University Center, especially Andrea Jackson and to David Fort, David Langbart, Stephanie Coon, Christina Jones, and the rest of the staff at the National Archives and Record Administration in College Park who have always been available and helpful. Their vast knowledge informed my own dives into US government documents. Thank you to Kerrie Williams at the Auburn Avenue Research Library for trusting my untrained hands with unprocessed papers, and thank you to Joellen ElBashir and the fine staff at the Moorland-Spingarn Reading Room at Howard University for always pointing me in the direction I needed to go.

The community of scholars is not the only community I owe debts to. In moving to Durham to pursue my PhD studies at Duke, I found a community beyond the History Department that nevertheless contributed to my work and my writing. Thank you to Sarah Almond, Lindsay Andrews, Alec Ferrell, everyone at Nido Durham, and the hardworking baristas at the Joe Van Gogh Coffee Roastery for innumerable conversations and discussions. Thank you to the Gray family—David,

Roxanne, Hudson, Archer, and Cohen—for the frequent use of your spare bedroom. I also want to thank the Fowler family—Shaun, Chandra, Pierce, and Rowan—for their wonderful hospitality whenever I found myself in Atlanta. Joel Ross, Thomas Ross, and Jessica Ross, thank you for always having a bed for me in Washington. To Abbey, Charles, and Jason Graf, friends like you are hard to come by. Thank you for always making time for us. Candice Moore offers more than just coffee and kind words, and I thank her so much for her support. I also thank Kathryn Marsden for her long friendship and willingness to commiserate. I don't think either of us ended up where we expected to be, but it's been a fun ride, nonetheless.

One of my only disappointments is that Marilyn B. Young, whose mentorship at New York University was the reason I ended up at Duke, did not live to see the completion of this project. Marilyn's support as a professor, a thesis adviser, a confidant, and a sounding board of an older student who was far too confident for his own good will not be forgotten.

Through my comrade Sandy Placído, I was fortunate enough to make the acquaintance of Rafael Mayfield, Emiliano's son Julian Hudson Mayfield, and Joan Cambridge. I am deeply indebted to all of them. Without their support and many conversations, I do not think this book would have been written. In particular, my 2018 visit to Georgetown, Guyana, gave me insights into that nation's role in the broader discourse on Pan-Africanism and Black nationalism that helped me better understand both.

Without a doubt, my biggest cheerleaders during the last decade have been my family. I want to thank Therese McKinney, Steven Tyroler, and Lee Spector for welcoming me into their family and giving me support and love. My sister, Megan Gosma, and her family—Jimmy, Jackson, Camden, and Hudson—have never faltered in their support. Rae Stein's editorial eye was much appreciated on earlier drafts, and I thank her and Barry Stein for a lifetime of support and love. My parents, Helene and Doug Romine, were my first teachers, and their support has been foundational at every step of the way. I lack the words to properly thank them for all that they have done for me. Thank you for giving me life, and thank you for never discouraging me in my desire to know more.

To Seb, who preceded this project, and to Desmond, who arrived shortly after it began in earnest, being your father has been the most challenging, humbling, joyful, and important job that I have ever taken on. Seb, by dint of his age, became a remarkably effective cheerleader in the final months and never stopped encouraging me to finish this project. Desi's presence and eagerness to understand the world humble me every day. I am so glad that both of you exist.

Finally, there is no one in the world who deserves more credit than Lis Tyroler for the completion of this project. Since my first tentative steps in 2010 to the writing of this acknowledgments section, she has been beside me. As a partner and a spouse, she has never faltered on a single step of this journey, never yielding in her support and always there to pick me up when I fell. Not only is she a partner in life, but she is also a valuable interlocutor, an insightful critic, and a seemingly bottomless wellspring of emotional support. For those reasons, and many more, this book is dedicated to her.

Notes

Introduction

1. Hollie I. West, "The Goal of Julian Mayfield: Fusing Art and Politics," *Washington Post*, July 7, 1975, B1.

2. Mayfield, "Into the Mainstream and Oblivion," in *The American Negro Writer*, 29–30.

3. "The American Negro Writer and His Roots" was sponsored by the American Society of African Culture and took place at the Henry Hudson Hotel in Midtown Manhattan between February 28 and March 1, 1959. See Mayfield, *The American Negro Writer*; and Lorraine Hansberry, "The Negro Writer and His Roots: Toward a New Romanticism," *Black Scholar* 12, no. 2 (March–April 1981): 2–12.

4. Mayfield, "Into the Mainstream," 31.

5. Mayfield, 30.

6. Minter, Hovey, and Cobb, *No Easy Victories*, 115.

7. Julian Mayfield, "Basner Misses Malcolm X's Point," *Ghanaian Times*, May 19, 1964, 2.

8. This claim of the use of archive is asserted by Mayfield's second wife, Joan Cambridge, but is borne out in discussions with archivists at the Schomburg. See Joan Cambridge, "Remembering Maya Angelou," *Stabroek News*, June 6, 2014, www.stabroeknews.com/2014/opinion/letters/06/06/remembering-maya-angelou/. Mayfield figures prominently in the most comprehensive historical portrait of the Black cultural Left in Harlem during the 1940s and 1950s, Welch, "Black Art and Activism in New York, 1950–1965," PhD diss. As a founding member of the Fair Play for Cuba Committee, Mayfield is cited in Gosse, *Where the Boys Are*; Reitan, *Rise and Decline of an Alliance*; and Young, *Soul Power*. For studies of Black Power, see Tyson, *Radio Free Dixie*; and Peniel Joseph, "Waiting till the Midnight Hour: Reconceptualizing the Heroic Period of the Civil Rights Movement, 1954–1965," *Souls: A Critical Journal of Black Politics, Culture, and Society* 2 (2000): 6–17. For Black literature and film, see Munby, *Under a Bad Sign*; Sieving, *Soul Searching*; and Jackson, *The Indignant Generation*.

9. Hanchard, *Party/Politics*, 8.

10. William J. Maxwell's literary analysis of these FBI files, which considers the FBI's response to modern Black American writing as a counterliterature, is especially instructive of how anti-Black racism combined with antiradicalism and anticommunism to produce the FBI's interest in Black writing from the 1920s until the 1970s. See Maxwell, *F.B. Eyes*, 12–13.

11. See Walter B. Rideout's foreword in Cook and Henderson, *Militant Black Writer in Africa*.

Chapter 1

1. Julian Mayfield, "Autobiographical Manuscript," Julian Mayfield Papers, Schomburg Center for Research in Black Culture, New York Public Library (hereafter SCH, JMP), box 15, folder 9, 82. Mayfield's fragmentary autobiographical manuscript exists in two distinct phases with two titles. The first title was "Which Way Does the Blood Red River Run?" and was begun in January or February 1969. The other, "Send Me My Grandmother!," reflected attempted revisions in 1971 and 1982. These fragments at the Schomburg run over two hundred pages, but substantial pieces of the autobiography are missing, including a section from Mayfield's childhood, his time in Puerto Rico, his time in Ghana, and his work on the Paramount film *Uptight*. The location of these missing sections remains unknown.

2. Mayfield, "Autobiographical Manuscript," 82–83.

3. Ultimately, the men "found lodgings with a little old black lady who was afraid she was overcharging us at fifty cents a day." See Mayfield, "Autobiographical Manuscript," 83.

4. Mayfield's account of the incident in his autobiographical manuscript claimed that the reason for the stop was that some of the actors had made a joke about smoking marijuana while at a restaurant on Sunset Boulevard. Their comments were apparently overheard by a police informant, and the group was stopped under suspicion of narcotics trafficking. Mayfield's experience jibes with other interracial groups during that time period, such that even in spaces where the color line was not enforced with violence, interracial groups were suspect. See Mayfield, "Autobiographical Manuscript," 82.

5. Neville Brand was then a former GI and up-and-coming actor who would later go on to play a series of tough guys and villains, such as Al Capone in the short-lived TV series *The Untouchables* (1959–61) and *The George Raft Story* (1961), the henchman Chester in *D.O.A.* (1949), and Duke in *Stalag 17* (1953). Brand died in 1992 at the age of seventy-one. See "Death Takes Tough-Guy Actor Neville Brand, 71," *The Bulletin*, April 19, 1992; "Private Service Planned for Neville Brand," *Los Angeles Times*, April 19, 1992, 13; and Hannsberry, *Bad Boys*.

6. Edward Escobar, a professor of Chicana/o studies at Arizona State University, has conducted extensive research into the relationship between Mexican Americans and the LAPD. In his accounts, Chicanos and the LAPD had a long-standing antagonistic relationship with violence, harassment, and sexual assault. Escobar makes no mention of Mexican Americans working within the LAPD, but contemporary newspaper accounts suggest that there were a handful of Mexican American police officers on the force dating back to the 1910s and 1920s, including one Joseph J. Romero Jr., who was killed in the line of duty in 1919. I am unable to find reliable statistics or demographic information relating to race and the LAPD with regard to Mexican Americans and thus am unable to identify this officer. See Edward J. Escobar, "Bloody Christmas and the Irony of Police Professionalism: The Los Angeles Police Department, Mexican Americans, and Police Reform in the 1950s," *Pacific Historical Review* 72, no. 2 (2003): 171–99; and Escobar, *Race, Police, and Political Identity*.

7. See Hughes, *I Wonder as I Wander*; Lacy, *Rise and Fall of a Proper Negro*; Fuller, *Journey to Africa*; Himes, *The Quality of Hurt*; Baraka, *Autobiography of Leroi Jones/Amiri Baraka*; Angelou, *All God's Children Need Traveling Shoes*; and Murray, *Song in a Weary Throat*. Although not an autobiography in a strict sense, Fuller's *Journey to Africa* was derived in part from his unpublished autobiographical manuscript, housed at Robert W. Woodruff Library of the Atlanta University Center.

8. W. E. B. Du Bois, "My Evolving Program for Negro Freedom," in Logan, *What the Negro Wants*, 37–38.

9. Lewis, *W. E. B. Du Bois*, 56–57.

10. The long civil rights movement thesis takes its name from historian Jacquelyn D. Hall's essay "The Long Civil Rights Movement and the Political Uses of the Past," *Journal of American History* 91, no. 4 (March 2005): 1233–63. Additionally, historian Robert Korstad has argued that the "civil rights unionism" of the 1930s and 1940s was not "just a precursor of the modern [civil rights movement]. It was its first phase." Robert O. Self argued that the 1954–65 framework minimized the impact of the "black radical tradition" and foregrounded the liberal Black political activists of the era, many of whom were anticommunist. Self also contends that this "long movement" was extant in both national and international politics. In general, the "long movement" thesis is useful for tracing the development of ideas, strategies, and tactics as well as the ways that intergenerational organizing had an important impact on the civil rights movement. See Self, *American Babylon*. However, as Cha-Jua and Lang point out, the necessity of periodization for historical analysis and the role of regional difference point to the limitations of the "long movement" thesis. See Sundiata Cha-Jua and Clarence Lang, "The 'Long Movement' as Vampire: Temporal and Spatial Fallacies in Recent Black Freedom Studies," *Journal of African American History* 92, no. 2 (Spring 2007): 265–88. For more on the "long movement" thesis and the connections between the Old Left and the civil rights movement of the 1950s and 1960s, see Korstad, *Civil Rights Unionism*; Hall, "The Long Civil Rights Movement and the Political Uses of the Past"; Theoharis and Woodward, eds., *Freedom North*; Theoharis and Woodard, eds., *Groundwork*; Countryman, *Up South*; Gilmore, *Defying Dixie*; Levy, *Civil War on Race Street*; Singh, *Black Is a Country*; and Kruse and Tuck, *Fog of War*.

11. Cha-Jua and Lang, "The 'Long Movement' as Vampire," 265.

12. Mayfield, "Autobiographical Manuscript," 23.

13. Julian Mayfield, "Greer Journal," 1982, SCH, JMP, box 1, folder 6, 1.

14. "Second Perrett Family Reunion," July 30–31, 1983, SCH, JMP, box 40, folder 6, 7.

15. Based on email communication with Rafael Mayfield and census records, Hudson Mayfield's mother, Mattie Perrett, was born on September 15, 1879, and died on November 18, 1962. She married Henry Mayfield, who was born sometime in the late 1870s and, according to census records, lived in Chick Springs, some fifteen miles west of Greer.

16. According to Julian's FBI file, his father, Hudson Mayfield, was born in Greer in 1906, and his mother, Annie Mae Prince, was born the following year. However, Mayfield's own sources indicate that Hudson was born in 1905, and Annie Mae was

born in 1906. Hudson attended Allen University in Columbia for a year between 1925 and 1926, suggesting that his family had some means or had established connections with the AME (African Methodist Episcopal) Church, but he did not graduate. Mayfield's own recollections emphasize his parents' working-class roots as well as their aspirations for him and his sister to rise above the poverty that they had been born into. Mayfield never spoke of why his father did not finish the degree that he started, but Hudson's marriage to Annie Mae Prince in 1927 and the birth of Julian in June 1928 suggest that the pressures of fatherhood were contributing factors to his decision. Mayfield makes note of his parents' names and personal details in his autobiography, but most of the details of birth dates and marriage dates were provided by his FBI file. See Julian Mayfield FBI File, SAC WFO (Special Agent in Charge, Washington Field Office) 100-30570, 2.

17. According to information gathered by the FBI, Hudson was hired as an orderly at the Oteen Veterans Administration Hospital in nearby Swannanoa township. He would work there for three years before relocating to Washington. See Julian Mayfield FBI File, SAC WFO (Special Agent in Charge, Washington Field Office) 100-30570, 3.

18. Annie Mae was already pregnant with their second child when the family arrived in Asheville in February 1930. Edith was born shortly after their arrival in February. In the 1930 census, she is listed as an infant two months of age, but by the end August she had developed a fever and died on September 1. Her death certificate lists the cause of death as "intestinal obstruction." She was seven months old. It is unclear if Mayfield was aware of his deceased sister; he never mentioned her in his writing. See Edith May Mayfield, Death Certificate, North Carolina State Archives, Raleigh, North Carolina, North Carolina Death Certificates.

19. Julian Mayfield FBI File, Subject file, SAC WFO, WFO 100-30570, 2.

20. Mayfield, "Autobiographical Manuscript," 208–9; Julian Mayfield interviewed by Malaika Lumumba, May 13, 1970, Ralph Bunche Collection, Moorland-Spingarn Research Center, Howard University, Washington, DC, 552–55.

21. Yellin's *Racism in the Nation's Service* argues that it was the Wilsonian Progressives who engaged in the effort to "whiten" federal service beginning in 1913. See Yellin, *Racism in the Nation's Service*.

22. Mayfield, "Autobiographical Manuscript," 24.

23. Mayfield, 23.

24. Mayfield, 31.

25. Mayfield, 23.

26. Hundley, *The Dunbar Story, 1870–1955*, 33.

27. Julian Mayfield interviewed by Malaika Lumumba, May 13, 1970, 552–56.

28. According to the special agent in charge of the Washington field office, "the subject is shown to have an I.Q. of 110 in 1943 and that his attendance and deportment were satisfactory. See Julian Mayfield FBI File, Subject file, SAC WFO 100-30570, 2.

29. The prize was US$50. See "Prize Winner in National Contest," *New Journal and Guide* (1916–2003), Norfolk, VA, April 6, 1946, 22.

30. Mayfield, "Autobiographical Manuscript," 33.

31. In particular, the experiences of Harold Cruse, Ossie Davis, and Hoyt Fuller, who all served abroad during World War II, are relevant comparisons. John H. Clarke, who did his service primarily at Kelley Field, Texas, did not experience combat, and neither did James Forman, who was present in Japan during the Korean War. However, both of the latter men nevertheless experienced military life during wartime, which contrasted with Mayfield's experiences in the peacetime army. See Cruse, *Rebellion or Revolution?*, 168–70; Letter from John Clarke to the *Atlantic Monthly*, March 28, 1946, Schomburg Center for Research in Black Culture, John H. Clarke Papers; Dee and Davis, *With Ossie and Ruby*, 124, 128; Hoyt W. Fuller, "Autobiographical Manuscript," Atlanta University Center (hereafter AUC), Hoyt W. Fuller Papers, box 6, folder 1, 78, 82–83; and Forman, *The Making of Black Revolutionaries*, 242–43.

32. "I learned to roll the dice in such a way that every roll of the bones out of my hand reduced the odds radically in my favor." Mayfield, "Autobiographical Manuscript," 78.

33. In Mayfield's FBI file the bureau reported that Mayfield served as a typist and played trumpet and trombone in a military band. He was diagnosed with an ulcer in November 1947 and was transported to Fairfield-Suisun Army Airfield outside Berkeley, California, for treatment. Two days later on November 28, 1947, he was honorably discharged and given a train ticket to Washington. See Julian Mayfield FBI File, Subject file, SAC WFO 100-30570, 3; and "Discharge Certificate," October 13, 1954, box 2, folder 3, 1.

34. Lincoln University became a public university in 1972 and currently has a second location in University City, Philadelphia. See "Lincoln University Fact Book," Fall 2015, www.lincoln.edu/sites/default/files/pdf/institutional-research/2015FactBook.pdf, accessed June 12, 2018.

35. The Blackfriars Theatre was founded in 1931 by two Dominicans, Father Urban Nagle, O.P., and Brother Fabian Carey, O.P. Taking their name from the sixteenth-century private theater of the same name in London, Carey and Nagle opted to produce original works that were both spiritually and intellectually challenging. More importantly for Mayfield and his peers, the Dominican Order in New York's diocese was committed to integration and regularly made parts available to Black actors and actresses. See "Guide to the Blackfriars Guild Collection, 1921–1997," Phillips Memorial Library, Special and Archival Collections, Providence College, Providence, RI, 2.

36. In Mayfield's autobiography, he recalls that "I do remember that sometime in the early fifties a number of the younger men decided that Paul should not be allowed to walk the streets alone, that hooligans hired by right-wingers were perfectly capable of killing our hero. We used to vie for the privilege of walking beside Paul wherever he went. Sometimes our entourage would include Sidney Poitier, Leon Bibb and Harry Belafonte. Looking back now it somehow seems amusing. Although Paul was in his early fifties, he was in very good health, and a former All-American from Rutgers who stood taller than six foot four inches. We must have been a great nuisance to Paul, but I think at this . . . time, when some of his former friends of the celebrity world had deserted him, and there was a group of young

men who wanted to be seen with him, he allowed us to tag along." See Mayfield, "Autobiographical Manuscript," 99–101.

37. It was not the first time that Mayfield received a role in this manner. In April 1949, the Blackfriars Guild Theatrical Company put on a production of *City of Kings*, with Elwood Smith and Urban Nagle, O.P., starring. According to news reports, Elwood Smith, who played Martin de Porres, took ill, and Mayfield stepped into the role "without a rehearsal and gave a brilliant performance." See "'City of Kings' Stars," *New York Age*, April 30, 1949, 6; and Goudsouzianm, *Sidney Poitier*, 59–60.

38. Anderson, *Lost in the Stars*.

39. Margaret Taylor-Burroughs was born Victoria Margaret Taylor on November 1, 1915, in Saint Rose, then a small town about twenty miles west of New Orleans. Around 1920, the Taylor family moved north to Chicago and settled on the South Side. Burroughs attended Englewood High School along with poet Gwendolyn Brooks. Burroughs and Brooks, along with Edward Bland, William Couch, and Margaret Cunningham Danner went on to found the South Side Writers' Project. See Ian Rocksborough-Smith, "Margaret T. G. Burroughs and Black Public History in Cold War Chicago," *Black Scholar* 41, no. 3 (Fall 2011): 26–42; and William Grimes, "Margaret T. Burroughs, Archivist of Black History, Dies at 95," *New York Times*, November 27, 2010, Online edition, www.nytimes.com/2010/11/28/arts/28burroughs.html.

40. Gwendolyn Brooks recalled that "you might meet any *Per-sonality* there, white or black. You might meet Paul Robeson. You might meet Peter Pollack. On any night you might meet Frank Marshall Davis, the poet, Robert A. Davis, the actor, artists Eldzier Cortor, Hughie Lee-Smith, Charles White, Elizabeth Catlett. . . . [I]n Margarett's barn apartment sculpture, rich fabrics, books, paintings and pain addressed you everywhere. Margaret, then a rebel, lived *up from the root*." See Brooks, *Report from Part One*, 112; and Mullen, *Popular Fronts*, 96–97.

41. Charles Burroughs was the eldest son of dedicated communist activist Williana "Liana" Jones Burroughs, the CPUSA's candidate for New York comptroller in 1933 and the party's candidate for lieutenant governor of New York in 1934. A prominent voice in defense of the Scottsboro Boys, Williana joined the Communist Party in 1928 and traveled to Moscow that year for the Sixth Congress of the Communist International as a representative of the American Negro Labor Congress. Burroughs and her husband subsequently traveled internationally for the Comintern, leaving their two sons, Eric and Charles, to be taught in Moscow. According to Mayfield, a daughter was also left in Switzerland. Burroughs and her children were reunited in Moscow in 1937 after being apart for nearly nine years, but due to the lack of dedicated American communists in the Soviet Union, she was persuaded to remain in Moscow for the duration of World War II. Eric Burroughs went on to become an actor and worked with Orson Welles's all-Black Federal Theatre Project production of *Macbeth*. Charles returned to the United States in 1945 after serving in the US Army and settled in Chicago, where he met Margaret Taylor and the two were married. See Klehr, Haynes, and Firsov, *Secret World of American Communism*, 199–201; Mickenberg, *American Girls in Red Russia*, 279–80, 394n30; and Carew, *Blacks, Reds, and Russians*, 85–87.

42. Mayfield, "Autobiographical Manuscript," 40.

43. Mayfield, 41.

44. Mayfield recounted that despite being a "working actor who must avoid injury of every kind [and] . . . are very particular about our faces," he had met a young woman named Geri at the Burroughses' home and "could not appear chicken in front of [her]." Upon returning to the Burroughses' home uninjured, he was disappointed to see that "she never gave me any indication that she was impressed." See Mayfield, "Autobiographical Manuscript," 76–77.

45. Trumbull Park Homes was located at 105th Street and Yates Avenue and was designed by architect John A. Holabird. In 1953, the project was "accidentally" integrated when a light-skinned Black woman named Betty Howard moved her family into the project. Beginning in August 1953, white residents and whites from neighboring areas attacked the building that the Howard family lived in while police did nothing to stop them. In October, the Chicago Housing Authority attempted to move ten more Black families into the complex, but violence prevented them from doing so. It was not until 1963 that Black families were able to move into the projects without police protection. See D. Bradford Hunt, "Trumbull Park Homes Race Riots, 1953–1954," *Encyclopedia of Chicago*, http://encyclopedia.chicagohistory.org/pages/2461.html.

46. Mayfield, "Autobiographical Manuscript," 77.

47. According to the *Chicago Daily Tribune*, *Lost in the Stars* opened in San Francisco on August 7, 1950, and played the Edwin Theater in Los Angeles four nights a week, ending its California run on September 30, 1950. The show then returned to New York until closing in December 1950. See "Theater Notes," *Chicago Daily Tribune* (1923–63), March 26, 1950, G4.

48. According to Mayfield, the producers planned an international tour of the production as well, and he applied for his first passport and was in the process of procuring the necessary visas when the producers "decided to quit while they were ahead." See Mayfield, "Autobiographical Manuscript," 79.

49. Mayfield, "Autobiographical Manuscript," 64.

50. There seems to be some confusion in secondary sources as to whether Mayfield was a founding member of the Harlem Writers Guild. Some sources claim that he was a founding member, while others leave his name off the list of people associated with the group entirely. John O. Killens's papers at Emory University related to the guild note that Mayfield joined early but was not a founding member. See John O. Killens Papers, Emory University, boxes 113 and 114.

51. Clarke, *My Life in Search of Africa*, 16–17.

52. Founder John O. Killens estimated that over three hundred published works of fiction, nonfiction, poetry, plays, and screenplays were created by members of the Harlem Writers Guild. Past members include Grace F. Edwards, Rosa Guy, Rachel DeAragon, Walter Dean Myers, Louise Meriwether, Karen Robinson, Dr. Olubansile Abbas Mimiko, Sarah E. Wright, Audre Lorde, Paule Marshall, Terry McMillan, Robert McNatt, Lofton Mitchell, Wilbert Oliver, Funmi Osoba, Sidney Poitier, Charles Russell, K. C. Washington, Minnette Coleman, Gammy Singer, Wilbert Tatum, Brenda Wilkinson, Valerie Wilson Wesley, Sandra L. West, Doris Jean Austin,

William H. Banks Jr., Wesley Brown, Rosemary Bray, Irving Burgie, Judy C. Andrews, Godfrey Cambridge, Andrea Broadwater, Alice Childress, Ossie Davis, Ruby Dee, James DeJongh, Lonnie Elder III, Donis Ford, Bill William Forde, Lorraine Hansberry, Bob Desverney, Dr. Beryl Dorsett, Sheila Doyle, Lloyd Hairston, Robert Hooks, Rose James, Alfonso Nicks, and Betty Ann Jackson. See Gerald D. Jaynes, "Harlem Writers Guild."

53. Mayfield, "Autobiographical Manuscript," 90–91.

54. Mayfield, 91.

55. Mayfield, 16.

56. Mayfield, 91.

57. Welch, "Black Art and Activism in Postwar New York, 1950–1965," PhD diss., 8.

58. According to census data, the Black population of New York increased from 1.8% in 1900 to nearly 10% in 1950, with nearly all of that growth confined to Harlem. Notably, this figure includes Afro-Caribbean migration from the West Indies (including Haiti, Jamaica, the Dominican Republic, the US Virgin Islands, and Windward Islands, with estimates of nearly twenty thousand to thirty thousand individuals but does not include Puerto Rican migration, which is considered a separate trend due to Puerto Ricans holding US citizenship. See Campbell Gibson and Kay Jung, "Historical Census Statistics on Population Totals By Race, 1790 to 1990, and By Hispanic Origin, 1970 to 1990, for Large Cities and Other Urban Places in the United States," Working Paper No. 76, February 2005, Population Division, US Census Bureau, https://www.census.gov/content/dam/Census/library/working-papers/2005/demo/POP-twps0076.pdf; and "Urban and Rural Population," Department of Commerce, Bureau of the Census, Sixteenth Census Reports, Population II, Part 1.

59. Julian Mayfield, "Civilian Deaths in Korea," *Washington Post*, February 2, 1952, 6.

60. Other early members included Rosa Guy, Ossie Davis, Audre Lorde, and Alice Childress.

61. Alice Childress, who also used the names Louise Henderson and Alice Herndon prior to her marriage to Alvin Childress in 1934, was born in Charleston but relocated to New York with her grandmother in 1925 when her parents divorced. A high school dropout, Childress received her education in drama in the American Negro Theater starting in 1939. She later performed in such plays as *On Striver's Row* (1940) and *Natural Man* (1941) and won acclaim when *Anna Lucasta* (1944) moved downtown to Broadway, becoming the longest-running all-Black play in theater history. Costars in *Anna Lucasta* included Canada Lee, Hilda Sims, and Frederick O'Neal. Childress died in Astoria at the age of seventy-seven in 1994. See Mary Helen Washington, "Alice Childress, Lorraine Hansberry, and Claudia Jones: Black Women Write the Popular Front," in *Left of the Color Line*, ed. Mullen and Smethurst, 186; and Sue Woodman, "Obituary of Alice Childress—A Testimonial to Black America," *The Guardian*, September 14, 1994.

62. *Candy Store* focused on a local boycott against a New York chain drugstore in a thinly veiled version of Harlem, encouraging residents not to patronize estab-

lishments that treated them poorly, a concept that would be repurposed a decade later during the height of the civil rights movement as "don't buy where you can't work." See McDonald, *Feminism, the Left, and Postwar Literary Culture*, 33–34.

63. Other plays Mayfield acted in or directed during this time included William Branch's *A Medal for Willie*, *The Big One*, and *The Other Foot*.

64. Marvin E. Gettleman, "'No Varsity Teams': New York's Jefferson School of Social Science, 1943–1956," *Science & Society* 66, no. 3 (Fall 2002): 336–59.

65. Craig Thompson, "Here's Where Our Young Communists Are Trained," *Saturday Evening Post* 221 (March 12, 1949): 38.

66. Marvin E. Gettleman, "Jefferson School of Social Science," in *Encyclopedia of the American Left*, ed. Buhle, Buhle, and Georgakas, 389–90.

67. Advertisement, *The Crisis*, July 1951, 233.

68. According to Larry Rubin, who grew up in Philadelphia and became an important member of the Student Nonviolent Coordinating Committee, Paul Robeson performed at many of these camps during the 1940s and 1950s, and W. E. B. Du Bois was also known to attend. Larry Rubin, interview with author, July 7, 2016.

69. Garment, *Crazy Rhythm*, 15.

70. Autobiographical accounts by saxophonist Sidney Bechet, Art Hodes, and Willie "The Lion" Smith provide accounts of how some artists chafed against the party dictates about what songs they could play and the food provided. According to his autobiography, *Hot Man*, Art Hodes recalled that he was asked to refrain from celebrating the South in "Dear Old Southland" and leisure in "Summertime." In an exchange with an unknown camp organizer, Hodes asked, "What's wrong with 'Summertime'?" The answer was the lyrics, particularly "the living is easy." Life and living, Hodes's critic declared, "was never easy." See Chilton, *Sidney Bechet*, 144–45; Hodes, *Hot Man*, 79–80; Finkelstein, *Jazz*; and Denning, *The Cultural Front*.

71. In her biography of Johnson, his widow Mayme Hatcher Johnson makes no mention of either communists or Camp Unity. See Johnson and Miller, *Harlem Godfather*.

72. Mayfield, "Autobiographical Manuscript," 104.

73. Mayfield notes that both Puerto Rico and Cuba were integrated during this time as well. See Mayfield, "Autobiographical Manuscript," 105.

74. Mayfield, 105.

75. Despite the surfeit of documentation about the second Peekskill concert and its violent aftermath, I have been unable to verify Johnson's presence at the event. The violent response that Robeson faced at Peekskill was prompted by remarks falsely attributed to the singer by the Associated Press from the April 20, 1949, World Congress of Partisans for Peace in Paris. Among those to perform were Woodie Guthrie, Pete Seeger, and Sylvia Kahn. Seeger later used rocks that shattered the windows in the car he was riding in to build a chimney at his cabin in the town of Fish Kill, New York. See Robeson, *The Undiscovered Paul Robeson*, 143–44; Duberman, *Paul Robeson*, 366; and Jim Reisler, "To Pete Seeger, It's Still the Song of the River," *New York Times*, June 13, 1999, www.nytimes.com/1999/06/13/nyregion/to-pete-seeger-it-s-still-the-song-of-the-river.html?.

76. Mayfield, "Autobiographical Manuscript," 105–6.
77. Mayfield, 30.
78. Mayfield, 32.
79. Julian Mayfield, "Lorraine Hansberry: A Woman for All Seasons," *Freedomways* 19, no. 4 (1979): 266.
80. Letter from Julian Mayfield to Mark Crawford, June 5, 1974, SCH, JMP, box 29, folder, 2, 1.
81. Mayfield also notes that he was asked to sign a loyalty oath in order to get an unnamed television drama produced. "I grandly told everyone concerned to go to hell," he wrote, but the amount under discussion was only about $2000.00." See Mayfield, "Autobiographical Manuscript," 23, 91.

Chapter 2

1. Although the panel was held on February 28, 1959, Baldwin was unable to attend and did not provide the American Society of African Culture with his essay. I am unable to ascertain the reason for his absence.
2. Mayfield, "Into the Mainstream and Oblivion," 33.
3. The idea of "Puerto Rican invisibility" originates in the work of Frances Negrón-Muntaner and Ramón Grosfoguel, who have pointed to the "general unawareness concerning American colonial history" among both scholars and the general public as evidence of said invisibility. Negrón-Muntaner and Grosfoguel, *Puerto Rican Jam,* 22.
4. Mayfield, "Into the Mainstream and Oblivion," 33.
5. Mayfield, "Autobiographical Manuscript," SCH, JMP, box 15, folder 9, unnumbered page with the heading "Chapter Nine."
6. Mayfield, "La Borinqueña," SCH, JMP, box 1, folder 12, 1.
7. Sydenham Hospital was founded as a small, private hospital that served African American patients in 1892. Run out of a Harlem brownstone, the clinic's staff remained white, despite the hospital's entirely Black clientele, until the 1940s. In 1924, the hospital relocated to 125th Street and Lenox Avenue (now Malcolm X Avenue) in a building with over two hundred beds. The hospital's staff and administration were highly integrated following the end of World War II, but the financial difficulties of the late 1970s prompted Mayor Ed Koch to close the hospital in 1977. Despite a grassroots effort led by the Coalition to Save Sydenham, which included hospital workers from District Council 37 of the American Federation of State, County and Municipal Employees, the hospital was closed in 1980 and subsequently turned into 102 apartments aimed at elderly and handicapped individuals. See David W. Dunlap, "Harlem Scenes: Sydenham Hospital Gets a New Role," *New York Times,* December 4, 1986, B1; and Ronald Sullivan, "Sydenham Scene of Office Seizure on Its Final Day," *New York Times,* September 17, 1980, B1.
8. Mayfield, "La Borinqueña," 1.
9. Mayfield, "Autobiographical Manuscript," 88.
10. Mayfield, "La Borinqueña," 3.

11. Mayfield, 2.

12. Correspondence from the time period also suggests that this relationship affected Mayfield's position in the Committee for the Negro in the Arts and prompted his resignation in February 1954. In a statement announcing his resignation, Mayfield decried the "organized campaign of slanderous gossip directed against me." He expressed further disappointment at the "petty gossip" and "personal malice" that, he declared, had "no place among honorable men and women banded together in common struggle." The statement does not mention Cordero, but I speculate that his relationship with Cordero during the final months of her marriage and subsequent divorce in late 1953 were related to the gossip that Mayfield was subject to. See Julian Mayfield, "Statement of Resignation," February 12, 1954, SCH, JMP, box 7, folder 13, 1.

13. "Certificado de Matrimonio," filed November 8, 1954, SCH, JMP, box 2, folder 3, 1.

14. Mayfield, "La Borinqueña," 1.

15. Mayfield, 2.

16. In a *New York Times* article from 1954, Edward S. Lewis, executive director of the Urban League of Greater New York, reported that "tensions found here between Negroes and Puerto Ricans barely exist in Puerto Rico." See "Minimum Racial Bias Noted in Puerto Rico," *New York Times*, September 28, 1954, 38.

17. Iglesias was the former secretary of the Puerto Rican Communist Party, a fact that was not lost on Mayfield or the FBI agents from San Juan. Mayfield alludes several times to Ana Livia's early radicalism but does not go into detail about it. Work by Sandy Placído, whose research uncovered Cordero's papers and deposited them at Harvard, will shed light on that subject. One fact that is clear is that her participation in radical politics was aided by her father's position as a Roosevelt-appointed auditor and comptroller on the island. Don Rafael I. T. Cordero's job protected the family from political retribution from the radical politics of Ana Livia and her mother. See Mayfield, "La Borinqueña," 1.

18. Pablo Garcia Rodriguez Cordero was not related to Dr. Ana Livia Cordero. See "Round Up Puerto Rico Reds: Police Nab 6; Hunt 4 Main Party Bosses; 2 Women among First Arrested," *Chicago Daily Tribune*, March 8, 1954, 1; "Police Round Up Puerto Rico Reds: Top Leaders Evade Arrest in Island Purge of Subversives," *Los Angeles Times*, March 8, 1954, 1; and "Puerto Rico Pushes Drive against Radical Group Leaders; 40 Nationalist Party Bigwigs, 6 Reds Nabbed; Island's Four Top Communists among Several Trouble Makers Still At Large," *Miami News-Record*, March 8, 1954, 2.

19. Mayfield, "La Borinqueña," 5.

20. Mayfield, 2.

21. Pedro Albizu Campos, "Puerto Rican Nationalism," in *La Conciencia nacional puertorriqueña*, ed. Maldonado-Denis, 44–45, translation by author.

22. The Ponce Massacre resulted in nineteen deaths and dozens of injuries after police opened fire into a large crowd of nationalist demonstrators. In spite of early claims by Roosevelt-appointed governor Blanton Winship that the island's police had acted "with great restraint" and "in self defense," the findings of the Hays

Commission concluded that "the facts show that the affair of March 21 in Ponce was a 'MASSACRE.'" See Tovar, *Albizu Campos*; Denis, *War against All Puerto Ricans*, 52–54; and Bolland, ed., *Birth of Caribbean Civilisation*.

23. On October 31, 1950, nationalist groups organized simultaneous small-scale revolts across the country. The following day, November 1, 1950, two nationalists living in the United States, Oscar Collazo and Griselio Torresola, approached President Truman's temporary residence, Blair House. Located on Pennsylvania Avenue northwest of the White House, Blair House was the executive mansion's official guest residence, and Truman was residing there while the White House was in the midst of renovations. Collazo and Torresola approached the house in broad daylight as Truman napped on the second floor and attacked officers and Secret Service agents guarding him, killing one and wounding three. Torresola was shot and killed along with White House police officer Leslie W. Coffelt, but Collazo survived to be captured. Collazo recovered and stood trial in federal court. His death sentence was commuted by Truman in 1952, and Collazo was freed in 1979 by President Jimmy Carter and returned to Puerto Rico. Collazo died in 1994. See "400 in Puerto Rico Lay Down All Arms: Puerto Rican Nationalist Leader Arrested," *New York Times*, November 3, 1950, 1; Johnson, *Trials of the Century*, 388; Kessler, *In the President's Secret Service*, 9; and Hunter and Bainbridge, *American Gunfight*, 251. The full quote was "The biggest gunfight in Secret Service history was over in forty seconds. A total of twenty-seven shots had been fired." See Kessler, *In the President's Secret Service*, 8.

24. Puerto Rican nationalists Lolita Lebrón, Rafael Cancel Miranda, Andres Figueroa Cordero, and Irving Flores Rodríguez entered the observation deck known as the Ladies Gallery and unfurled a Puerto Rican flag while Lebrón shouted "¡Viva Puerto Rico Libre!" The group fired over thirty shots from semiautomatic weapons at the 240 representatives of the 83rd United States Congress in the midst of debating an immigration bill when the shooting began. Five representatives were wounded in the attack, which was quickly broken up by Capitol Security. Alvin M. Bentley (R-MI) was shot in the chest, Clifford Davis (D-TN) was shot in the leg, and Ben F. Jensen (R-IA) was shot in the back. George Hyde Fallon (D-MD) and Kenneth A. Roberts (D-AL) were also injured in the attack. See Clayton Knowless, "Five Congressmen Shot in House by 3 Puerto Rican Nationalists; Bullets Spray from Gallery," *New York Times*, March 2, 1954, 1.

25. In a 2012 report about the decline of the Puerto Rican sugar industry, researchers Benjamin Bridgman (Bureau of Economic Analysis), Michael Maio (University of Minnesota and Federal Reserve Bank of Minneapolis), and James A. Schmitz Jr. (Federal Reserve Bank of Minneapolis) argued that "in the 1930s and 1940s, the local Puerto Rican government enacted policies to stifle the growth of large cane-farms. As a result, farm size fell, mechanization of farms essentially ceased, and the Puerto Rican sugar industry's productivity (relative to Louisiana) rapidly declined until the industry collapsed." See James A. Schmitz Jr., Arilton Teixeira, Benjamin Bridgman, and Michael Maio, "What Ever Happened to the Puerto Rican Sugar Manufacturing Industry?," Staff Report 477, Federal Reserve

Bank of Minneapolis, December 27, 2012, www.minneapolisfed.org/research/staff-reports/what-ever-happened-to-the-puerto-rican-sugar-manufacturing-industry.

26. See David M. Helfeld, "Discrimination for Political Beliefs and Associations," 25 *Revista del Colegio de Abogados de Puerto Rico* (1964): 5; Mayfield, "La Borinqueña," 2. The Smith Act was also known as the Alien Registration Act of 1940. It was passed by the 76th United States Congress, 3rd session, chap. 439, 54 Stat. 670, 18 USC § 2385.

27. Mayfield, "La Borinqueña," 3.

28. Mayfield, 3.

29. The organization was renamed the Federal Bureau of Investigation in 1935. "History," www.fbi.gov/history/timeline.

30. Other sources on FBI history, especially that of COINTELPRO and the focus on Black radicals, can be seen in the works of Tim Weiner, William Maxwell, and Athan Theoharis, to name a few. See Athan Theoharis, *Spying on Americans* Tim Weiner, *Enemies*; and William J. Maxwell, *F.B. Eyes*.

31. Professor William Maxwell observed that "in the manner of a state museum the FBI collected, preserved, and educationally labeled works of black art, exhibiting foreign objects it intended to defang but came to emulate." By applying literary analytical techniques to the memos and writings produced by the FBI regarding modern Black writers, Maxwell points to the ways that African American writing was in fact a dialogue between Black writers and the state, such that each influenced the other in novel and often unseen ways. Julian Mayfield, as one of the writers whom Maxwell concerns himself, along with James Baldwin, Fank London Brown, Langston Hughes, Alice Childress, and Alice Windom, shows how the FBI influenced Black literature in ways reminiscent of the ways the bureau shaped the strategies and tactics of the civil rights movement. See Maxwell, *F.B. Eyes*, 11.

32. According to the memo, Mayfield was reported to be the "Chairman of the Subcommittee on Unemployment, Committee for Negro in the Arts, 1951; appeared in a play under auspices of CRC [Civil Rights Congress], 1953; appeared in musical presented at Camp Unity, 1953; was staff writer at Camp Unity Interracial Gala Program, 1953; active on behalf of WILLIE MCGEE, 1951; spoke at a rally for the defense of V. J. Jerome, 1953; participated in a People's Rights Party Nominating Petition for George Blake Charney, 1953; enrolled with ALP [American Labor Party], 1952; spoke at conference called by the NY Council of the Arts, Sciences and Professions, 1951; denounced American intervention in Korea, 1950; took part in places and activities which were against "witchhunting" and handling of prisoner of war issue." See Julian Mayfield FBI File, SAC, New York (100-120145), Memo dated February 18, 1955, 1–3.

33. According to his FBI file, Mayfield missed almost an entire year of school (between November 1940 and September 1941) due to a rheumatic heart, a consequence of rheumatic fever. The file also included an arrest for larceny and "depredation of private property" on April 3, 1940. Records from Mayfield's military service include a diagnosis of a duodenal ulcer, the reason for his discharge in 1947. See Julian Mayfield FBI File, SAC WFO, WFO 100-30570, 3.

34. According to communications with the FBI conducted by Dr. Sandy Placído, the FBI opened a file on Dr. Cordero at some point, but that file has been lost or destroyed. Conversation with Sandy Placído, email, March 6, 2017.

35. Julian Mayfield FBI File, Untitled report dated November 30, 1955 (47 of 217, second PDF).

36. The unnamed agent stated that he had mailed the recordings to Washington, but the file makes no further mention of them. My attempts to locate these recordings been unsuccessful.

37. While that report noted Mayfield's connection with Juan Saez Corales, Pablo Garcia Rodriguez, and Ramon Mirabel Carrion, it did not seem to recognize any connection with Iglesias, ironic given that it was César and Jane Iglesias who hosted the party. See Julian Mayfield FBI File, Report dated November 30, 1955 (47 of 217, second PDF).

38. The spy ring was known as Mocase, based on the association with Boris Morros, a Hollywood producer, member of the Communist Party of the United States of America, and FBI double agent. According to the FBI, Mayfield met with Rand and asked her to talk up some of his plays in New York. The origin of Mayfield's friendship with Rand is unknown, but the context suggests that she was associated with the New York theater business. Rand was known to the FBI as an associate of Jacob Albam, Robert Soble (Soblen), his brother Jack Soble, and Jack's wife Myra, who were all convicted of conspiracy for receiving and obtaining national defense information and transmitting it to [a] foreign government (18 USC. §793). The FBI could not link Mayfield to the Sobles and did not pursue that connection any further. In 1957, Myra and Jack were sentenced to five and a half and seven years in prison, respectively, and Jack died soon after his release in 1967. Myra Soble was later pardoned by George H. W. Bush in 1991. Robert Soble committed suicide in London as he was being deported back to the United States after an unsuccessful suicide attempt and having sought asylum in Israel. The Sobles and Albam were all convicted based on testimony from Boris Morros. See Morros, *My Ten Years as a Counter-Spy*; Edward Ranzal, "Brother of Soble Is Seized as a Wartime Soviet Spy: Psychiatrist Is Linked to Ring Headed by Beria," *New York Times*, November 30, 1960, 1; Robert Merry, "Soblen Death Suicide, Says British Jury: How Spy Got Pills Is Still Mystery," *Chicago Daily Tribune*, October 10, 1962, 24; and Conant, *A Covert Affair*, 326.

39. Julian Mayfield FBI file, Report dated November 30, 1955 (47 of 217, second PDF).

40. It was Mayfield's fellow Harlem Writers Guild alumnus John H. Clarke who brought these books to editors at Vanguard.

41. The numbers game (also known as the numbers racket) was an informal gambling system prominent in New York during the first half of the twentieth century. The "numbers" originated at the New York Clearing House on Cedar Street in Lower Manhattan, which posted two figures that were combined each day in order to derive the winning number. Those figures were typically (1) the daily clearances among member banks of the exchange and (2) the Federal Reserve Bank of New York's credit balance. New York residents could bet as little as a penny and

as much as a few dollars on a three-digit number. *417*, the title of Mayfield's original play, was what protagonist Hubert Cooley bet each day. The phrases "hitting the number" and "I hit" were how players described winning numbers. See White et al., *Playing the Numbers*.

42. Langston Hughes, "Lord, Please Let That Number Be 417," *New York Herald Tribune*, October 20, 1957, unknown page.

43. Like *The Hit*, *The Long Night*'s story revolved around the numbers racket. That story had as its protagonists young Steely Brown, who was sent by his mother to pick up her winnings so she can pay rent. When Steely is robbed on his way home, he spends the rest of the night desperately searching for a way to bring home the money that his mother needs. See Julian Mayfield, *The Hit* (New York: Vanguard, 1957); and Mayfield, *The Long Night*.

44. One exception is a single mention of Toussaint L'Ouverture in *The Long Night* and the character Black Papa. Black Papa was a homeless man who crosses protagonist Steely Brown's path twice during the novel chanting what Steely believed to be gibberish. However, the words "Cina, Cina, Cina Dogwe sang, cina lo-ge," which Mayfield spells out in the text, are in fact Haitian Creole and part of songs sung in praise of the lwa of the seas, Agwé. This marks Black Papa as an Afro-Caribbean figure who is embedded within midcentury Harlem. See Mayfield, *The Long Night*, 37, 47; and Steven Belletto, "Julian Mayfield and Alternative Civil Rights Literatures," *Twentieth-Century Literature* 63, no. 2 (June 2017): 125.

45. In a series of hearings in the fall of 1959 held in both New York and San Juan, the House Un-American Activities Committee heard testimony from undercover New York City police investigators about the various Puerto Rican nationalist and communist groups that were organizing. See Committee on Un-American Activities, *Communist Activities among Puerto Ricans*, 1528–29.

46. Mayfield, "Into the Mainstream," 34.

47. Mayfield, 31.

48. These conclusions would also prefigure Emmanuel's decision to turn his back on the United States and relocate to Europe in the early 1980s after his son, James A. Emmanuel Jr., was brutally beaten by Los Angeles police officers and later committed suicide. Emmanuel Sr. died in Paris in 2013. See Emanuel, *Dark Symphony*, 242; and William Yardley, "James A. Emanuel, Poet Who Wrote of Racism, Dies at 92," *New York Times*, October 11, 2013, www.nytimes.com/2013/10/12/books/james-a-emanuel-poet-who-wrote-of-racism-dies-at-92.html.

Chapter 3

1. Julian Mayfield, "Challenge to the Negro Leadership," *Commentary*, April 1961, 1.

2. Steven Preston, "A Searching Insight," *Worcester Telegram & Gazette*, July 22, 1961, Newspaper clipping, SCH, JMP, box 10, folder 12, 1.

3. *The Grand Parade* was retitled *Nowhere Street* and reprinted as a paperback in 1963 by Warner Paperback Library.

4. Washington, *The Other Blacklist*, 267.

5. Leopold Kohr, then a professor of economics and public administration at the University of Puerto Rico, suggested that it was Mayfield's hope of getting *The Hit* turned into a film that prompted his departure from Puerto Rico, although corroborating evidence for that assertion is minimal. In another letter, Poitier was associated with the project. See Letter from Leopold Kohr to Julian Mayfield, October 12, 1960, SCH, JMP, box 7, folder 2, 1; and Letter from Benjamin Pepper to Julian Mayfield, April 20, 1960, SCH, JMP, box 7, folder 2, 1.

6. *Virgin Island* was adapted from the 1953 memoir *Our Virgin Island*, written by Robb White III. The film featured Cassavetes and Maskell as a young Anglo-American couple who settle on a small uninhabited island in the British Virgin Islands. The island where White and his wife settled, known as Marina Cay, now uses the home they constructed as a reading room for an exclusive private resort. See White, *Our Virgin Island*.

7. Mayfield used the pseudonym "Gerald Orsini" for this writing, for unstated reasons. Considering that he had only recently left the Communist Party and was not then a member of the Screenwriter's Guild of America, I suspect that this was a political as well as a financial decision. I have been unable to uncover a script for the episode or even notes in Mayfield's archive, but contemporary newspaper accounts indicate that the episode Mayfield wrote, "Viva Paco!," revolved around a friend of the lead character Johnny Staccato. Paco, an up-and-coming Puerto Rican boxer, disappears before his bout with the champion. Cassavetes's eponymous character goes to Spanish Harlem to find Paco, who had been kidnapped, so that he may fight and protect his reputation. Contemporary newspapers indicate that this episode aired first in October 1959 and was seen on television several times between then and 1962. See "Untitled," *The Sun* (Baltimore, MD), October 18, 1959, A13; "Today's Programs on Television," *Washington Post and Times Herald*, April 24, 1960, 145; and "Wednesday Television Programs" *Washington Post and Times Herald*, June 13, 1962, D8.

8. *The Adventures of Huckleberry Finn* was released on August 3, 1960, and starred Eddie Hodges as the titular character, Archie Moore as Jim, Neville Brand as Pap Finn, and Tony Randall as the King of France. See "Author-Actor," *New York Age*, September 26, 1959, 4; and William Leonard, "Huck Finn Movie Fine Family Fare: The Adventures of Huckleberry Finn," *Chicago Daily Tribune*, August 29, 1960, B5.

9. When James Baldwin had pronounced the protest novel dead in his 1949 essay "Everybody's Protest Novel," he declared his intention to move beyond the sterile categories of "Negro-ness" in his writing. Baldwin made little distinction as to whether those categories were products of white racism or defensive constructs by Blacks, a move that frustrated many of his contemporaries, Mayfield included. Rather, Baldwin's concern was "to prevent myself from becoming merely a Negro; or, even merely a Negro writer." Baldwin recognized that "the world tends to trap and immobilize you in the role you play," and he saw little distinction in whether that trap was the result of hatred or an uneasy sort of kindness. However, it would be a mistake to regard many of the Black-themed works that emerged in the 1950s from the Harlem cultural Left as protest novels descended from *Native Son*, although

they were often marketed as such. Instead, as Lawrence Jackson has argued in *The Indignant Generation*, those writers sought an audience for Black drama that "neither emphasized white relationships nor grounded itself in comedy, song, [or] dance." In short, while the works of writers such as John O. Killens, Rosa Guy, Alice Childress, and Mayfield himself were focused on "Negro-ness," they resisted the urge to "bring greater freedom to the oppressed," as Baldwin described. Furthermore, theirs was an effort to produce socially conscious works for a Black audience. Mayfield, who was critical of Baldwin during this period, would later embrace the writer and his work. See Jackson, *The Indignant Generation*, 457; and Baldwin, *Notes of a Native Son*, 157.

10. Evelyn Cunningham, "N.Y. Courier's Bookshelf," *New Pittsburgh Courier*, national edition, August 19, 1961, 7.

11. "Wilkins Scorns 'Token Integration,'" *Washington Post and Times Herald*, February 28, 1959, B6.

12. Dwight D. Eisenhower, "Address Accepting the Presidential Nomination at the Republican National Convention in Chicago," July 11, 1952, www.presidency.ucsb.edu/documents/address-accepting-the-presidential-nomination-the-republican-national-convention-chicago-0.

13. Gainesboro's proximity to Baltimore and Washington suggests that the city is located in eastern Maryland, as it has numerous parallels with Cambridge, Maryland, prior to and during the civil rights movement.

14. Mayfield, *The Grand Parade*, 35–37.

15. The formation of White Citizens Councils began in 1954 and 1955 in Mississippi, Alabama, and Georgia. The councils organized resistance to desegregation efforts, in addition to working closely with the Ku Klux Klan and other violent, vigilante organizations to intimidate and terrorize activists who opposed Jim Crow. See Dittmer, *Local People*; and McMillen, *The Citizens' Council*.

16. Steven Preston, "A Searching Insight," *Worcester Telegram & Gazette*, July 22, 1961, SCH, JMP, box 10, folder 3, 1.

17. Joseph Blotner, "Racial Tensions in Gainesboro," *New York Times*, June 18, 1961, B26.

18. Brown's powerful novel *Trumbull Park* examined the integration of a Chicago Housing Authority project on the South Side. The novel presented a grim story of white supremacist violence that evoked none of the stereotypes about desegregation common to the era. Of Brown's debut novel, Sterling Stuckey wrote that it "signaled the advent of a new and brilliant flowering of creative effort on the part of Negro writers." Brown, who was born in Chicago in 1927 and would go on to sign his name to the Fair Play for Cuba Committee ad alongside Mayfield in the *New York Times* in April 1961, died suddenly in 1962. See Brown, *Trumbull Park*; and Guzman, *Black Writing from Chicago*, 155.

19. *The Hit*, for example, was adapted from a one-act play *417* that he had begun during the summer he spent at Camp Unity. *The Hit* went through several drafts, evidence of which are present in Mayfield's archive.

20. The town of Oak Ridge was established in 1942 as living quarters for workers at the four enrichment plants that would produce uranium for the Manhattan

Project, and in December 1953, Oak Ridge's town council resolved to integrate the high school, several months in advance of the *Brown* decision of May 17, 1954. With integration scheduled to start at the beginning of the 1955 school year following the *Brown* decision, some citizens urged a school boycott, but the first day of school was peaceful and uneventful. According to journalist Bob Fowler, two African American students made the Oak Ridge basketball team that year, but they were not permitted to play in away games since segregation was still in force throughout the rest of Tennessee. The smooth transition of Oak Ridge in comparison to Clinton has been attributed to the former's status as a federal enclave, as the city was under the jurisdiction of the Atomic Energy Commission (later folded into the Department of Energy in 1977). See James Sparrow, "Behind the Atomic Curtain: School Desegregation and Territoriality in the Early Cold War," *Tocqueville Review/ La revue Tocqueville* 33, no. 2 (June 2018): 115–39; Russell Olwell, "Help Wanted for Secret City: Recruiting Workers for the Manhattan Project at Oak Ridge, Tennessee, 1942–1946," *Tennessee Historical Quarterly* 58, no. 1 (April 1999): 52–69; Janice M. McClelland, "A Structural Analysis of Desegregation: Clinton High School, 1954–1958," *Tennessee Historical Quarterly* 56, no. 4 (December 1997): 294–310; and Bob Fowler, "Before Clinton or Little Rock, Oak Ridge Integration Made History," *Knoxville News Sentinel*, February 16, 2009, http://archive.knoxnews.com/news /local/before-clinton-or-little-rock-oak-ridge-integration-made-history-ep -410364049-359586141.html.

21. That case, originally filed in 1950, was known as *McSwain et al. v. County Board of Education of Anderson County, Tennessee*. After ruling against the plaintiffs in 1952, Johnson was forced to hear the case once more in the aftermath of *Brown v. Board of Education,* and the 1956 decision reflects the decision's impact. While that story was not as dramatic as the one Mayfield tells in *The Grand Parade,* it would go on to have important ramifications on future desegregation initiatives, especially in Memphis and Nashville, prolonging the process through legal and illegal means. See "McSwain v. Bd. of Ed. of Anderson County," *Hastings Law Journal* 9 (January 1957): 175–90; and Janice M. McClelland, "A Structural Analysis of Desegregation: Clinton High School, 1954–1958," *Tennessee Historical Quarterly* 56, no. 4 (December 1997): 294–310.

22. Born in 1929, John Kasper learned of Pound's works as an undergraduate student at Columbia. In 1950, Kasper sent the poet a letter comparing him favorably to Friedrich Nietzsche. Pound responded positively, and the men struck up a friendship, exchanging hundreds of letters between 1950 and 1963. During the early 1950s, Kasper opened a bookstore called Make It New in Greenwich Village and featured Pound's works prominently alongside other far-right, anti-Semitic, and white nationalist literature. Kasper relocated to Washington, DC, in 1954 and opened another bookstore in order to be able to visit Pound regularly while the poet was imprisoned in St. Elizabeth's Hospital. Kasper reacted to the 1954 *Brown* decision by declaring that racial integration was "a Jewish plot" and founded the Seaboard White Citizens Council in Washington to prevent that city's schools from following federal desegregation mandates. When he received word that Clinton High School was set to integrate in 1956, he moved again, bringing with him Asa Carter, a young

man he had met in Washington. A detailed analysis of Kasper and Pound's relationship has recently been written by Alex Marsh, who examined the voluminous correspondence between the two and asserts that "Kasper was more than a rabble rouser; he was a serious transmitter of Pound's ideas who imagined himself as the successor to James Laughlin as Pound's publisher. Pound's idiosyncratic Confucianist, Fascist, Jeffersonianism, and Kasper's homegrown Christian anti-Semitism fed off each other, influencing Pound's great poem and Kasper's 'southern strategy'—ultimately having an obscure but real effect on the American political landscape." Pound's biographer, J. James Wilhelm, argued that the poet's association with Kasper was one of the reasons Pound remained imprisoned until 1958, despite passionate pleas by friends such as Ernest Hemingway. In an interview with George Plimpton in 1958, Hemingway told Plimpton that Pound should be released to write in Italy. Of Kasper, Hemingway told Plimpton, "I would be happy to see Kasper jailed as soon as possible," noting that "I am sure that it will take a footnote to this paragraph in ten years to explain who Kasper was." See Marsh, *John Kasper and Ezra Pound*, xiv–xv; Wilhelm, *Ezra Pound*, 204–6, 208; and Ernest Hemingway, "The Art of Fiction No. 21," *Paris Review* 18 (Spring 1958).

23. A year after the events in Clinton, Kasper moved farther south to Florida, where he once again joined forces with those defending Jim Crow from new legislation. However, despite organizing White Citizens Councils in Jacksonville, offhand comments about dancing with Black women in interracial clubs in New York landed him in hot water with his hosts. Fred B. Hockett, who had helped Kasper found the Seaboard White Citizens Council of Washington, DC, publicly denounced Kasper in March 1957. In an article in the *Atlanta Constitution*, Hockett was quoted as saying that Kasper was "doing more to hurt segregationist organizations in Florida than anything else." Homer Bars, the executive secretary of the Association of Citizens Councils of Florida, similarly rebuked Kasper and was quoted as saying that Kasper had "done a disservice to legitimate segregation organizations" and that he "ought to get out of Florida." The following year after a conviction based on a contempt charge resulting from the Clinton Riot, Kasper was sent to the Tallahassee Federal Correctional Institute. Assaulted by a fellow inmate, Kasper was then transferred to the federal prison in Atlanta to finish his sentence. Upon release, he reiterated his support for segregation even as he renounced violence as a means to achieve it while complaining bitterly about the integrated conditions in the prisons in both Florida and Atlanta. See "Florida Segregationists Snip Ties with Kasper," *Atlanta Constitution*, March 13, 1957, 2; Harold Parr, "Kasper Free, Faces Term in Tennessee," *Atlanta Constitution*, December 17, 1959, 5; and "Inmate Slugs John Kasper in Federal Pen," *Chicago Defender*, national edition, August 8, 1959, 1.

24. Ironically, following the destruction of Clinton High School, students were bused to nearby Oak Ridge High School while their school was rebuilt. With the aid of Reverend Billy Graham, local columnist Drew Peterson, and others, the school was quickly rebuilt at the cost of $500,000. See June N. Adamson, "Few Black Voices Heard: The Black Community and the Desegregation Crisis in Clinton, Tennessee, 1956," *Tennessee Historical Quarterly* 53, no. 1 (1994): 30–41; and Neil R.

McMillen, "Organized Resistance to School Desegregation in Tennessee," *Tennessee Historical Quarterly* 30, no. 3 (1971): 315–28.

25. In *The Strange Career of Jim Crow*, C. Vann Woodward differentiates Tennessee, Texas, Arkansas, and Florida as mid-South states (as opposed to border or Deep South states). In the first edition of the book, published in 1955, he points to how those states were "inclining toward the example of the border states rather than in the opposite direction" (i.e., the Deep South). Citing examples from Longview, Texas, as well as Tulsa, Oklahoma, and Elaine, Arkansas, Woodward notes that while opposition to Jim Crow seemed to waver initially, it was soon shorn up by legislative and executive pressure. Citing the "Declaration of Constitutional Principles," which managed to get 101 out of 128 legislators from eleven states, Woodward points to the interplay between factions within the broader southern region, which was differentiated politically and socially. See Woodward, *Strange Career of Jim Crow*, 161.

26. Mayfield's decision to make Bryant a Mississippi native suggests that he may have believed that a white supremacist from New Jersey would be less convincing, despite the actual details of Kasper's life.

27. Mayfield, *The Grand Parade*, 242.

28. Mayfield, 243.

29. Mayfield, 242.

30. Woodward, *Strange Career of Jim Crow*, 61.

31. While *The Grand Parade*'s narrative ends following the confrontation at the school and Mayor Taylor's death, in real-life Clinton the riot was only a prelude to more violence. See June N. Adamson, "Few Black Voices Heard: The Black Community and the Desegregation Crisis in Clinton, Tennessee, 1956," *Tennessee Historical Quarterly* 53, no. 1 (1994): 30–41.

32. Julian Mayfield interviewed by Malaika Lumumba, May 13, 1970, Ralph Bunche Collection, Moorland-Spingarn Research Center, Howard University, Washington, DC, 552-21.

33. Following Mayfield's resignation from the Committee for the Negro in the Arts in February 1954, he remained active in the CPUSA until his departure from New York in March, when he and Dr. Cordero left for Puerto Rico. In his autobiographical manuscript, he examined his decision to leave the party and concluded, "Not ever having been a public Communist I felt no need to resign publicly." He also reflected on this decision: "Leaving the party was no great strain on me. I have observed that I was in the party for my own purposes, mainly to use it to achieve my objectives and I was leaving it now that it had become clear to me that my membership in it would not further these objectives." Of his time in Puerto Rico, he recalled that "my main regret was the expectation that many comrades whom I respected most might now begin to regard me as a traitor and an enemy. (They did not.)" See Mayfield, "Autobiographical Manuscript," SCH, JMP, box 15, folder 9, 32–33.

34. Julian Mayfield interviewed by Malaika Lumumba, 552-17.

35. "Popular Front" refers specifically to the association of socialist, social-democratic, communist, and center-leftist groups that collaborated on political, labor, and cultural issues between 1934 and 1939. See McKenzie, *Comintern and*

World Revolution, 159; Denning, *The Cultural Front*, xv–xvi; Mark Naison, "Remaking America: Communists and Liberals in the Popular Front," in *New Studies in the Politics and Culture*, ed. Michael Brown, 45–76; Mullen, *Popular Fronts*; and Biondi, *To Stand and Fight*.

36. In particular, Mayfield cites the Communist Party's defense of the Scottsboro Boys and the Martinsville Seven and opposition to the execution of Willie McGee. See Mayfield, "Autobiographical Manuscript," 43, 55–56; Eric W. Rise, "Race, Rape, and Radicalism: The Case of the Martinsville Seven, 1949–1951," *Journal of Southern History* 58, no. 3 (August 1992): 461–90; and Heard, *Eyes of Willie McGee*.

37. Julian Mayfield interviewed by Malaika Lumumba, 552–25.

38. Mayfield interview, 552–23.

39. The "secret speech," whose actual title was "On the Cult of Personality and Its Consequences," was given by Soviet premier Nikita Khrushchev at the 20th Congress of the Communist Party of the Soviet Union on February 25, 1956. Rumors of Khrushchev's denunciation of Stalin and Stalinism reached the West by early March, but a full text of the speech was not received by the Eisenhower administration until April 13, 1956, via Israeli intelligence. Allen Dulles leaked the speech to the *New York Times* in June of that year, and the US State Department officially published it on June 5, 1956. See Dulles, *The Craft of Intelligence*, 80–81; and Harrison E. Salisbury, "Khrushchev Talk on Stalin Bares Details of Rule Based on Terror; Charges Plot for Kremlin Purges: US Issues a Text," *New York Times*, June 5, 1956, 1.

40. Mayfield, *The Grand Parade*, 201.

41. The National Negro Congress was founded in 1935 at Howard University as a collaborative organization with the goal of fighting for Black liberation and was affiliated with the Communist Party. The party worked to forge relationships between white and Black workers during the Great Depression, fighting against war, fascism, and racial discrimination. In addition to Randolph, major figures involved with the organization included John P. Davis and James W. Ford. The organization survived Randolph's departure in 1939 but merged with other labor groups in 1946 to form the Civil Rights Congress in 1946. See Gellman, *Death Blow to Jim Crow*.

42. Randolph cited in Padmore, *Pan-Africanism or Communism?*, 310.

43. The fictional dispute was grounded in various attempts by factions within the CPUSA to resist Moscow's influence and control. The most well-known example was Jay Lovestone, who attempted to steer the party away from the Soviet Union in the 1930s and was excommunicated for his efforts. Unlike Lovestone, who later joined forces with the AFL-CIO and provided intelligence on the party, Lonnie Banks remains an ideologically committed communist. See Alexander, *The Right Opposition*; and Morgan, *A Covert Life*.

44. The article was revised and later published as one of six essays in Koestler, *The God That Failed*.

45. Hughes, who appeared before the House Un-American Activities Committee on March 24–26, 1953, spoke in a circumspect manner about his associations with the Communist Party. Although he refused to identify his comrades, he did testify about its organizational structures, its goals, and its impact on his writing. Hughes

was forthcoming about his own seduction by and slow rejection of communist ideology. According to biographer Laurie F. Leach, Hughes announced his intention to appear as a "friendly witness" and even rehearsed his testimony with his lawyer, Frank D. Reeves, and with Roy Cohn. In contrast, Max Yergan, one of the founders of the Council on African Affairs and a defiant Communist Party member during the 1930s, became an informant to the Federal Bureau of Investigation and reported on the extent of his associates and former friends' activities in the party, including Paul Robeson, Louis Burnham, Shirley Graham Du Bois, and Alphaeus Hunton. See Leach, *Langston Hughes*, 134–36; and Anthony, *Max Yergan*.

46. Shirley Graham, "The Time Is Now," *Freedomways* 1, no. 2 (Summer 1961): 223.

47. Graham, "The Time Is Now," 219.

48. Mayfield, *The Grand Parade*, 120.

Chapter 4

1. Gosse, *Where the Boys Are*; Reitan, *Rise and Decline of an Alliance*; and Moore, *Castro, the Blacks, and Africa*.

2. Cynthia Young, "Havana Up in Harlem," *Science & Society* 65, no. 1 (Spring 2001): 13.

3. It is unclear which date this call was received. Mayfield's response to the Senate Internal Subcommittee on Security suggests that he added his name as a matter of course, perhaps failing to consider potential consequences, but his desire to avoid testifying may make his recollections unreliable.

4. Other signatories included Simone de Beauvoir, Frank London Brown, Truman Capote, Jean-Paul Sartre, Robert G. Colodny, Richard Gibson, Maurice Green, Edmonde Haddad, Donald Harrington, John O. Killens, Sidney Lens, Norman Mailer, Elva dePue Matthews, Eugene Noble, John Papandrew, James Purdy, Joseph Quintana, Alan Sanger, John Singleton, Robert Taber, G. A. Thurston, Kenneth Tynan, Dan Wakefield, and Sidney Weinstein.

5. FPCC Ad, *New York Times*, April 6, 1960.

6. Following the publication of *The Hit*, surveillance on Mayfield appears to have ceased entirely. There is a gap in his FBI file from April 1957 that lasts until March 1960.

7. The article, published online on May 15, 2018, reveals that Gibson's identity as an informant and asset of the CIA was revealed through the 2017 release of documents relating the assassination of President John F. Kennedy. Gibson, who was still alive as of the publication of this article, has not commented on this accusation, nor has further research uncovered what Gibson shared with the CIA. See Jefferson Morley, "CIA Reveals Name of Former Spy in JFK Files—And He's Still Alive," *Newsweek*, May 15, 2018, www.newsweek.com/richard-gibson-cia-spies-james-baldwin-amiri-baraka-richard-wright-cuba-926428.

8. While Hoover's statement could be regarded as alarmism for the sake of reinforcing the prominence of his agency, the amount of documentation on the FPCC and those associated with it suggest that the FBI regarded the organization and its

association with the Cuban government as a significant threat to national security. Hoover, quoted in Gosse, *Where the Boys Are*, 243.

9. Theoharris, *FBI and American Democracy*, 158; and Morley, *The Ghost*, 94.

10. Díaz was the personal pilot of Fidel Castro until his defection in the spring of 1959. Díaz claimed that many of Castro's lieutenants and aides were communists. He stated that the Cuban leader was now taking orders from Moscow. See "Communist Threat to the United States through the Caribbean," Díaz testimony, 25, Senate Internal Security Subcommittee report cited in Annis, *Big Jim Eastland*, 1837.

11. Mayfield was again subpoenaed in April 1961, the result of a subsequent ad placed by the FPCC titled "An Appeal to Conscience" that denounced the Bay of Pigs invasion. While Gibson testified in July 1961, Mayfield claims that his lawyer, Leonard Boudin, called the subcommittee's secretary and let it slip that Mayfield was not white, and the committee rescinded its subpoena. Mayfield writes that it was Paul Robeson's forceful repudiation of the committee during his testimony in 1956 that meant that "since then, committees with Southern chairmen—and most committees have Southern chairmen—had avoided summoning black radicals whenever possible." See Mayfield, "Autobiographical Manuscript," SCH, JMP, box 15, folder 9, 215–17.

12. John H. Clarke, "Journey to the Sierra Maestre," *Freedomways* 1, no. 2 (Spring 1961): 32.

13. Mayfield's contribution, a Spanish translation of his short story "The Last Days of Duncan Street," was republished in Pelecanos, ed., *D.C. Noir 2*.

14. In a poignant section of his autobiography, Mayfield relates an encounter with the Afro-Cuban poet Nicolas Guillén, who was appointed as the head of Unión Nacional de Escritores de Cuba after his return to the island in 1959. At a cocktail party held shortly after their arrival, Guillén arrived and loudly demanded of the visitors, "Where is Langston Hughes? He is one of my oldest friends. He should be here!" Guillén, who had met Hughes during the American's first trip to Havana in 1921, was saddened when he learned that his old friend was not present. For the same reason that Hughes had felt compelled to keep his name off the FPCC letter in the *New York Times*, he was also reticent to travel to a country that was already fending off charges of communist sympathies. Those present understood that having already sat before the House Un-American Activities Committee in 1951, Hughes might not be eager to do so again. Like Hughes, men and women who had received invitations through the FPCC decided the extent of their participation with one eye on the response their attendance might generate. See Mayfield, "Autobiographical Manuscript," 213–14.

15. Mayfield, "Autobiographical Manuscript," 191.

16. The July 26th Movement was named for the attack on the Moncada Barracks in the city of Santiago de Cuba on July 26, 1953. See Chomsky, *History of the Cuban Revolution*.

17. LeRoi Jones, "Cuba Libre," *Evergreen Review* 4, no. 15 (November–December 1960): 2–15. See also Baraka, *Autobiography of LeRoi Jones*, 243.

18. Julian Mayfield, "The Cuban Challenge," *Freedomways* 1, no. 2 (Summer 1961): 187.

19. Mayfield, "Autobiographical Manuscript," 191.

20. Mayfield, "Autobiographical Manuscript," 191–92. Unfortunately, Mayfield does not seem to have been aware of a number of examples to the contrary, in particular the uprising of African American soldiers returning from World War I in Houston, Texas, and the number of returning World War II veterans who became important leaders in racial justice struggles in New York, Mississippi, Alabama, Georgia, and Illinois. These examples suggest that while some African American veterans may have laid down their arms, they were still willing to fight for their citizenship rights. See Lentz-Smith, *Freedom Struggles*; and Williams, *Torchbearers of Democracy*.

21. Carlos Moore, an Afro-Cuban scholar and early proponent of the revolution, has written several scathing accounts of the racism within the Cuban Revolution and the failed promise of its antiracism, confirming many of Mayfield's suspicions. See Moore, *Pichón*; Moore, "Afro-Cubans Push Back," *Journal of Pan African Studies* 4, no. 2 (December 2010): 457; and Moore, *Castro, the Blacks, and Africa*.

22. During the long train ride from Havana to Santiago de Cuba that he recounted in his autobiography, Mayfield recalled what had happened when the train carrying "los negros Americanos" pulled into small Cuban towns. "As a measure of how bad things must have been before the revolution, the [Cubans] would often go and awaken a poor guy whom I supposed to be the only black man in town and hold his hand up to show [Robert] Williams that blacks and whites were now united in revolution." Mayfield, "Autobiographical Manuscript," 194.

23. Castro also repeated these remarks at a National Press Club luncheon the following day in Washington, DC. See "Reds' Alleged Role in Castro's Regime Alarming Havana," *New York Times*, April 24, 1959, 1.

24. Accounts of this conflict have been explored elsewhere in more detail, especially in Cynthia Young's article "Havana Up in Harlem." According to Castro, the Shelbourne demanded a $10,000 deposit, and Castro refused to pay. Media accounts from New York tabloids cited barbaric behavior of the visiting Cubans, portraying them as "uncouth primitives" who had "killed, plucked, and cooked chickens in their rooms at the Shelbourne and extinguished cigars on expensive carpets." There is also a minor debate over who was responsible for Castro's move uptown. According to Mayfield, it was Richard Gibson who suggested that Castro move uptown to Hotel Theresa. In contrast, Van Gosse claims it was Robert Taber who suggested the Theresa to Castro (Gosse, *Where the Boys Are*, 151). Ralph Crowder, writing in 2000, claimed that "Raul Roa Kouri . . . communicated with Richard Gibson and Robert Taber, leaders of the Fair Play for Cuba Committee (FPCC) about hotel accommodations in Harlem. Taber informed the young diplomat that '[Malcolm X] had already suggested that we use the [Theresa] in Harlem.'" The recent book by Rosemari Mealy repeats Crowder's claim, suggesting that it was Malcolm X who had the initial idea and that Taber and Gibson handled the logistics. Whoever was ultimately responsible, the Cuban delegation took over the hotel for the entirety of their stay. See Ralph L. Crowder, "Fidel Castro and Harlem: Political, Diplomatic,

and Social Influences of the 1960 Visit to the Hotel Theresa," *Afro-Americans in New York Life and History* 24, no. 1 (January 31, 2000): 79; and Mealy, *Fidel and Malcolm X*, 122.

25. Plummer, *Rising Wind*, 17.

26. Alvin White, "Fidel Calls Harlem 'An Oasis in the Desert,'" *The Afro-American*, September 24, 1960, 1.

27. Partial letter from Julian Mayfield to "Maga," September 25, 1960, SCH, JMP, box 7, folder 13, 2.

28. Mayfield, "Autobiographical Manuscript," 192.

29. "Harlem Labels Castro's Visit as Propaganda," *Chicago Defender*, October 1, 1960, 1.

30. The African Memorial Bookstore remained in operation until 1974, although it was forced to relocate due to the construction of the State Harlem Office Building in 1968. See Davis, *From Head Shops to Whole Foods*.

31. John Young III, "The Negro in Castro's Cuba," *New York Amsterdam News*, February 7, 1957, 1.

32. Young, "The Negro in Castro's Cuba," 1, 11.

33. "Harlem Labels Castro's Visit as Propaganda," 2.

34. Julian Mayfield, "Cuba Has Solution to Race Problem," *Baltimore Afro-American*, October 1, 1960, 9.

35. Mayfield, 9.

36. Williams's book, *Negroes with Guns*, cited in Mayfield, "Challenge to the Negro Leadership," *Commentary*, April 1961, 2.

37. Mayfield, "Challenge to the Negro Leadership," 1.

38. Mayfield, 1.

39. Tyson, *Radio Free Dixie*, 72.

40. Tyson, 80.

41. Mayfield, "Challenge to the Negro Leadership," 2.

42. After Williams refused to heed Wilkins's demands that he should refrain from repeating this statement in interviews, Wilkins sent a telegram demanding that Williams suspend his activities as local NAACP president. Several weeks later, Williams attended the NAACP national conference, and a hearing was held which Mayfield dubbed *Wilkins vs. Williams*, that made his suspension official. See Mayfield, "Challenge to the Negro Leadership," 2–3.

43. Mayfield, "Challenge to the Negro Leadership," 2.

44. One of the main reasons Williams set his sights on the Works Progress Administration swimming pool, Tyson argues, was that the "black children barred from these [swimming safety] programs swam in isolated farm ponds, muddy creeks, and abandoned quarries—and they drowned all too frequently." See Tyson, *Radio Free Dixie*, 83–84.

45. "Ike Deplores, but Won't Act in Monroe Kissing Case," *Baltimore Afro-American*, January 3, 1959, 1.

46. Williams's book, *Negroes with Guns*, cited in Mayfield, "Challenge to the Negro Leadership," 2.

47. Tyson, *Radio Free Dixie*, 50.

48. Mayfield, "Autobiographical Manuscript," 200.

49. Mayfield, 201.

50. Williams directly influenced the foundation of the Revolutionary Action Movement in 1962, and his book was cited by Black Panther Party founders Huey P. Newton and Bobby Seale. See Joseph, *Waiting 'Til the Midnight Hour*.

51. Mayfield, "Autobiographical Manuscript," 203.

52. Mayfield, 203.

53. Mayfield, 202.

54. Julian Mayfield, "Tales of the Lido," SCH, JMP, box 15, folder 11, 27.

55. Mayfield, 28–29.

56. Mayfield, 28.

57. According to Mayfield's account in notes from "Tales of the Lido," Williams cautioned the Freedom Riders against this planned picketing. However, Freedom Rider James Forman's account indicates that he was leery of the plan, "but Williams was in favor of the plan. 'We can't stop now,' he said excitedly. 'Things are hot but we have to know how to make them hotter.' I didn't agree with him, but if he felt it was necessary than [sic] I was willing to help him with the picketing." See Mayfield, "Tales of the Lido," 30; and Forman, *Making of Black Revolutionaries*, 189, 192–93.

58. John Lowery Oral history, interviewed by Elsa Knight Thompson and Mike Tigar, American Archive of Public Broadcasting, May 4, 1962, http://americanarchive.org/catalog/cpb-aacip_28-h707w67k6x.

59. Mayfield, "Tales of the Lido," 30.

60. Mayfield, 31.

61. According to James Forman, Julian Mayfield's car was being driven by a man named Paul Brooks. Mayfield's account, however, does not specify which car he was driving but does mention that it had a New York license plate, suggesting that it was his. See Forman, *Making of Black Revolutionaries*, 197–98.

62. Notably, Lowery's oral history includes no mention of Mayfield or of this incident on the bridge. Lowery had arrived in Monroe by way of Jackson, Mississippi, and had recently been let of jail along with James Forman. According to Lowery, a Reverend Vivian of Mississippi told him that "Williams wanted freedom riders to come up and form an integrated picket line," but Williams's own discussion of the incident challenges this idea. According to his oral history, Lowery was also present at the Williams house following the arrival of the Stegalls, and it was Lowery who moved their car away from the angry mob after the Stegalls entered the Williams household. For this, Lowery would be indicted, along with Mae Mallory and two men from Monroe, on charges of kidnapping.

63. My efforts to discern the Stegallses's motivation to drive through New Town did not shed any light on their reasoning. It appears that they drove to the other side of town solely out of morbid curiosity.

64. Mayfield, "Tales from the Lido," 36; and Tyson, *Radio Free Dixie*, 181.

65. The supporter, Richard Crowder, was later arrested and tried by the State of North Carolina. The home where Crowder and Mayfield buried the weapons belonged to Crowder's mother. These two submachine guns had been trans-

ported to Monroe by Mayfield during an earlier trip. In the "Tales of the Lido" fragment that focuses on Monroe, Mayfield wrote that they had been procured by "a famous writer [who] made touch with a gangster in New Jersey." Tim Tyson, during interviews, revealed that this famous writer was in fact Amiri Baraka (aka LeRoi Jones). See Tyson, *Radio Free Dixie*, 179; and Mayfield, "Tales from the Lido," 36.

66. Mayfield, "Tales from the Lido," 36–37. I have been unable to determine if these men were members of law enforcement from other jurisdictions, unofficial police auxiliaries, or state police forces, but the implication of accounts from Mallory, Mayfield, and Williams is that it was some combination of all three.

67. Julian Mayfield FBI File, "Memorandum, Subject: Justification for continuation of technical or microphone surveillance," October 10, 1961, 1.

68. Mayfield FBI File, 2a.

69. Mayfield FBI File, "Memorandum from C. H. Stanley to Mr. Evans," September 5, 1961, 2.

70. Curiously, this passport contains a visa from the Ghanaian Consulate in New York dated November 8, 1961. It is unclear if Mayfield traveled all the way to New York City from Canada in order to acquire it or if Cordero provided this for him. See "Passport 1961," SCH, JMP, box 2, folder 3.

71. O'Brien, *Interviews with Black Writers*, 146.

Chapter 5

1. Mayfield obtained his first passport for this trip, apparently not being required to hold a passport for the Havana trip the previous year.

2. Julian Mayfield, "Ghanaian Sketches," in *Young Americans Abroad*, ed. Klein, 177–78.

3. The title of Klein's volume alluded to a widely read book published in 1852 titled *Young Americans Abroad, or, Vacation in Europe: Travels in England, France, Holland, Belgium* by John Overton Choules (1801–56).

4. Myrdal, *An American Dilemma*. For more on the history of Myrdal's famous study, see Jackson, *Gunnar Myrdal and America's Conscience*; and Southern, *Gunnar Myrdal and Black-White Relations*.

5. Julian Mayfield, "The Lonely Warrior," draft manuscript, SCH, JMP, box 13, folder 10, 9.

6. Mayfield, "The Lonely Warrior," 9.

7. This visit, which occurred on November 9–20, was hotly contested by much of the British government at the time. In October, former prime minister Winston Churchill wrote to Harold Macmillan expressing his fears for the queen's security, as Nkrumah had already experienced two assassination attempts during his short tenure. After having canceled a proposed trip in 1959, the queen was determined to show her support for Nkrumah especially as the Soviet Union had begun to make overtures to the small West African nation. Despite tensions between the African socialism of Nkrumah and the role of the United Kingdom in the history of Ghana, Queen Elizabeth and Prince Philip were welcomed warmly by crowds wherever

they went. Special cloth was made bearing the queen's face, and her motorcade was thronged by well-wishers wherever she went.

8. Henry Tanner of the *New York Times* estimated that nearly 500,000 Ghanaians turned out to see Queen Elizabeth II and Prince Philip upon their arrival to Ghana on November 10, 1961. The public outpouring of support for the queen surprised Mayfield, who recalled that "many of the market women wore ankle-length dresses emblazoned with photographs of Dr. Nkrumah and Queen Elizabeth." This stood in stark contrast to the fiery denunciations of British imperialism that were a constant feature of Ghanaian newspapers in the years following independence. See Henry Tanner, "Ghanaians Hail Queen in Parade: Nkrumah Vows Continuation of Esteem for Elizabeth," *New York Times*, November 11, 1961, 7; and Mayfield, "Ghanaian Sketches," 182–83.

9. It was an Akan custom to name children after the day of the week they were born. Kwame, for instance, is for a child born on Saturday. The other names are as follows: Kwasí, Sunday; Kwadwó, Monday; Kwabená, Tuesday; Kwakú, Wednesday; Yaw, Thursday; and Kofí, Friday. See Nkansa-Kyeremateng, *The Akans of Ghana*.

10. Historian David Levering Lewis called *Black Power* a "dyspeptic book" in his short memoir of his time in Ghana, "Ghana 1963." He also noted the irony that Wright's daughter, Julia Wright Hervé, "clearly shared none of her father's aversion to Nkrumah's one-party state." Kevin Gaines, though noting the flawed nature of Wright's book, insisted that it "demands our attention for his revisionist reading of the condition of blacks in the diaspora, which he understands dialectically as the product of slavery, dispersion, and oppression, and simultaneously, as the necessary condition for black modernity and the forging of an anti-imperialist critique of Western culture." Furthermore, the book should be considered an important "account of the interface of global black radical projects with the configurations of hegemonic power they confronted" as well as a challenge to the reified "Diaspora-Homeland binary." One of the few Black journalists to praise Wright was Charles Walker of the *New York Amsterdam News*. Walker urged readers not to be put off by Wright's "irritating mannerisms" because there is "no other book which can present so well the Africa of today to the descendants of the people who were torn away from it centuries ago and to whom Africa is not even a memory." See Charles Walker, "Africa Talks Back: Richard Wright Discovers Africa," *New York Amsterdam News*, city edition, October 9, 1954, 17; David Levering Lewis, "Ghana 1963: A Memoir," *American Scholar* 68, no. 1 (Winter 1999): 39–60; and Kevin K. Gaines, "Revisiting Richard Wright in Ghana: Black Radicalism and the Dialectics of Diaspora," *Social Text* 19, no. 2 (Summer 2001): 75–101.

11. Michael Clarke, "A Struggle for the Black Man Alone?" *New York Times*, September 26, 1954, BR3; and David E. Apter, "A Negro's Dim View of Africa's Gold Coast," *Chicago Daily Tribune*, October 10, 1954, U6.

12. Wright, *Black Power*.

13. While this "uplift" perspective on Africa is present in early Pan-African writings, especially in the early writings of W. E. B. Du Bois, Marcus Garvey, and George Padmore, by the 1940s most had abandoned the idea that diasporic Africans

needed to "save" Africa. Du Bois in particular chose to renounce his American citizenship in 1961 and relocate to Ghana, where he worked diligently in service of Nkrumah's vision of Pan-Africanism for the remainder of his life. While Kevin Gaines characterized Wright's anticolonialism as a means of recasting "diaspora as the mobilization of black modernity toward a transnational, transracial community of struggle," the articulation of an African American modernity remained deeply embedded with the shared language of Western superiority. Gaines asks, "What were the conditions either facilitating or mitigating the production and dissemination of knowledge between these intellectuals and audiences and vice versa? These questions move beyond issues of location framed by the diaspora [sic] 'return' to the ancestral homeland as a gauge of authenticity. Their ultimate aim is an account of the interface of global black radical projects with the configurations of hegemonic power they confronted. Wright's reflections on black modernity are exemplary and necessary for our response to the enduring material and spiritual crises of underdevelopment in Africa and among New World blacks." See Gaines, "Revisiting Richard Wright in Ghana," 75–77.

14. Wright, *Black Power*, 237.

15. Mannoni's *Prospero and Caliban: The Psychology of Colonization* was published in 1950. In it, Mannoni abstracted his experience during the Malagasy Uprising (1947–48) in Madagascar to all colonized peoples, arguing that their psychology was inherently "dependent" and that they would seek security in any kind of authority they could find. The Lacan-trained psychoanalyst was rebuked in 1952 by Frantz Fanon's *Black Skin, White Masks*, but by then his analysis of colonial "dependence" had become a mainstay of popular and bureaucratic discussions of colonial peoples. See Mannoni, *Prospero and Caliban*; Fanon, *Black Skin, White Masks*; and Wright, *Black Power*, 350.

16. Mayfield, "Ghanaian Sketches," 180.

17. Harold Isaacs, "A Reporter at Large: Back to Africa," *New Yorker*, May 13, 1961, 108.

18. Estimates of the size of this community vary. According to Kevin Gaines, this community's population fluctuated, numbering between 150 and 200 depending on the time. Leslie A. Lacy, an African American sociologist from Louisiana, claimed that the group numbered over 300 at its height. Class and social differences between different social and national groups, combined with the fluidity associated with an expatriate community where people were constantly arriving and departing, however, suggest that a comprehensive census is impossible. See Gaines, *American Africans in Ghana*, 7, 151; and Lacy, *Rise and Fall of a Proper Negro*, 22.

19. This line in fact comes from a speech given by Nkrumah in New York but was repeated often in other contexts. Peter Kihss, "Harlem Hails Ghanaian Leader as Returning Hero," *New York Times*, July 28, 1958, A9.

20. Mayfield, "Ghanaian Sketches," 183.

21. Mayfield, 188.

22. Julian Mayfield, "Uncle Tom Abroad: Genus Tomus Americanus in Africa," *Negro Digest* 12, no. 8 (June 1963): 37.

23. Mayfield, "Uncle Tom Abroad," 38.

24. While Mayfield did not mention anyone by name in "Uncle Tom Abroad," he made references in correspondence to the types of men and women he saw playing this role. In particular, Mayfield singled out Adger Emerson Player as one of the "skunks and judases" who worked at the American embassy in Accra. This was in reference to Player's role in the February 1964 protest by Afros at the US embassy. When the US flag was lowered by protesters, Player retrieved it and rushed it back into the embassy compound to prevent it from being damaged. For this he was criticized in the Ghanaian press, but after formal complaints by the Johnson administration, an apology was issued. See "Saves Old Glory," *Afro-American*, February 15, 1964, 1. Mayfield also made reference to African American businessmen traveling to Ghana who hoped to take advantage of African naivete in his draft manuscript of "Tales of the Lido" and in his play *Fount of the Nation*.

25. Mayfield, "Uncle Tom Abroad," 39.

26. W. E. B. Du Bois famously criticized African American attendees at the first African Writer's Conference in Paris in 1956 after he had been denied a passport by the US Department of State. Under the terms of 1950 McCarran Act, Du Bois was required to remain in the United States and had his passport revoked in 1952. It was not returned to him until 1958. Despite being prevented from attending in person, Du Bois sent a telegram to Alouine Diop, who read the telegram aloud at the meeting's opening. In the telegram, Du Bois condemned the African American attendees, which included James Ivy (National Association for the Advancement of Colored People), William Fontaine, Horace Mann Bond, Richard Wright, and James Baldwin (who wrote about the meeting for *Encounter*). "I am not present at your meeting today because the United States government will not grant me a passport for travel abroad. Any Negro-American who travels abroad today must either not discuss race conditions in the United States or say the sort of thing, which our State Department wishes the world to believe. It would be a fatal mistake if new Africa becomes the tool and cat's paw of the colonial powers and allows the vast power of the United States to mislead it into investment and exploitation of labor. I trust [that] the black writers of the world will understand this and will set themselves to lead Africa toward the light and not backward toward a new colonialism where hand in hand with Britain, France and the United States, black capital enslaves black labor again." See Kiuchi and Hakutani, *Richard Wright*, 338.

27. Mayfield, "Uncle Tom Abroad," 40.

28. Mayfield, "Ghanaian Sketches," 181. Here Mayfield is not referring to the long history of kidnapping and slave trading on the Bight of Benin that gave the area one of its old monikers, the Slave Coast. Instead, he is specifically referring to the modern form of governance that came about in the late nineteenth and early twentieth centuries following the 1885 Berlin Conference, which partitioned the continent into competing zones of European colonialism. In contrast to settler colonies such as Rhodesia, South Africa, and Kenya, Ghana (then the Gold Coast) did not see the formation of a settler class or the implementation of plantation-style agriculture. In contrast, the Gold Coast was considered a hardship posting and was administered by civil servants who exercised power largely through cooperation with ruling local elites.

29. Nkrumah's writings on this subject can be seen in various volumes, including Nkrumah, *I Speak of Freedom*; Biney, *Political and Social Thought*; Gordon, *Revisiting Kwame Nkrumah*; and Nkrumah and Obeng, eds., *Selected Speeches of Kwame Nkrumah*. Padmore considered African unity a necessary component of any meaningful resistance to both Western capitalism and Eastern communism, the two threats that he believed posed the most significant threats to modern Africa.

30. Mayfield, "Ghanaian Sketches," 183.

31. Shirley Graham, "Nation Building in Ghana," *Freedomways* 2, no. 4 (Fall 1962): 373.

32. In his 1983 treatise on nationalism, Benedict Anderson argued that these "communities are to be distinguished, not by their falsity or genuineness, but in the style in which they are imagined." See Anderson, *Imagined Communities*, 49.

33. More books have been published on Kwame Nkrumah than perhaps any other African leader, past or present, covering nearly every aspect of his life. A search of the WorldCat online database returns 7,893 results.

34. Russell Howe, "Strangers in Africa," *The Reporter* 24, no. 13 (June 22, 1961): 34.

35. Isaacs, "A Reporter at Large," 108.

36. Blyden used the term "African Personality" to distinguish intrinsic differences between the "European" and "African" character. He saw the former as competitive, combative, harsh, and individualistic, while the latter he presented as empathic, sympathetic, and highly spiritual. Rather than worshipping science and industry and expressing hypermaterialist ideas, Blyden outlined the "African Personality" as collectivist, warm, and welcoming, the opposite of what he saw in modern Europe. See Biney, *Political and Social Thought*, 119–20.

37. Nkrumah quoted in Quaison-Sackey, *Africa Unbound*, 35–36.

38. Quaison-Sackey, *Africa Unbound*, 35.

39. African Americans were not the only non-Ghanaians to serve the government of Ghana in this capacity. The framework Nkrumah envisioned was a broad enough category to contain anyone whose interests aligned with that of a united Africa free of colonial influence. This made for alliances that did not always align with Ghanaian nationalism and continental racialism. While invitations to join the Ghanaian Pan-African political project were aimed at Afro-Americans and Afro-Caribbeans, white South African communist in exile H. M. Basner and former Nazi glider pilot Hanna Reitsch joined the Nkrumah government in pursuit of African sovereignty. This also meant that African Americans who came to Ghana in search of markets for their products or who worked for the US Department of State were rejected, often to their surprise, by Ghanaian Pan-Africanists. Race remained but a single point of understanding, particularly for Afro expatriates, but national and class identities, Mayfield and other Afros wrote, could not be separated from racial ties. Unity lay at the intersection of these identities, and Mayfield joined other Africans and expatriates in Flagstaff House in writing within this framework for speaking about and interacting with the broader geopolitical discourses about Africa. See Bernhard Rieger, "Hanna Reitsch (1912–1979): The Global Career of a Nazi Celebrity," *German History* 26, no. 3 (2008): 383–405.

40. Ironically, Nkrumah and many of his closest ministers from the Convention People's Party had also been educated abroad. Nkrumah himself had graduated from Lincoln University in Pennsylvania and the London School of Economics.

41. David Levering Lewis, who taught at the University of Ghana at Legon during the early 1960s, recalled Mayfield as being exceedingly busy and difficult to reach during this era. "One usually got to see Mayfield by invitation only—unless one was accompanied by [Preston] King, who seemed to have the widest possible entrée. Mayfield was preoccupied with the startup vexations of *West Africa*, a monthly journal he hoped to make the *Encounter* of the region (though it was subsidized by Ghanaian special funds, of course, rather than, as with *Encounter*, by the CIA)." It is unknown if Lewis misquoted the title, as the magazine was titled *The African Review* upon publication of its first issue in May 1965, or if the name of the project changed at some point. See Lewis, "Ghana 1963," 47.

42. Mayfield, "Ghanaian Sketches," 198.

43. A. Morales-Carrion, "Seizing the Initiative on the Civil Rights Issue," June 13, 1963, RG 59, Classified Records of Assistant Secretary for African Affairs G. Mennem Williams 1961–1966, box 3, NN3-59-90-13, National Archives and Record Administration, College Park, MD.

44. William J. Jorden, "US Race Relations and American Foreign Policy," June 12, 1963, RG 59, Classified Records of Assistant Secretary for African Affairs G. Mennem Williams 1961–1966, box 3, NN3-59-90-13, National Archives and Record Administration College Park, MD.

45. Von Eschen, *Satchmo Blows up the World*.

46. Mayfield, "Ghanaian Sketches," 198–99.

47. Mayfield, "The Lonely Warrior," 16–17.

48. The series began with an article titled "Save Mae Mallory! Frame-Up in Monroe" and continued with three articles under the headline "Why They Want to Kill Mae Mallory!": "Monroe, No Man's Land," "Monroe USA: The Powderkeg Explodes," and "Monroe, USA: The Frame-up" published on March 29, 30, and 31 and April 3, respectively.

49. According to Meriwether, Kennedy saw the efforts to bring African students to the United States and the offer of foreign aid to new African governments as a way to convince African Americans of his commitment to racial issues without angering the Southern Democrats, whose votes in Congress he depended on. As the title of his article suggests, Kennedy saw that African intervention was "worth a lot of Negro votes" in the United States. See James H. Meriwether, "'Worth a Lot of Negro Votes': Black Voters, Africa, and the 1960 Presidential Campaign," *Journal of American History* 95, no. 3 (2008): 737–63.

50. Julian Mayfield, "Save Mae Mallory! Frame-Up in Monroe," *Ghana Evening News*, March 29, 1962, 5.

51. While it is true that Mallory spent much of her time in Monroe at the home of the Williamses and not with the Freedom Riders or drilling with Williams's defensive militia, it is inaccurate to claim that she played no significant role. Not only was her presence integral to protecting the Stegalls from mob violence when their car was surrounded upon entering Newtown, but she also served as a key person in

the support network that aided Williams's militia, ensuring that the self-defense committee was able to function. Mayfield's claims in this article were likely an attempt to present her as a more sympathetic figure for African audiences. In doing so, however, he succeeded in minimizing her role and contributing to the silencing of her long history of radicalism, which has only recently been reconsidered by scholars. See Ashley Farmer, "Maladjusted Negro: The Political Thought and Activism of Mae Mallory," manuscript in possession of the author.

52. Harold Reape's name is rendered as "Reepe" in some sources.

53. Julian Mayfield, "Save Mae Mallory! Frame-Up in Monroe," 5.

54. Arrested in Cleveland in October 1961, Mallory was released on bail for nearly a year. In October 1962 the Ohio Supreme Court rejected attorney Warren Haffner's plea to stop extradition to North Carolina, and she was returned to prison. In December 1963, the US Supreme Court rejected appeals by attorneys Len Holt and Warren Haffner to stop Mallory's extradition, and she was sent to North Carolina in January 1964. In February, an all-white Union County jury deliberated for thirty-two minutes before finding Mallory, Crowder, Reape, and Lowery guilty of kidnapping. Mallory was given the harshest sentence, while Crowder, Reape, and Lowery were given shorter sentences. In January 1965, the Supreme Court of North Carolina threw out the Union County verdict against Mallory and her three codefendants on the grounds that the jury had systematically excluded African Americans from the selection process. Mallory was freed, although the court reserved the right to indict her and her codefendants again in the future. See Farmer, "Maladjusted Negro."

55. "Plain Speaking," *Evening News*, April 13, 1962, North Carolina Central University, Shepherd Library, Microform Serial, January 1, 1962–July 1, 1962.

56. *Look Pretty for the People*, Mayfield's fictionalized account of life among the Black cultural Left in Harlem, was completed and sent to publishers in November 1962.

57. Nana Kobina Nketsia IV, who died in 1995, remains a celebrated figure in independence and politics due in part to his successful navigation of the partisan politics of postwar Ghana. During his short visit to Ghana in 1964, Malcolm X recalled in *The Autobiography of Malcolm X*, "Nana Nketsia . . . said that as an African his concept of freedom is a situation or condition in which he, as an African, feels completely free to give vent to his own likes and dislikes and thereby develop his own African personality." Maya Angelou, a close friend of Mayfield, arrived in Ghana in 1962 following her son Guy's involvement in a serious car accident. Their relationship, which Angelou alluded to in *All God's Children Need Traveling Shoes*, has been speculated on by Mary Jane Lupton. Lupton noted that Angelou was close with another couple, Molly and Kwesi Brew, who spent time with Nana Nketsia in Mexico City and had Angelou as their guest. Mayfield's archive mentions Nana several times in letters with Angelou and with his friend, Tom Feelings. See also Haley and Malcolm X, *Autobiography of Malcolm X*; Lupton, *Maya Angelou*; Letter from Maya Angelou to Julian Mayfield, September 5, 1970, SCH, JMP, box 4, folder 4, 2; and Letter from Julian Mayfield to Tom Feelings, July 19, 1971, SCH, JMP, box 5, folder 1, 1.

58. "Black Cultural Nationalism" was perhaps most profoundly articulated by Ron Karenga of US Organization in 1967 and 1968. See Ron Karenga, "On Black Art," *Black Theater* 3 (1968): 9–10.

59. The ideological debate between these different forms of nationalism maps the fault lines between Black Power movements during the mid- to late 1960s. Cultural nationalism, which Huey P. Newton derisively called "pork chop" nationalism, explicitly rejected the Marxist-Leninist framework, while the Black Panther Party's "revolutionary nationalism" emphasized it. Newton accused Karenga's US Organization of being "concerned with returning to the old African culture and thereby regaining their identity and freedom." Karenga's response to Newton was similarly derisive. "A lot of brothers play revolutionary; they read a little Fanon, a little Mao, and a little Marx. Although this information is necessary, it is not sufficient, for we must develop a new plan for revolution for Black people here in America." Newton and Karenga cited in Robinson, *Black Nationalism in American Politics*, 68.

60. Mayfield, "The Lonely Warrior," 249.

61. Mayfield, 250.

62. Publicly, Mayfield was supportive and laudatory toward the women writers in his orbit, including Maya Angelou, Rosa Guy, and Alice Windom, who examined their own experiences through the intersecting lenses of race, class, and gender. In his home, however, Mayfield expected his partners to fulfill traditional gender roles, as select correspondence with Ana Livia Cordero and Sandra Drake indicates. See Letter from Sandra Drake to Julian Mayfield, August 15, 1968, SCH, JMP, box 4, folder 14, 2–3.

63. In particular, "Black on Black" recalled Du Bois's 1928 novel *Dark Princess*. That novel examined the romance and union of an African American man, Matthew Towns, and the eponymous Princess Kautilya of Bwodpur, India. In Du Bois's story, the connections between Pan-Africanism and Pan-Asianism overcame the obstacles that divided the lovers, including racist violence in the United States and revolutionary activism in Europe. Written almost four decades later, "Black on Black" offered a vision of a union of Africa and its diaspora although smaller in scope, which suggested that Du Bois's utopian vision had soured in the intervening years. By then, his vision of unity had become fragmented and precarious, challenged by broader geopolitical issues and riven with internal tensions. See Du Bois, *Dark Princess*.

64. Notably, Nana Kiboda Nketsia IV did not share Nkrumah's public persona and in this way reveals the character of Nana to be a fictionalized composite.

65. Angelou's reasons for leaving Ghana were many, as she notes in her autobiographical accounts, marking Bessie as a composite character as well.

66. The fictional attempt to modernize a harbor in Songhay was a composite of various efforts in Ghana, including the construction of the damn on the Upper Volta River, the modernization of the port of Sekondi, and other capital projects that Nkrumah solicited while publicly criticizing neoimperialism and American interventions on the African continent. Mayfield, *Fount of the Nation*, Long version, SCH, JMP, box 2, folder 15, 138.

67. Mayfield, "The Lonely Warrior," 7.

68. Mayfield, 6.

69. Mayfield, 18.

70. Mayfield, 259.

71. Mayfield's choice to relocate to Ibiza marked the beginning of a formal separation from Dr. Cordero, but in a letter to David Du Bois, he expressed surprise that Cordero had not joined him. My own research indicates that Mayfield lived in a house belonging to Jan Carew, a Guyanese writer and intellectual who took over editorial duties at the *African Review* upon Mayfield's departure. See Julian Mayfield, "Letter from Julian Mayfield to David Du Bois," April 7, 1968, SCH, JMP, box 4.

72. Placído's groundbreaking dissertation "A Global Vision: Dr. Ana Livia Cordero and the Puerto Rican Liberation Struggle, 1931–1992" is currently being revised into a book manuscript.

73. A more recent blog post about Cordero explains her legacy thusly: "Cordero developed insights and implemented strategies that are as relevant to transnational liberation struggles today as they were during the years that she lived. As a Puerto Rican female doctor who traveled widely and maintained relationships with prominent leaders throughout the African diaspora, she had a keen understanding of the ways that racism and imperialism intertwined. Her global perspective and activism speak to the tensions and solidarities that continue to evolve in Afro-Diasporic communities. A greater awareness of Cordero's life will contribute to the bridges that need to be built and strengthened between Black, Latinx, African, and Latin American studies and communities." See Sandy Placído, "A Global Vision: Ana Livia Cordero and the Puerto Rican Liberation Struggle," *Black Perspectives*, December 10, 2016, www.aaihs.org/a-global-vision-ana-livia-cordero-and-the-puerto-rican-liberation-struggle/.

74. In a letter to David Du Bois, Mayfield noted that writing was easy in the laid-back climate of the Balearic Island, "but it is hell when you need to do research." Letter from Julian Mayfield to David Du Bois, April 4, 1966, SCH, JMP, box 4, folder 15, 1.

75. Letter from Maya Angelou to Julian Mayfield and Ana Livia Cordero, undated ["1966" written later], SCH, JMP, box 4, folder 11, 1.

Chapter 6

1. According to his passport, Julian Mayfield arrived at the Port of New York on May 27, 1967. He sailed aboard the SS *France*, having departed on May 22 from Southampton in the United Kingdom. According to his FBI file, he traveled in a two-berth room accompanied by a "Mrs. Mayfield." However, Ana Livia Cordero had been arrested in Ghana and deported earlier that year and was living in Puerto Rico at the time. Correspondence indicates that the woman traveling with him was Sandra Drake and that the two had a romantic relationship between 1966 and 1967. See passport issued November 25, 1966, SCH, JMP, box 2, folder 4, 3.

2. This quotation is taken from a memo dated August 23, 1967, from J. Edgar Hoover on the Counterintelligence Program (COINTELPRO) that was sent to all

offices within the FBI. See vault.fbi.gov/cointel-pro/cointel-pro-black-extremists/cointelpro-black-extremists-part-01-of/view, 3.

3. Biondi, *Black Revolution on Campus*; and Kendi, *The Black Campus Movement*.

4. It is unclear if Mayfield was aware of the social programs offered by the Black Panther Party in Oakland. While the performative militancy of Black berets, leather jackets, and long guns were relevant to his analysis, the free breakfast programs, the medical program, literacy efforts, and community patrols—all part of the party's appeal in East Bay communities—were not mentioned by him in his criticism. For more on such programs, see Abu-Jamal, *We Want Freedom*; Alkon, and Agyeman, eds., *Cultivating Food Justice*; Bloom and Martin, *Black against Empire*; and Brown, *A Taste of Power*.

5. Julian Mayfield, SCH, JMP, box 23, folder 12, "The Black Writer and Revolution," 1.

6. Mayfield, 3.

7. Letter from Julian Mayfield to William Marshall, February 18, 1973, SCH, JMP, box 6, folder 8, 1.

8. Peniel Joseph, "The Black Power Movement: A State of the Field," *Journal of American History* 96, no. 3 (December 2009): 752.

9. The full paragraph from the FBI's memo on COINTELPRO reads as follows: "The purpose of this new counterintelligence endeavor is to expose, disrupt, misdirect, discredit, or otherwise neutralize the activities of black nationalist, hate-type organizations and groupings, their leadership, spokesmen, membership, and supporters, and to counter their propensity for violence and civil disorder. The activities of all such groups of intelligence interest to this Bureau must be followed on a continuous basis so we will be in a position to promptly take advantage of all opportunities for counterintelligence and to inspire action in instances where circumstances warrant. The pernicious background of such groups, their duplicity, and devious maneuvers must be exposed to public scrutiny where such publicity will have a neutralizing effect." See Memo from Director of FBI, "Counterintelligence Program," August 25, 1967, 383, http://docs.noi.org/fbi_august_25_1967.pdf.

10. There were some independent projects that did not fit this dichotomy, and it therefore is limited to films produced by major Hollywood studios, such as Paramount, Palomar, and Universal, that received widespread distribution in the United States and Europe. Other "integrationist" films include *The Defiant Ones* (1957), *Odds Against Tomorrow* (1959), *The World, the Flesh and the Devil* (1959), *Lilies of the Field* (1963), *The Bedford Incident* (1965), and *To Sir, With Love* (1967). These films emphasized themes of interracial cooperation, integration, and understanding. Most featured Black and white characters overcoming their differences and cooperating amid extraordinary circumstances.

11. "Blaxploitation," a portmanteau of "Black" and "exploitation," first came into use following the release of the 1972 film *Superfly*. Response to that film prompted Junius Griffin, president of the Hollywood chapter of the National Association for the Advancement of Colored People, to organize a panel that would rate portrayals of Black characters in films such that "our children are not constantly

exposed to a diet of so-called black movies that glorify black males as pimps, dope pushers, gangsters, and super-males with vast physical prowess but no cognitive skills." Cedric Robinson argued in 1998 that "with a few exceptions blaxploitation was a degraded cinema." In an article that emphasized the negative social and political impact of these films, he historicized the emergence of the genre as capitalism's response to Black anger and frustration: the production of a constant stream of negative imagery. The sexualized and hypermasculine caricatures of Black liberation activists depicted in those films further solidified a link between Black radicalism and criminality. Blaxploitation, Robinson argued, was Hollywood's response to Black Power. In making films that emphasized the violence, sexuality, and degraded nature of Black life, Hollywood was "sustaining a more muted integrationism, while conceding that Black social protest was an emergent force from a community with a historical dimension and an urgent moral impulse." Author Sam Greenlee pointed out that "the vast majority of the films are not black films, insomuch as they are produced, directed, and written mostly by white folks for black consumption. If anybody is obsessed with sex and violence, it is the people who make the films." Addison Gayle pointedly wrote that "the best example of this kind of nihilism/irresponsibility are the Black films; here is freedom pushed to its most ridiculous limits; here are writers and actors who claim that freedom for the artist entails exploitation of the very people to whom they owe their artistic existence." See "Panel Formed to Combat 'Blaxploitation' in Movies," *Afro-American*, August 26, 1972, 22; Cedric J. Robinson, "Blaxploitation and the Misrepresentation of Liberation," *Race & Class* 40, no. 1 (1998): 2; T. Prescott Simms, "Black Films: What Next, Now That Whitey's Been Stomped?," *Chicago Tribune*, October 13, 1974, J70; and Addison Gayle, "The Black Aesthetic," *Black World* 24, no. 2 (December 1974): 40.

12. Sugrue, *Sweet Land of Liberty*, 255.

13. Letter from Julian Mayfield to Connor Cruise O'Brien, 1966, SCH, JMP, box 6, folder 12.

14. This plan was ultimately unsuccessful. In April 1969, a number of Cornell's Black students armed themselves with rifles and occupied William Straight Hall during parents' weekend. Mayfield, along with Dr. Gloria Joseph, would play minor roles as intermediaries between the students and the administration. Mayfield only made veiled references to the events in his autobiography and did not speak publicly about them. His presence is noted in one monograph. However, in a letter between Mayfield and gallery owner and artist Ivan Spence, Mayfield bragged that "you probably saw three students emerging from a sit-in at Cornell. Two of the youths were my students last year . . . and the fellows had reason to arm themselves." See Downs, *Cornell '69*; and Letter from Julian Mayfield to Ivan Spence, undated, SCH, JMP, box 7, folder 13, 2.

15. "Puerto Rican Doctor Jailed and Expelled from Ghana," June 11, 1966, SCH, JMP, box 36, 1–2.

16. Mayfield, "The Black Writer and Revolution," 2.

17. Julian Mayfield, "Negro Goals as Reflected in Negro Writing," 1967, SCH, JMP, box 26, folder 3, 1–6.

18. Letter from Julian to Max Black, April 4, 1967, SCH, JMP, box 26, folder 11, 1.

19. Mayfield's archive contains a fragmentary untitled draft that makes no mention of King and an outline for "The Black Writer as Revolutionary," which reflects substantive changes made in the wake of King's assassination. See "The Black Writer as Revolutionary: Outline," undated, SCH, JMP, box 23, folder 2, 2.

20. Mayfield, "The Black Writer and Revolution," 4.

21. Mayfield, 2.

22. Mayfield, 5.

23. A month later, Carmichael would step down from the position of chairman of SNCC, elevating Louisiana-born firebrand Hubert "Rap" Brown to the post. "I'm going to leave for the field to organize," Carmichael told reporters, "and you fellows can have the pleasure of taking your potshots at Brother Brown during the next year." See Jack Nelson, "Another SNCC Militant Replaces Carmichael," *Los Angeles Times*, May 13, 1967, 14; and Joseph, *Stokely*.

24. Stokely Carmichael, bereft over King's death, proclaimed an end to the peaceful program and the disruptive, nonviolent action of the civil rights era. In contrast, Bayard Rustin reaffirmed his commitments to nonviolence, citing examples of the changes wrought in the wake of King's assassination. While he argued that "Dr. King's death marked the end of one stage of the Negro struggle and the beginning of another," Rustin cited the full-page newspaper ad that Levitt and Sons (the real estate development firm responsible for the Levittown subdivisions with racially restrictive covenants) took out. The ad read in part that "as a tribute to Dr. King, this Company has adopted a new policy—effective immediately—eliminating segregation in any place it builds—whether in the US or any other country in the world. We ask all our colleagues to adopt a similar policy without delay." See Joseph, *Stokely*, 258; and Bayard Rustin, "Tears Are Cheap; Action, Alas, So Dear," *Philadelphia Tribune*, April 20, 1968, 7.

25. Mayfield, "The Black Writer and Revolution," 5.

26. Mayfield, 6.

27. Mayfield, 6.

28. Mayfield, 7.

29. Mayfield, 13.

30. Julian Mayfield, "Autobiographical Manuscript," SCH, JMP, box 15, folder 9, 16.

31. Mayfield, "The Black Writer and Revolution," 4.

32. Mayfield, 16.

33. Rhodes Johnson, "Writer: Negroes' Only Hope Is Destruction of US 'System,'" *Nashville Tennessean*, April 20, 1968, in Julian Mayfield Papers, SCH, JMP, box 1, folder 12, 1.

34. It is not lost on this historian that the Civil Rights Congress's 237-page pamphlet was titled "We Charge Genocide." The document, presented before the United Nations in 1951, provided an exhaustive and detailed documentation of lynching, wrongful execution, racist prosecution of Black defendants, and institutionalized anti-Black racism as "domestic genocide" directed toward African Americans. "We Charge Genocide" also argued that US anticommunism obscured human rights abuses against nonwhite Americans, linking institutionalized anti-

Black violence in the United States with anticommunist rhetoric against the "Red Menace" in China and Korea. Thus, at the same moment that anticommunist persecutions of men and women such as Paul Robeson, Claudia Jones, William and Louise Patterson, and W. E. B. Du Bois were being submitted to the United Nations and called "genocide," the potential for the use of Title II of the Internal Security Act provided a more efficient means to carry out this violence. Julian Mayfield, who was a member of the Communist Party of the United States of America at this time, published numerous articles about many of the crimes listed in the document—including the lynching of Willie McGhee and the execution of the Martinsville Seven—indicating that he was aware of the document, not to mention closely affiliated with many in the Civil Rights Congress, including Paul Robeson. See Civil Rights Congress, "We Charge Genocide: The Historic Petition to the United Nations for Relief from a Crime of the United States against the Negro People" (New York, 1951; reprint, New York: International Publishers, new ed., 1970), 7.

35. Internal Security Act of 1950 (McCarran Act) US Statutes at Large, 81st Cong., II Sess., Chap. 1024, Title II Emergency Detention, Section 100, 14.

36. According to the *Chicago Daily Tribune*, "The Truman administration is busy preparing two concentration camps in Arizona and another in Oklahoma for purposes described as the housing of potential spies and saboteurs in the event of war." In that article, the author suggests that Title II was inserted by Senators Herbert H. Lehman (D-NY), Hubert Humphrey (D-MN), and Estes Kefauver (D-TN) in order to force Truman to veto the bill. The article, however, continues an analysis of the constitutionality of the section of the McCarran bill, harshly criticizing any potential for the subversion of constitutional rights. See "Concentration Camps for America," *Chicago Daily Tribune*, January 4, 1952, 14.

37. P. L. Prattis, "The Horizon: The US Is Set to Fill Its Concentration Camps Now—Or Did You Know It?," *Pittsburgh Courier*, May 12, 1951, 20.

38. Williams, *The Man Who Cried*, 307–12.

39. The fictitious description ends with the "O" Committee Report, a chilling allusion to the extermination camps of the Third Reich, which Williams euphemistically describes as "Production." "Survey shows that, during a six-year period, Production created 9,000,000 objects, or 1,500,000 each year. Production could not dispose of the containers, which proved a bottleneck. However, that was almost twenty years ago. We suggest that vaporization techniques be employed to overtime the Production problems inherent in King ALFRED." See Williams, *The Man Who Cried*, 312.

40. Rhetoric similar to that around the King Alfred Plan can be seen in the response to Project 100,000. This project was approved by Defense Secretary Robert McNamara to recruit soldiers who were below the standard mental and medical standards then extant in the military. In practice, the plan increased the number of nonwhite men drafted without reducing college deferments, which disproportionately affected white men. Implemented in late 1966 as Secretary McNamara escalated the Vietnam conflict, Project 100,000, Kimberly Phillips has argued, was soon folded into President Johnson's "Great Society." Phillips's recent monograph links discourse critical of Project 100,000 to warnings by Black radicals in SNCC

and nationalist groups that "the survival of blacks in America" was at stake in the aftermath of King's assassination. Tracing the deep roots of antiwar activism as a catalyst for civil rights activism, Phillips notes how many activists considered Project 100,000 an effective form of genocide against nonwhite Americans. See Phillips, *War! What Is It Good For?*; and Hall, *Peace and Freedom*, 144.

41. The first mention of the King Alfred Plan in print media that I have been able to locate is in a *Chicago Tribune* article published on October 9, 1970. A young man named Clive De Patton of Des Moines, Iowa, testified before the House Intelligence Subcommittee that "many blacks believe in the existence of a plan to exterminate them." When representatives told the former Black Panther Party member that the scheme was entirely fictitious and a product of Williams's novel, De Patton insisted that it was true. "This plan is for use in case of a major uprising of the blacks in the entire United States—not in an isolated place like Chicago or New York," De Patton was reported to have said. "The first thing the white would do is send the 'black leaders' into the ghetto to try and quiet the people. If this doesn't work, then someone presses a button and the plan goes into effect." See "Ex-Panther's Tale Denied," *The Sun*, October 9, 1970, A7; and William Kling, "Undercover Cop Tells of 'Bomb School': I Was Trained to Kill Policemen, He Says," *Chicago Tribune*, October 9, 1970, 4.

42. Notably, Mayfield pointed out that "the fact of the matter is they don't need the labor of most White people but they—the message hasn't reach them yet." See *Black Journal*, Episode 7, 06:32:50.

43. *Black Journal*, Episode 7, 06:32:51.

44. *Uptight*, Dir. Jules Dassin, 1968.

45. According to Herb Boyd, Williams photocopied pages from the final page proofs of *The Man Who Cried I Am* and deliberately left the pages on the New York City subway. Not only did the publicity promote the book, but it also contributed toward its broader integration into Black culture beyond the five boroughs. See Herb Boyd, "The Man and the Plan: Conspiracy Theories and Paranoia in Our Culture," *Black Issues Book Review*, March 1, 2002, 1.

46. Sylvan Fox, "Radicals See Pretrial Detention as a Step to Fascism," *New York Times*, March 7, 1969, 48.

47. Laurence H. Tribe, "An Ounce of Detention: Preventive Justice in the World of John Mitchell," *Virginia Law Review* 56, no. 3 (April 1970): 371.

48. Ethel Payne, "Top Leaders Hold Secret Meeting with Atty. General Mitchell," *New Pittsburgh Courier*, November 1, 1969, 2.

49. Fleming, *Yes We Did?*, 72–73.

50. "Army Spy Confirms Black Control Plan," *Chicago Daily Defender*, January 2, 1971, 1.

51. Yette, *The Choice*, 16.

52. Another one of Yette's arguments in *The Choice* was that Nixon's declaration of the "War on Drugs" was a smokescreen to harass, repress, and marginalize African American communities. Although little attention was paid to this claim at the time, subsequent research has borne out Yette's argument. In a now-famous 1994 interview with John Ehrlichman, Dan Baum of *Harper's Magazine* quoted the former policy chief for the White House as stating that "the Nixon campaign in 1968,

and the Nixon White House after that, had two enemies: the antiwar Left and black people. You understand what I'm saying? We knew we couldn't make it illegal to be either against the war or black [people], but by getting the public to associate the hippies with marijuana and blacks with heroin, and then criminalizing both heavily, we could disrupt those communities. We could arrest their leaders, raid their homes, break up their meetings, and vilify them night after night on the evening news. Did we know we were lying about the drugs? Of course we did." Yette, who went on to teach at Howard University, remained committed to his arguments about the obsolescence of African Americans for the remainder of his life. He died in 2011. See Sundiata Cha-Jua, "We Need to Move beyond 'War on Drugs,'" *News Gazette*, April 10, 2016, C3; and Dan Baum, "Legalize It All: How to Win the War on Drugs," *Harper's Magazine,* April 2016, https://harpers.org/archive/2016/04/legalize-it-all/.

53. The Non-Detention Act did not ban detention outright but instead specified that congressional authorization for such detention is now required. Passed as Public Law 92-128, 85 Stat. 347 (1971), it was codified at 18 USC. § 4001(a).

54. Not only was Mayfield not mentioned in Yette's book, but it also appears that the two men did not correspond. Mayfield, however, made mention of *The Choice* in letters during the early 1970s indicating that he was at least aware of Yette's book.

55. My research indicates that this "English friend" was likely Robert "Robin" Cecil Romer Maugham, an author and later member of the House of Lords. Maugham was a friend and neighbor of Ivan Spence, a gallery owner, and the men were friends with Mayfield in 1966–67 when he lived on Ibiza. Mayfield and Spence exchanged numerous letters between 1969 and 1971 with references to a "Robin," whom I believe to be Maugham. See Julian Mayfield, "By Force and Violence," SCH, JMP, box 13, folder 10, 1; and Letters between Julian Mayfield and Ivan Spence, SCH, JMP, box 7, folder 13 (various pages).

56. Mayfield, "By Force and Violence," 2.

57. Julian Mayfield, "Everybody Loves the Africans of Rhodesia," SCH, JMP, box 21, folder 6, 5.

58. Julian Mayfield, "Black Techniques of Survival," Emory University, John O. Killens Papers, box 70, 2.

59. Mayfield, "Black Techniques of Survival," 5.

60. Mayfield, 6.

61. Mayfield, 11.

62. Hollie I. West, "The Goal of Julian Mayfield: Fusing Art and Politics," *Washington Post*, July 7, 1975, B1.

63. Mayfield, "The Black Writer and Revolution," 13.

64. Contemporary media reported that Jones accepted a part in *The Great White Hope* on May 10, 1968, and I believe this was the reason why he was unable to commit to Dassin for *Uptight*. See "Great White Hope Will Open on Oct. 3," *New York Times*, May 10, 1968, 57.

65. Julian Mayfield, "*Uptight* Notes—Blk Film Institute," undated (ca. 1979), SCH, JMP, box 18, folder 2, 1.

66. Letter from Max Black to Julian Mayfield, May 20, 1968, SCH, JMP, box 26, folder 1, 1.

Chapter 7

1. Julian Mayfield and Richard B. Moore, eds., *Black Journal*, produced by William W. Greaves, Volume 7, 1968, 06:31:10.
2. Mayfield and Moore, 06:32:50–06:35:41.
3. Mayfield and Moore, 06:35:33.
4. Kay Bourne, "Julian Mayfield," *Bay State Banner*, February 6, 1969, 1.
5. Julian Mayfield, "Explore Black Experience," *New York Times*, February 2, 1969, D9.
6. A British film based on O'Flaherty's book, also titled *The Informer*, was released in 1928 and is now both less well known and less well regarded.
7. O'Flaherty, *The Informer*.
8. According to Dassin, in 1948 Darryl F. Zanuck told him that he would soon be blacklisted but that he still would be able to make a film for Fox Pictures. Dassin was able to shoot the film, *Night and the City*, but was not allowed to edit it or oversee the score. Following this, Dassin fled to France, where he went on to direct eight films, including *Rififi* (1954), *He Who Must Die* (1957), *Never on Sunday* (1960), and *Topkapi* (1964). *Uptight* went on to be the final film he made in the United States, as he returned to shooting in Europe soon after. See Dan Georgakas, *Cineaste* 32, no. 2 (Spring 2007): 72.
9. Dassin quoted in Vernon Scott, "Dassin Hopes Negro Film Will Teach Whites," *Cleveland Press*, July 17, 1968, G3.
10. Dassin, who had been raised in Harlem, later told a reporter at the Cleveland-based *Call and Post* that "I try hard to understand the Negro problem, which is the white problem. I feel and care and think I understand. However, no white man can really say he knows what it is to be black." See "'Uptight' Premiered in Cleveland Tuesday," *Call and Post*, February 8, 1969, 3B.
11. Dee and Davis, *With Ossie and Ruby*, 326–27.
12. Julian Mayfield, "The Black Writer and Revolution," SCH, JMP, box 23, folder 12, 5, 13.
13. Letter from Lily Veidt to Jules Dassin, April 25, 1968, SCH, JMP, box 18, folder 2, 1.
14. Julian Mayfield, *The Betrayal*, undated (ca. May 1968), SCH, JMP, box 18, folder 1, handwritten comments on inside cover page of script draft.
15. Interviews with the film's writers indicate that there was a great deal of disagreement about this ending, with Dee and Mayfield intending for Tank to die solely from suicide, while Dassin intended him to die after being shot by a fellow militant. See Connie Harper, "'Up Tight' Gets Glamorous Hollywood Send Off," *Call and Post*, December 17, 1968, C1; and Lindsay Patterson, "It's Gonna Blow Whitey's Mind," *New York Times*, August 25, 1968, D13 (clippings and photocopies of articles present in Mayfield's papers at the Schomburg).
16. The handwritten commentary on the film scripts is in Mayfield's handwriting, and available correspondence in his archive is between him and Dassin. Due to the lack of textual evidence of Dee's contributions, Mayfield's influence is most prominent in this analysis. However, I believe that Dee's papers or some other

archive will shed more light on her specific contributions to the film beyond what is already known.

17. Michael Baseleon and Dick Anthony Williams, *Uptight*, DVD, Dir. Jules Dassin, Paramount, 1968.

18. See "SNCC Staff Meeting at Peg Leg Bates Club," SNCC Digital Gateway, https://snccdigital.org/events/sncc-staff-meeting-peg-leg-bates-club/.

19. It is unclear which of the three cowriters were ultimately responsible for Teddy's would-be redemption. Production notes and letters do not specify. Mayfield had expressed his distrust of interracial activism frequently and linked it to his time with the Communist Party, but he had also expressed his frustration with ideological orthodoxy. His overall pragmatism and generally strategic embrace of allies suggest that even if he was not responsible for the direction of Teddy's character, he likely approved of this wrinkle in his story.

20. In 1966, members of the SNCC-affiliated Vine City Project in Atlanta wrote a document titled "Black Power," in reference to Stokely Carmichael's recent statements in Mississippi. Among its conclusions, the document stated that white activists were harming the movement in the wake of the rising tide of Black consciousness; instead, the document suggested, white members of SNCC would better serve the organization by organizing in white communities and leaving Black communities to Black members. See "Black Power: Position Paper for the SNCC Vine City Project," Civil Rights Movement Archive, www.crmvet.org/docs/6604_sncc _atlanta_race.pdf.

21. Julian Mayfield, Jules Dassin, and Ruby Dee, *Betrayal*, second draft screenplay, 51.

22. Tank's motivation for this betrayal is made clear earlier in the film when he confronts Laurie, played by Ruby Dee, at her dilapidated house where her children are sleeping. During a conversation about money, a welfare agent arrives for an inspection, and Laurie hustles Tank out the back door. However, the agent spies Tank and accuses Laurie of welfare fraud, threatening to cut off her benefits. Not only is Tank's masculinity undermined by his inability to keep a job or maintain the discipline to participate in militant revolutionary activism, but his character's mere presence also threatens to undermine the livelihood of the woman he loves.

23. Mayfield, Dassin, and Dee, *Betrayal*, 70.

24. Norman Nadel, "Portrait of Unrest in Authentic Setting," *Memphis Press-Scimitar*, January 3, 1969, C1.

25. Nelson and Meranto, *Electing Black Mayors*, 360.

26. The Hough Uprising, also known as the Hough Riots, was a five-day confrontation between local residents of Hough, a working-class Black neighborhood, and Cleveland's white police and fire departments. Although Hough's population in 1966 was nearly 90 percent Black, most businesses and properties were owned by whites. The immediate cause of the violence was a series of confrontations between the white owners of the Seventy-Niner Café, on the corner of Hough Avenue and East 79th Street, and local residents. According to historical accounts, the café owners began barring certain residents from the café, especially those suspected of prostitution or drug dealing. In July, the café refused to serve water to either

patrons or local residents, and one of the staff allegedly posted a sign reading "No Water for Niggers." Following this incident, which took place on or about July 18, the café was robbed. After reports of the crime circulated, a crowd of approximately three hundred people gathered outside the café and began throwing rocks and threatening the owners. Abe Feigenbaum, who owned the bar with his brother Dave, reportedly responded to taunts by exiting the bar armed with a high-caliber rifle. When calls from the police went unanswered, the Feigenbaum brothers called the fire department, which responded and notified the police of a large crowd of rioters. According to the Feigenbaums, the rioters dispersed and headed down Hough Avenue, looting stores and setting fires as they went. Violence spread from there, and over the next five days, roving groups of youths, adults, and senior citizens battled police, fire officials, and subsequently National Guard troops. On July 23 violence and property damage were reported to have stopped, but National Guard units did not withdraw from the area until July 31. Although historical accounts indicate that the violence was spontaneous and fueled by poverty and poor living conditions, a grand jury called in August issued a seventeen-page report that alleged that "the outbreak of lawlessness and disorder was both organized, precipitated, and exploited by a relatively small group of trained and disciplined professionals of this business. They were aided and abetted willingly or otherwise by misguided people of all ages and colors, many of whom are avowed believers in violence and extremism, and some of whom are either members of, or officers in the Communist Party." In other words, the city claimed that the violence was the result of Black nationalists aided by communists. In total, nearly US$2 million of property damage was reported as well as dozens of injuries and four civilian deaths. See Moore, *Carl B. Stokes*, 42–45; Kerr, *Derelict Paradise*, 180–87; Kerr, "Who Burned Cleveland, Ohio? The Forgotten Fires of the 1970s," in *Flammable Cities*, ed. Bankoff, Lübken, and Sand, 330–32; "Guardsmen Leaving Cleveland," *New York Times*, July 31, 1966, 53; "First Troops Leave Area in Cleveland," *New York Times*, July 27, 1966, 27; "Grand Jury Called in Cleveland Riots," *New York Times*, July 26, 1966, 24; and Stradling and Stradling, *Where the River Burned*, 79.

27. Moore, *Carl B. Stokes*, 79.

28. Norman Jordan was born in Ansted, West Virginia, in 1938 but moved to Cleveland as a young boy. He was one of the most celebrated and widely published Affrilachian poets. Jordan's work included two published volumes, *Destination: Ashes* (1967) and *Above Maya* (1971). In Cleveland, Jordan became a leading voice in the Cleveland Poetry Movement and worked closely with Karamu House, one of the oldest Black theaters in the United States. He died in 2015. See the website Norman Jordan African American Arts and Heritage Academy, https://normanjordanaaaha.com; and Sieving, *Soul Searching*, 137.

29. "Producer Sees Mayor after Film Interruption," *Cleveland Press*, June 5, 1968, C9.

30. Patterson, "It's Gonna Blow Whitey's Mind," D13.

31. Sieving, *Soul Searching*, 139.

32. Special agent in charge to director of FBI, May 22, 1968, *Uptight* Motion Picture Files, #157-9534-1.

33. Sieving, *Soul Searching*, 139.

34. Sieving, 140.

35. The incident, known as the Glenville Shootout, began during a confrontation between members of the Republic of New Libya and the Cleveland Police Department. It is unclear who fired first, but the resulting gun battle lasted nearly an hour and resulted in seven deaths. Four days of property damage, violence, and assaults followed until the National Guard arrived and enforced a mandatory curfew. Local Black nationalist Fred "Ahmed" Evans, a prominent member of the Republic of New Libya, was ultimately convicted of the deaths of four police officers—Leroy C. Jones, Louis E. Galonka, Willard J. Wolff, and James E. Chapman—and sentenced to death. Following the federal moratorium on capital punishment (*Furman v. Georgia*, 1972), Evans's sentence was commuted to life in prison, where he died of cancer in 1978. See Masotti and Corsi, *Shoot-Out in Cleveland*, 97–100; and "Execution Stay Won by Evans," *Toledo Blade*, September 15, 1969, 10.

36. Zannes, *Checkmate in Cleveland*, xii.

37. Dassin quoted in Alex Madsen, "The Race Race!! or Too Late Blues," *Take One*, May–June 1968, 16–17.

38. Although the film was never officially released on VHS, bootleg versions of the film circulated in New York City during the 1980s and 1990s. The film was officially released on DVD and Blu-Ray for the first time in 2012 by a small film-publishing firm, Olive Films. However, the film's soundtrack, composed and recorded by Booker T and the MGs, had sold well and went through at least one reissue on vinyl. The soundtrack was also released on cassette and compact disc. Blu-Ray and vinyl record in possession of author; and email communication with Michael A. Gonzales, May 3, 2018.

39. Patterson, "It's Gonna Blow Whitey's Mind," D13.

40. Clifford Terry, "Acting, Script Both Stilted in 'Up Tight,'" *Chicago Tribune*, February 23, 1969, F12.

41. "On Film: Militants on a Pedestal," *Wall Street Journal*, December 19, 1968, 18.

42. Renata Adler, "Critic Keeps Her Cool on 'Up Tight,'" *New York Times*, December 29, 1968, D1.

43. Hazel Garland, "Stanley Theatre Movie Stars All-Black Cast," *New Pittsburgh Courier*, February 1, 1969, 20.

44. This piece, now located in Neal's archive at the Schomburg Center for Research in Black Culture, is also present in the FBI file on *Uptight*, surreptitiously photocopied likely by an informant. See Larry Neal, "Why Save America?," SCH, Larry Neal Papers, box 7, folder 28, 17; and "Motion Picture Entitled 'Up Tight,'" August 1, 1968, Motion Picture Files, #157-1471-17, FBI.

45. Laurie, played by cowriter Ruby Dee, offered viewers a rare portrait of a Black woman on film who was neither seductress nor loyal wife. Instead, Laurie's independence and determination to survive in spite of Tank illuminated for Giovanni the "triple oppression" of poor Black women in the United States and how her social class, gender, and race rendered her vulnerable to different institutional

forms of oppression. Nikki Giovanni, "And What about Laurie?," *Black Dialogue* 4 (Spring 1969): 14.

46. Bernard L. Drew, "Our Critic Reviews the Movie . . . and Then the Audience," *Hartford Times*, December 29, 1968, G1, G3.

47. Ruth Jett was born in Alabama in 1920 and relocated to New York in 1940. As a member of the Committee for the Negro in the Arts, she was responsible for producing William Branch's 1953 play *A Medal for Willie*, which featured Julian Mayfield. Jett later went on to be the executive director of the Cinque Gallery in Soho, which featured African American fine artists and opened in 1969. Jett died in 2014. See Victoria Horsford, "What's Going On," *New York Beacon*, May 22, 2014, 17.

48. Drew, "Our Critic Reviews the Movie," G3.

49. The student was referencing the Moynihan Report's conclusion about the supposed disintegration of the African American family as a result of poverty. S. Craig Watkins, writing in 1998, argued that Moynihan, "concluded that the structure of family life in the black community constituted a 'tangle of pathology . . . capable of perpetuating itself without assistance from the white world,' and that 'at the heart of the deterioration of the fabric of Negro society is the deterioration of the Negro family. It is the fundamental source of the weakness of the Negro community at the present time.' Also, the report argued that the matriarchal structure of black culture weakened the ability of black men to function as authority figures. That particular notion of black familial life has become a widespread, if not dominant, paradigm for comprehending the social and economic disintegration of late 20th-century black urban life." See Watkins, *Representing*, 218–19.

50. Ken Barnard, "Mayfield Stays Loose, Wins 'Up Tight' Role," *Detroit News*, January 19, 1969, 7C.

51. Sieving, *Soul Searching*, 158–59.

52. In his manifesto on the subject, "The Black Arts Movement," Neal argues that "a main tenet of Black Power is the necessity for Black people to define the world in their own terms. The Black artist has made the same point in the context of aesthetics. The two movements postulate that there are in fact and in spirit two Americas—one black, one white." However, in an unpublished chronicle of *Uptight*, Neal praised the film, its writers, and its actors. See Larry Neal, "The Black Arts Movement," *Drama Review* 12 (Summer 1968): 30; and Neal, "Why Save America?," 2.

53. Sieving, *Soul Searching*, 149.

54. Jesse H. Walker, "Theatricals," *New York Amsterdam News*, February 15, 1969, 20.

55. Sieving, *Soul Searching*, 151.

56. In contrast to *Uptight*, another Black-themed film helmed by a formerly blacklisted director, Herbert Biberman's *Slaves* was financially successful during the same era. The film starred Dionne Warwick as an enslaved protagonist who engages in a sexual and emotional relationship with the man who purchased her, played by Stephen Boyd. Ossie Davis had a supporting role. *Slaves*, according to contemporary critics, was more akin to an "art film" (aka pornography) than a serious drama. Despite these issues, *Slaves* was profitable and popular, which contrib-

uted toward studio decisions to shelve other "political" films in favor of the more exploitative and racy content. See Sieving, *Soul Searching*, 151–52.

57. One exception to this trend was Ivan Dixon's *The Spook Who Sat by the Door*, based on a novel by Sam Greenlee, that was released in 1973. However, due to FBI pressure, the film was removed from theaters and was "lost" by its distributor, United Artists. Rediscovered in 2004, the film was released on DVD. See Karen Bates, "Profile: Importance of the Movie 'The Spook Who Sat by the Door' on the Release of a 30th Anniversary DVD," *All Things Considered*, National Public Radio, March 2, 2004.

58. Audre Lorde, "The Master's Tools Will Never Dismantle the Master's House," in *Sister Outsider*, 110.

59. Sieving, *Soul Searching*, 149.

60. Ed Lacy was the pen name of Leonard "Len" Zinberg, a New York writer who was active in leftist and Jewish causes during the 1930s and 1940s. Zinberg published over two dozen novels including *Room to Swing*, which introduced what Ed Lynskey called "the first credible African-American PI" character in fiction. *Walk Hard, Talk Loud* was Zinberg's debut novel, published in 1940, and introduced Andy Whitman, a scrappy Black boxer on the cusp of turning pro. In the story, a gangster who runs the boxing racket opposes Andy, while a kind-hearted communist activist named Ruth saves him in the end. Highlighting discrimination, racism, and white gangsters' exploitation of Black athletes, *Walk Hard, Talk Loud* was critically lauded for its detailed portrayal of racial politics in pre–World War II boxing. See Ed Lynskey, "Ed Lacy: New York City Crime Author," *Mystery File*, no. 45, August 2004, 1.

61. Ruby Dee cited in Michael A. Gonzales, "UP TIGHT: 1st Blaxploitation Movie was a Baaad Mutha . . . ," *Ebony*, January 14, 2012, www.ebony.com/entertainment-culture/up-tight-1st-blaxploitation-movie-was-a-baaad-mutha.

62. Hoberman cited in Michael A. Gonzales, "'The Long Night': A Novel by Julian Mayfield," *Catapult*, https://catapult.co/stories/the-long-night-a-novel-by-julian-mayfield.

63. Mayfield, *Ten Times Black*, 5–6.

64. Julian Mayfield, "You Touch My Black Aesthetic and I'll Touch Yours," in *The Black Aesthetic*, ed. Gayle, 65–66.

65. Letter from Julian Mayfield to Maya Angelou, June 9, 1973, SCH, JMP, box 4, folder 3, 2.

Chapter 8

1. Julian Mayfield, "Political Refugees and the Politics of Guyana," *Black Scholar* 4, no. 10 (July–August 1973): 34.

2. Russell Rickford, "African-American Expats, Guyana, and the Pan-African Ideal in the 1970s," in *New Perspectives on the Black Intellectual Tradition*, ed. Blain, Cameron, and Farmer, 233.

3. Letter from Julian Mayfield to Preston King, September 11, 1971, SCH, JMP, box 6, folder 2, 1.

4. Tom Feelings, "Towards Pan-Africanism: A Letter from Tom Feelings to Julian Mayfield," *Black World*, August 1971, 27.

5. Tom Feelings was born on May 19, 1933, in Bedford-Stuyvesant, Brooklyn, and by all accounts was artistic from an early age. He attended the George Westinghouse Vocational High School in downtown Brooklyn, majoring in art. Following his graduation, he received numerous scholarships and published his first comic art as early as 1953. He visited Ghana in 1964, where he befriended Julian Mayfield, leaving sometime after the coup in 1966. Between the mid-1960s and his death in 2003, Feelings focused mainly on children's books, illustrating the writing of others as well as producing his own prints. The friendships he made while in Ghana, especially with Jan Carew and Sidney King (later Eusi Kwayana), encouraged Feelings's interest in Guyana, and he emigrated in late 1969, residing there until 1975. Feelings's papers are currently being processed at the Schomburg Center for Research in Black Culture in Harlem. See Feelings, *Black Pilgrimage*.

6. Five years later in 1976, *Black World* published its final issue after the Johnson Publishing Company fired Hoyt Fuller and retired the title. Fuller subsequently founded another magazine, *First World*, geared toward Black readers determined to stay abreast of international events. See Fenderson, "'Journey toward a Black Aesthetic.'"

7. As of 2023, Guyana now has overland connections with Brazil and Suriname, although the roads from Georgetown to the Brazilian city of Boa Vista are unpaved and often impassable during the rainy season. There is still no road connecting Venezuela and Guyana, but the porous border has become a flashpoint of tension as Venezuelan migrants, fleeing economic dislocation in the Bolivarian Republic of Venezuela, have been making the crossing more frequently since 2015–16.

8. Daryl M. Scott, "How Black Nationalism Became Sui Generis," *Fire!!!* 1, no. 2 (Summer/Winter 2012): 6.

9. Scott, "How Black Nationalism Became Sui Generis," 8.

10. This is not an oversight on Scott's part but rather a result of his narrow definition of nationalism, which limits expressions of nationalism to the borders of the United States. However, the nationalist impulse among African Americans has long transcended the boundaries of US political power both rhetorically and functionally, as figures such as Edward Blyden, Martin Delaney, and Marcus Garvey demonstrate.

11. Letter from Tom Feelings to Julian Mayfield, April 22, 1971, SCH, JMP, box 5, folder 1, 4. This letter was the basis of Feelings's open letter published in *Black World* that August. Mayfield joked with Preston King in another letter that was the result of Feelings "being a lazy writer, and having promised H. Fuller of *Black World* an article, Tom turned it into an open letter to yours truly." See Letter from Julian Mayfield to Preston King, September 11, 1971, SCH, JMP, box 6, folder 2, 1.

12. Following the formation of Tanzania from the nations of Tanganyika and Zanzibar in 1964, the new president, Julius Nyerere, invited African-descended peoples from around the world to join his Pan-African project. Among those who spent time in the nation were Student Nonviolent Coordinating Committee veterans such as Judy Richardson, Charles Cobb Jr., Robert P. Moses, and Courtland Cox and Black

Panthers such as Felix "Pete" O'Neal. Seth Markle has argued that "Tanzania played a significant role in shaping the anti-imperialist/pan Africanist politics of Black Power militants on a profound level." However, as a largely Swahili-speaking nation on the shores of the Indian Ocean, Tanzania proved linguistically, culturally, and geographically challenging for many African Americans who chose to be expatriates or sought sanctuary. The geographical proximity of Guyana and its anglophone history proved appealing to many. See Markle, "'We Are Not Tourists.'"

13. Mayfield, "Political Refugees and Politics," 35.

14. A more detailed account of the colony's founding and first two centuries can be found in McGowan, *Atlantic Slave Trade, Slavery and Guyana*; and Rodney, *History of the Guyanese Working People*.

15. British Guiana in 1946 was also approximately 10 percent Amerinidians and 2 percent Chinese immigrants. The remaining 8 percent were Portuguese and British, who controlled much of the sugar trade. See "World Population Prospects—Population Division," United Nations Department of Economic and Social Affairs, Population Division, https://population.un.org/wpp/.

16. Perhaps the only Caribbean nation whose demographics approach the unique breakdown that Guyana has is Trinidad, which saw a similar influx of Indian indentured laborers in the 1840s. In Trinidad, sugar planters also turned to indentured labors, as slavery was in the process of being formally abolished, but Trinidad only imported about half the number of Indian laborers that Guiana did, and they were never a majority in the island nation. See Rodney, *History of the Guyanese Working People*, 16–17.

17. Jagan was born in the rural village of Port Mourant in Berbice, and Burnham was born in Kitty, a suburb of the capital Georgetown. Both men attended Queen's College in Georgetown and left the colony to pursue advanced degrees. Despite the name, Queen's College is in fact a secondary school and was established by Anglican Bishop William Piercy Austin in 1844 to train the children of the colonial elite. Jagan went to the United States and sought a four-year degree in dentistry, and Burnham pursued Economics in the United Kingdom. Both men were politically active, Jagan at Howard University and later Northwestern University in the United States and Burnham at the London School of Economics. There Burnham joined the small cadre of Anglophone colonial students, including Errol Barrow and Kwame Nkrumah, in protesting British imperialism and the slow pace of decolonization. See Rodney, *History of the Guyanese Working People*, 144–46.

18. See Hinds, *Ethno-Politics and Power Sharing*; Hope, *Guyana*; Premdas, *Party Politics and Racial Division*; and Singh, *Guyana*.

19. Newspaper reports cited the links between leaders of the PPP and the "international Communist movement" as the pretense for Macmillan to order naval forces to Georgetown on October 7, 1953. The Colonial Office "felt it necessary to send naval and military forces to Georgetown . . . to preserve peace and safety of all classes." See "'Communist Threat' in British Guiana: Colonial Office Statement on Movement of Troops," *Manchester Guardian*, October 7, 1953, 1.

20. Letter from Winston Churchill to Colonial Secretary Oliver Lyttleton, May 27, 1953, cited in Rabe, *US Intervention in British Guiana*, 13.

21. Diplomatic historian Stephen Rabe has documented this history in more detail, examining how the Kennedy and Johnson administrations used the CIA to ensure that Jagan lost the election (despite winning a majority) and ensuring that "our man in Georgetown" (Forbes Burnham) was prime minister when Guyana declared independence in 1966. See Rabe, *Most Dangerous Area in the World*.

22. Following the 1961 election and a narrow victory for the PPP, the PNC was awarded more seats, resulting in widespread interracial violence between Afro-Guyanese and Indo-Guyanese groups. Jagan, however, became premier. See John Bland, "Leftist Parties Easily Sweep to Control of British Guiana Legislature in Election: Freedom Demand Expected 80 Per Cent Vote," *Washington Post and Times Herald*, August 23, 1961, B5.

23. Accusations of voter fraud were rampant during this election, with both Jagan and Burnham's erstwhile ally D'Aguilar claiming irregularities, intimidation, and miscounting in 1968. See Rabe, *US Intervention in British Guiana*, 65.

24. H. J. Maidenberg, "Guyana Proclaimed a Republic; Ties with British Crown Broken," *New York Times*, February 24, 1970, 3.

25. Between 1970 and Burnham's death in 1985, the PNC successively increased its majority in the Guyanese parliament as a result of rigged elections. During the 1970s and 1980s, the PPP provided limited support for Burnham's policies. See Nohlen, *Elections in the Americas*, 363.

26. Hopkinson, *Mouth Is Always Muzzled*, 167.

27. In fact, most of the maneuvering against Jagan to install Burnham was done so secretively that few were aware of it in the period between the 1961 election and independence. However, by 1967, newspaper accounts of CIA influence over data tabulation related to elections and the role of the AFL-CIO began to trickle out. It does not appear that African Americans and other Black peoples took these reports seriously, as many indicated their support for Burnham throughout the 1960s. See Paul L. Montgomery, "Jagan Assails Guyana's Drive to Register Voters: Election Rigging Foreseen," *New York Times*, December 17, 1967, 24; and Neil Sheehan, "C.I.A. Men Aided Strikes in Guiana against Dr. Jagan: Worked under the Cover of US Union in 1962 Drive on Marxist Premier," *New York Times*, February 22, 1967, 1.

28. Julian Mayfield, "Burnham of Guyana," draft manuscript, 42. This biography of Burnham remains unpublished. According to correspondence, Mayfield began the manuscript in early 1972 shortly after his arrival in the country. The book was supposed to be published by Paula Giddings at Howard University Press the following year, but disagreements between Mayfield and his editor over the focus of the book led to multiple delays and rewrites and the eventual termination of the project.

29. Mayfield, "Burnham of Guyana," 43.

30. The Black Power uprisings in Trinidad and Tobago the previous year, which had been the response to the police killing of an unarmed protester, resulted in the proclamation of a state of emergency by then prime minister Eric Williams. Subsequent strikes and mutinies led Williams to propose a new "Public Order Act" that would drastically curtail civil liberties, but the bill was never passed. In Jamaica, the 1968 disturbances known as the Rodney Riots (after Guyanese-born scholar-

activist Walter Rodney) were the result of nearly two decades of suppression of Black nationalist movements, which the government of Hugh Shearer (and his predecessor Alexander Bustamante) saw as inherently subversive. Rodney would later be expelled from Jamaica for his role in the uprisings. Other challenges to established governments occurred in Bermuda, the US Virgin Islands, and Curaçao as young Afro-Caribbeans rejected policies in response to calls for Black liberation elsewhere in the hemisphere and the world. See Quinn, ed., *Black Power in the Caribbean*.

31. Letter from Julian Mayfield to Joan Cambridge, September 24, 1971, SCH, JMP, box 1, folder 4, 1.

32. Mayfield, "Burnham of Guyana," 64.

33. Mayfield, 63.

34. Mayfield, 79.

35. Mayfield's use of the phrase "getting his hands dirty" was deliberate, as he argued that Burnham was at heart a farmer. In "Burnham of Guyana," Mayfield described how the prime minister worked his own farm, where he grew cassava, potatoes, and beans. Burnham also favored horseback riding and fishing over more hedonistic pursuits, although he was known to drink rum on the campaign trail. This, Mayfield argued, profoundly influenced Burnham's politics and his embrace of autarky. Unlike Kwame Nkrumah, who "was a sucker for almost any proposed publishing project," Burnham "did not possess a keen news sense. His thing is construction and farming. Go to him with a plan to form a co-operative in either of these areas, or even to set up your own farm, and you have got his support." See Mayfield, "Burnham of Guyana," 102–3.

36. Mayfield, "Burnham of Guyana," 96.

37. Eusi Kwayana was born Sidney King in Lusignan, Guyana, on April 4, 1925. Raised primarily in Buxton, a suburb of Georgetown, he became a cabinet minister with the PPP in 1953. Though he had been detained by the British Army after their intervention in 1953–54, Kwayana remained active in politics. At some point during the mid-1960s he was present in Ghana, where he made the acquaintance of Julian Mayfield, Tom Feelings, and Maya Angelou. After Kwayana returned to Guyana, he emerged as a dissenting voice against Burnham's rise to power, earning the prime minister's ire. In 1968 Kwayana met and married Ann F. Cook, who had been born in Buena Vista, Georgia. She later changed her name to Tchaiko Kwayana. Eusi Kwayana still lives in Guyana, and his life is worthy of further study. Tchaiko Kwayana died in Atlanta, Georgia, in 2017. See "An Interview with Eusi Kwayana: Caribbean Left's Legacy," *Against the Current*, no. 112 (2004); Rupert Roopnaraine, "Resonances of Revolution: Grenada, Suriname, Guyana," *Interventions* 12, no. 1 (2010): 11–34; and David Hinds, "Remembering Sister Tchaiko Kwayana," *Guyana Chronicle*, May 16, 2017, http://guyanachronicle.com/2017/05/16/remembering-sister-tchaiko-kwayana.

38. ASCRIA was a grassroots movement founded by Kwayana in the early 1960s. In its first incarnation, as the separatist African Society for Racial Equality, the organization promoted the partition of Guyana into three sections: an African section, an Indian section, and one section that was mixed. The failure of this scheme

to gain traction among the populace inspired Kwayana to found ASCRIA, which served as a cultural front for the PNC. See Eusi Kwayana, "Burnhamism, Jaganism, and the People of Guyana," *Black Scholar* 4, nos. 8–9 (May–June 1973): 42–43.

39. Mayfield, "Burnham of Guyana," 200–201.

40. Mayfield, "Political Refugees and the Politics of Guyana," 34–35.

41. Feelings, "Towards Pan-Africanism," 27.

42. Burnham, "Motion on Federation with the West Indies: 20th August, 1958," in *Linden Forbes Sampson Burnham, O.E., S.C. National Assembly Speeches*, 78.

43. Festus Brotherson Jr., "The Foreign Policy of Guyana, 1970–1985: Forbes Burnham's Search for Legitimacy," in "The International Dynamics of the Commonwealth Caribbean," special issue, *Journal of Interamerican Studies and World Affairs* 31, no. 3 (Autumn 1989): 9.

44. Julian Mayfield, "Guyana Public Relations Abroad," SCH, JMP, box 34, folder 21, 2.

45. Although Cordero and Mayfield had agreed on a divorce in 1966 when Mayfield was in Ibiza and Mayfield had apparently signed and notarized the papers there, when he decided to marry Cambridge he learned that he was still technically married to Cordero. After an exchange of letters, the couple agreed to divorce, and documents in Mayfield's archive indicate that this was carried out in Georgetown in late June 1972. Aside from a few letters in which Mayfield makes mention of his interest in Cambridge to friends, his archive does not contain much material about their relationship or their courtship. However, according to Ms. Cambridge, it was brief and intense, and the two were aligned not only romantically but also politically and ideologically. See "Mayfield vs. Mayfield," June 28, 1972, SCH, JMP, box 1, folder 3, 1. I am indebted to Sandy Placído for providing documents from Dr. Cordero's archive, including letters from September 4, 1966, and April 12, 1972, Papers of Ana Livia Cordero, Schlesinger Library, Harvard University, Cambridge, MA; and to conversation with Joan Cambridge, January 20, 2019, Georgetown, Guyana. Notes in possession of the author.

46. Mayfield's archive contains multiple proposals by him and Cambridge for projects as diverse as a documentary film on CARIFESTA '72 (an art and culture festival held in Georgetown), lesson plans for public schools, and the quarterly journal *New Nation International*, which Mayfield modeled after the *African Review*, founded in Accra in 1965. See Julian Mayfield Papers, SCH, JMP, box 32, box 33.

47. Mayfield, "Burnham of Guyana," 79.

48. Booker Sugar Estates Limited was founded in 1834 as Booker Brothers & Co. by George, Josias, and Richard Booker. In 1815 shortly after the Demerara colony was claimed by the British, Josias Booker took a job managing a cotton plantation and, seeing potential in sugar as a crop, invited his brothers to invest in its cultivation in the colony. In 1834 the brothers purchased their first ship in order to transport their product across the Atlantic. Through a series of advantageous purchases and marriages, the Booker family controlled most of the sugar plantations in Guyana by the middle of the nineteenth century. By the turn of the twentieth century the company, now named Booker, McConnell Ltd., oversaw large estate

holdings in Trinidad, Barbados, Jamaica, Nigeria, Canada, India, and British East Africa. By the mid-twentieth century Booker and its subsidiaries controlled 75 percent of the sugar industry in Guyana, in addition to cattle ranching, wholesale shipping, and the retail sale of consumer goods, which meant that Booker controlled the majority of the nation's economy. The company's influence in the colony was so great that the term "Booker's Guiana" was often used to highlight their power. Following the formation of the Guyanese Cooperative Republic in 1970, most of the Booker holdings in Guyana were nationalized, although by 1971 Burnham had quietly rehired many former estate managers in order to run the plantations more efficiently. In 1968, Booker, McConnell Ltd. began sponsoring a literary prize, now known as the Man Booker Prize, that awards winners a sum of £50,000 each year. See Natalie Hopkinson, "The Booker Prize's Bad History," *New York Times*, October 17, 2017, www.nytimes.com/2017/10/17/opinion/man-booker-bad-history.html.

49. Following the appropriation of its massive sugar holdings, Booker retained its presence in mundane aspects of Guyanese society. Mayfield's archive contains numerous invoices from retailers, storage facilities, and other businesses identifying them as Booker subsidiaries. See Julian Mayfield Papers, SCH, JMP, box 32, for examples, including documents from "Bookers Stores Limited" and "Bookers Storage."

50. It is unclear to what extent Mayfield contributed to these documents. While drafts exist with marginalia written in his handwriting, the cadence of the documents reflects Burnham's speech patterns more so than Mayfield's. In some cases, multiple copies of these documents exist in Mayfield's archive with annotations and edits indicating that he revised them. In other cases, handwritten notes by Mayfield are affixed to the typed documents indicating how they are to be printed and distributed. My research suggests that Mayfield's role in these documents was that of an editor and researcher, working alongside Joan Cambridge and other staff at the Ministry of Information and Culture to prepare them for distribution to PNC party conferences and government meetings. While Mayfield might not have composed them, he clearly contributed to their construction in substantive ways.

51. Julian Mayfield, "The Ideology of Our Party: The Leader Extract Part III," undated, SCH, JMP, box 33, folder 8, 9.

52. Mayfield, "Burnham of Guyana," 39.

53. Mayfield, 98–99.

54. Mayfield, 99.

55. Mayfield, 101–2.

56. The undated memo, likely from 1973, was addressed to Minister Elvin McDavid. In it, Mayfield argued that "television for Guyana would be dangerous because (1) a small, relatively poor nation embarked on a genuine socialist revolution, cannot afford to experiment with capitalist matches over which it cannot hope to retain control; (2) Guyana is a non-white nation and the images which the PNC and the Government set before its people must reflect the racial composition of the population, and not the white images of the colonial era; (3) Under no circumstances can Guyana now or in the near future hope to produce enough of its own indigenous programs to satisfy the never-ending demands of TV; (4) It would be politically foolhardy for the PNC government to introduce TV *at this time* because

when it followed the inevitable capitalist course as it has in every other small nation in the West and in Africa, it could be pointed to as a glaring example of PNC failure . . . ; (5) All countries outside the Communist bloc[,] . . . despite brave starts, have eventually succumbed to the temptation to fill their empty TV hours with cheap, canned programmes from the United States. The message carried in all of these programs militate against the message of the PNC government. . . . TV—with its double-barreled audio-visual impact—is much more effective than radio can ever be." Memo to Elvin McDavid, "RE: Television for Guyana," undated, SCH, JMP, box 32, folder 20, 2–3.

57. Julian Mayfield, "Women's Work Not Appreciated Says Elvin McDavid," undated, SCH, JMP, box 32, folder 12, 1.

58. It is unclear if Mayfield was aware of Hill during the filming of *Uptight* in Cleveland or if he was aware of the cultlike nature of the House of Israel, the organization that Hill had founded in Cleveland and brought with him to Guyana, but his letter to the prime minister indicates that he welcomed any ally of the PNC to Guyana. According to contemporary newspaper accounts, Hill, along with Jim Raplin and Reverend Ernest Hilliard (also known as local radio personality Prophet Frank Thomas), founded the House of Israel in Cleveland sometime in the mid-1960s. Espousing a militant Black separatist ideology, Hill dubbed himself Rabbi Hill and soon attracted a number of followers. During the late 1960s, Rabbi Hill initiated a boycott against local white-owned businesses, urging locals to "buy black." In 1968 Hilliard was found murdered, and Hill and Raplin were discovered to have fled the country. According to Mayfield's letter to Burnham, Hill stopped over in Trinidad, running out on a hotel bill, before arriving in Georgetown in late 1971. In 1972, Hill was convicted of blackmail in absentia in relation to his boycott of white businesses in Cleveland, but by then he had already been allowed to settle in Guyana, where he became an organizer and an enforcer with the PNC. See "Raplin Faces 20-Year Sentence for Blackmail," *Call & Post*, City edition, May 13, 1972, 1A; and Alvin Ward, "Rabbi Hill Still Missing from Trial," *Call & Post*, City edition, November 20, 1971, 1A.

59. Mamadou Lumumba was born Kenneth M. Freeman in October 11, 1938. A graduate of the University of San Francisco in 1960, Lumumba took his name based on his resemblance to Congolese prime minister Patrice Lumumba. In 1965 Mamadou Lumumba founded the quarterly journal *Soulbook* along with Donald Freeman, Isaac Moore, Carroll Holmes, and Ernie Allen. Lumumba was a member of the Revolutionary Action Movement and founding member of the Black Panther Party for Armed Self-Defense in Oakland, California. See Akinyele Umoja, "From One Generation to the Next: Armed Self-defense, Revolutionary Nationalism, and the Southern Black Freedom Movement," *Souls* 15, no. 3 (2013): 218–40, www.academia.edu/5193708/From_One_Generation_to_the_Next_Armed_Self-defense_Revolutionary_Nationalism_and_the_Southern_Black_Freedom_Movement.

60. The Pan-African Secretariat emerged in 1966 as the San Francisco Pan-African People's Organization (which had been founded as the Afro-American Institute) and was again reorganized by organizer Oba T'Shaka and the San Francisco chapter of the Congress of Racial Equality. Largely an umbrella organization,

made up of smaller liberatory and Pan-African groups, the Pan-African Secretariat was explicitly dedicated to African liberation on the continent and in the diaspora.

61. Kwayana, "Burnhamism, Jaganism and the People of Guyana," 45.

62. Mayfield, "Political Refugees and the Politics of Guyana," 34–35.

63. Letter from Julian Mayfield to Forbes Burnham, undated, SCH, JMP, box 7, folder 6, 1–2. Mayfield was referring here to any number of incidents involving the Black Panther Party and Ron Karenga's "Organization Us." Between 1968 and the early 1970s the FBI deliberately stoked tensions between the groups, which resulted in the deaths of Alprentice "Bunchy" Carter and John Higgins during elections of the Afro-American Studies Center at the University of California at Los Angeles.

64. The WPA was a fusion of multiple groups, including the Working People's Vanguard Party, ASCRIA, the Indian Political Revolutionary Associates, and Ratoon (an Indo-Guyanese working-class party). See Rickford, "African-American Expats, Guyana, and the Pan-African Ideal in the 1970s," 5.

65. According to Kwayana, after settling in Guyana Hill refounded the House of Israel and adopted the name "Rabbi Washington." He became affiliated with the PNC. Rabbi Washington attracted a following of Guyanese men and women who considered him a prophet and declared in the *New York Times* that "it is safe to say that I am the first and last word," a deliberate reference to the New Testament Book of Revelation, 1:8, in which the author declares that he is the "alpha and the omega." The House of Israel subsequently evolved into a paramilitary wing of the PNC and violently broke up a WPA rally in Georgetown on August 22, 1979. Eusi Kwayana, who witnessed the violent response, reported that "a squad of uniformed policemen, including Rabbi Washington's men dressed in police uniform and carrying no regulation numbers, attacked the meeting which they claimed was illegal. It was a total assault with batons on the crowd of peaceful citizens by a crowd of well-armed policemen of the Tactical Service Unit (Riot Squad). . . . Scores of people were beaten by the police. They were on fire with venom not noticed before. This was due to the House of Israel." Mayfield's archive indicates that he came to regret taking Hill's case to the prime minister. In an undated handwritten letter addressed to Burnham, Mayfield referenced this violent encounter, expressing his sadness at hearing of the violence. "I deplore hooliganist violence against dissenters directed by the fraudulent Rabbi Washington for whose introduction into Guyana you and I are largely responsible." Although the letter is undated, Mayfield signed it, indicating that he was writer-in-residence at Howard University, a position he held between 1979 and his death in 1984. See Kwayana, *Walter Rodney*, 15; Joseph B. Treaster, "Black Supremacist Heads Guyana Cult," *New York Times*, October 21, 1979, 7; and Letter from Julian Mayfield to Forbes Burnham, undated, SCH, JMP, box 32, folder 19.

66. Letter from Julian Mayfield to Forbes Burnham, undated, SCH, JMP, box 32, folder 19, 2.

67. Mayfield, "Burnham of Guyana," 204.

68. Mayfield, 205.

69. Walter Rodney was assassinated by a car bomb on June 13, 1980, in Georgetown following independence celebrations for the new nation of Zimbabwe.

A member of the Guyanese Defense Force, Gregory Smith, is reported to have given the bomb to Rodney. This has led many in Guyana and abroad to connect his assassination with Forbes Burnham, suggesting that Burnham ordered Rodney's killing. Burnham died in 1985 at the age of sixty-two. See "Guyanese Leader, Dead at 62, Had a Reputation for Ruthlessness," *Globe and Mail*, August 7, 1985, 10.

70. Walter Rodney, "Contemporary Political Trends in the English-Speaking Caribbean," *Black Scholar*, September 1975, 15, 21.

71. Rodney, "Contemporary Political Trends," 20.

72. Conversation with Joan Cambridge, January 20, 2019, Georgetown, Guyana.

73. Letter from Dr. Marvin S. Belsky, MD, undated, SCH, JMP, box 32, folder 12, 1.

74. Cambridge's first novel, *Clarise Cumberbatch Want to Go Home*, was published in 1987. Written in Guyanese Creole, the novel traces the eponymous Guyanese woman's journey to the United States to find her wayward African American husband, Harold. Portraying a Third World feminist perspective on the masculine militancy of African American radical movements, the protagonist is continuously dismissed, marginalized, and ignored by the very people who claim to be acting in her interest. In one of the novel's most poignant scenes, she encounters a young Afghan woman, and the two women bond over the recent invasions of Grenada and Afghanistan by the United States and the Soviet Union, respectively. The encounter offers a poignant example of how even radical African American critiques of the Cold War were inadequate when it came to issues of gender, class, and relationships that crossed into the Global South. See Cambridge, *Clarise Cumberbatch*.

Chapter 9

1. Julian Mayfield, *King Christophe*, second draft, SCH, JMP, box 18, folder 2, 120.

2. There has been a renewed interest in Christophe and the northern Kingdom of Haiti (as distinguished from the Southern Haitian Republic) in recent years. See Doris L. Garraway, "Empire of Freedom, Kingdom of Civilization: Henry Christophe, the Baron De Vastey, and the Paradoxes of Universalism in Postrevolutionary Haiti," *Small Axe* 16, no. 3 (2012): 1–21; Doris L. Garraway, "Print, Publics, and the Scene of Universal Equality in the Kingdom of Henry Christophe," *L'Esprit Créateur* 56, no. 1 (2016): 82–100; Cole, *Christophe, King of Haiti*; Moran, *Black Triumvirate*; Newcomb, *Black Fire*; and James, *The Black Jacobins*.

3. According to historical accounts, Christophe had recently suffered a stroke, and a number of his officers, who chafed under his discipline, sought to overthrow him. They were joined by tens of thousands of Haitian peasants, who marched on the Citadel at Cap Haitien. Rather than face a mutiny and the anger of his subjects, Christophe shot himself. Reportedly, he did so with a silver bullet fired from his own pistol. See Vandercook, *Black Majesty*; and Walcott, *The Haitian Trilogy*.

4. Although Burnham would not institute forced labor or legally bind peasants to sugar plantations, in the late 1970s he would encourage political violence against his rivals in the opposition and is suspected to have ordered the assassination of scholar and political activist Walter Rodney by a car bomb in 1980.

5. Despite ongoing communication with Marshall's son, Tariq, I have not been able to access the personal papers of William Marshall.

6. Vandercook's novel, ostensibly a biography, is not a scholarly work. Despite this, it has been cited by generations of Black historians, including John H. Clarke, John Hope Franklin, and C. L. R. James, for its sympathetic portrait of Christophe and the Haitian government following the deaths of Toussaint L'Ouverture and Jean-Jacques Dessalines.

7. Anthony Quinn (aka Antonio Rodolfo Quinn Oaxaca) was the son of an Irish father and a Mexican mother. He was born in Chihuahua in 1915 amid the Mexican Revolution. Coincidentally, Jean-Claude Duvalier was married to one of King Henry I's descendants. Michèle Bennett, the mother of his two children, was a great-great-great-granddaughter of Henri Christophe.

8. It is unclear the extent to which President Jean-Claude Duvalier was involved in either Quinn's or Marshall's efforts to film a movie in Haiti or if he was involved at all. His father, François Duvalier, was well known as a patron of the arts, but Jean-Claude was known for delegating most of his responsibilities to his advisers and taking very little interest in governing Haiti, especially early on in his administration.

9. William Marshall and Tony Quinn, "An Exchange between William Marshall and Anthony Quinn: The Black King Must Be Black," *Black Scholar* 3, no. 10 (Summer 1972): 50.

10. See Sepinwall, *Slave Revolt on Screen*.

11. While dates are not given in the film, the fact that Haiti's generals are making preparations for the invasion led by General LeClerc places the action sometime between 1800 and 1801.

12. I am indebted to the master's thesis of Alan Lipke for a well-researched and thoughtful analysis of King Dick's life and story. Alan Thomas Lipke, "The Strange Life and Stranger Afterlife of King Dick Including His Adventures in Haiti and Hollywood with Observations on the Construction of Race, Class, Nationality, Gender, Slang Etymology and Religion," Digital Commons, 2013, http://scholarcommons.usf.edu/etd/4530.

13. Julian Mayfield, "Autobiographical Manuscript," SCH, JMP, box 15, folder 9, 94.

14. James L. Hicks, "Negro Actors Steal Film Premiere," *Cleveland Call and Post*, May 24, 1952, 1B. Hicks's comments may have been somewhat exaggerated, as no criticisms of Marshall escorting Francis to the premiere have been discovered in contemporary newspaper accounts.

15. Hazel L. Lamarre, "All the World's a Stage," *Los Angeles Sentinel*, July 3, 1952, B2.

16. See Ellen Holly, "Living a White Life—for a While," *New York Times*, August 10, 1969, D13; Agnes Nixon, "What Do Soaps Have to Do to Win Your Approval?," *New York Times*, May 28, 1972, D13; Abernathy, "African Americans' Relationship with Daytime Serials," PhD diss.; and Libby Slate, "One Life, 25 Years: ABC Serial Hits a Quarter Century Still the Soap with a Social Conscience," *Los Angeles Times*, July 11, 1993, 74.

17. Ellen Holly, "Black History Does Not Need Tony Quinn," *New York Times*, June 11, 1972, D1.

18. Holly, D1.

19. Pamala Haynes, "Right On," *New Pittsburgh Courier*, September 16, 1972, 7.

20. Emily F. Gibson, "She Gets Vibrations re 'Black Majesty,'" *Los Angeles Sentinel*, September 20, 1973, A7.

21. This claim came from the *Caribbean Daily*, a tabloid published in New York for Anglophone West Indian expatriates in the United States and Canada. In an article published on July 23, 1973, Edwini Walker examined *Haiti Hebdo* and reported that Anthony Quinn was paying Haitian journalists Frantz Pratt and Richard Kayatt to operate the new magazine as a front for sympathetic perspectives on his plan to film *Black Majesty* on the island. See Edwini Walker, "A Gimmick—Haitian US Mission Charges Actor Anthony Quinn," *Caribbean Daily*, July 23, 1973, 4.

22. Gibson, "She Gets Vibrations,'" A7.

23. Letter from William Marshall to Julian Mayfield, August 11, 1975, SCH, JMP, box 5, folder 1, 1–2.

24. Alix Matheiu and Pierre-Michel Fontaine, "A Haitian Hero," *New York Times*, July 9, 1972, D12.

25. Letter from Julian Mayfield to Tom Feelings, June 5, 1973, SCH, JMP, box 5, folder 1, 1.

26. According to newspaper accounts, the SGA went on strike against the Association of Motion Picture and Television Producers on March 6, 1973, demanding pay raises for one-hour filmed programming. The strike ended on June 24, 1973, after the Director's Guild joined the strike, but a contract would not be signed until March 1977. The strike forced NBC, CBS, and ABC to delay much of their fall programming. See "Writers Go on Strike against TV Producers, Motion Picture Firms," *Wall Street Journal*, March 7, 1973, 4; "Writers Guild Strikes Major Producers on Coast; Union Seeks Almost Fourfold Increase in Wages," *New York Times*, March 7, 1973, 35; Albin Krebs, "Networks Struck by Writers Guild," *New York Times*, April 13, 1973, 7; "Writers Approve Pacts with the Networks, Movie, TV Producers," *Wall Street Journal*, March 3, 1977, 11; and Letter from Julian Mayfield to Tom Feelings, June 5, 1973, box 5, folder 1, 1.

27. Oral history with Joan Cambridge, January 10, 2019, Georgetown, Guyana.

28. Letter from Julian Mayfield to William Marshall, February 18, 1973, SCH, JMP, box 32, folder 15, 1.

29. Letters in Mayfield's archive indicate that Marshall contacted, among others, John Johnson of Johnson Publishing Company, producer Berry Gordy, Sidney Poitier, and Harry Belafonte.

30. This idea has only recently gained traction in scholarship about the Haitian Revolution. See Chris Davis, "Before They Were Haitians: Examining Evidence for Kongolese Influence on the Haitian Revolution," *Journal of Haitian Studies* 22, no. 2 (2016): 4–36; Christina Frances Mobley, "The Kongolese Atlantic: Central African Slavery and Culture from Mayombe to Haiti," Duke University ProQuest Dissertations and Theses, 2015.

31. Julian Mayfield, *Christophe* film treatment draft, Undated, SCH, JMP, box 18, folder 9, 2.

32. Christophe personally oversaw the development of a system of Haitian peerage beginning in 1808. The new Haitian noble class included four princes, eight dukes, twenty-two counts, forty barons, and fourteen knights. He also founded the College of Arms to create heraldic visuals. For his own coat of arms, Christophe used a crowned phoenix rising from flames. Underneath the phoenix was the motto "Je renais de mes cendres" (I rise from my ashes). See James, *The Black Jacobins*, 199.

33. In an odd twist, Mayfield wrote a letter to Burnham following his return to Guyana after his second meeting with Marshall asking the prime minister to consider shooting the film in Guyana. The letter made note of the resemblance of Rupununi, a region in southern Guyana, to the highlands of Haiti's interior. "In view of the present economic crisis . . . there is no reason why the Rupununi should not be used for making such a motion picture, and my view is that Guyana should strive to become a motion picture capital of the world." No reply from Burnham about this subject is present in Mayfield's archive. See Letter from Julian Mayfield to Forbes Burnham, undated, SCH, JMP, box 18, folder 8, 1.

34. Among other changes, in Mayfield's draft Christophe dies of a stroke rather than taking his own life. Christophe did have a stroke shortly before his suicide in 1820, but he survived until the Citadel of Sans Souci was taken by renegade forces accompanied by Haitian peasants. See Julian Mayfield, *Christophe*, second draft, undated, SCH, JMP, box 18, folder 8, 97.

35. The claim that Christophe shot himself, either in the heart or the head, with a silver bullet from one of his own pistols is commonly cited in scholarly and popular accounts of the king's death.

36. Letter from William Marshall to Julian Mayfield, August 11, 1975, SCH, JMP, box 5, folder 1, 1–2.

Epilogue

1. Email from Wahneema Lubiano to author, April 27, 2019.
2. Julian Mayfield, "Greer Journal," August 12, 1982, SCH, JMP, Box 1, 9.
3. Mayfield, "Greer Journal," 1.
4. At issue were a public disclosure in early February of Jackson's receipt of US$200,000 from the Arab League, a 1979 visit with the Palestine Liberation Organization's Yasser Arafat, and criticism of previous comments made by Jackson related to Jewish control of the media by the Jewish Defense League. See Mark Shields, "Arabs, Jews and Jackson," *Washington Post*, February 10, 1984, A19; and Dennis Farney, "What Makes Jesse Run: He Is Impelled by a Haunting Fear—Jackson's Boyhood Plays Role in Presidential Campaign; Syria Move Shows Instinct," *Wall Street Journal*, Eastern edition, January 3, 1984, 1.
5. "The Post said a nameless, faceless person said it," Jackson told reporters on a flight after the story was published. "In the story they do not have a source. It's a rumor and whoever said it should expose his face and say the reason why." See

"Jackson Denies He Said Jews Are Hymies," *Atlanta Constitution*, February 19, 1984, 13A.

6. "Jesse Admits, Apologizes for 'Hymie' Remark," *Philadelphia Daily News*, February 27, 1984, 4.

7. Joyce Purnick and Michael Oreskes, "Jesse Jackson Aims for the Mainstream," *New York Times*, November 29, 1987, 34.

8. Carl T. Rowan, "Muslim Leader's Actions Hurt Jackson, All Blacks," *Atlanta Constitution*, April 11, 1984, 15A.

9. Carl T. Rowan, "A Threat to All Blacks," *Washington Post*, April 4, 1984, A23.

10. Julian Mayfield, "Sorting Us Out," *Washington Post*, April 20, 1984, A15.

11. Julian Mayfield, "Is He Really a Scoundrel?," *Washington Post*, July 8, 1984, D7.

12. *The Giant That Many Overlooked* was a play for children written by Obi Egbuna Jr. and Joan Cambridge. In it, Egbuna and Cambridge invite children to dramatize important events in Mayfield's life, his influences, and those whom he influenced speaking as important figures, such as Mae Mallory, Robert F. Williams, Paul Robeson, Maya Angelou, Alice Windom, and W. E. B. Du Bois. Most recently, *The Giant That Many Overlooked* was performed by the Mass Emphasis Children's Theater in Washington, DC. See "The Giant That Many Overlooked," YouTube, June 8, 2014.

13. Joan Cambridge, "Letter to the Editor," November 2, 1984, SCH, JMP, box 1, folder 4, 1.

Bibliography

Primary Sources

Archives

Atlanta, GA
    Harold Cruse Papers, Auburn Avenue Research Library
    Hoyt Fuller Papers, Clark Atlanta University, Robert W. Woodruff Library, Special Collections
    John O. Killens Papers, Stuart A. Rose Manuscript, Archives, and Rare Book Library, Emory University

Cambridge, MA
    Ana Livia Cordero Papers, Arthur and Elizabeth Schlesinger Library on the History of Women in America, Radcliffe Institute for Advanced Study, Harvard University

College Park, MD
    National Archives and Record Administration
        Record Group 59 (General Records of the Department of State)
        Record Group 84 (General Records of State Department Foreign Service Posts)
        Record Group 286 (General Records of the United States Agency of International Development)
        Record Group 306 (General Records of the United States Information Agency)

New York, NY
    First World Festival of Negro Arts United States Committee, Schomburg Center for Research in Black Culture, New York Public Library
    John H. Clarke Papers, Schomburg Center for Research in Black Culture, New York Public Library
    Julian Mayfield Papers, Schomburg Center for Research in Black Culture, New York Public Library
    Larry Neal Papers, Schomburg Center for Research in Black Culture, New York Public Library
    Maya Angelou Papers, Schomburg Center for Research in Black Culture, New York Public Library
    St. Claire Drake Papers, Schomburg Center for Research in Black Culture, New York Public Library
    Tom Feelings Papers, Schomburg Center for Research in Black Culture, New York Public Library

Interviews

Cambridge, Joan. Interview with the author, Georgetown, Guyana, January 20, 2019.
Greaves, Louise. Phone interview with the author, November 2, 2013.
Lubiano, Wahneema. Email interview with the author, April 27, 2019.
Rubin, Larry. Email interview with the author, July 7, 2016.

Periodicals

Against the Current
All Things Considered
Atlanta Constitution
Atlanta Journal
Atlanta Journal and Constitution
Bay State Banner
Black Dialogue
Black Journal
Black Scholar
Black World
Caribbean Daily
Catapult
Chicago Daily Defender
Chicago Defender
Chicago Tribune
Cineaste
Cleveland Call & Post
Cleveland Press
Crisis
Detroit News
Drama Review
Ebony
Economic and Political Weekly
Fire!!!
First World
Ghana Evening News
Ghanaian Times
Globe and Mail
Guyana Chronicle
Harper's Magazine
Hartford Times
History Workshop Journal
Interventions
Journal of American Studies
Journal of Interamerican Studies and World Affairs
Journal of Social History
Los Angeles Sentinel
Los Angeles Times
Memphis Press-Scimitar
Mystery File
Negro Digest
New Pittsburgh Courier
News Gazette
New Statesman
New York Amsterdam News
New York Beacon
New York Times
New York Times Magazine
Pacific Historical Review
Philadelphia Daily News
Plains Dealer
Province
Puerto Rico World Journal
Stabroek News
Take One
Toledo Blade
Wall Street Journal
Washington Post
William and Mary Quarterly

Films/Television

Black Journal, Dir. William Greaves, PBS Broadcasting, 1968–70
The Defiant Ones, Dir. Stanley Kramer, United Artists, 1958
The Informer, Dir. Arthur Robison, Wardour Films, 1929
The Informer, Dir. John Ford, RKO Radio Pictures, 1935
The Long Night, Dir. Woodie King Jr., Woodie King Productions, 1976
Lydia Bailey, Dir. Jean Negulesco, 20th Century Fox, 1952
Our Virgin Island, Dir. Pat Jackson, British Lion Film Corp., 1958
Slaves, Dir. Herbert Biberman, Slaves Co., Theatre Guild Films, and Walter Reade Organization, 1969
The Spook Who Sat by the Door, Dir. Ivan Dixon, United Artists, 1973

Superfly, Dir. Gordon Parks Jr., Warner Brothers Pictures, 1972
Uptight, Dir. Jules Dassin, Paramount, 1968
What Happened, Miss Simone? Dir. Liz Garbus, Netflix, Web, 2017

Vinyl Recordings

Amiri Baraka, "Nation Time," *It's Nation Time*, Vinyl Recording, 1970
Booker T. and the MGs, *Uptight*, Vinyl Recording, 1968
Gil Scott-Heron, "King Alfred Plan," *Free Will*, Vinyl Recording, 1972

Online Sources

Civil Rights Movement Veterans. http://crmvet.org
Student Nonviolent Coordinating Committee Digital Gateway. http://snccdigital.org

Secondary Sources

Books

Abu-Jamal, Mumia. *We Want Freedom: A Life in the Black Panther Party*. Cambridge, MA: South End, 2004.
Addo, Ebenezer Obiri. *Kwame Nkrumah: A Case Study of Religion and Politics in Ghana*. Lanham, MD: University Press of America, 1997.
Agyeman, Opoku. *Nkrumah's Ghana and East Africa: Pan-Africanism and African Interstate Relations*. Cranbury, NJ: Fairleigh Dickinson University Press, 1992.
Alexander, Robert J. *The Right Opposition: The Lovestoneites and the International Communist Opposition of the 1930s*. Westport, CT: Greenwood, 1981.
Alkon, Alison Hope, and Julian Agyeman, eds. *Cultivating Food Justice: Race, Class, and Sustainability*. Cambridge, MA: Massachusetts Institute of Technology Press, 2011.
Anderson, Benedict. *Imagined Communities: Reflections on the Origin and Spread of Nationalism*. New York: Verso, 1991.
Anderson, Maxwell. *Lost in the Stars: The Dramatization of Alan Paton's Novel Cry, the Beloved Country*. New York: W. Sloane Associates, 1950.
Angelou, Maya. *All God's Children Need Traveling Shoes*. New York: Random House, 1986.
——. *The Collected Autobiographies of Maya Angelou*. Toronto: Random House, 2004.
Annis, J. Lee. *Big Jim Eastland: The Godfather of Mississippi*. Jackson: University Press of Mississippi, 2016.
Anthony, David H. *Max Yergan: Race Man, Internationalist, Cold Warrior*. New York: New York University Press, 2006.
Arhin, Kwame. *A View of Kwame Nkrumah, 1909–1972: An Interpretation*. Accra, Ghana: Sedco Publishing, 1990.
Baker, Jean H. *The Politics of Continuity: Maryland Political Parties from 1858 to 1870*. Baltimore: Johns Hopkins University Press, 1973.
Baldwin, James. *Notes of a Native Son*. Boston: Beacon, 2012.

Bankoff, Greg, Uwe Lübken, and Jordan Sand, eds. *Flammable Cities: Urban Conflagration and the Making of the Modern World*. Madison: University of Wisconsin Press, 2012.

Baraka, Amiri. *The Autobiography of Leroi Jones/Amiri Baraka*. New York: Freundlich Books, 1984.

Basner, H. Miriam. *Am I an African? The Political Memoirs of H. M. Basner*. Johannesburg: Witwatersrand University Press, 1993.

Bell, Daniel. *The End of Ideology: On the Exhaustion of Political Ideas in the Fifties*. Cambridge, MA: Harvard University Press, 2000.

Biney, Amy. *The Political and Social Thought of Kwame Nkrumah*. New York: Palgrave Macmillan, 2011.

Biondi, Martha. *The Black Revolution on Campus*. Berkeley: University of California Press, 2012.

———. *To Stand and Fight: The Struggle for Civil Rights in Postwar New York City*. Cambridge, MA: Harvard University Press, 2003.

Birmingham, David. *Kwame Nkrumah*. London: Cardinal, 1990.

Blackstock, Nelson. *Cointelpro: The FBI's Secret War on Political Freedom*. New York: Vintage Books, 1976.

Blain, Keisha N., Christopher Cameron, and Ashley D. Farmer, eds. *New Perspectives on the Black Intellectual Tradition*. Evanston, IL: Northwestern University Press, 2018.

Bloom, Joshua, and Waldo E. Martin Jr. *Black against Empire: The History and Politics of the Black Panther Party*. Berkeley: University of California Press, 2013.

Bolland, O. Nigel, ed. *The Birth of Caribbean Civilisation: A Century of Ideas about Culture and Identity, Nation and Society*. Kingston, Jamaica: Ian Randle Publishers, 2004.

Borstelmann, Thomas. *The Cold War and the Color Line: American Race Relations in the Global Arena*. Cambridge, MA: Harvard University Press, 2001.

Botwe-Asamoah, Kwame. *Kwame Nkrumah's Politico-Cultural Thought and Policies: An African-Centered Paradigm for the Second Phase of the African Revolution*. New York: Routledge, 2005.

Broadwater, Jeff. *Adlai Stevenson and American Politics: The Odyssey of a Cold War Liberal*. New York: Maxwell Macmillan International, 1994.

Brooks, Gwendolyn. *Report from Part One*. Detroit: Broadside, 1972.

Brown, Elaine. *A Taste of Power: A Black Woman's Story*. New York: Anchor Books, 1994.

Brown, Frank London. *Trumbull Park*. Chicago: Regnery, 1959.

Brown, Michael, ed. *New Studies in the Politics and Culture of US Communism*. New York: Monthly Review Press, 1993.

Brugger, J. Robert. *Maryland: A Middle Temperament*. Baltimore: Johns Hopkins University Press, 1996.

Budu-Acquah, Kwame. *Kwame Nkrumah: The Visionary*. Accra, Ghana: Service and Method Agency, 1992.

Buhle, Mari Jo, Paul Buhle, and Dan Georgakas, eds. *Encyclopedia of the American Left*. New York: Garland, 1990.

Burnham, Forbes. *Linden Forbes Sampson Burnham, O.E., S.C.: National Assembly Speeches, Vol. 1, September 1957–November 1958.* Georgetown: Caribbean Press, 2013.

Calloway, Bertha W., and Alonzo Nelson Smith. *Visions of Freedom on the Great Plains: An Illustrated History of African Americans in Nebraska.* Marceline, MO: Walsworth Publishing, 1998.

Cambridge, Joan. *Clarise Cumberbatch Want to Go Home.* New York: Ticknor & Fields, 1987.

Carew, Joy Gleason. *Blacks, Reds, and Russians: Sojourners in Search of the Soviet Promise.* New Brunswick, NJ: Rutgers University Press, 2008.

Chilton, John. *Sidney Bechet: The Wizard of Jazz.* New York: Oxford University Press, 1987.

Chomsky, Aviva. *A History of the Cuban Revolution.* Hoboken, NJ: Wiley, 2015.

Churchill, Ward. *The Cointelpro Papers: Documents from the FBI's Secret Wars against Dissent in the United States.* Cambridge, MA: South End, 2002.

Clarke, John Henrik. *My Life in Search of Africa.* Chicago: Third World Press, 1994.

Cole, Hubert. *Christophe, King of Haiti.* New York: Viking, 1967.

Committee on Un-American Activities. *Communist Activities among Puerto Ricans in New York City and Puerto Rico.* Washington, DC: US Government Printing Office, 1960.

Conant, Jennet. *A Covert Affair.* New York: Simon & Schuster, 2011.

Cook, Mercer, and Stephen E. Henderson. *The Militant Black Writer in Africa and the United States.* Madison: University of Wisconsin Press, 1969.

Countryman, Matthew. *Up South: Civil Rights and Black Power in Philadelphia.* Philadelphia: University of Pennsylvania Press, 2006.

Cronon, E. David. *Black Moses: The Story of Marcus Garvey and the Universal Negro Improvement Association.* Madison: University of Wisconsin Press, 1969.

Cruse, Harold W. *Rebellion or Revolution?* Minneapolis: University of Minnesota Press, 2009.

Davidson, Basil. *Black Star: A View of the Life and Times of Kwame Nkrumah.* Boulder, CO: Westview, 1989.

Davis, Joshua Clark. *From Head Shops to Whole Foods: The Rise and Fall of Activist Entrepreneurs.* New York: Columbia University Press, 2017.

Dee, Ruby, and Ossie Davis. *With Ossie and Ruby: In This Life Together.* New York: It Books, 2000.

Delmont, Matthew F. *Why Busing Failed: Race, Media, and the National Resistance to School Desegregation.* Berkeley: University of California Press, 2016.

Denis, Nelson A. *War against All Puerto Ricans: Revolution and Terror in America's Colony.* New York: Nation Books, 2015.

Denning, Michael. *The Cultural Front: The Laboring of American Culture in the Twentieth Century.* New York: Verso, 2010.

Dittmer, John. *Local People: The Struggle for Civil Rights in Mississippi.* Urbana: University of Illinois Press, 1994.

Dodoo, Vincent. *Africa's Many Divides and Africa's Future: Pursuing Nkrumah's Vision of Pan-Africanism in an Era of Globalization.* Cambridge: Cambridge Scholars Publishing, 2015.

Dongen, Luc van, Stéphanie Roulin, and Giles Scott-Smith, eds. *Transnational Anti-Communism and the Cold War.* London: Palgrave Macmillan, 2014.

Downs, Donald Alexander. *Cornell '69: Liberalism and the Crisis of the American University.* Ithaca, NY: Cornell University Press, 1999.

Drew, David. *Kurt Weill: A Handbook.* Los Angeles: University of California Press, 1987.

Duberman, Martin. *Paul Robeson.* New York: The New Press, 1995.

Du Bois, W. E. B. *Dark Princess: A Romance.* Millwood, NY: Kraus-Thomson, 1974.

Dudziak, Mary L. *Cold War Civil Rights: Race and the Image of American Democracy.* Princeton, NJ: Princeton University Press, 2000.

——. *Exporting American Dreams: Thurgood Marshall's African Journey.* New York: Oxford University Press, 2008.

Dulles, Allen. *The Craft of Intelligence.* New York: HarperCollins, 1963.

Ellison, Ralph. *Invisible Man.* New York: Vintage International, 1995.

Emanuel, James A. *Dark Symphony: Negro Literature in America.* New York: Free Press, 1968.

Engerman, David C. *Staging Growth: Modernization, Development, and the Global Cold War.* Amherst: University of Massachusetts Press, 2003.

Escobar, Edward J. *Race, Police, and the Making of a Political Identity: Mexican Americans and the Los Angeles Police Department, 1900–1945.* Berkeley: University of California Press, 1999.

Fanon, Frantz. *Black Skin, White Masks.* New York: Grove, 2008.

——. *The Wretched of the Earth.* New York: Grove, 2004.

Feelings, Tom. *Black Pilgrimage.* Lothrop: Lee & Shepard, 1972.

Fields, Barbara. *Slavery and Freedom on the Middle Ground: Maryland during the Nineteenth Century.* New Haven, CT: Yale University Press, 1987.

Finkelstein, Sidney. *Jazz: A People's Music*, edited by Jules Halfant. New York: Citadel Press, 1948.

Fleming, Cynthia Griggs. *Yes We Did? From King's Dream to Obama's Promise.* Lexington: University Press of Kentucky, 2009.

Forman, James. *The Making of Black Revolutionaries.* Seattle: University of Washington Press, 1997.

Frazier, Nishani. *Harambee City: The Congress of Racial Equality in Cleveland and the Rise of Black Power Populism.* Fayetteville: University of Arkansas Press, 2017.

Freire, Paulo. *Pedagogy of the Oppressed.* New York: Bloomsbury, 2000.

Fuller, Harcourt. *Building the Ghanaian Nation-State: Kwame Nkrumah's Symbolic Nationalism.* New York: Palgrave Macmillan, 2014.

Fuller, Hoyt W. *Journey to Africa.* Chicago: Third World Press, 1971.

Gaines, Kevin K. *American Africans in Ghana: Black Expatriates and the Civil Rights Era.* Chapel Hill: The University of North Carolina Press, 2006.

Garment, Leonard. *Crazy Rhythm: From Brooklyn and Jazz to Nixon's White House, Watergate, and Beyond.* New York: Da Capo, 2001.

Gayle, Addison, ed. *The Black Aesthetic.* New York: Doubleday, 1971.

Gellman, Erik S. *Death Blow to Jim Crow: The National Negro Congress and the Rise of Militant Civil Rights.* Chapel Hill: The University of North Carolina Press, 2012.

Gibbs, James. *Ghanaian Theatre: A Bibliography of Primary and Secondary Sources.* Llangynidr, Wales: Nolisment Publications, 2006.

Gilman, Nils. *Mandarins of the Future: Modernization Theory in Cold War America.* Baltimore: Johns Hopkins University Press, 2003.

Gilmore, Glenda Elizabeth. *Defying Dixie: The Radical Roots of Civil Rights, 1919–1950.* New York: Norton, 2008.

Gilroy, Paul. *The Black Atlantic: Modernity and Double Consciousness.* Cambridge, MA: Harvard University Press, 1993.

Gordon, Jacob U. *Revisiting Kwame Nkrumah: Pathways for the Future.* Trenton, NJ: Africa World, 2017.

Gosse, Van. *Where the Boys Are: Cuba, Cold War America and the Making of a New Left.* London: Verso, 1993.

Goudsouzianm, Aram. *Sidney Poitier: Man, Actor, Icon.* Chapel Hill: The University of North Carolina Press, 2011.

Guzman, Richard. *Black Writing from Chicago: In the World, Not of It?* Carbondale: Southern Illinois Press, 2006.

Haley, Alex, and Malcolm X. *The Autobiography of Malcolm X.* New York: Grove, 1965.

Hall, Simon. *Peace and Freedom: The Civil Rights and Antiwar Movements in the 1960s.* Philadelphia: University of Pennsylvania Press, 2005.

Hanchard, Michael. *Party/Politics: Horizons in Black Political Thought.* New York: Oxford University Press, 2006.

Hannsberry, Karen Burroughs. *Bad Boys: The Actors of Film Noir.* Jefferson, NC: McFarland, 2003.

Harris, William C. *Lincoln and the Border States: Preserving the Union.* Lawrence: University Press of Kansas, 2011.

Heard, Alex. *The Eyes of Willie McGee: A Tragedy of Race, Sex, and Secrets in the Jim Crow South.* New York: Harper, 2010.

Higashida, Cheryl. *Black Internationalist Feminism: Women Writers of the Black Left, 1955–1995.* Urbana: University of Illinois Press, 2011.

Himes, Chester B. *The Quality of Hurt: The Autobiography of Chester Himes.* London: Joseph, 1973.

Hinds, David. *Ethno-Politics and Power Sharing in Guyana: History and Discourse.* Washington, DC: New Academia Publishing, 2011.

Hodes, Art. *Hot Man: The Life of Art Hodes.* Urbana: University of Illinois Press, 1992.

hooks, bell. *Black Looks: Race and Representation.* Boston: South End, 1992.

Hope, Kempe Ronald, Sr., *Guyana: Politics and Development in an Emergent Socialist State.* Oakville, Canada: Mosaic, 1985.

Hopkinson, Natalie. *A Mouth Is Always Muzzled: Six Dissidents, Five Continents, and the Art of Resistance.* New York: The New Press, 2018.

Hughes, Langston. *I Wonder as I Wander: An Autobiographical Journey.* New York: Rinehart, 1956.
Hundley, Mary Gibson. *The Dunbar Story, 1870–1955.* New York: Vantage, 1965.
Hunter, Stephen, and John Bainbridge Jr. *American Gunfight: The Plot to Kill Harry Truman—And the Shoot-Out That Stopped It.* New York: Simon & Schuster, 2005.
Jackson, Kenneth T. *The Encyclopedia of New York City.* New York: The New York Historical Society and Yale University Press, 1995.
Jackson, Lawrence P. *The Indignant Generation: A Narrative History of African American Writers and Critics, 1934–1960.* Princeton, NJ: Princeton University Press, 2011.
Jackson, Walter A. *Gunnar Myrdal and America's Conscience: Social Engineering and Racial Liberalism, 1938–1987.* Chapel Hill: The University of North Carolina Press, 1990.
James, C. L. R. *The Black Jacobins: Toussaint L'Ouverture and the San Domingo Revolution.* New York: Vintage Books, 1963.
Jaynes, Gerald D. "Harlem Writers Guild." In *Encyclopedia of African American Society.* New York: Sage, 2005.
Johnson, Mayme Hatcher, and Karen E. Quinones Miller. *Harlem Godfather: The Rap on My Husband, Ellsworth "Bumpy" Johnson.* New York: Oshun Publishing, 2008.
Johnson, Scott P. *Trials of the Century: An Encyclopedia of Popular Culture and Law,* Vol. 1. Santa Barbara, CA: ABC-CLIO, 2011.
Jones, LeRoi, and Larry Neal, eds. *Black Fire: An Anthology of African-American Writing.* New York: Morrow, 1968.
Joseph, Peniel. *Stokley: A Life.* New York: Civitas Books, 2014.
———. *Waiting 'Til the Midnight Hour: A Narrative History of Black Power in America.* New York: Henry Holt, 2006.
Kendi, Ibram X. *The Black Campus Movement: Black Students and the Racial Reconstitution of Higher Education, 1965–1972.* New York: Palgrave Macmillan, 2012.
Kerr, Daniel. *Derelict Paradise: Homelessness and Urban Development in Cleveland, Ohio.* Amherst: University of Massachusetts Press, 2011.
Kessler, Ronald. *In the President's Secret Service.* New York: Random House, 2010.
Kiuchi, Toru, and Yoshinobu Hakutani. *Richard Wright: A Documented Chronology, 1908–1960.* Jefferson, NC: McFarland, 2014.
Klehr, Harvey, John Earl Haynes, and Fridrikh Igorevich Firsov. *The Secret World of American Communism.* New Haven, CT: Yale University Press, 1995.
Klein, Roger H., ed. *Young Americans Abroad.* New York: Harper & Row, 1962.
Koestler, Arthur. *The God That Failed.* New York: Harper & Bros., 1949.
Korstad, Robert R. *Civil Rights Unionism: Tobacco Workers and the Struggle for Democracy in the Mid-Twentieth-Century South.* Chapel Hill: The University of North Carolina Press, 2003.
Kruse, Kevin M., and Stephen Tuck, eds. *Fog of War: The Second World War and the Civil Rights Movement.* New York: Oxford University Press, 2012.

Kwayana, Eusi. *Walter Rodney*. Georgetown, Guyana: Working People's Alliance, 1988.

Lacy, Leslie Alexander. *The Rise and Fall of a Proper Negro: An Autobiography*. New York: Macmillan, 1970.

Larsen, Lawrence H., and Barbara J. Cottrell. *The Gate City: A History of Omaha*. Lincoln: University of Nebraska Press, 1982.

Latham, Michael E. *Modernization as Ideology: American Social Science and "Nation Building" in the Kennedy Era*. Chapel Hill: The University of North Carolina Press, 2000.

Leach, Laurie F. *Langston Hughes: A Biography*. Westport, CT: Greenwood, 2004.

Lentz-Smith, Adriane. *Freedom Struggles: African Americans and World War I*. Cambridge, MA: Harvard University Press, 2011.

Levy, Peter B. *Civil War on Race Street: The Civil Rights Movement in Cambridge, Maryland*. Gainesville: University Press of Florida, 2003.

Lewis, David Levering. *W. E. B. Du Bois: A Biography*. New York: Macmillan, 2009.

Logan, Rayford. *What the Negro Wants*. Chapel Hill: The University of North Carolina Press, 1944.

Lorde, Audre. *Sister Outsider: Essays and Speeches*. New York: Crossing Press, 1984.

Lupton, Mary Jane. *Maya Angelou: The Iconic Self*. Santa Barbara, CA: ABC-CLIO, 2016.

Malavet, Pedro A. *America's Colony: The Political and Cultural Conflict between the United States and Puerto Rico*. New York: New York University Press, 2004.

Maldonado-Denis, Manuel. *La Conciencia nacional puertorriqueña*. Mexico City: Siglo Veintiuno Editores, 1972.

Mannoni, Octave. *Prospero and Caliban: The Psychology of Colonization*. Ann Arbor: University of Michigan Press, 1990.

Marsh, Alec. *John Kasper and Ezra Pound: Saving the Republic*. New York: Bloomsbury, 2015.

Masotti, Louis H., and Jerome R. Corsi. *Shoot-Out in Cleveland: Black Militants and the Police: A Report to the National Commission on the Causes and Prevention of Violence*. Washington, DC: US Government Printing Office, 1969.

Maxwell, William J. *F.B. Eyes: How J. Edgar Hoover's Ghostreaders Framed African American Literature*. Princeton, NJ: Princeton University Press, 2015.

Mayfield, Julian. "Into the Mainstream and Oblivion." In *The American Negro Writer and His Roots*, edited by John Aubrey Davis Sr. New York: American Society of African Culture, 1960.

———, ed. *Ten Times Black*. New York: Bantam, 1971.

———. *The Grand Parade*. New York: Vanguard, 1961.

———. *The Hit*. New York: Vanguard, 1957.

———. *The Long Night*. New York: Vanguard, 1958.

McDonald, Kathlene. *Feminism, the Left, and Postwar Literary Culture*. Jackson: University Press of Mississippi, 2012.

McGowan, Winston. *The Atlantic Slave Trade, Slavery and the Demographic History of Guyana*. Turkeyen: University of Guyana, 2006.

McKenzie, Kermit E. *Comintern and World Revolution, 1928–1943: The Shaping of a Doctrine.* New York: Columbia University Press, 1964.

McMillen, Neil R. *The Citizens' Council: Organized Resistance to the Second Reconstruction, 1954–64.* Urbana: University of Illinois Press, 1971.

Mealy, Rosemari. *Fidel and Malcolm X: Memories of a Meeting.* New York: Black Classic, 2013.

Mickenberg, Julia L. *American Girls in Red Russia: Chasing the Soviet Dream.* Chicago: University of Chicago Press, 2017.

Millay, Edna St. Vincent. *Collected Poems.* New York: Harper and Brothers, 1956.

Minter, William, Gail Hovey, and Charles E. Cobb Jr. *No Easy Victories: African Liberation and American Activists over a Half Century, 1950–2000.* Trenton, NJ: Africa World, 2008.

Moon-Ho Jung. *Coolies and Cane: Race, Labor, and Sugar in the Age of Emancipation.* Baltimore: Johns Hopkins University Press, 2006.

Moore, Carlos. *Castro, the Blacks, and Africa.* Los Angeles: Center for Afro-American Studies, University of California, 1988.

———. *Pichón: A Memoir: Race and Revolution in Castro's Cuba.* Chicago: Lawrence Hill Books, 2008.

Moore, Leonard N. *Carl B. Stokes and the Rise of Black Political Power.* Urbana: University of Illinois Press, 2002.

Moran, Charles. *Black Triumvirate: A Study of Louverture, Dessalines, Christophe—the Men Who Made Haiti.* New York: Exposition, 1957.

Morgan, Ted. *A Covert Life: Jay Lovestone: Communist, Anti-Communist, and Spymaster.* New York: Random House, 1999.

Morley, Jefferson. *The Ghost: The Secret Life of CIA Spymaster James Jesus Angleton.* New York: St. Martin's, 2017.

Morros, Boris. *My Ten Years as a Counter-Spy.* London: Werner Laurie, 1959.

Moukoko, Pierre Mbonjo. *The Political Thought of Kwame Nkrumah: A Comprehensive Presentation.* Lagos: University of Lagos Press, 1998.

Mullen, Bill V. *Popular Fronts: Chicago and African-American Cultural Politics, 1935–46.* Urbana: University of Illinois Press, 2010.

Mullen, Bill, and James Edward Smethurst, eds. *Left of the Color Line: Race, Radicalism, and Twentieth-Century Literature of the United States.* Chapel Hill: The University of North Carolina Press, 2003.

Munby, Jonathan. *Under a Bad Sign: Criminal Self-Representation in African American Popular Culture.* Chicago: University of Chicago Press, 2011.

Murray, Pauli. *Song in a Weary Throat: An American Pilgrimage.* New York: Harper & Row, 1987.

Myrdal, Gunnar. *An American Dilemma: The Negro Problem and Modern Democracy.* New Brunswick, NJ: Transaction Publishers, 1996.

Negrón-Muntaner, Frances, and Ramón Grosfoguel. *Puerto Rican Jam: Rethinking Colonialism and Nationalism.* Minneapolis: University of Minnesota Press, 2008.

Nelson, William E., and Philip J. Meranto. *Electing Black Mayors: Political Action in the Black Community.* Columbus: Ohio State University Press, 1986.

Newcomb, Covelle. *Black Fire: A Story of Henri Christophe.* New York: Longmans, Green, 1940.

Nkansa-Kyeremateng, K. *The Akans of Ghana: Their Customs, History and Institutions.* Accra, Ghana: Sebewie Publishers, 2004.

Nkrumah, Kwame. *I Speak of Freedom: A Statement of African Ideology.* New York: Praeger, 1961.

Nkrumah, Kwame, and Samuel Obeng, eds. *Selected Speeches of Kwame Nkrumah.* Accra, Ghana: Afram Publications, 1977.

Noble, Peter. *The Negro in Films.* London: Skelton Robinson, 1948.

Nohlen, D. *Elections in the Americas: A Data Handbook,* Vol. 1, *North America, Central America, and the Caribbean.* New York: Oxford University Press, 2005.

O'Brien, John. *Interviews with Black Writers.* New York: Liveright, 1973.

O'Flaherty, Liam. *The Informer.* New York: Mariner Books, 1980.

O'Reilly, Kenneth. *Racial Matters: The FBI's Secret File on Black America, 1960–1972.* London: Free Press, 1989.

Padmore, George. *Pan-Africanism or Communism?* London: Dobson Books, 1956.

Paton, Diana. *No Bond but the Law: Punishment, Race, and Gender in Jamaican State Formation, 1780–1870.* Durham, NC: Duke University Press, 2004.

Patterson, William L. *We Charge Genocide: The Historic Petition to the United Nations for Relief from a Crime of the United States against the Negro People.* New York: International Publishers, 1951.

Pelecanos, George, ed. *D.C. Noir 2: The Classics.* New York: Akashic Books, 2008.

Phillips, Kimberley L. *War! What Is It Good For? Black Freedom Struggles and the US Military from World War II to Iraq.* Chapel Hill: The University of North Carolina Press, 2012.

Plummer, Brenda Gayle. *In Search of Power: African Americans in the Era of Decolonization, 1956–1974.* New York: Cambridge University Press, 2013.

———. *Rising Wind: Black Americans and US Foreign Affairs, 1935–1960.* Chapel Hill: The University of North Carolina Press, 1996.

———. *Window on Freedom: Race, Civil Rights, and Foreign Affairs, 1945–1988.* Chapel Hill: The University of North Carolina Press, 2003.

Premdas, Ralph R. *Party Politics and Racial Division in Guyana.* Denver: University of Denver, 1973.

Quaison-Sackey, Alexander. *Africa Unbound: Reflections of an African Statesman.* New York: Praeger, 1963.

Quinn, Kate, ed. *Black Power in the Caribbean.* Gainesville: University Press of Florida, 2014.

Rabe, Stephen G. *The Most Dangerous Area in the World: John F. Kennedy Confronts Communist Revolution in Latin America.* Chapel Hill: The University of North Carolina Press, 1999.

———. *US Intervention in British Guiana: A Cold War Story.* Chapel Hill: The University of North Carolina Press, 2005.

Reitan, Ruth. *The Rise and Decline of an Alliance: Cuba and African-American Leaders in the 1960s.* East Lansing: Michigan State University Press, 1999.

Robeson, Paul, Jr. *The Undiscovered Paul Robeson: Quest for Freedom, 1939–1976*. New York: Wiley, 2010.

Robinson, Dean. *Black Nationalism in American Politics and Thought*. New York: Cambridge University Press, 2001.

Rodney, Walter. *A History of the Guyanese Working People, 1881–1905*. Baltimore: Johns Hopkins University Press, 1981.

Rosenberg, Rosalind. *Jane Crow: The Life of Pauli Murray*. New York: Oxford University Press, 2017.

Said, Edward. *Representations of the Intellectual*. New York: Vintage Books, 1996.

Sbardellati, John. *J. Edgar Hoover Goes to the Movies: The FBI and the Origins of Hollywood's Cold War*. Ithaca, NY: Cornell University Press, 2012.

Schrecker, Ellen, and Phillip Deery. *The Age of McCarthyism: A Brief History with Documents*. Boston: Bedford/St. Martin's, 2017.

Self, Robert O. *American Babylon: Race and the Struggle for Postwar Oakland*. Princeton, NJ: Princeton University Press, 2003.

Sepinwall, Allison Goldstein. *Slave Revolt on Screen: The Haitian Revolution in Film and Video Games*. Oxford: University of Mississippi Press, 2021.

Sieving, Christopher. *Soul Searching: Black-Themed Cinema from the March on Washington to the Rise of Blaxploitation*. Middletown, CT: Wesleyan University Press, 2011.

Singh, Chaitram. *Guyana: Politics in a Plantation Society*. Stanford, CA: Hoover Institution Press, 1988.

Singh, Nikhil Pal. *Black Is a Country: Race and the Unfinished Struggle for Democracy*. Cambridge, MA: Harvard University Press, 2004.

Solomon, Mark. *The Cry Was Unity: Communists and African Americans, 1917–1936*. Oxford: University Press of Mississippi, 1998.

Southern, David W. *Gunnar Myrdal and Black-White Relations: The Use and Abuse of an American Dilemma, 1944–1969*. Baton Rouge: Louisiana State University Press, 1987.

Speltz, Mark. *North of Dixie: Civil Rights Photography beyond the South*. Los Angeles: J. Paul Getty Museum, 2016.

Stradling, David, and Richard Stradling. *Where the River Burned: Carl Stokes and the Struggle to Save Cleveland*. Ithaca, NY: Cornell University Press, 2015.

Sugrue, Thomas J. *Sweet Land of Liberty: The Forgotten Struggle for Civil Rights in the North*. New York: Random House, 2008.

Theoharis, Athan G. *Chasing Spies: How the FBI Failed in Counterintelligence but Promoted the Politics of McCarthyism in the Cold War Years*. Chicago: Ivan R. Dee, 2002.

——. *The FBI: A Comprehensive Reference Guide*. New York: Oryx, 1999.

——. *The FBI and American Democracy: A Brief Critical History*. Lawrence: University of Kansas Press, 2004.

Theoharis, Jeanne, and Komozi Woodard, eds. *Freedom North: Black Freedom Struggles Outside the South, 1940–1980*. New York: Palgrave Macmillan, 2003.

——. *Groundwork: Local Black Freedom Movements in America*. New York: New York University Press, 2005.

Torrence, Ridgely. *The Story of John Hope*. New York: Macmillan, 1948.
Tovar, Federico Ribes. *Albizu Campos: Puerto Rican Revolutionary*. New York: Plus Ultra Educational Publishers, 1971.
Tyson, Timothy B. *Radio Free Dixie: Robert F. Williams and the Roots of Black Power*. Chapel Hill: The University of North Carolina Press, 1999.
Vandercook, John W. *Black Majesty: The Life of Christophe, King of Haiti*. New York: Editions for the Armed Services, 1944.
Von Eschen, Penny M. *Race against Empire: Black Americans and Anticolonialism, 1937–1957*. Ithaca, NY: Cornell University Press, 1997.
———. *Satchmo Blows up the World: Jazz Ambassadors Play the Cold War*. Cambridge, MA: Harvard University Press, 2004.
Walcott, Derek. *The Haitian Trilogy*. New York: Farrer, Straus and Giroux, 2002.
Washington, Mary Helen. *The Other Blacklist: The African American Literary and Cultural Left of the 1950s*. New York: Columbia University Press, 2014.
Watkins, S. Craig. *Representing: Hip Hop Culture and the Production of Black Cinema*. Chicago: University of Chicago Press, 1998.
White, Robb. *Our Virgin Island*. New York: Doubleday, 1953.
White, Shane, Stephen Garton, Stephen Robertson, and Graham White, eds. *Playing the Numbers: Gambling in Harlem between the Wars*. Cambridge, MA: Harvard University Press, 2010.
Wilford, Hugh. *The Mighty Wurlitzer: How the CIA Played America*. Cambridge, MA: Harvard University Press, 2004.
Wilhelm, James J. *Ezra Pound: The Tragic Years, 1925–1972*. University Park: Pennsylvania State University Press, 1994.
Williams, Chad. *Torchbearers of Democracy: African American Soldiers in the World War I Era*. Chapel Hill: The University of North Carolina Press, 2010.
Williams, John A. *The Man Who Cried I Am*. New York: Signet Books, 1967.
Williams, Rhonda Y. *Concrete Demands: The Search for Black Power in the 20th Century*. New York: Routledge, 2015.
Williams, Robert Franklin. *Negroes with Guns*. New York: Marzani and Munsell, 1962.
Williams, Yohuru R. *Rethinking the Black Freedom Movement: American Social and Political Movements of the Twentieth Century*. New York: Routledge, 2015.
Woods, Jeff. *Black Struggle, Red Scare: Segregation and Anti-Communism in the South, 1948–1968*. Baton Rouge: Louisiana State University, 2004.
Woodward, C. Vann. *The Strange Career of Jim Crow*. New York: Oxford University Press, 2002.
Wright, Richard. *Black Boy*. New York: Harper, 1945.
———. *Black Power: A Record of Reactions in a Land of Pathos*. New York: Harper & Brothers, 1954.
———. *Blueprint for Negro Literature*. New York: 1937.
Yellin, Eric S. *Racism in the Nation's Service: Government Workers and the Color Line in Woodrow Wilson's America*. Chapel Hill: The University of North Carolina Press, 2013.
Yette, Samuel. *The Choice*. New York: Putnam and Sons, 1971.

Young, Cynthia A. *Soul Power: Culture, Radicalism, and the Making of a US Third World Left*. Durham, NC: Duke University Press, 2006.
Zannes, Estelle. *Checkmate in Cleveland: The Rhetoric of Confrontation during the Stokes Years*. Cleveland, OH: Case Western Reserve University Press, 1972.
Zinberg, Len. *Walk Hard, Talk Loud*. New York: Lions Books, 1949.

Dissertations and Theses

Abernathy, Gloria E. "African Americans' Relationship with Daytime Serials," PhD diss., University of Wisconsin, Madison, 1992.
Fenderson, Jonathan. "'Journey toward a Black Aesthetic': Hoyt Fuller, The Black Arts Movement, and the Black Intellectual Community." PhD diss., University of Massachusetts, 2011.
Markle, Seth. "'We Are Not Tourists': The Black Power Movement and the Making of 'Socialist' Tanzania, 1960–1974." PhD diss., New York University, New York, 2011.
Ono-George, Meleisa. "'Coolies,' Containment, and Resistance: The Indentured System in British Guiana." Manuscript in possession of the author.
Placído, Sandy. "A Global Vision: Dr. Ana Livia Cordero and the Puerto Rican Liberation Struggle, 1931–1992." PhD diss., Harvard University, Cambridge, MA, 2017.
Welch, Rebeccah E. "Black Art and Activism in Postwar New York, 1950–1965," PhD diss., New York University, New York, 2002.

Index

Abernathy, Ralph David, 124
Adams, Paul, 155, 172
Adler, Renata, 144
Adventures of Huckleberry Finn, The (film, 1960), 218n8
African American identity, 91, 98, 105, 195–97, 218n9. *See also* African diaspora; Black liberation; Black Power
African diaspora: African Americans centering their experiences, 186; Africans and African Americans, 95–97; Afro-Caribbean culture in Harlem, 217n44; Black Power in, 164; Cuban Revolution, 70–71, 72–74, 75, 77; FBI concern over, 45, 46; framing Black liberation, 49–50; intersection of political economy, gender, class, and culture, 105–8; in *King Christophe* (film project), 188–89; and Julian Mayfield, 2–3; requirements for solidarity, 107–8; social relationships in Africa, 98, 105–6, 108–9; solidarity across, 92–97, 130, 233n29; sources of disunity, 95–96, 98, 105–8. *See also* African unity; colonialism; Ghana; Guyana
African Society for Cultural Relations with Independent Africa (ASCRIA), 162, 171, 253n38
African unity: Afro-diasporic solidarity and, 92–97, 130, 233n29; and disunity, 95, 96, 98, 105, 108; and Tom Feelings, 154; nationalism conflated with, 156; nation-state's role in, 153; Pan-Africanism, 92; as resistance to neocolonialism, 109

Ahmad, Muhammad (Max Stanford), 172
Albam, Jacob, 216n38
Albizu Campos, Pedro, 39–40
Allen, Ernie, 170, 256n59
Allen, Samuel W., 2
American Left: Black radical thought and New Left, 70–71, 72–74; interwar years, 63–64; marginalization of, 63, 64, 67, 68; white activists in, 135–36, 245n20. *See also* Black Left
Anderson, Benedict, 233n32
Anderson, Maxwell, 19
Angelou, Maya: Cuban Revolution and US race relations, 73; and Julian Mayfield in Ghana, 109; and Julian Mayfield's return to United States, 110–11; in Ghana, 12, 100, 105, 235n57, 236n65
anticolonialism: African independence and Richard Wright, 94; anticommunism and, 158; Ana Livia Cordero's influence on Julian Mayfield, 35, 37, 48–49; Cuban Revolution, 72, 74, 75, 78–79; land and decolonization, 155; post–WWII increases in, 39; power as solution to, 48–49. *See also* Guyana; nationalism; Puerto Rico
anticommunism: anti-Black racism and, 7, 240n34; anticolonialism and, 158; Black Left and, 65; Cuban Revolution, 72, 76; FBI, 27, 72; and obscuring of human rights abuses, 240n34
anti-imperialism, 48–49, 110. *See also* anticolonialism

antiracism: Cuban Revolution, 71, 72, 73, 74, 75, 79–80, 226n21; of Fidel Castro, 70, 79–80; in Guyana, 153–54, 155; and state power, 80
Apter, David E., 94
ASCRIA (African Society for Cultural Relations with Independent Africa), 162, 171, 253n38
Augusto, Gerí, 3–4

Baker, Josephine, 12
Baldwin, James, 12, 31, 71, 73, 218n9, 232n26
Baraka, Amiri, 70, 173, 228n65
Barnett, Claude, 123
Barrow, Errol, 164
Bars, Homer, 221n23
Baseleon, Henry, 135
Basner, H. M., 233n39
Batista, Fulgencio, 72, 158
Baum, Dan, 242n52
Bechet, Sidney, 211n70
Belafonte, Harry, 179, 207n36
Bennett, Michèle, 259n7
Bentley, Alvin M., 214n24
Bibb, Leon, 207n36
Biberman, Herbert, 248n56
Black, Max, 118, 128–29
Black aesthetic, 146–47, 151
Black Arts Movement, 143, 146, 151
blackface, 94, 178–79, 183–84, 186
Black Left: Black radical thought and, 70–71, 72–74; and Alice Childress, 26; communism and anticommunism and, 65, 66–68; in *The Grand Parade* (Mayfield), 65–66, 67, 68; long civil rights movement, 65, 205n10; race and political economy, 25; in *Uptight* (film), 134. *See also* American Left
Black liberation: Black male leaders, 80–81, 83, 84–85, 120; Ana Livia Cordero and Julian Mayfield, 37; diasporic frame, 49–50; future of in Guyana, 154; and national coherence, 164; nationalism and, 33, 141, 155–56, 250n10; National Negro Congress, 66, 223n41; and power, 48–49, 80, 152; Puerto Rico and, 37, 43; writers' responsibilities to, 119, 120–21. *See also* Black Power; Black radicalism; genocide of African Americans; *Uptight* (film)
Black masculinity: in blaxploitation films, 238n11; in *Clarise Cumberbatch Want to Go Home* (Cambridge), 258n74; in *King Christophe* (film project), 190; and male leaders, 80–81, 83, 84–85, 120; masculinist militancy, 112–14; in Moynihan Report, 248n49; state power and, 114; in *Uptight* (film), 137, 245n22
Black Panther Party, 112, 114, 134, 236n59, 238n4. *See also* militancy and armed self-defense
Black Power: *Black Power* (Wright), 94, 230n10; "Black Power" position paper, 136; Black working class and, 64, 81, 120–21; and blaxploitation films, 238n11; and Forbes Burnham, 159; collapse of movement, 160; defining world in Black people's terms, 248n50; in diaspora, 164; divisions over nationalism, 236n59; *The Grand Parade* as analytic frame for, 52–53; Julian Mayfield's theater career and, 113–14, 149–50; militant vs. revolutionary, 112–14; and nonviolent tactics, 64; popular fascination with, 112, 115; response to MLK Jr.'s assassination, 118–20; revolutionary ideology vs. pragmatic politics, 113; separatism from white activists, 135–36; solidarity and, 149–50; white Americans' misunderstanding of, 126–27. *See also* Black liberation; Black radicalism; genocide of African Americans; *Uptight* (film)
Black radicalism, 3, 13, 20. *See also* Black Left; Black Power

Black working class: art for, 29–30; Black Power and, 64, 81, 120–21; and Julian Mayfield, 5–6, 13–14, 19, 205n16; and nonviolence tactics, 139; *Uptight*'s message for, 133, 138, 139, 146

Black writers: as agents of change, 7; American dream and, 2; Black Writer's Conference, 112–14, 118–21, 128; FBI surveillance of, 7, 44–45, 46, 47, 203n10, 214n31; Harlem Writers Guild, 23–24, 209n50, 209n52; and "Negroness," 218n9; protest novels and, 218n9; and Black liberation, 119, 120–21; role of, 128; symbiosis with revolution, 119; travel's role among, 12; women writers and Julian Mayfield, 236n62. See also *individual writers*

Bland, Edward, 208n39
Blankfort, Michael, 181
blaxploitation films, 115, 148, 150, 238n11
Blotner, Joseph, 58
Blyden, Edward, 99, 233n36
Bond, Horace Mann, 18, 232n26
Bontemps, Arna, 2
Booker Sugar Estates Ltd., 167, 254n48, 255n49
Boudin, Leonard, 225n11
Bourne, Kay, 131
Boyd, Herb, 242n45
Boyd, Stephen, 248n56
Branch, William, 26
Brand, Neville, 11, 204n5, 218n8
Brando, Marlon, 180, 184
Brew, Kwesi, 235n57
Brew, Molly, 235n57
Bridgman, Benjamin, 214n25
Briggs, Cyril, 44
Brooks, Gwendolyn, 7, 22, 208nn39–40
Brooks, Paul, 228n61
Brotherson, Festus, Jr., 165
Brown, Frank London, 7, 59, 147, 219n18
Brown, Hubert "Rap," 124, 145–46, 149, 240n23
brownface, 184

Brown v. Board of Education, 219n20
Bunche, Ralph, 77–78
Bundy, McGeorge, 76
Burnham, Forbes: assassination of Walter Rodney and, 257n69, 258n4; autarky of, 156, 162, 166, 252n30; biography, 157–58, 159, 251n17; "Burnham of Guyana" (Mayfield), 166–67, 169, 173–74, 253n35; Henri Christophe and, 190; and cooperative socialism, 163, 167; downfall of, 160, 174; and intellectuals and artists, 159–60; Machiavellian pursuit of legitimacy, 165; Julian Mayfield on, 161; Julian Mayfield's relationship with, 166, 174–75; Julian Mayfield's support for, 152, 160, 161–63, 164, 165–68; overtures to Soviet bloc, 159; party affiliations, 157–59; paternalism toward Guyanese, 168–69; rivalry with Eusi Kwayana, 162, 163, 171, 172; Third World radicalism and Pan-Africanism of, 156, 159, 162. See also Guyana

Burnham, Louis E., 24
Burroughs, Charles, 21–22, 208n41
Burroughs, Eric, 208n41
Burroughs, Williana "Liana" Jones, 208n41

Cambridge, Joan: *Clarise Cumberbatch Want to Go Home*, 175, 258n74; *The Giant That Many Overlooked*, 262n12; *King Christophe* (film project), 188; and Julian Mayfield's archive, 4; and Julian Mayfield's relationship with Forbes Burnham, 174–75; and propaganda in Guyana, 165–66; relationship with Julian Mayfield, 161, 165, 254n45; on Ronald Reagan, 198
Cancel Miranda, Rafael, 214n24
capitalism, 19, 127, 187, 238n11. See also class; economic oppression
Carew, Jan, 237n71, 250n5
Carey, Fabian, 207n35

Index 279

Carmichael, Stokely, 58–59, 119–20, 137, 240nn23–24
Carrion, Ramon Mirabel, 216n37
Carter, Alprentice "Bunchy," 257n63
Carter, Asa, 60, 220n22
Carter, Jimmy, 214n23
Cassavetes, John, 53, 218n6
Castro, Fidel: African American reaction to, 77–79; antiracism of, 70, 79–80; communism and anticommunism, 76, 225n10; and Julian Mayfield, 74–75, 79–80; race in United States and, 74–75, 76–78, 80; UN speech, 78; visit to Harlem, 76–79, 226n24. *See also* Cuban Revolution
Cavett, Dick, 178
Central Intelligence Agency (CIA), 72, 158
Césaire, Aimé, 183
Cha-Jua, Sundiata, 13, 205n10
Chapman, James E., 247n35
Chicago, IL, 21, 22–23, 209n44, 219n18
Childress, Alice: biography, 210n61; Black Left activism, 26; Cuban Revolution and, 73; FBI surveillance of, 7; and Harlem Writers Guild, 23; and Julian Mayfield in Ghana, 109; and "Negro-ness," 218n9
Christmas, Walter, 23, 26
Christophe, Henri: *Black Majesty* (Vandercook), 178; death of, 258n3, 261nn34–35; *Le Tragedie du Roi du Christophe* (Césaire), 183; policies in Haiti, 176–77, 190, 261n32; relevance to Julian Mayfield, 187, 189–91. See also *King Christophe* (film project)
Churchill, Winston, 158, 229n7
CIA (Central Intelligence Agency), 72, 158
Civil Rights Congress, 26, 240n34
civil rights movement: and class, 51–52; under Eisenhower, 56, 83–84; equal rights vs. improved material conditions, 2; Freedom Riders, 86–88, 103, 135, 228n57, 228n62; long civil rights movement and Black Left, 64, 65, 205n10; Julian Mayfield's criticism of, 51–52, 53, 55, 60; US foreign relations and, 100–101. *See also* Black Panther Party; Black Power; integration politics; National Association for the Advancement of Colored People (NAACP); nonviolence tactics; segregation; Student Nonviolent Coordinating Committee (SNCC); *individual leaders*
Clark, Ed, 73
Clarke, John Henrik: African American writing and American dream, 2; Afro-American nationalism, 33; Cuban Revolution, 71, 73; Harlem Writers Guild, 23, 26; military service of, 207n31; Monroe Defense Committee, 83
Clarke, Michael, 94
class: and civil rights movement, 51–52; liberalism's inadequacy addressing, 58–59; *Lost in the Stars* tour and, 11; Julian Mayfield's working-class origins, 5–6, 13–14, 19, 205n16; nationalism and, 58; socioeconomic status and race, 11, 25, 37, 42–43, 67. *See also* Black working class; economic oppression
Cleveland, OH, 140–43, 170, 245n26, 247n35
Cobb, Charles, Jr., 250n12
Coffelt, Leslie W., 214n23
Cohn, Roy, 223n45
Cold War, 2–3, 7, 76–77, 92, 158–59. *See also* communism; Cuban Revolution; US imperialism
Coleman, Milton, 195–96
Collazo, Oscar, 40–41, 214n23
Collier, Eugenia, 194
colonialism: African Americans and, 31–32; colonial mentality, 159, 169–70, 173–74, 231n15; English colonialists vs. white Americans, 126; foreign media, 169–70, 255n56; ideological interpretations of, 101–2; Jim Crow and, 34; local culture vs., 42, 96–97; Monroe, NC, and Africa,

280 Index

103; neocolonialism, 96, 109, 174, 232n24; and newly independent nations, 161, 169–70, 173; as product of white supremacy, 103; race and economic oppression, 42–43, 157; "Social Responsibility and Social Protest" conference, 31–32; and solidary of colonized peoples, 32; Western superiority and, 230n13, 231n15; Western tropes about Africa, 94–95. *See also* African diaspora; African unity; anticolonialism; neocolonialism; Puerto Rico; racism

color. *See* race and color

communism: "African socialism" as, 94; Black Left and, 66–68; Fidel Castro and, 225n10; diversity of socialisms, 168; Guyana and, 251n19; Hough Uprising blamed on, 245n26; HUAC testimony, 223n45; National Negro Congress and, 66, 223n41; in Puerto Rico, 46, 213n17, 217n45. *See also* socialism

Communist Party of the United States of America (CPUSA): calls for local control of, 66–67; Camp Unity, 25, 27–29, 211n68, 211n70; Committee for the Negro in the Arts, 25, 213n12, 222n33; in *The Grand Parade* (Mayfield), 66, 67, 68; Jefferson School of Social Science, 25, 26–27; Julian Mayfield's membership in, 11, 24, 28–30, 35, 63, 67, 222n33; party duties, 25; policy on interracial organizing, 27–29; resistance to Julian Mayfield's marriage to Ana Livia Cordero, 35–36, 213n12; Soviet spy ring, 47, 216n38

Congress of Racial Equality, 86, 134, 256n60

Conyers, John, 124

Cook, Ann F. *See* Kwayana, Tchaiko

Cordero, Ana Livia: biography, 35–36; Cuban Revolution, 72, 73–74; FBI's interest in, 46, 89, 216n34; influence on Julian Mayfield, 33, 34–35, 37, 48–49; as personal physician to W. E. B. Du Bois, 104; political ideology and activism, 46, 110, 216n34, 237n73; relationship with and marriage to Julian Mayfield, 35–36, 38, 43, 89–90, 213n12; separation and divorce from Julian Mayfield, 110, 117, 237n71, 254n45; work in Ghana, 89–90, 104, 110, 117; work in Puerto Rico, 110, 117, 213n17

Cordero, Pablo Garcia Rodriguez, 37, 213n18, 216n37

Cordero, Rafael I. T., 36, 213n17

Cordero, Vivi, 36

Cornell University, 113, 116, 117–18, 128–29, 239n14

Couch, William, 208n39

Cox, Courtland, 250n12

CPUSA. *See* Communist Party of the United States of America (CPUSA)

Crafus, Richard "King/Big Dick," 180–82

Crawford, Mark, 30

Crowder, Ralph, 226n24, 235n54

Crowder, Richard, 103, 228n65

Cruse, Harold, 6, 7, 66–67, 70, 73

Cuban Revolution: African diaspora and, 70–71, 72–74, 75, 77; anticolonialism, 72, 74, 75, 78–79; anticommunism, 72; antiracism, 71, 72, 73, 74, 75, 79–80, 226nn21–22; Black radical thought and New Left, 70–71, 72–74; and CIA, 72; Fair Play for Cuba Committee (FPCC), 71–72, 73, 224n8, 225n11, 225n14; *The Grand Parade* (Mayfield) and, 68–69; Janet Rosenberg Jagans's support for, 158; and Julian Mayfield, 70, 71, 73–75; propaganda campaign and African Americans, 78, 79; racial discourse and policies, 70, 226nn21–22; revolutionary nationalism, 69; "What is really happening in Cuba?," 71; white supremacy, 73, 75, 79–80. *See also* Castro, Fidel

Cunningham, Evelyn, 54

D'Aguiar, Peter, 159
Danner, Margaret Cunningham, 208n39
Dassin, Jules: blacklisting of, 132, 244n8; filming *Uptight*, 140, 141–42; film panel at *Uptight*'s premier, 145–46; pitch for *Uptight*, 132; and racial issues, 128, 132–33, 244n10; *Uptight*'s impact on career of, 148, 149, 150; work with Julian Mayfield, 113, 131. See also *Uptight* (film)
Davis, Clifford, 214n24
Davis, John P., 223n41
Davis, Ossie, 23, 26, 133, 145, 248n56
Dee, Ruby: 2008 showing of *Uptight*, 150; impact of *Uptight* on, 148; performance in *Uptight* praise, 145; *Uptight* script writing, 116, 129, 133, 135. See also *Uptight* (film)
De Patton, Clive, 242n41
desegregation. See integration politics
Dessalines, Jean-Jacques, 176–77, 180, 190
Díaz Lanz, Pedro L., 72, 225n10
Diop, Alouine, 232n26
Dixon, Ivan, 111, 151, 249n57
Dohm, Bernadine, 124
Dorvillier, William J., 43
Drake, Sandra, 237n1
Drew, Bernard L., 145
Du Bois, Shirley Graham, 68, 93, 97
Du Bois, W. E. B.: African Writer's Conference in Paris, 232n26; *Dark Princess*, 236n63; in Ghana, 93, 104; Pan-Africanism, 230n13, 236n63; travel's influences on, 12
Dulles, Allen, 223n39
Dunne, Philip, 181
Duvalier, Jean-Claude "Baby Doc," 178, 259nn7–8

Earle, Arnold, 79
Eastland, James O., 72
economic oppression: and Black racial discourse, 20; colonialism and, 42–43, 157; genocide and, 124–25; and liberalism, 58–59; race and, 25, 37, 42–43. See also class; political economy
Egbuna, Obi, Jr., 262n12
Ehrlichman, John, 242n52
Eisenhower, Dwight D., 35, 56, 83–84
Eisenstein, Sergei, 179
Elizabeth II (queen), 93, 229n7, 230n8
Emmanuel, James, 50, 217n46
Emmanuel, James, Jr., 217n46
empire. See US imperialism
Escobar, Edward, 204n6
Evans, Fred "Ahmed," 247n35

Fair Play for Cuba Committee (FPCC), 71–72, 73, 224n8, 225n11, 225n14
Fallon, George Hyde, 214n24
Fanon, Franz, 231n15
Farrakhan, Louis, 196
FBI (Federal Bureau of Investigation): and Black activist groups, 257n63; and Black cultural and political work, 44–45, 215n31; communism and, 27, 72; Counter Intelligence Program (COINTELPRO), 44, 115, 128, 142, 238n9; Cuban government as national security threat, 224n8; Cuban Revolution, 71–72; diasporic connections concerns, 45, 46; monitoring of militant groups by, 141; and Puerto Rican nationalist movement, 39, 41; surveillance of African American activists, 7, 46, 89, 216n34, 238n9; surveillance of Black writers, 7, 44–45, 46, 47, 203n10, 215n31; and *Uptight* (film) production, 131, 142–43
FBI surveillance of Mayfield: communist activity, 46–47, 216n38; concern over diasporic connections, 46; in Cuba, 45–46, 71–72; early reports, 45–46, 215nn32–33; family background checks, 46; file on, 6, 7; in Ghana, 45–46; initiation of, 44; Julian Mayfield's reporting for

282 Index

WHOA, 43; and Monroe, NC violence, 89; Puerto Rico's centrality, 44, 45, 46–47; reduction in, 47, 224n6; tactics, 45; writings of primary interest, 46, 47
Feelings, Muriel, 154
Feelings, Tom, 154, 155–56, 157, 164, 187, 250n5
Feelings, Zamani, 154
Feigenbaum, Abe, 245n26
Feigenbaum, Dave, 245n26
Ferguson, Herman, 155
Figueroa Cordero, Andres, 214n24
film career. *See* theater and film career
Fisk University: Black Writer's Conference, 112–14, 118–21, 128; *Uptight* (film) and Julian Mayfield's speech at, 131, 133, 136–37, 140
Fontaine, Pierre-Michel, 186
Fontaine, William, 232n26
Ford, James W., 223n41
Ford, John, 131–32
Forman, James, 86, 207n31, 228n57
Fowler, Bob, 219n20
FPCC. *See* Fair Play for Cuba Committee (FPCC)
Francis, Anne, 182
Freedom Riders, 86–88, 103, 135, 228n57, 228n62
Freeman, Donald, 256n59
Freeman, Kenneth M. *See* Lumumba, Mamadou
Fuller, Hoyt, 154, 250n6

Gaines, Kevin, 230n10, 230n13, 231n18
Galonka, Louis E., 247n35
gambling, 18, 216n41, 217n43
Garland, Hazel, 145
Garvey, Marcus, 44, 149, 230n13
Gayle, Addison, 151, 238n11
gender politics, 106, 236n62, 247n45. *See also* Black masculinity
genocide of African Americans: African American survival, 126–28; economic oppression and, 124–25; fears of, 114, 121–24, 127, 130, 137; Geneva Conventions, 125; genocidal character of white racism, 127; King Alfred Plan, 121–26, 241nn39–40, 242n41; *The Man Who Cried I Am* (Williams), 122–23, 125–26, 241n39; Non-Detention Act, 126, 243n53; Project 100,000, 241n40; "We Charge Genocide" (Civil Rights Congress), 240n34
Ghana: Afro expatriates in, 100, 101, 105–10, 231n18, 233n39; British royal visit to, 93, 229n7, 230n8; criticism of Julian Mayfield in, 109; foundation for Julian Mayfield's nationalist rhetoric, 109; language bridge and barrier with US, 100–101, 104; Julian Mayfield in, 99–100, 102, 104, 109; national, class, and racial identities in, 233n39; nation building, 99–100; outdooring ceremony and sense of welcome, 93, 95; Publicity Secretariat, 100, 102, 104; Puerto Rico shaping Julian Mayfield's approach to, 34; race and power in, 92; sovereignty and Pan-Africanism, 164; US foreign policy and, 100–101. *See also* African diaspora; Nkrumah, Kwame
Gibson, Emily F., 184–85
Gibson, Richard, 71, 72–73, 77, 85, 224n7, 226n24
Giddings, Paula, 252n28
Gilmore, Glenda, 65
Giovanni, Nikki, 143, 145
Glenville Shootout, 247n35
Glover, Danny, 179–80
Gonzales, Michael A., 150
Gordy, Berry, 191
Gosse, Van, 70, 226n24
Graham, Billy, 221n24
Grand Parade, The (Mayfield): American progress narrative challenged in, 55–56; author's overview, 51–52, 55, 59; betrayal of African American patriots, 75; Black Left in, 65–66, 67,

Index 283

Grand Parade, The (Mayfield) (cont.) 68; and Black Power, 52–53; challenging civil rights movement, 55, 60; Clarke Bryant (character), 61–63; Communist Party in, 66, 67, 68; critical reception of, 57–58, 68; Cuban Revolution and, 68–69; educational role, 65; integration politics critique in, 51–52, 54–55, 56–58, 59, 61–62, 90; and liberalism, 49–50, 52, 55–56, 57–58; Lonnie Banks (character), 65–66, 67, 68; marginalization of American Left, 63, 64, 68; nationalism and critique of class relations, 58; racial justice struggles, 49–50, 63; real-life inspiration for, 54, 59–61, 66–67; tension between message and audience, 53–54, 59

Greaves, William, 10, 21, 123, 149

Greenlee, Sam, 238n11, 249n57

Greer, SC, 13–14, 194–95

Griffin, Herman, 78, 79

Griffin, Junius, 238n11

Grosfoguel, Ramón, 33, 40, 212n3

Guillén, Nicolas, 225n14

Gussin, Sylvia, 188, 191

Guthrie, Woodie, 211n75

Guy, Rosa, 23, 218n9

Guyana: African American expatriates in, 153, 155, 157, 161, 170–73; Afro-diasporic polities in, 153, 160, 161, 162, 170–72; ASCRIA, 162, 171, 253n38; author's overview, 155, 157, 250n7, 251n15; Black liberation's future in, 154; Black radicals and, 155–56, 157, 160, 170, 172–73; Joan Cambridge's propaganda role in vision for, 165–66; during Cold War, 158–59; and colonialism after independence, 169–70, 173, 255n56; colonial mentality in, 159, 169–70, 173–74; communism and, 251n19; foreign policy, 165, 167, 174; Guyanese Cooperative Republic, 159, 162, 164, 167; "The Ideology of Our Party" (Mayfield), 167; independence from Britain, 157–159, 162, 252nn21–23; Julian Mayfield's decision to leave, 174–75; Julian Mayfield's reasons for moving to, 151, 153–54, 157, 160–61; Julian Mayfield's writing themes while in, 152, 162–63, 165–166, 167–68, 169–70, 171–72; Lumumba and Umoja incident, 170–72; Ministry of Information and Culture, 160, 162–63, 164, 165–67; nation building in, 152, 156, 160, 163–64, 165, 170–73; as neocolonial state, 174; as one-party state, 159; Pan-Africanism in, 154–56, 162, 163–64, 171; People's Progressive Party (PPP), 157–59, 252n25; race in, 156–58; resisting US hegemony and anti-Black racism, 153–54, 155; sovereignty and nationalism, 155, 156, 162–64, 167, 171, 173; state apparatus as mechanism for change, 162–63; sugar industry in, 157, 167, 174, 251n15, 254n48, 255n49; US State Department's involvement in, 158–59, 252n21, 252n27; Working People's Alliance (WPA), 172. *See also* Burnham, Forbes; *King Christophe* (film project); People's National Congress (PNC)

Haffner, Warren, 235n54

Haiti, 176–77, 182, 183, 186, 187

Haitian Revolution on film: author's overview, 178–80; Ellen Holly and Black Hollywood, 183–84; *Lydia Bailey*, 180–83; nationalism and Black history, 184–86; Anthony Quinn's blackface project, 178–79, 183–85, 186. See also *King Christophe* (film project)

Hall, Jacquelyn D., 65, 205n10

Hampton, Fred, 149

Hanchard, Michael, 5

Hansberry, Lorraine, 2, 7, 23, 29, 31

Harlem, NY: Afro-Caribbean culture in, 217n44; Black population growth in,

284   Index

210n58; Fidel Castro in, 76–79, 226n24; Harlem Writers Guild, 23–24, 209n52, 209n50; Hotel Theresa, 76, 77, 226n24; Lenox Avenue and 125th Street, 79; in Julian Mayfield's writing, 48, 235n56; Sydenham Hospital, 212n7; theatrical community, 19

Harlem Godfather. *See* Johnson, Ellsworth "Bumpy"

Harvey, William K., 72

Hatcher, Richard, 124

Hawaii, 18

Haynes, Pamela, 184–85

Hemingway, Ernest, 220n22

Hervé, Julia Wright, 230n10

Hicks, James L., 182

Higgins, John, 257n63

Hill, David, 170, 172–73, 256n58, 257n65

Hilliard, Ernest (Prophet Frank Thomas), 256n58

Himes, Chester, 12

Hoberman, J., 150

Hockett, Fred B., 221n23

Hodes, Art, 211n70

Holabird, John A., 209n44

Holly, Ellen, 180, 183–84

Hollywood: blackface in, 178–79, 183–84, 186; blaxploitation films, 115, 148, 150, 238n11; brownface in, 184; interracial relationships and red carpet, 182; *Lydia Bailey*, 180–83; racial inequality in, 178–81, 183, 184–85, 187, 188; racial representation on screen, 184, 185–86; Screenwriters Guild of America strike, 187–88, 260n26. *See also* Haitian Revolution on film; *King Christophe* (film project); Paramount Pictures; *Uptight* (film); *individual actors*

Holmes, Carroll, 170, 256n59

Holt, Len, 235n54

Hoover, John Edgar, 7, 44, 72, 142

Hough Uprising, 141, 143, 245n26

House Un-American Activities Committee (HUAC), 2, 24, 72, 217n45, 223n45

Howard, Betty, 209n44

Howard University, 175, 193–94, 223n41

Howe, Russell, 98

Hughes, Langston: communism and, 12, 68, 223n45; Cuban Revolution, 73, 225n14; FBI surveillance of, 7; and Julian Mayfield, 22; praise for *The Hit* (Mayfield), 47–48

Humphrey, Hubert, 241n36

Ibiza, Spain, 110, 117, 237n71

Iglesias, César, 37, 213n17, 216n37

Iglesias, Jane, 37, 216n37

imperialism. *See* US imperialism

Informer, The (film), 131–32, 135

integration politics: *Brown v. Board of Education*, 219n20; Clinton High School (TN), 60–61, 220n22, 221n24, 222n31; critique of in Julian Mayfield's writing, 31–32, 38, 49–52, 54–58, 59, 61–62, 90; integrated civil rights movement, 135–36, 139, 245n20; as interregional battle, 62; liberal integrationists and segregationists, 61–62; Julian Mayfield's rejection of, 28–30; *McSwain et al. v. County Board of Education of Anderson County, Tennessee*, 220n21; potential to succeed in through tragedy, 57, 59; "Social Responsibility and Social Protest" conference, 31–32; white motivations for, 58

Internal Security Act (McCarran Act), 122, 123, 124, 240n34, 241n35

intersectionality, 105–8, 233n39

Isaacs, Harold, 95–96, 97

Ivy, James, 232n26

Jackson, Jesse, 195–97, 261nn4–5

Jackson, Lawrence, 218n9

Jagan, Cheddi, 157–58, 251n17, 252n21

Jagan, Janet Rosenberg, 158

Jamaica, 252n30

James, C. L. R., 179

jazzy diplomacy, 101

Index 285

Jefferson School of Social Science, 25, 26–27
Jenkins, Mr., 15
Jenkins, Timothy, 124
Jensen, Ben F., 214n24
Jett, Ruth, 145, 248n47
Jewish Americans, 195–96, 261n4
Jim Crow: celebration of, 61; colonialism and, 34; in Los Angeles, CA, 11; mid-South vs. Deep South states, 222n25; in Omaha, NB, 10, 23; as product of white supremacy, 103; in Washington, DC, 14–17; White Citizens Councils, 219n15, 220n22. *See also* Williams, Robert F.
Johnny Staccato (tv show), 53
Johnson, Ellsworth "Bumpy," 28, 48, 211n75
Johnson, John H., 191
Johnson, Lyndon B., 114, 241n40
Johnson, Mayme Hatcher, 211n71
Johnson, Rhodes, 121
Jones, James Earl, 128
Jones, LeRoi, 72, 73, 74, 75, 228n65
Jones, Leroy C., 247n35
Jordan, Norman, 141, 246n28
Joseph, Peniel, 115
Julien, Max, 134

Kahn, Sylvia, 211n75
Kasper, John, 60, 220n22, 221n23
Kayatt, Richard, 260n21
Kazan, Elia, 184
Kefauver, Estes, 241n36
Kelley, Robin D. G., 65
Kennedy, John F., 102, 103–4, 234n49
Kennedy, Robert, 115
Khrushchev, Nikita, 76, 223n39
Killens, John O.: Black Writers Conference, 113; Cuban Revolution, 73; focus on "Negro-ness," 218n9; Harlem Writers Guild, 23, 26, 209n52; "Social Responsibility and Social Protest" panel, 31
King, Coretta Scott, 124

King, Martin Luther, Jr., 58, 118–20
King, Preston, 109, 157
King, Sidney. *See* Kwayana, Eusi
King Alfred Plan, 121–26, 241nn39–40, 242n41. *See also* genocide of African Americans
King Christophe (film project): Afro-diasporic ideology in, 188–89; Black masculinity in, 190; commentary on postcolonial nations, 176–77, 189–91; deviations from historical fact, 189–91, 261n34; filming in Guyana (proposed), 261n33; Hollywood's discomfort with, 177–78; Julian Mayfield' work on, 176, 186–87, 188–90; and Julian Mayfield's work in Guyana, 177, 189; project's end, 191–92; project's origin, 178, 187–88. *See also* Marshall, William
Koch, Ed, 212n7
Kohr, Leopold, 218n5
Korstad, Robert, 205n10
Kotto, Yaphet, 180
Kraft, Joseph, 197
Kunstler, William, 124, 196
Kwayana, Eusi: biography, 253n37; and Tom Feelings, 250n5; on House of Israel violence, 257n65; rivalry with Forbes Burnham, 162, 163, 171, 172
Kwayana, Tchaiko, 170, 253n37

Lacy, Ed, 149, 249n60
Lacy, Leslie, 109, 231n18
Lamarre, Hazel L., 182
Lamming, George, 173
Lang, Clarence, 13, 205n10
Leach, Laurie F., 223n45
Lebrón, Lolita, 214n24
Lee, Canada, 210n61
Leeman, Clive, 196
Lehman, Herbert H., 241n36
Lewis, David Levering, 12, 109, 230n10, 234n41
Lewis, Edward S., 213n16

liberalism, 57–59, 69. *See also* American Left
Library of Congress, 15
Lincoln University, 18
linguistic barriers, 100–101, 104, 106, 107
Lipke, Alan, 259n12
Locher, Ralph S., 141
Lorde, Audre, 24
Los Angeles, CA, 11
Lost in the Stars (musical), 10–11, 13, 19–23
L'Ouverture, Touissaint, 176–77, 180, 190
Lovestone, Jay, 223n43
Lowery, John, 87, 103, 228n62, 235n54
Lubiano, Wahneema, 193–94
Lumumba, Malaika, 63
Lumumba, Mamadou, 170–71, 256n59
Lunes de Revolución, 73
Lupton, Mary Jane, 235n57
Luyt, Richard, 159
Lydia Bailey (film), 180–83
Lynskey, Ed, 249n60

Macmillan, Harold, 158, 229n7, 251n19
Magloire, Paul Eugène, 182
Maio, Michael, 214n25
Mallory, Mae, 87–88, 102–4, 234n51, 235n54
Mamoulian, Rouben, 19
Manley, Michael, 164
Mannoni, Dominique-Octave, 94–95, 231n15
Marcus, Sidney, 195
Markle, Seth, 250n12
Marsh, Alex, 220n22
Marshall, William: Black nationalist sentiments, 185; hiring of Julian Mayfield onto *King Christophe*, 176, 186–87; *King Christophe* project, 176, 178–79, 185, 186–88, 191–92; as King Dick in *Lydia Bailey*, 180–83; relationship with Julian Mayfield, 114, 187, 191. *See also King Christophe* (film project)
Mathieu, Alex, 186
Maugham, Robert "Robin" Cecil Romer, 243n55
Maxwell, William J., 203n10, 215n31
Mayfield, Annie Mae Prince (mother), 14, 46, 205n16, 206n18
Mayfield, Dorothy (sister), 14, 194
Mayfield, Emiliano (son), 93, 95, 117
Mayfield, Henry (grandfather), 205n15
Mayfield, Hudson (father), 14, 46, 83, 194, 205n16, 206n17
Mayfield, J. C. (uncle), 194
Mayfield, Joseph (great-grandfather), 14
Mayfield, Julian: archive at Schomburg Center for Research in Black Life, 4–5, 6; autobiography, 11; career overview, 1–4, 7–8; challenging assumptions about United States, 2–3, 49–50, 55–56; childhood, 13–17; education, 16–17, 18–19, 25–27; escape to Canada, 88, 89; family history, 14, 205n16, 206n18; financial difficulties, 193; Fulbright Fellowship, 192; fungibility of ideological framework and politics, 104, 113; gender roles, 106, 236n62; heart attack and death, 197–98; marginality of in scholarship, 4–5, 203n8; military career, 17–18, 196, 207n33; power central to intellectual project of, 69; working-class origins of, 5–6, 13–14, 19, 205n16 (*see also* Black liberation; Black masculinity; Black Power; Cambridge, Joan; Communist Party of the United States of America (CPUSA); Cordero, Ana Livia; Cuban Revolution; Ghana; Guyana; militancy and armed self-defense; power; Puerto Rico; Mayfield, Julian: teaching career; Mayfield, Julian: theater and film career; Mayfield, Julian: writing career)

Index 287

—teaching career: abroad, 192; African American survival, 126–28; Black masculinity and power, 114; Black radical activism and, 150; "Black Techniques of Survival," 127; Black thought through literature, 117–18, 193; "The Black Writer in the Revolution," 114; "By Force and Violence," 126; Cornell University, 113, 116, 117–18, 128–29, 239n14; "Everybody Loves the Africans of Rhodesia," 127; Howard University, 175, 193–94, 223n41; on militancy, 114; "Negro Goals as Reflected in Negro Writing," 117–18; New York University, 113, 126; popularity of courses, 193–94; "The Quagmire of the Black American Writer," 127; return to United States, 116, 117; SUNY Cortland, 113, 126, 127; teaching philosophy, 127–28; Third World nationalisms, 127; University of Maryland, 175, 193

—theater and film career: adaptation of novels for screen, 53, 149; after *Lost in the Stars*, 23; American Negro Theater, 25; art for Black working class, 29–30; Blackfriars Theatre, 19, 207n35, 208n37; Black Power and, 113–14, 149–50; *Candy Store*, 26, 210n62; Chaka Productions, 149; commentary on postcolonial governments, 176, 177; compromises when working with whites, 131; film adaptations, 53; Harlem Black theatrical community, 19; impact of *Uptight* on, 148, 149; *Johnny Staccato* (tv show), 53; *Lost in the Stars*, 10–11, 13, 19–23; loyalty oaths, 212n81; Marcus Garvey biopic, 149; pursuit of film career, 128–29; *Virgin Island* (film), 53 (*see also* Hollywood; *King Christophe* (film project); *Uptight* (film); Mayfield, Julian: writing career)

—writing career: ambitions, 17; Committee for the Negro in the Arts, 24, 25, 213n12, 222n33; fiction's advantages, 104–5; financial struggles, 24–25, 38; "Gerald Orsini" (pseudonym), 218n7; for Guyanese government and Forbes Burnham, 152, 162–63, 165–72; Harlem Writers Guild, 23–24, 209n50; influence of Puerto Rico, 48; journalism, 38, 43–44, 102–4, 193, 195; for Kwame Nkrumah and Ghanaian government, 99–100, 102–4; motivations for, 23; New York literary scene, 53; skepticism from Julian Mayfield's in-laws, 36; writer-in-residence at Howard University, 175, 193–94; writing as political act, 1 (*see also* Mayfield, Julian: theater and film career)

—writing career, individual works, 38, 219n19; "Black on Black," 105–8, 236n63; "The Black Writer and the Revolution," 112–13, 114, 118–21; "Burnham of Guyana," 166–67, 169, 173–74, 253n35; "The Cuban Challenge," 74; *Fount of the Nation*, 108–9; "Ghanaian Sketches," 91, 93, 94, 95, 98, 105; *The Hit*, 30, 43–44, 47–48, 219n19; The Ideology of Our Party," 167; "Into the Mainstream and Oblivion," 31–32, 48, 49–50; "The Lonely Warrior," 107; *The Long Night*, 30, 43–44; *Look Pretty for the People*, 235n56; "Monroe, No Man's Land," 102–4; "Monroe, USA: The Powderkeg Explodes," 102–4; "Save Mae Mallory! Frame-up in Monroe," 102–4; "Sorting Us Out," 196–97; "Tales from the Lido," 109, 194; *Ten Times Black*, 150; "Uncle Tom Abroad," 96, 232n24; "Which Way Does the Blood River Run," 194; "Why They Want to Kill Mae Mallory," 102–4; "You Touch My Black Aesthetic and I'll Touch Yours," 151 (see also *Grande Parade, The* (Mayfield))

—writing career, publication outlets: *African Review*, 100, 234n41; *Baltimore*

288   Index

Afro-American, 79–80; *Black Scholar*, 152, 163, 171; *Cleveland Call & Post*, 83; *Commentary*, 81; *Evening News*, 102–4; *Freedom*, 24, 26; *Lunes de Revolución*, 73; *Negro Digest*, 96; "Plain Speaking" column, 104; *Puerto Rican World Journal*, 43–44; *Time Capsule*, 193; *Washington North Star*, 193; *Washington Post*, 195–97
—writing career, subjects and themes: African American writing and American dream, 2; African diaspora, 49–50, 94, 108–9, 153; Afro-diasporic solidarity, 95–98, 102, 105–6; anti-Black racism as institutional force, 150–51; anticolonialism, 31–32, 93–95, 173–74; art for Black working class, 29–30; Black aesthetic, 150–51; Black Power, 52–53; challenging liberalism, 49–50, 52, 55–56, 57–58; and civil rights movement, 51–52, 53, 55, 60; communism and Communist Party, 66, 67, 68; constructing Kwame Nkrumah's "African Personality," 99; criticism of Korean War, 25–26, 32; Cuban Revolution, 71, 73, 74, 79–80; cynical realism in, 104; Harlem in novels, 48; ideological interpretations between cultures, 100–102, 104; integration politics, 31–32, 49–52, 54–58, 59, 61–62, 90; and JFK, 102, 103–4; "Monroe Frame-Up," 102–4; political economy's intersections with class, gender, culture, 105–8; political roots of everyday life, 108; protecting Black culture, 49–50; responses to Eusi Kwayana, 163, 164, 171; role of Black writers, 128; uniting Africa, 99; US imperialism, 32; writing for television, 53, 218n7 (*see also* Ghana; *Grand Parade, The* (Mayfield); Guyana; *King Christophe* (film project); *Uptight* (film))
Mayfield, Rafael (son), 14, 43, 89, 93, 117
McCarran Act (Internal Security Act), 122, 123, 124, 240n34, 241n35

McDavid, Elvin, 167, 175, 255n56
McDonald, Kathleen, 26
McKay, Claude, 7
McNamara, Robert, 241n40
McSwain et al. v. County Board of Education of Anderson County, Tennessee, 220n21
Mealy, Rosemari, 226n24
Meriwether, James, 102, 234n49
Mexican Americans, 204n6
Michaux, Lewis H., 79
militancy and armed self-defense: African Americans not ready for, 75; alienation from Black working class, 139; Black militias, 84; in Cleveland, OH, 140, 141, 143; mass-movement tactics and, 138–39; militant vs. revolutionary, 112–14; MLK Jr.'s assassination and, 120; Monroe, NC, 85–86, 87, 89, 113; and nonviolence, 131, 133–34, 135–38, 140; post-war militarism, 25–26; Puerto Rico's influence on Julian Mayfield, 34, 43; *Uptight* (film) and, 114–15, 123, 140, 144, 147, 150; Robert F. Williams and, 82, 83, 84–85, 113. *See also* nonviolence tactics
military career, 17–18, 196, 207n33
Mitchell, John, 124
Mitchell, Loften, 26
mobility. *See* travel
Monroe, NC: and Africa under colonialism, 103; author's overview of, 82; extrajudicial violence in, 103; Freedom Riders, 86–88, 103, 228n57, 228n62; influence on struggles elsewhere, 102–4, 170; and JFK, 102, 103–4; Jim Crow and NAACP chapter, 82–84; Julian Mayfield's defense of activists, 102–4; militancy and armed self-defense in, 85–86, 87, 89, 113; "Monroe Frame-up," 103–4, 234n51, 235n54; and nonviolent, passive resistance, 87, 89, 103
Moore, Archie, 218n8

Moore, Carlos, 70, 226n21
Moore, Isaac, 170, 256n59
Moore, Juanita, 134, 182
Moore, Richard B., 123, 130
Moore, Willard, 23
Morales-Carrion, A., 100–101
Morros, Boris, 216n38
Moses, Robert P., 250n12
Moynihan, Daniel, 146, 248n49
Moynihan Report (*The Negro Family*), 146, 248n49
Muñoz Marín, Luis, 33, 41
Murray, Pauli, 12
Myrdal, Gunnar, 91–92

NAACP. *See* National Association for the Advancement of Colored People (NAACP)
Nagle, Urban, 207n35, 208n37
Nasser, Gamal Abdul, 76
National Association for the Advancement of Colored People (NAACP): and grassroots movements, 81; Julian Mayfield's critique and criticism of, 49–51, 81, 83; Monroe, NC, 82–84; praise for *Lydia Bailey* (film), 182–83; suspension and expulsion of Robert F. Williams, 81, 82–83, 227n42
nationalism: African American, 75, 105–6, 141, 155–56, 250n10; Afro-American, 33–34, 38; "The Bitchers," 95–96; Black history and, 184–86; class relations and, 58; in Cuba, 69; cultural vs. revolutionary nationalism, 105–6, 236n59; in Ghana, 109, 233n39; in Guyana, 155, 163–64, 167, 171, 173; Pan-Africanism vs., 99, 152, 155, 163–64, 171, 186; in Puerto Rico, 33–34, 38, 48–49, 110, 117, 213n17, 217n45; question of land, 155–56, 157, 185; race relations and, 98, 156; sovereignty and, 163–64, 167, 171, 173; Third World nationalisms, 71, 127; transnationalism, 153; utility for overthrowing ruling class, 35

National Negro Congress (NNC), 66, 223n41
National Rifle Association, 84
nation-state: cooperative republics, 164, 167; *King Christophe's* commentary on, 176–77, 189–91; national sovereignty, 163; Pan-Africanism vs., 153; postcolonial nation-state, 152, 153, 176; role in African unity, 153; romanticized view of, 155. *See also* Cuban Revolution; Ghana; Guyana; Haiti; sovereignty
Neal, Larry, 143, 145, 146, 248n50
Negro Family, The (Moynihan Report), 146, 248n49
Negrón-Muntaner, Frances, 33, 40, 212n3
Negulesco, Jean, 181
Nehru, Jawal, 76, 78
neocolonialism, 96, 109, 174, 232n24
Newton, Huey P., 112, 139, 236n59
New York University, 113, 126
Nixon, Richard, 124, 126, 242n52
Nketsia, Nana, IV, 105, 235n57
Nkrumah, Kwame: "African Personality," 98, 99, 233n36; African socialism of, 94; Afro-diasporic solidarity, 95, 233n29; Fidel Castro's UN speech, 78; Henri Christophe and, 190; confidence in Julian Mayfield, 104; criticisms of, 107, 109–10; fall of, 109; fictionalized in *Fount of the Nation* (Mayfield), 108–9; "The Lonely Warrior" (Mayfield), 107; Julian Mayfield reflecting arguments of, 107; Pan-Africanism, 97, 109–10, 233n39. *See also* Ghana
nonviolence tactics: alienation from Black working class, 139; futility of, 87, 89, 103; Julian Mayfield on, 51, 64, 69, 87, 89, 103, 140; militancy and, 131, 133–34, 135–38, 140; politics of respectability, 38. *See also* militancy and armed self-defense; *Uptight* (film)
Nyerere, Julius, 250n12

290 Index

Oak Ridge, TN, 60, 219n20
O'Brien, Connor Cruise, 116
O'Connor, John J., 144
O'Flaherty, Liam, 131–32
Omaha, NB, 10, 23
O'Neal, Felix "Pete," 250n12
O'Neal, Frederick, 210n61

Padmore, George, 97, 230n13, 233n29
Pan-Africanism: "African Personality," 99; African unity, 92; Black radical traditions and, 97; of Forbes Burnham, 156, 159, 162; challenging Cold War structures, 92; *Dark Princess* (Du Bois), 236n63; in Ghana, 97, 109–10, 164, 233n39; in Guyana, 154–56, 162, 163–64, 171; as imperialist chauvinism, 163; Julian Mayfield on, 99, 163; national and imperial realities threatening, 186; nationalism vs., 99, 152, 155, 163–64, 171, 186; nation-state vs., 153; Pan-African Secretariat, 170–71, 256n60; racial solidarity ideal, 174; in Tanzania, 250n12; "Uncle Tomus Americanus" undermining, 96, 232n24; uplift perspective on Africa, 230n13
Papich, Sam, 72
Paramount Pictures: and FBI pressure to halt *Uptight* (film), 131, 142–43; lack of support for *Uptight*, 144, 147–48, 150; risks in taking on *Uptight* (film), 131, 132. *See also* Hollywood; *Lydia Bailey* (film)
Paton, Alan, 19, 20
Patterson, Lindsay, 144
Paul Laurence Dunbar High School, 16–17
Payne, Ethel, 124
People's National Congress (PNC): corruption in, 171, 172, 174, 252n25; criticism of Forbes Burnham, 164–65; formation of, 158; House of Israel, 173, 256n58, 257n65; relations with ASCRIA, 172, 253n38; rhetoric and policies, 153; suppression of opposition parties, 159. *See also* Burnham, Forbes; Guyana
Perrett, Mattie (grandmother), 205n15
Persaud, Bernadette, 159
Peters, Brock, 180
Peterson, Drew, 221n24
Phillips, Kimberly, 241n40
Piñero, Jesús T., 41–42
Placído, Sandy, 33, 213n17
Player, Adger Emerson, 232n24
Plimpton, George, 220n22
Plummer, Brenda Gayle, 39, 76
PNC (People's National Congress). *See* People's National Congress (PNC)
Poitier, Sidney, 19–20, 53, 179, 207n36
political economy, 25, 105–8. *See also* economic oppression
Pontecorvo, Gillo, 180
Popular Front, 63–64, 65, 222n35
Pound, Ezra, 60, 220n22
power: Black liberation and, 48–49, 80, 152; Blackness vs. Americanness, 196–17; as central to Julian Mayfield's thought, 4, 198; land and, 155–56; race and, 92; as solution to imperialism and colonialism, 48–49. *See also* Black Power; colonialism; economic oppression; militancy and armed self-defense; racism; sovereignty; state power; US imperialism; white supremacy
Pratt, Frantz, 260n21
Prattis, P. L., 122
President's Commission on Civil Rights, 56
Preston, Steven, 57
Prince, Annie Mae (mother), 14, 46, 205n16, 206n18
Prince, Van, 21
Project 100,000, 241n40

Puerto Rico: Afro-American nationalism, 33–34, 38; as colonized space, 33, 36, 42; communism in, 46, 213n17, 217n45; economic and social transformation, 41–42; independence struggle, 33–34, 36–37, 38–44, 213n22, 214nn23–24; influence on Julian Mayfield, 33, 34, 35, 36–37, 42–43, 48–49; integration politics and, 56; Ley de la Mordaza ("Gag Law"), 41–42; local culture vs. colonialism, 42; and Julian Mayfield's approach to Ghana, 34; Julian Mayfield's journalism in, 38; nationalism in, 33–34, 38, 48–49, 110, 117, 213n17, 217n45; out-migration, 39, 42; Partido Nacionalista de Puerto Rico, 40; poverty of, 36–37; "Puerto Rican invisibility," 38–39, 40, 44, 212n3; radical influences, 32; segregation in, 35, 36–37; sugar industry in, 41–42, 214n25; US imperialism and, 32, 39, 41

Queimada/Burn! (film), 180
Quinn, Anthony, 178–79, 183–85, 186, 259n7, 260n21

Rabe, Stephen, 252n21
race and color: art criticizing, 54; aspects of seen through US travel, 10–11, 12–13; Fidel Castro and US race relations, 74–75, 76–78, 80; importance of in Guyana, 156–58; in Lydia Bailey, 180–83; in Pan-Africanism, 174; political economy and, 25; racial representation on screen, 184; salience of national identity, 98; socioeconomic status and, 11, 25, 37, 42–43, 67; US foreign policy and race relations, 100–101, 156
racism: anticommunism and, 7, 240n34; blackface, 178–79, 183–84, 186; and colonialism, 97; in Cuban Revolution, 70, 226n21; genocidal character of, 127; interracial relationships and red carpet, 182; Lost in the Stars tour, 10–11, 13, 20–21; racial capitalism, 127, 187; US foreign relations and, 100–101; white paternalism, 61–62. See also antiracism; genocide of African Americans; Hollywood; segregation; white supremacy
Rand, Esther, 47, 216n38
Randall, Tony, 218n8
Randolph, A. Philip, 32, 66
Raplin, Jim, 256n58
Reagan, Ronald, 198
Reape, Harold, 103, 235n54
Redding, Saunders, 2
Reeves, Frank D., 223n45
Reitan, Ruth, 70
Reitsch, Hanna, 233n39
Republic of New Afrika, 114, 141
Republic of New Libya, 143, 247n35
revolution: advocacy for, 102; Black aesthetic and, 151; Black writers and, 119; local control over, 127; as series of practical actions, 170–73; Uptight (film) and, 131, 133. See also Cuban Revolution; Haiti; Puerto Rico
Richardson, Judy, 250n12
Rickford, Russell, 153, 173
Rideout, Walter, 9
Roberts, Kenneth A., 180, 181, 183, 214n24
Robertson, Dale, 180–81, 182
Robeson, Paul, 19, 24, 28, 64, 207n36, 211n75
Robinson, Cedric J., 3, 148, 238n11
Robinson, Jackie, 77
Rodney, Walter, 172, 174, 252n30, 257n69, 258n4
Rodríguez, Irving Flores, 214n24
Romero, Joseph J., Jr., 204n6
Roosevelt, Theodore, Jr., 41
Rowan, Carl T., 196
Rubin, Larry, 211n68
Rustin, Bayard, 64, 141, 240n24

Saez Corales, Juan, 37, 216n37
Santos Rivera, Juan, 37
Scarupa, Harriet Jackson, 198
Schmitz, James A., Jr., 214n25
SCLC (Southern Christian Leadership Conference), 38, 51
Scott, Daryl Michael, 155
Scott-Heron, Gil, 125
Seale, Bobby, 112
Seeger, Pete, 211n75
segregation: in Chicago, 21, 22–23, 209n44, 219n18; criticism of in *The Grand Parade* (Mayfield), 61–62; and Cuban Revolution, 74; informal color lines, 56; in Omaha, NB, 23; in Puerto Rico, 35, 36–37; *Trumbull Park* (Brown), 219n18; *Uptight* set and filming, 141–42. *See also* Jim Crow; racism; white supremacy
Self, Robert O., 205n10
Senate Internal Security Subcommittee, 72, 224n3
Shearer, Hugh, 252n30
Sieving, Christopher, 146
Silvera, Frank, 113, 128, 135, 147
Sims, Hilda, 210n61
Smith, Elwood, 208n37
Smith, Gregory, 257n69
Smith, Willie "The Lion," 211n70
Smith Act, 42, 215n26
SNCC (Student Nonviolent Coordinating Committee), 49–50, 81, 134, 136
Soble, Jack, 216n38
Soble, Myra, 216n38
Soble (Soblen), Robert, 216n38
socialism, 94, 163, 167, 168. *See also* communism
socially conscious art, 21–22
Southern Christian Leadership Conference (SCLC), 38, 51
sovereignty: Black Power as threat to, 164; in Ghana, 164; in Guyana, 156, 162–64, 167, 171, 173; and local sensitivity, 163, 167; nationalism and, 163–64, 167, 171, 173

Soviet Union, 100–101. *See also* Cold War; communism
Spence, Ivan, 239n14, 243n55
Spook Who Sat by the Door, The (film), 151, 249n57
Stahl, Leslie, 195
Stanford, Max (Muhammad Ahmad), 172
Stanley, C. H., 89
State Department: in Ghana, 100–101; involvement in Guyana, 158–59, 252n21, 252n27; race relations and foreign policy, 100–101; sensitivity of to African affairs, 102. *See also* US imperialism
state power: Black liberation and, 80, 152; inaccessibility of positions of power to Black people, 130–31, 137; masculine articulations of, 114; mechanism for change, 92–93, 162–63. *See also* nation-state; US imperialism
State University of New York at Cortland (SUNY Cortland), 113, 126, 127
Stegall, Mrs. Bruce, 87–88, 228nn62–63, 234n51
St. Jacques, Raymond, 135, 144
Stokes, Carl B., 141, 142, 143
Stuckey, Sterling, 219n18
Student Nonviolent Coordinating Committee (SNCC), 49–50, 81, 134, 136
Sugrue, Tom, 116

Taber, Robert, 85, 226n24
Tanner, Henry, 230n8
Tanzania, 250n12
Taylor, Robert, 60
Taylor-Burroughs, Margaret, 21–22, 208n39
Terry, Clifford, 144
Theoharris, Athan, 72
Thomas, Frank (Ernest Hilliard), 256n58
Thompson, Craig, 27
Torresola, Griselio, 40–41, 214n23

Touré, Sekou, 76, 78
transdiasporic activism. *See* African diaspora; Puerto Rico
transnationalism, 153
travel: aspects of race in United States seen through, 10–11, 12–13; capitalism and, 19; criticism of capitalism and, 19; and critique of integration politics, 56; and Julian Mayfield, 10–12, 20–21; as theme among Black writers, 12. *See also* Ghana; Guyana; Puerto Rico
Trinidad and Tobago, 251n16, 252n30
Truman, Harry, 33–34, 40–41, 56, 214n23, 241n36
T'Shaka, Oba, 256n60
Tugwell, Rexford, 41
Tyson, Tim, 82, 228n65

Umoja, Shango, 170–71
University of Maryland, 175, 193
Uptight (film): audience reception, 145–47; author's overview, 113–14, 131–32; Black Left in, 134; Black masculinity in, 137, 245n22; Black militancy in, 114–15, 123, 140, 144–45, 147, 150; Black Power and radicalism depicted in, 113–14, 115–16, 135–37, 140; Black women in, 247n45; Black working class audience, 133, 138, 146; as blaxploitation, 148, 150; challenging schema of Black-oriented films, 115; as character study of social movement, 134–35; FBI's attempts to disrupt filming, 131, 142–43; filming in Cleveland, OH, 140–43; film panel at premier, 145–46; Fisk speech by Julian Mayfield and, 131, 133, 136–37, 140; ideological project, 115–16, 131, 133, 137–39; impact on Black films in Hollywood, 148, 150–51; lacking vision for Black freedom struggle, 147; marginalization of Black Left, 134; Julian Mayfield's defense of, 145–46, 148–49; and Julian Mayfield's fears of genocide, 123, 137; militancy, nonviolence, and backlash, 131, 133–34, 135–38, 140; plot overview, 134–40; reception of, 143–49, 150; script writing by Julian Mayfield, 128–29, 131, 133–34, 135; script writing by Ruby Dee, 116, 129, 133, 135; segregated set for, 141–42; source material, 131–32, 134–35; white liberal activists in, 135–36, 245n20
US imperialism: and African Americans, 186; Cuban Revolution and, 78; cultural hegemony, 42; Hawaii and, 18; ideological interpretations of, 101–2; Korean War, 32; political power as solution to, 48–49; Puerto Rico, 32, 39, 41; and US hegemony, 2–3, 32, 153–54, 155. *See also* colonialism; State Department; state power

Vandercook, John W., 178, 259n6
Vernon, Scott, 133
Virgin Island (film), 53, 218n6
Viva Zapata! (film), 184
Voice of America (radio network), 101

Walker, Charles, 230n10
Walker, Edwini, 260n21
Walker, Jesse, 148
Warden, Donald, 170
War on Drugs, 242n52
Warwick, Dionne, 248n56
Washington, DC, 14–17
Washington, Mary, 52
Watkins, S. Craig, 248n49
Watts, Dan, 123
Weill, Kurt, 19, 20
Welch, Rebeccah E., 25
West, Hollie I., 1, 128
White, Rob, III, 218n6
White, Walter, 182
White Citizens Councils, 219n15, 220n22

white supremacy: Blackness vs. Americanness, 196–97; colonialism and Jim Crow, 103; and colorblindness, 196–97; Cuban Revolution and, 73, 75, 79–80; cultural distance in African diaspora, 96–97; direct confrontation of, 83, 84–85, 87–88, 89; geographic scope across United States, 10–11; grassroots movements against, 81; Guyana's resistance of, 155; in Hollywood, 150; inaccessibility of positions of power to Black people, 130–31, 137; and integration, 55; intransigent and transnational nature, 37; justice system under, 103; and Pan-Africanism, 92; and "Uncle Tomus Americanus," 96, 232n24; white paternalism, 61–62
Wilhelm, J. James, 220n22
Wilkins, Roy, 55, 82–83, 227n42
Williams, Dick Anthony, 135
Williams, Eric, 164
Williams, G. Mennen "Soapy," 100, 101
Williams, Hosea, 124
Williams, John A., 7, 122–23, 125–26, 241n39
Williams, Mabel, 89
Williams, Robert F.: Cuban Revolution, 71, 72–73, 89; escape to Canada, 88; friendship with Julian Mayfield, 69, 80–81, 83, 84–85, 87–88; insurrection charges against, 87–88; Julian Mayfield's recollections of, 84–85; militancy and armed self-defense, 82, 83, 84–85, 113; Monroe Defense Committee, 83; NAACP career, 81, 82–83, 227n42; Revolutionary Action Movement, 228n50. *See also* Monroe, North Carolina
Wilson, Harold, 159
Wilson, Woodrow, 15
Winship, Blanton, 41, 213n22
Wolff, Willard J., 247n35
Woodward, C. Vann, 62, 222n25
Wright, Richard: African Writer's Conference in Paris, 232n26; anticolonialism and Pan-Africanism, 93–95, 173, 230n13; *Black Boy*, 16; Black modernity, 230n13; *Black Power*, 93–95, 230n10; renunciation of communism, 67–68; travel's influences on, 12
Wright, Sarah E., 2, 31, 73

X, Malcolm, 77, 78, 109, 226n24, 235n57

Yellin, Eric S., 15, 206n21
Yergan, Max, 68, 223n45
Yette, Samuel, 124–25, 127, 242n52
Young, Andrew, 195
Young, Cynthia A., 70, 226n24
Young, Whitney, 124

Zanuck, Darryl F., 244n8
Zinberg, Leonard "Len." *See* Lacy, Ed

www.ingramcontent.com/pod-product-compliance
Lightning Source LLC
LaVergne TN
LVHW051940060925
820435LV00015B/107